The Secret Wars

Volume II

Intelligence, Propaganda and Psychological
Warfare, Covert Operations, 1945–1980

The Secret Wars: A Guide to Sources in English

"The Secret Wars: A Guide to Sources in English"

Volume II

Intelligence, Propaganda and Psychological Warfare, Covert Operations, 1945–1980

MYRON J. SMITH, JR.

With a Foreword by

HARRY HOWE RANSOM

ABC-Clio

Santa Barbara, California   Oxford, England

Library of Congress Cataloging in Publication Data

Smith, Myron J.
   The secret wars, a guide to sources in English.

   (War/peace bibliography series; no. 12–14)
   Includes indexes.
   CONTENTS: v. 1. Intelligence, propaganda and psychological warfare, resistance movements, and secret operations, 1939–1945.—v. 2.
Intelligence, propaganda and psychological warfare, covert opera-
tions, 1945–1980.
   1. Military intelligence—Bibliography. 2. Espionage—Bibliogra-
phy. 3. Psychological warfare—Bibliography. 4. World War, 1939–
1945—Underground movements—Bibliography. 5. World War,
1939–1945—Secret service—Bibliography. 6. Commando troops—
Bibliography. 7. Guerrilla warfare—Bibliography. 8. Terrorism—
Bibliography. I. Title.
Z6724.17S63 [UB250] 016.3553'43   79–25784
ISBN 0–87436–303–9 (v. 2)

ABC-Clio, Inc.
Riviera Campus
2040 Alameda Padre Serra, Box 4397
Santa Barbara, California 93103

Clio Press, Ltd.
Woodside House, Hinksey Hill
Oxford OX1 5BE, England

The War/Peace Bibliography Series

RICHARD DEAN BURNS, EDITOR

This Series has been developed in cooperation with the Center for the Study of Armament and Disarmament, California State University, Los Angeles.

About the War/Peace Bibliography Series

With this bibliographical series, the Center for the Study of Armament and Disarmament, California State University, Los Angeles, seeks to promote a wider understanding of martial violence and the alternatives to its employment. The Center, which was formed by concerned faculty and students in 1962–63, has as its primary objective the stimulation of intelligent discussion of war/peace issues. More precisely, the Center has undertaken two essential functions: (1) to collect and catalogue materials bearing on war/peace issues; and (2) to aid faculty, students, and the public in their individual and collective probing of the historical, political, economic, philosophical, technical, and psychological facts of these fundamental problems.

This bibliographical series is, obviously, one tool with which we may more effectively approach our task. Each issue in this series is intended to provide a comprehensive "working," rather than definitive, bibliography on a relatively narrow theme within the spectrum of war/peace studies. While we hope this series will prove to be a useful tool, we also solicit your comments regarding its format, contents, and topics.

RICHARD DEAN BURNS
SERIES EDITOR

Other Bibliographies by Myron J. Smith, Jr.

Navies in the American Revolution. Vol. 1 of the American Naval Bibliography Series.

The American Navy, 1789–1860. Vol. II of the American Naval Bibliography Series.

American Civil War Navies. Vol. III of the American Naval Bibliography Series.

The American Navy, 1865–1918. Vol. IV of the American Naval Bibliography Series.

The American Navy, 1918–1941. Vol. V of the American Naval Bibliography Series.

The European Theater. Vol. I of *World War II at Sea: A Bibliography of Sources in English.*

The Pacific Theater. Vol. II of *World War II at Sea: A Bibliography of Sources in English.*

General Works, Naval Hardware, Home Fronts, Special Studies, and the "All Hands" Chronology (1941–1945). Vol. III of *World War II at Sea: A Bibliography of Sources in English.*

General Works, European and Mediterranean Theaters of Operations. Vol. I of *Air War Bibliography, 1939–1945: English-language Sources.*

The Pacific Theater; Airpower, Strategy and Tactics; Escape, Evasion, Partisan, and POW Experiences. Vol. II of *Air War Bibliography, 1939–1945: English-language sources.*

Multi-theater Studies and the Air Forces. Vol. III of *Air War Bibliography, 1939–1945: English-language Sources.*

The Aircraft. Vol. IV of *Air War Bibliography, 1939-1945: English-language Sources.*

World War I in the Air: A Bibliography and Chronology.

Cloak-and-Dagger Bibliography: An Annotated Guide to Spy Fiction, 1937–1975.

Air War Southeast Asia, 1961–1973: An Annotated Bibliography and 16mm Film Guide.

Men-at-Arms: A Fiction Guide.

The War Stories Guide: An Annotated Bibliography of Military Fiction.

Sea Fiction Guide. With Robert C. Weller.

for Stu Godfrey and Sue Webreck,
colleagues and friends

There is an old saying that victory has a hundred
fathers and defeat is an orphan.
—President John F. Kennedy
April 21, 1961

Contents

Foreword

We shall probably never know the full story of the secret side of the Cold War during the 1945–1980 period. By the early 1950s three-fourths of the resources of the United States Central Intelligence Agency were being allocated to clandestine operations. Hundreds of millions of dollars annually were expended for operations beyond public view and much of this activity was in reaction to similar covert activities by major Soviet bloc adversaries, designed to influence the course of world politics.

The history of this secret side of the Cold War remains unwritten, but the ingredients for such a history have been accumulating at an accelerating pace since the late 1960s. By the "secret side" of the Cold War I mean the use of such coercive foreign policy instruments as counterintelligence, espionage, propaganda, and psychological warfare, and even more extreme forms of coercion such as covert political intervention as a means of toppling governments, assassination of political leaders, and in some cases, paramilitary operations.

Aside from official secrecy, a major factor complicating our understanding of this subject is its confusing terminology. Little consistency can be found in the literature in the use of such terms as intelligence, espionage, counterintelligence and covert action. In common misusage, the word "intelligence" may be used to cover a wide range of disparate activities, some of them unrelated to intelligence in its true meaning. Such chaos of terminology reflects conceptual confusion which may be, at least in part, the consequence of secrecy and the result of deliberate deception and "disinformation" which are the trademarks of secret operations. The confusion over terminology also reflects the weakness of intelligence and covert action theory. It may be useful to suggest some basic definitions, although the reader must not expect the literature to display much precision in the use of these terms.

Intelligence means evaluated information and commonly refers to information required in national strategic (foreign and defense policy) decision making. Intelligence will be drawn from an unlimited variety of sources, will be developed in a complex series of steps and will be reported to "consumers" in a variety of forms; but keep in mind this essential point: intelligence is evaluated information. Espionage, on the other hand, commonly called "spying," is one of many ways of collecting data to be fed into the intelligence process. The chief characteristic of espionage is that it is illegal. There is nothing inherently illegal about intelligence work, but gathering certain kinds of information that a state wishes to keep secret is, by definition, illegal. Since the world remains a collection of sovereign states often in competition or conflict, and since knowledge or information is potential power, espionage has always been a major enterprise of nations. Here enters another and often confused term—counterintelligence (or counter-espionage). This refers to a police and security function, designed to protect one nation's secrets from penetration by the espionage agents of another nation. While primarily a negative function, counterintelligence can produce useful positive intelligence, for it can indicate the deficiencies of another nation's information or suggest clues to that nation's intentions.

Covert action, in its simplest definition, refers to the efforts by a nation to influence the affairs of other nations by secret, deceptive or unattributable means. Covert action goes forward under a number of euphemistic labels. For many years the covert action branch of the CIA operated under a directorate labeled "Plans." Sometimes these activities were classified under the rubric "clandestine services." More recently, the term "special activity" has been suggested as a cover label.

If one were to catalog the various activities that take place under the general covert action label, the following would be included: (a) political advice and counsel to foreign political leaders, sometimes to those in power, at other times to those in opposition; (b) secret financial subsidies to selected foreign individuals believed to be working in support of one's own national interests; (c) financial support and other forms of specialized assistance to foreign political parties or favored political groups; (d) support of non-government foreign organizations, such as business firms, labor unions, cooperatives, and other special interest groups; (e) secret training of individuals, e.g., foreign security police, including secret exchange of personnel; (f) secret foreign aid, sometimes on a massive scale, for economic development, or technical assistance, or outright bribery; and (g) paramilitary, psychological warfare or other forms of secret action designed to overthrow or support a foreign regime.

Professor Smith's bibliography is a valuable and necessary step toward a better understanding of the Cold War. His extensive earlier bibliographical works have demonstrated his impressive ability to command and control a vast array of publications. For the scholar or general reader there are snares and pitfalls at every turn. Much of the literature included here is self-serving, even deliberately deceptive, and some is very likely the product of a "disinformation" battle waged by opposing secret services. Professor Smith properly warns us of this in his introduction.

Covert actions of all kinds have become multi-billion dollar activities, often occurring in the gutters of world politics. Dean Rusk, the United States Secretary of State, is reported to have said that a bitter struggle was going on in the back alleys of international politics, and the United States could little afford to refrain from this kind of struggle. More recently, Henry Kissinger argued that the United States needs a capability somewhere between doing nothing and sending the Marines to a crucial area of the world where United States' interests are at stake. President Carter, in his 1980 State of the Union address, noted the necessity of dealing with the world as it is rather than with the world as we would like it to be. The President went on to call for the removal of some Congressional restraints that had been placed on covert action.

Such assertions are made in the context of the dominating assumption that the world is involved in a kind of secret World War III. This war commenced within a year or so of the end of World War II. Note the observation of a veteran of that secret war, Harry Rositzke, in *The CIA's Secret Operations* (p. 1): "In the spring of 1948 the White House saw war with the Soviet Union as imminent." A few months later, the CIA's new Office of Special Operations targeted the Soviet Union and mobilized secret missions. Writes Rositzke (p. 13): "The Soviet Union was the enemy, and the 'Soviet target' our intelligence mission. We were professionally and emotionally committed to a single purpose. We felt ourselves as much a part of the American crusade against Stalin as we had against Hitler."

From that period onwards the hidden Cold War escalated, involving allies on both sides of the "Iron Curtain." A wide variety of covert actions became a routine, albeit highly secret, instrument of American foreign policy. The focus was initially in Western Europe and in the late 1950s began to shift to the developing areas of the world commonly referred to as the "Third World." Early success in controlling events in Italy and France and later Greece and Turkey led to even bolder moves in Guatemala and Iran. This was heady wine for the covert operators, who were able to persuade presidents and secretaries of state that they could, on assignment, manipulate political events in almost any part of the world, at low cost to the United States. Recent Congressional studies reveal that by 1953 major covert operations were under way in 48 countries. These operations included propaganda, paramilitary action, and a variety of secret political intervention. By the 1960s, with such operations numbering in the hundreds, covert action came to have the following official definition: "any clandestine activity designed to influence foreign governments, events, organizations or persons in support of United States foreign policy." It is assumed that most of this activity was in response to perceived similar activity by the "other side," i.e., Communist bloc activity.

Assumptions about the necessity for all of this secret intervention are best understood by quoting from a 1954 special Hoover Commission subcommittee, chaired by General James Doolittle, which stated in a confidential report to the President:

> It is now clear that we are facing an implacable enemy whose avowed objective is world domination by whatever means and at whatever cost. There are no rules in such a game. Hitherto acceptable norms of human conduct do not apply. If the United States is to survive, long-standing American concpets of 'fair play' must be reconsidered. We must develop effective espionage and counterespionage services and must learn to subvert, sabotage and destroy our enemies by more clever, more sophisticated, and more effective methods than those used against us.

Motivated by such principles, covert action programs became the dominant part of the CIA's activities in the 1950s and 1960s. Presumably this escalated the secret war with adversaries who responded in kind. With the United States' withdrawal from Southeast Asia in the early 1970s and the beginning of a new era labeled "detente," followed by increasing disclosures and criticisms of some CIA covert actions, programs for secret operations declined sharply in the late 1970s. There was little evidence that America's Cold War adversaries had curtailed their activities, which presumably went forward under tight controls against disclosure. With the beginning of the 1980s, a great and, as of this writing, unresolved debate began regarding the future policy, organization and control of United States covert operations.

Undoubtedly covert action is a controversial foreign policy instrument of all major foreign powers. This is because the institutions created for carrying out such activities are double-edged swords. Clandestine activity can silently defend against foreign enemies but, as a weapon that cuts both ways, it can also be internally dangerous. It constitutes secret power and secret power is a threat to any regime, democratic or totalitarian. Note that in the past more than one head of the Soviet Secret Service has been executed; that the President of South Korea was assassinated by the chief of the Korean Central Intelligence Agency. As onetime United States CIA Director Allen Dulles said: "An intelligence agency is an ideal vehicle for a conspiracy."

The 1945–1980 international political period has been shaped by both open and secret diplomacy, by attributable propaganda and covert propaganda and psychological warfare, by massive public foreign aid programs as well as secret financial subsidies, by open as well as secret support of dissidents in foreign lands, and by overt military intervention (as in Korea and Vietnam) as well as secret wars (as in Laos and Angola).

The task of the historian and analyst of world politics, therefore, goes beyond an examination of the overt record of diplomacy and events data. Historians and analysts must try to ferret out the facts of the covert record if we are to understand why events transpired as they did. This is an extremely difficult task of scholarly detective work. But the secret has been too massive and influential to ignore. Professor Smith has provided us with some of the essential tools for such an understanding. Our task as analysts of the world is to serve as constant and faithful revisionists, in the true sense of that term. The task of understanding the 35 years of Cold War between 1945–1980 has just begun. Professor Smith's bibliography will serve as an indispensable guide to a fuller historical understanding of one of the most turbulent periods of modern history.

HARRY HOWE RANSOM
Professor of Political Science
Vanderbilt University

Preface

Background

A vast "secret war" is being fought around the globe today, a continuation of a decades old conflict of competing ideologies. Its progress has been unimpeded and has ebbed and flowed under a nuclear presence through various changes in political atmosphere labeled "cold war" or "detente." The role of the principal undercover instruments—intelligence and counterintelligence, propaganda and psychological warfare, and covert, often paramilitary, operations—can hardly be overemphasized as nation states maneuver for security and advantage in the world arena.

Since 1945, a "secret war" literature has evolved seemingly to keep pace with events. Fanned by novels and films, this production, at least three quarters of which has been published in English or German, can be of great or small value to the lay reader and requires of this book certain analytical introductory remarks.

In his article "Strategic Intelligence and Foreign Policy," Professor Harry Howe Ransom suggests that the literature of which we speak may be classified in three different ways. First, there is the "memoir," a publication by a former member of the secret war establishments which, with some exceptions, has official blessing. Next, there is the "muckraking" product, a whistle-blowing exposé which can often provide certain insight but usually fails the standard tests of serious scholarship. Finally, there is the "objective analysis," a scholarly work prepared by a professional specialist in history or another social science which examines "how the system works in specific historical contexts."[1]

Another scholar, David H. Hunter, takes Professor Ransom's categories into account and in a recent article goes further to suggest that "the overall attitudinal tenor" of secret war literature has undergone changes determined by certain time frames and events. In accounts published before the mid-1960s, the view of agencies, agents, and activities was usually favorable and often glamorizing. With the coming of the Vietnam-Watergate era, the tenor abruptly changed and almost all publications, especially those prepared in the U.S., demonstrated veiled or outright hostility to the concept and operations of a secret war. "Muckraking" became extremely stylistic and certain authors apparently competed to see how much "dirt" could be uncovered and trumpeted. By 1977, the heights of outright hostility had apparently been reached. In the years closing the decade, secret war literature appears to have settled onto a middle course with reactions "both reflected and accompanied by the appearance of more attitudinally balanced" commentary.[2]

Given the ups and downs of the literature one other point should, in all honesty, be addressed. How accurate is the literature of the post World War II secret struggle and how much of it can you believe? Despite the comments of experts, this is still a difficult question to answer.

In many Commonwealth countries for example, including Britain, Australia, and Canada, it is official government policy never to openly provide information concerning secret war activities. The existence of an Australian intelligence apparatus was not even acknowledged until 1977. Any information becoming available to the press is severely censored by a series of guidelines known in Britain, at least, as "D Notices." For that reason, readers will find virtually no solid information on recent secret war activities by Commonwealth nations and will note that what is available usually has followed in the wake of spectacular defections or scandals.

On the other hand, the literature appearing in the media of Communist and certain leftist countries has, over the years, been so filled with ideology, propaganda, and inaccuracy that it remains virtually impossible to unravel the truth from the lie. Some of this production has been translated into English and published in some Western-based journals.

In the United States, the literature, as noted by Professors Ransom and Hunter above, has fluctuated according to time and purpose. The most accurate journal, the CIA's quarterly *Studies in Intelligence,* is classified and not available to the public. Two others, *Counterspy: The Quarterly Journal of the Fifth Estate* and the *Covert Action Information Bulletin,* manifest extreme hostility to secret war activities and organizations, even to the point of actively attempting to identify American agents. These, while not classified, are extremely difficult to obtain by the layman. In time, the trend towards balanced works, coupled with the Freedom of Information Act, should provide American citizens with a fairly abundant amount of scholarly and useful information.

Our problem, right now, is in dealing with the literature available to us since 1945. The problem is compounded by an actual disinformation game being played on the reader in many instances by various secret agencies and legislatures around the world. To improve their images and blacken that of their opponents, agencies as different as the KGB and the U.S. Senate Internal Security Subcommittee have provided official and semi-official disclosures and testimony and have backed the preparation of general histories and the memoirs of various individuals.

During the early phase of preparation for this guide, an older intelligence hand suggested to me that only about 10 percent of the secret war literature currently available is accurate and that it reports on only about 20 percent of what has actually occurred. This is understandable; if everyone knew what was going on and truthfully reported it, the secret war would not be secret.

As a rule of thumb, therefore, secret war literature must be treated with certain skepticism. Adopt the code of "investigative" journalists and accept no fact that cannot be verified in at least two or three overt sources. Recognize the aim of authors, many of whom have given themselves away through their titles, and always examine footnoting and bibliographic information carefully. In these ways, you can begin to protect yourself from falling into literary "boobietraps."

Objectives

In preparation for this work, I found only a few bibliographies in English devoted to the secret war as it has been fought since 1945. Several guides have appeared on intelligence as a subject from ancient times to the present and at least two (Blackstock/Schaf and Zuehlke) are extremely well annotated. Most of these contain at best only a few hundred citations, are unpublished, or are out of date. The principal reason for this state of affairs appears to be that until the great intelligence flap of 1974–1976 the secret war was not considered a suitable target for bibliographic enterprise.

This bibliography is intended to serve as a "working" guide to English-language sources concerning intelligence, counterintelligence, propaganda, psychological warfare, espionage, and covert operations written during the years 1945 to mid-1979. While aimed primarily at scholars and especially graduate and undergraduate students, it should also prove useful to librarians, general readers, and journalists. It may also be interesting to specialized students known as "intelligence buffs."

This guide is not definitive, but it attempts comprehensiveness in that virtually all factors concerning the secret war are covered. As a reference tool, it will permit users to quickly determine what material is available and help them establish a basis for further research. In general, items are cited which the user might reasonably expect to find in large university, public, or government libraries. In practice, students should be able to find many of the more recent book titles at least in even small- or medium-sized college or public library collections. Should you be unable to turn up a given reference locally, keep in mind that many items cited are available through interlibrary loan, details of which service can be obtained at your nearest library.

The criteria for selection in this guide is the same as that for the first volume of this series, *Intelligence, Propaganda and Psychological Warfare, Resistance Movements, and Secret Operations, 1939–1945.* The following types of published material are represented below: books and monographs; scholarly papers; periodical and journal articles; government documents; doctoral dissertations; and masters theses. Although much has been included, it was necessary to draw a line somewhere and omit certain kinds of information. Excluded materials include fiction, obvious children's works, newspaper articles (unless reprinted in other works), poetry, and book reviews.

Arrangement

The four main sections of the Table of Contents form, with their subsections, a classified subject index to this guide and a key to the book's organization. Within the text, each alphabetically-arranged section includes a brief introduction outlining its task, often with a note on "further references" designed to guide the user to other sections containing related materials. References are not usually repeated.

Each citatation is numbered and entry numbers appear consecutively throughout the guide. The author index is keyed to the entry numbers. A few non-critical annotations are provided to clarify title contents or to warn of disinformation tactics. Unnumbered cross-references to joint (jt.) authors, editors, and spy aliases are provided within the body of the text where appropriate.

Other Features

The chronology of secret war events (1945–1979) following this preface was drawn from overt sources to whet the appetite of users; corrections or additions may be sent to the publisher for use in the next edition.

The literature of secret wars contains numerous terms, some cute and many confusing. In 1978, the American Intelligence Community under CIA direction prepared a "Glossary of Intelligence Terms and Definitions" for internal use. Unclassified aspects of this list were printed in the first annual report of the House Select Committee on Intelligence. In an effort to increase the limited circulation of that "sanitized" glossary and to be of assistance to the user with the latest official terminology, the House version is reprinted in Part V.

Acknowledgments

For their advice, assistance, or encouragement in the formulation, research, and completion of this endeavor, the following persons and libraries are gratefully acknowledged. Their involvement does not necessarily constitute an endorsement of this guide.

Dr. Dean C. Allard, Head, Operational Archives Branch, U.S. Naval Historical Center

Mr. Robert B. Lane, Director, Air University Library

Professor Lyman B. Kirkpatrick, Jr., Brown University

Hon. Birch Bayh, U.S. Senate Committee on Intelligence

Hon. Edward P. Boland, U.S. House Permanent Select Committee on Intelligence

Hon. John Ashbrook, U.S. House Permanent Select Committee on Intelligence

Mr. Charles E. Wilson, Chief, Plans and Policy Branch, U.S. Central Intelligence Agency

Public Information Office, U.S. Central Intelligence Agency

Dr. Walter Pforzheimer, Washington, D.C.

The Association of Former Intelligence Officers, McLean, Virginia

Mr. Lester L. Miller, Jr., Morris Swett Library, U.S. Army Field Artillery School

Ms. Donnie W. Draughon, Documents Expeditor, Exchange and Gift Division, Library of Congress

Ms. Joyce Eaking, Library Director, U.S. Army Military History Institute

Dr. Brian J. Winkel, Albion College (Mich.)

West Virginia University Library

Kanawha County (W.V.) Public Library

Harrison County (W.V.) Public Library

U.S. Navy Department Library

U.S. Air University Library

Interlibrary Loan Department, Central Intelligence Agency Library

Special appreciation is reserved for my colleagues at Salem College without whose backing and aid this project would not have been completed. President James C. Stam and Dean Ronald O. Champagne continuously supported and encouraged me to proceed. The Political Science Department, chaired by Dr. Jesse Kelly and including Dr. David

Lynch, provided stimulation, insight, and resources. Mrs. Sara J. Graham, Margaret Allen, Jacqueline Isaacs, and Sara Case of the Benedum Learning Resources Center staff gave bibliographic and interlibrary loan assistance.

To series editor Richard Burns and editor Shelly Lowenkopf go my appreciation for their support and guidance, to say nothing of their endurance.

Finally, hearty thanks is due to Professor Harry H. Ransom of the Political Science Department of Vanderbilt University, who in his many writings has objectively brought insight and wisdom to the postwar secret war story, for his excellent and kind historical foreword.

Notes

1. Harry Howe Ransom, "Strategic Intelligence and Foreign Policy," *World Politics,* XXVII (October 1974), 133.

2. David H. Hunter, "The Evolution of Literature on United States Intelligence," *Armed Forces and Society,* V (November 1978), 31–32.

Chronology

The selected incidents which follow were drawn from secret service histories, documents of Congressional committees, general espionage accounts, and other materials cited in the bibliography. A list of the principal sources employed follows the chronology.

The chronology is arranged by year or range of years and then by geographical area beginning with Northern Europe and ranging around the globe back to the United States.

1944–1957   **(USSR)** The Soviet ambassador to Canada (1944–1947), Britain (1947–1952), and the U.S. (1952–1957) is spymaster Georgi Zarubin.

1945   **(Canada)** Cipher clerk Igor Gouzenko defects in Ottawa reporting massive Soviet espionage against the Allied atomic bomb program.

(United States) President Harry S Truman's Executive Order 9621 disbands the Office of Strategic Services (OSS) and its functions are absorbed by the State and War Departments.

1945–1975   **(United States)** RCA and ITT make their customers' telegraphic communications available for surveillance purposes to the U.S. Army Signal Security Agency and its successor, the National Security Agency (NSA).

1946   **(Britain)** British scientist Dr. Alan N. May is convicted of passing atomic secrets to the Soviets.

(USSR) The Soviet NKGB is redesignated the Ministry for State Security (MGB) and Chairman Beria is elevated to the Politburo.

The NKVD is redesignated the Ministry for Internal Affairs (MVD) with Sergei N. Kruglov as director.

(Indochina) U.S. Central Intelligence Group (CIG) agents funnel covert funds to pro-French political parties.

(United States) President Truman signs a Presidential directive establishing the CIG to operate under the direction of the National Intelligence Authority (NIA).

Rear Admiral Sidney W. Souers, USNR, is appointed the first Director of Central Intelligence (DCI).

The Bureau of Intelligence and Research is created within the Department of State.

1947　　**(USSR)** The Committee of Information (KI) is established to carry out foreign intelligence work; it is comprised of the foreign intelligence units of the MVD and the General Staff's GRU.

(Europe) From transmitters in Western Europe, the Voice of America (VOA) begins to send Russian-language broadcasts to the Soviet Union.

(United States) The National Security Act of 1947 replaces the NIA with the National Security Council (NSC) and the CIG with the Central Intelligence Agency (CIA).

At its first meeting, the NSC issues a top secret directive granting the CIA authority to conduct covert operations abroad.

1947–1948　　**(Indochina)** CIA agents continue to funnel covert funds in an effort to buy off political leaders opposed to the French.

1947–1950　　**(United States)** Admiral Roscoe H. Hillenkoetter, USN, serves as the first CIA director and the second DCI.

1947–1975　　**(Italy)** The CIA is alleged to have funneled $75 million in covert financial aid to anti-Communist politicians and political parties.

During the same period, covert funds are funneled to Communist and leftist parties and politicians from Russian and Eastern European sources.

1948　　**(Europe)** The Soviets begin jamming incoming foreign radio broadcasts.

(USSR) The General Staff recovers its GRU units from the KI.

(Czechoslovakia) Soviet-supported Czech intelligence agents plot the death of Jan Masaryk.

(Yugoslavia) The Soviet MGB fails to predict Marshal Tito's break with Russia.

(France) The CIA begins to funnel covert financial aid to anti-Communist political parties and politicians.

(West Germany) With covert subsidies from the CIA-backed Radio Free Europe (RFE), the West German *Kampfgruppe gegen Unmenschlichkeit* ("Fighting Group Against Inhumanity") is established to support political prisoners and their families and to run secret commando missions into East Germany.

(Syria) CIA agent Stephen Meade engineers a coup against the government of President Shukri Quwatli.

(United States) President Truman establishes the Office of Policy Coordination, under Frank G. Wisner, Jr., to conduct U.S. covert operations separately from the CIA and the Office of Special Operations to conduct clandestine intelligence collection.

The CIA implements its National Intelligence Survey designed to provide basic data on every country in the world.

In testimony before the House Un-American Activities Committee, Whittaker Chambers admits to being a spy and condemns foreign officer Alger Hiss as a Soviet agent.

1948–1950   **(USSR-Albania)** The CIA unsuccessfully attempts to establish and nourish anti-Communist guerrilla movements in the Ukraine and Albania.

1948–1953   **(Japan)** MGB agents posing as Soviet newsmen mount an intense disinformation campaign against the United States and the American occupation of Japan.

1948–1956   **(Europe)** The U.S. flies aircraft equipped with various electronic sensors along the borders of the Soviet Union.

1948–1962   **(United States)** Prior to his retirement, CIA escape and evasion expert Stephen J. Meade, known as "The Whistler," made 32 incursions into the USSR, China, and North Korea to rescue agents or bring out defectors.

1948–1962   **(United States)** The Federal Bureau of Investigation (FBI) monitors the activities of persons and groups involved in the Civil Rights movement.

1949   **(USSR)** The USAF Long Range Detection Unit detects a large amount of radioactive dust giving the U.S. knowledge of the first Russian atomic blast.

(Britain) Dr. Klaus Fuchs is arrested and convicted of being a Soviet atomic spy from 1943–1946.

(West Germany) The British-sponsored Federal Office for the Protection of the Constitution (BfV) is formed as the West German secret service under Otto John.

The Association of Free German Jurists is organized with covert CIA subsidies.

(China) Aircraft of the CIA proprietary company Civil Air Transport support the Chinese Nationalist withdrawal to Formosa.

(United States) The Free Europe Committee is established with covert CIA funding.

Congress enacts the Central Intelligence Agency Act of 1949, supplementing the 1947 National Security Act by specifying fiscal and administrative procedures for the agency.

Department of Justice employee Judith Coplon is arrested and convicted as a Soviet agent.

1949–1954   **(USSR)** Camera-equipped CIA balloons are released in Western Europe, drift eastward over the Soviet Union, and those which survive are picked up in the Pacific Ocean.

1949–1964 (**Eastern Europe**) U.S. foreign officers uncover over 130 listening devices in American embassies.

1950 (**Eastern Europe**) The first Radio Free Europe broadcast is made into Eastern Europe from transmitters in West Germany.

(**Albania**) Soviet agent Harold "Kim" Philby leaks information on the CIA and British Secret Intelligence Service (SIS) infiltration of Albania resulting in the death of half the Western agents.

(**Israel**) The Israeli intelligence service Mossad is created.

(**Formosa**) The CIA begins operating under the cover of Western Enterprises, Inc., training nationalist Chinese commandos for raids on the mainland of China.

(**Korea**) After warning of the North Korean invasion of South Korea, Western spy Banda MacLeod, reportedly Mata Hari's daughter, is caught and executed by the North Koreans.
  The CIA is criticized for its handling of Chinese Communist intervention estimates.

(**India**) Chinese agents in Bombay attack Anadan Andrew, a courier, in an attempt to steal documents intended for the U.S. consulate.

(**United States**) The CIA transport proprietary company, the Pacific Corporation, is organized as a Delaware corporation.
  New CIA chief General Walter Bedell Smith, USA, reorganizes the agency's recruitment procedures.
  Harry Gold, Alfred D. Slack, David Greenglass, Abraham Brothman, Miriam Moskowitz, Morton Sobel, and Julius and Ethel Rosenberg are arrested by the FBI on charges of espionage.

1950–1952 (**North Korea**) CIA trained and backed South Korean agents are involved in several unsuccessful clandestine missions into North Korea.

1950–1953   **(Philippines)** Acting under CIA auspices, USAF Colonel Edward Lansdale advised and assisted Philippine leader Ramon Magsaysay in a struggle against Communist Huk guerrillas who are ultimately defeated.

(United States) General Smith serves as CIA Director.

1950–1954   **(Poland)** The CIA unsuccessfully attempts to set up an underground network in Poland; the Polish secret service co-opts the operation from the beginning luring anti-Communist emigres back (and into prison) and bilking the Americans of millions of dollars.

(USSR) USAF RB-36 aircraft conduct high altitude reconnaissance flights over the Soviet Union.

1950–1966   **(United States)** The anti-Communist Congress for Cultural Freedom is secretly financed by the CIA with over $1 million.

The Center for International Studies at the Massachusetts Institute of Technology is established with a secret CIA grant of $300,000; it received additional "grants" over the next sixteen years.

1950–1967   **(United States)** In the wake of the revelation that the CIA had subsidized the National Student Association, it is disclosed that the agency funded many other labor, business, church, university, and cultural organizations through a variety of foundation conduits, spending at least $12,422,925 in the process.

1950–1973   **(United States)** It was learned in 1973 that Radio Free Europe (RFE) and Radio Liberty (RL), purportedly "nonprofit, privately managed" American radio stations, had received most of their financing from the CIA; the combined budget of the two stations was found to be between $30 and $35 million with the CIA providing over 95 per cent of this amount.

1951   **(USSR)** MGB chief V. S. Abakumov is arrested and the KI is abolished.

(Britain) Under suspicion but warned by Kim Philby, Soviet agents Guy Burgess and Donald Maclean flee to Russia to avoid arrest.

(**East Germany**) Agents of the West German *Kampf-gruppe gegen Unmenschlichkeit* set fire to the State Trade Organization in East Berlin.

(**Burma**) Nationalist Chinese guerrillas who have fled to North Burma from China receive CIA support.

(**Thailand**) The CIA proprietary company, Sea Supply Corporation, begins operations in Thailand.

(**Korea**) Long-range U.S. radio intercepts reveal that Soviet pilots fly North Korean MIGs in combat against USAF and USN forces.

(**United States**) The U.S. Office of Policy Coordination and Office of Special Operations are combined into the CIA's Directorate of Plans.

Soviet agent Rudolf Abel enters the U.S. under the alias Emil R. Goldfus.

Accused foreign officer Alger Hiss is sentenced to a prison term of five years.

1951–1952	(**United States**) Thomas Braden, chief of the CIA's Division of International Organization, gives Walter Reuther, United Auto Workers, $50,000 in covert funds which was ultimately spent by Victor Reuther to support anti-Communist labor unions in West Germany.
1951–1954	(**Estonia**) MVD agents penetrate a British SIS network in Estonia.
1951–1965	(**United States**) Twenty-one residents of the U.S., all but two current or former CIA employees, are wiretapped by the agency in an effort to check on leaks of classified information.
1952	(**USSR**) Seman D. Ignatiev becomes director of the MGB. MVD agents disguised as workmen place 44 "bugs" in the new U.S. Embassy in Moscow.

(**West Germany**) Soviet agents kidnap Dr. Walter Linse, acting President of the Association of Free German Jurists.

(**Egypt**) The CIA supports a coup which overthrows King Farouk and brings Gamel A. Nassar to power.

(**Burma**) The CIA is accused of supporting a Thai invasion into eastern Burma.

(China) U Ba Thein, working for the CIA, organizes the first cross-border intelligence missions from Thailand into China.

Agents of the CIA's Special Operations Division begin attempts to develop resistance movements inside Communist China.

While organizing and training two teams of Nationalist Chinese to stir up mainland Chinese against their Communist government, CIA agents John Thomas Downey and Richard George Fecteau are captured on the mainland.

(United States) The U.S. Army Signal Security Agency is disbanded and its duties assumed by the new National Security Agency (NSA).

1952–1953　**(East Germany)** Railroad targets throughout East Germany are sabotaged by agents of the West German *Kampfgruppe gegen Unmenschlichkeit.*

1952–1966　**(United States)** In a successful effort to influence its activities and policies the CIA and NSA funnel some $3.3 million to the National Student Association or as much as 80 per cent of its budget in certain years.

1952–1972　**(Greece)** Greek military and political figures, including Georgios Papadopoulos who led the 1967 coup, receive covert subsidies from the CIA.

1953　　　**(Britain)** Sir Percy Sillitoe retires as Chief ("K") of MI5 and is succeeded by Sir Dick Goldsmith-White.

Soviet defector Ismail Akhmedoff describes the operations division of the GRU to Western intelligence agents.

(USSR) MVD chief Beria is arrested and later executed as the Soviet hierarchy undergoes a shake-up following Stalin's death.

(West Germany) The CIA establishes an independent West German intelligence service under former Nazi general Reinhard Gehlen.

West German agents break-up and arrest Polish members of a spy network which infiltrated the Amt Blank, an anti-Soviet NATO intelligence group.

(East Germany) Agents of Gehlen's organization operate in East Germany to encourage workers' riots.

The East German Ministry of State Security (MfS) is established under Soviet supervision.

(Iran) CIA agent Kermit "Kim" Roosevelt, grandson of President Theodore Roosevelt, organizes and directs the overthrow of Premier Mohammed Mossadegh's government. Mossadegh, with the connivance of the Iranian Communist Party, nationalized certain Western oil interests. The coup enables Shah Mohammed Reza Pahlevi to keep his throne.

(China) The Joint Office of Intelligence agenicies of the Chinese Central Peoples' Government is established under Chiang Chin-t'ao.

(United States) Radio Liberty is founded with covert CIA funds.

Having unknowingly taken LSD in a CIA drug experiment, Frank Olson commits suicide.

The CIA's Division of International Organizations operates or influences international organizations (through legitimate existing organizations) to counter Communist fronts in several areas.

The United States Information Agency is established as an independent agency to counter Communist propaganda.

1953–1956   **(Egypt)** The CIA maintains a close intelligence liaison with the Egyptian government.

1953–1958   **(Costa Rica)** The CIA works with forces opposed to President José (Pepe) Figueres's policy of granting asylum to Communists. Fugueres steps down when his candidate loses the Presidential election of 1958.

1953–1960   **(USSR)** The *Narodno-Troudoyov Soyouz* (National Alliance of Russian Solidarists), based in West Germany, sends 100 million propaganda leaflets, newspapers, and magazines into the Soviet Union by aerial balloon, water, and personal contact.

1953–1961   **(United States)** Allen W. Dulles serves as CIA Director.

1953–1967   **(United States)** In Project MK-ultra, the CIA's Directorate of Science and Technology conducts research on the effects of hallucinatory drugs on human beings.

1953–1973   **(United States)** To identify individuals in active correspondence with Russia and China, the CIA surveys and opens selected mail for counterintelligence purposes and to determine the nature and extent of censorship techniques.

1954   **(USSR)** The Committee on State Security (*Komitet Gosudarstvennoi Bezopastnosty*) is organized as the main Soviet police and intelligence organization.

(West Germany) The defection of Soviet agent Nikolai Khokhlov to West Germany reveals the existence of the Soviet murder/kidnap group SMERSH.
    Two *Narodno-Troudoyov Soyouz* officials are kidnapped in West Germany by MfS agents.

(East Germany) Seven agents of Gehlen's West German intelligence agency are convicted of stealing patents and documents from an East German electrical plant.

(Israel) In the "Lavon Affair," named after the Israeli defense minister Pinkas Lavon, Israeli intelligence agents plot to destroy the British and American information offices in Egypt in an effort to discredit Nassar; disclosure of the scheme leads to the resignation of the Ben-Gurion government.

(Australia) KGB agent Vladimir Petrov defects revealing information concerning Soviet espionage activities "down under."

(Japan) Soviet agent Yuri A. Rastvorov, who operates an Asian spy network centered in Japan, defects to the West.

(Indochina) Air drops to French troops at Dien Bien Phu are made by aircraft of the CIA proprietary company Civil Air Transport.
    Civil Air Transport aircraft fly refugees from North to South Vietnam and clandestinely fly agents and supplies from South to North Vietnam.

(Guatemala) The Communist-dominated regime of President Jacobo Arbenz Guzman in Guatemala is overthrown in a coup masterminded by the CIA which supplied arms, ammunition, and agency-piloted fighter bombers as well as training and support for the forces of Colonel Carlos Castillo-Armas who assumed power.

(United States) The U.S. Congress approves the death penalty for peacetime espionage.

The Attorney General grants the FBI sweeping authority to engage in microphone surveillance for counterintelligence purposes.

Lockheed chief engineer C. L. Johnson designs a high altitude research aircraft which will become known as the U(tility)-2.

The U.S. National Indications Center, an early warning group, is established subordinate to the U.S. Intelligence Board.

NSA employee Joseph S. Peterson, Jr., is prosecuted in connection with the misuse of documents concerning North Korean and Netherlands codes.

1954–1955   (South Vietnam) CIA agent Colonel Edward Lansdale engineers the overthrow of the Binh Xuyen bandits and engages in an underground war with French 2nd Bureau agents for control of Saigon.

1954–1963   (United States) As part of Project MK-ultra, the CIA covertly runs bars and prostitutes as cover for LSD experiments in "Operation Midnight Climax."

1954–1974   (United States) The Justice Department allows the CIA to investigate crimes allegedly committed by its agents.

1954–1976   (Canada) The Royal Canadian Mounted Police (RCMP) and Defence Force Security and Intelligence Agency engage in covert mail opening and burglary designed to combat espionage, subversion, and terrorism.

1955   (Eastern Europe) From bases in West Germany, agents of the *Narodno-Troudoyov Soyouz* send 14 million propaganda tracts into Eastern Europe via balloon.

(East Germany) CIA and Gehlen intelligence agents tap the main underground cables between Moscow and Soviet military headquarters in East Berlin.

Agents of the *Kampfgruppe gegen Unmenschlichkeit* burn an East Berlin radio station.

MfS agents capture several agents of the *Kampfgruppe gegen Unmenschlichkeit* engaged in covert operations against East German targets.

(Egypt) Two Egyptian Jews are executed as Israeli agents to end the "Lavon Affair."

(South Vietnam) CIA agents of Colonel Lansdale's team conduct a successful black propaganda campaign leading to the election of Ngo Dinh Diem.

(United States) The Second Hoover Commission investigates the structure of the U.S. government, including intelligence agencies.

Authority for authorizing CIA covert operations is given to the NSC Special Group.

1955–1959   **(South Vietnam)** Michigan State University is utilized by the CIA to conduct a covert police training program for the Diem government.

1956   **(USSR)** CIA agent Stephen Meade is parachuted into Soviet territory to rescue an American scientist whose plane crashed near the Iranian border.

(Britain) Sir Dick Goldsmith-White is named Chief ("C") of the SIS MI6, while Sir Henry Hollis becomes "K" of MI5.

Royal Navy frogman Commander Lionel Crabbe vanishes near a Soviet cruiser in Portsmouth Harbour.

(West Germany) The BND under Reinhard Gehlen is established as the official West German Federal Intelligence Agency.

(Hungary) During the Hungarian Revolution RFE broadcasts imply that American aid would be forthcoming to the rebels.

CIA and BND agents supply a limited number of arms to Hungarian patriots.

KGB agents kidnap Prime Minister Nagy and the leaders of the revolt are arrested at a dinner sponsored by the Soviet ambassador.

(Eastern Europe) RFE broadcasts information on the Polish uprising at Poznaw to other Communist satellites.

(Egypt) Mossad agents discover a team of former Nazi rocket experts working in Egypt.

The CIA warns the U.S. government about a forthcoming Israeli invasion of the Sinai.

(South Vietnam) The CIA-controlled First Observer Group is organized for operations against Viet Cong guerrillas.

(United States) The U.S. Senate rejects a bill setting up a Joint Committee on Intelligence.

Designed to promote public interest in the Far East, the Asia Foundation is established under a covert CIA subsidy.

1956–1960   **(USSR)** CIA pilots fly the U-2 over the Soviet Union to photograph missile and defense related installations.

(Europe) Czechoslovak intelligence mails neo-Nazi pamphlets to British, French, and American officials in Europe and commit a number of anti-Semitic acts designed to embarrass the West German government.

1956–1969   **(Pakistan)** The USAF maintains a spy plane base near Peshawar in West Pakistan.

1956–1972   **(United States)** In twelve separate cointelpro programs, the FBI carries out 2,370 covert buggings and burglaries against U.S. citizens and groups.

1957   **(USSR)** U.S. intelligence agencies predict the launching of the Soviet Sputnik earth-orbiting satellite.

(West Germany) MfS agents abduct Dr. Erwin Neuman, President of the Association of Free German Jurists.

SMERSH agent Bogdan Stashynsky kills Ukrainian anti-Communist leader Lev Rebet.

Soviet defector Nikolai Khokhlov narrowly escapes death by poisoning while attending a West German convention.

(Greece) British SIS agents in Athens tap the telephone of the Greek Prime Minister during the First Cyprus Crisis.

(Iran) The Iranian secret police and intelligence agency SAVAK is established, reportedly assisted by the CIA.

(Thailand) CIA agents who supported General Phao's police are dismissed from the country.

(Indonesia) Employing a look-alike, the CIA produces the film "Happy Days" in an effort to embarrass President Sukarno.

(United States) Following his betrayal by agent Eugene Hayhanen, Soviet agent Rudolf Abel is arrested by the FBI in New York.

In a decade of service as an FBI double agent, Boris Morros assisted in the arrests of Jacob Albam, Jack and Myra Soble, Albert and Martha Dodd Stern, and George and Jane Zlatovski for espionage.

Jack and Myra Soble and Jacob Albam are convicted of spying for the Russians.

1957–1976   **(Jordan)** King Hussein receives covert CIA funds.

1958   **(East Germany)** Various bridges in East Germany are attacked by agents of the *Kampfgruppe gegen Unmenschlichkeit*.

(France) The French intelligence services are reorganized into the *Service de Documentation Extérieure et de Countrespionage* (SDECE) and the *Direction de la Securité du Territoire* (DST).

(Rumania) Rumanian citizens receive information on a secret government criminal code by listening to RFE broadcasts.

(Egypt) Sami Sharaf, head of Egyptian intelligence, is subverted by the KGB.

(Lebanon) The CIA urges U.S. military intervention.

(South Vietnam) A clandestine radio, the Voice of the South Vietnamese Liberation Front, begins operation.

(Indochina) The CIA proprietary company Air America is established to support clandestine actions in Southeast Asia.

(Indonesia) Rebels on the island of Sumatra attempting to overthrow President Kukarno are given air support by CIA B-26's; agency pilot Allen L. Pope is shot down and captured by the Indonesians.

(United States) Having defected to the CIA, Polish spy Michael Goleniewski provides information which will eventually help break the Portland spy ring in Britain.

The CIA Directorate of Plans encourages its technicians to develop a spy satellite.

1958–1961   **(United States)** Camp Hale, near Leadville, Colorado, is established as a secret CIA training base for Tibetan troops loyal to the Dalai Lama; CIA trained guerrillas, occasionally led by contract mercenaries, conduct raids against the Communist Chinese in Tibet during this period.

1958–1962   **(USSR)** Alexandr Shelepin serves as Chairman of the KGB.

1958–1965   **(United States)** FBI agents burglarize the New York offices of the Socialist Workers Party.

1959   **(USSR)** The KGB's Disinformation Department or Department D is established.

(West Germany) The *Kampfgruppe gegen Unmenschlichkeit* is disbanded.

Anti-Communist Soviet exile Stefan Bandera is killed by SMERSH agent Bogdan Stashynsky.

MfS agents contaminate the food in the RFE cafeteria in Munich.

(Egypt) Egyptian intelligence chief Sami Sharaf arranges for joint Egyptian-KGB operations.

(Thailand) CIA-backed paramilitary operations begin in Thailand.

(Burma) KGB agents unsuccessfully plot to implant forgeries in the Burmese press.

(Tibet) A CIA trained radio operator helps the Dalai Lama to escape the Chinese conquest of Tibet.

The Commerical Academy of Lhasa is established as a cover for Chinese Secret Service operations to monitor the Soviet Union and India.

(United States) Polish agent Pawel Monat and Soviet agent Nikolai Shadrin defect.

KGB agents contact Richard Flink to cultivate him as an agent of influence in American politics.

The Double Check Corporation is established in Miami as a CIA proprietary company to provide air support for the operations of Cuban exile groups.

1959–1967   **(West Germany)** Posing as a photographer, KGB agent Heinz Sutterlein marries Lenore Heinz, secretary to a high Foreign Ministry official. She subsequently provides her husband with 2,900 sensitive documents, and when Sutterlein's cover is exposed Lenore commits suicide.

1960   **(USSR)** Francis Gary Powers, a CIA U-2 pilot, is shot down over Sverdlovsk; the incident causes Premier Khrushchev to cancel his scheduled Paris summit meeting with President Eisenhower.

The Soviets try pilot Powers in public court in Moscow, convict him of espionage, and sentence him to prison.

Soviet fighters down a U.S. RB-47 reconnaissance plane over international waters in the Barents Sea.

(West Germany) Espionage convictions in West Germany total 590 since 1951.

(China) The Chinese Secret Services establish a special Peking school to train Latin American Communists in subversion and terrorism.

(**Argentina**) Iser Harel's Mossad agents kidnap Adolf Eichmann and return him for trial to Israel.

(**Guatemala**) A CIA training camp is established to prepare Cuban exiles for the overthrow of the government of Fidel Castro.

When a rebellion breaks out against President Miguel Ydigoras Fuentes, CIA piloted B-26's attack the rebels and the insurgency is subsequently crushed.

(**Caribbean**) A CIA clandestine radio station is established on Swan Island to braodcast propaganda to Cuba.

(**Canada**) On trial for espionage, Soviet agent Victor Spencer receives a light sentence. Subsequent revelations lead to a Liberal/Conservative scandal, the Munsinger Affair.

(**United States**) After long surveillance, the FBI arrests Willi Hirsch and Igor Y. Melck as Soviet agents.

U.S. ambassador Henry Cabot Lodge of the U.N. displays a great seal of the U.S. given by the Soviets to the American embassy in Moscow and which was equipped with an electronic bug.

The CIA proprietary company Southern Air Transport is acquired to support possible South American interventions; the organization is sold in 1973.

The U.S. Intelligence Advisory Board is renamed the U.S. Intelligence Board.

NSA employees Bernon Mitchell and William H. Martin defect to the Soviet Union.

1960–1962   (**Egypt**) Mossad agents tail general Mahmoud Khalil and learn of Egyptian plans to establish a rocket industry with the aid of West German scientists.

1960–1970   (**United States**) French SEDECE liaison to the CIA Pierre de Vosjoli passes information to the Americans which later confirms events leading to the Cuban missile crisis.

(**Worldwide**) KGB agents attempt to suborn U.S. diplomats and citizens in 78 countries; citizens of other Western nations receive the same treatment.

1961

(USSR) Vladimir Semichastny succeeds Alexandr Shelepin as Chairman of the KGB and launches an effort to popularize the deeds of Soviet secret agents.

American student Marvin W. Makinen is convicted of espionage and sentenced to prison.

(Britain) Foreign officer George Blake is arrested as a Soviet agent.

Konan T. Molody, alias Gordon Lonsdale; Morris and Lorna Cohen, alias the Krogers; Harry Houghton and Ethel Gee are convicted of espionage in the Portland naval secrets case.

(East Germany) The CIA fails to provide adequate forewarning of the East German construction of the Berlin Wall.

During the Berlin Crisis, Georges Pacques delivers NATO's contingency plan for the defense of the city to the KGB.

(West Germany) KGB Department V assassin Bogdan Stashynsky defects to the West.

East German agent Guenther Maennel provides western intelligence with much data on MfS organization and practices.

(Italy) Italian Captain Luigi Spada is caught selling NATO secrets to an Albanian diplomat.

(Poland) American diplomat Irving C. Scarbeck is compromised in Warsaw and agrees to spy for Polish intelligence; he is caught and arrested within four months.

(Middle East) The CIA is criticized for failing to warn of the rift between Syria and the United Arab Republic (Egypt).

(Iran) SAVAK chair General Teimur Bakhtiar is accused of an anti-Shah plot and dismissed.

(Burma) Nationalist Chinese forces are pushed out of Burma after two decades of CIA support.

(North Vietnam) Transported in C-54's of the CIA-proprietary Vietnam Air Transport, agency-trained South Vietnamese rangers begin harassing raids on North Vietnam via Laos and the Gulf of Tonkin.

(Algeria) Despite denials, the CIA is accused of supporting rightist army plots in Algeria against the French government.

(Congo) The CIA is implicated in the overthrow of the first independent government of the Congo.

CIA plans the murder of Congolese Prime Minister Patrice Lumumba, but he is killed by agents of Katangan leader Moise Tshombe before the plot can come to fruition.

(Dominican Republic) Dominican dissidents armed with weapons allegedly obtained from CIA sources assassinate dictator Rafael Trujillo.

(Cuba) Prior to the scheduled invasion of Cuba by Cuban exiles, the CIA enlists ex-FBI agent Robert Maheu who recruits Mafia figure John Roselli to put together an assassination team to "hit" Fidel Castro. The first attempt is a failure.

Trained and equipped by the CIA, a force of Cuban exiles unsuccessfully invades Cuba at the Bay of Pigs in an effort to overthrow Fidel Castro's government; the invasion fails and some 300 exiles and four CIA pilots are killed.

Three CIA electronics technicians are convicted of tapping the wires of the New China News office in Havana.

(Ecuador) The government of President Jose Velasco Ibarra refuses to sever diplomatic relations with Cuba. The CIA backs efforts which result in Ibarra's downfall.

(Worldwide) The U.S. begins using reconnaissance satellites, the first being code-named SAMOS; reports indicate that photographs from these satellites enabled President Kennedy to inform Khrushchev that the Americans knew just how few strategic missiles the Russians had at the height of the Berlin Wall crisis.

(United States) CIA Director Allen W. Dulles and Deputy Director for Plans Richard W. Bissell, Jr., are forced from office as a result of the Bay of Pigs fiasco.

The U.S. President's Foreign Intelligence Advisory Board is established.

CIA headquarters is moved from various offices in Washington, D.C., to a large new building in Langley, Va.; the entrance drive is marked by a sign reading "Bureau of Public Roads."

The U.S. Defense Intelligence Agency is created to coordinate the intelligence operations of the Department of Defense.

CIA Directorate of Science and Technology employees working with Lockheed develop the A-11 reconnaissance aircraft.

Dr. Robert Soblen is convicted of espionage; after fleeing to England, he later commits suicide.

1961–1962   **(USSR)** GRU Colonel Oleg Penkovsky delivers 5,000 microframes of Soviet military secrets to the British SIS and U.S. CIA.

(Cuba) Pro-Soviet Cuban Communists, backed by the KGB, unsuccessfully attempt to depose Fidel Castro.

(United States) KGB agents in the U.S. are ordered to seek evidence of American war preparations.

1961–1963   **(Cuba)** The CIA sends five teams to assassinate Fidel Castro but all are unsuccessful.

1961–1964   **(Congo)** The CIA becomes involved in a political struggle in the Congo, paying cash to selected politicians and giving arms to supporters of Joseph Mobutu and Cyril Adoula before eventually sending in mercenaries and paramilitary experts to aid the new government.

(Africa) Operating in Ghana, the KGB establishes a Bureau of Technical Assistance ("Special African Service") which trains natives in espionage, subversion, and guerrilla warfare and dispatches graduates into Cameroon, Ivory Coast, Togo, Niger, Upper Volta, Congo Leopoldville, Sierra Leone, Chad, Sudan, Nigeria, Liberia, Tanzania, Gambia, Swaziland, Zambia, Malawi, Guinea, Mali, Congo Brazzaville, Rwanda, Burundi, Angola, Rhodesia, Portugese Guinea and Mozambique.

(Laos) CIA operatives organize a private army (*L'Armée Clandestine*) of Meo tribesmen, establish bases, and provide Air America aircraft to support it.

(South Vietnam) The CIA supports and organizes the South Vietnamese Civilian Irregular Defense Guards, which operate under the direction of U.S. Army Special Forces advisors.

(North Vietnam) CIA supported and directed South Vietnamese sea-borne commando raids are increased against North Vietnam.

1961–1965   **(United States)** The CIA Director is John A. McCone.

1961–1970   **(Cambodia)** The CIA allegedly carried out a covert campaign of sabotage, assassination, and attempted coups against the government and politicians of Prince Sihanouk.

         (Cuba) Following the Bay of Pigs fiasco, Cuban exiles are directed and paid by CIA agents to compile secret files on and watch over other Cubans and Americans; at the height of this Cuban "counterintelligence" operation, the main Florida office has some 150 informants on its payroll and on-going activities in Los Angeles, New York, San Juan, and Miami.

1961–1971   **(France)** Atomic engineer Dimitri Volokov passes secrets of the French nuclear force to the KGB.

         (Mexico) KGB agents plot to destroy the government and plunge the nation into civil war.

1961–1973   **(United Nations)** Viktor M. Lessiovsky, personal aide to Secretary General U Thant, provides the KGB advance

information on the inner workings of the U.N. Secretariat.

1962   **(USSR)** The Soviet MVD is renamed the Ministry of the
Defense of the Public Order.

GRU Colonel Oleg Penkovsky and his British contact
Greville Wynne are captured.

In the wake of the Penkovsky scandal, KGB Chairman Ivan Serov is disgraced and replaced by his First
Deputy, Petr I. Ivashutin.

The Soviets provide information on 23 Western
agents caught infiltrating Russia since 1951.

(Britain) Naval clerk John Vassall is arrested for passing defense secrets to the Soviets.

(France) Soviet agent Martel reveals that several
French ministries are infiltrated by the KGB and that a
ring known as "Sapphire" is at work inside the SDECE
itself.

Acting on this CIA-generated information, President Kennedy sends President DeGaulle a letter warning of the Soviet penetration of his government.

(Sweden) Chao Fu defects in Stockholm in the first
widely-publicized case of a Chinese Secret Service
officer "going over."

(East Germany) Francis Gary Powers and Rudolf Abel
are exchanged on an East Berlin bridge.

(West Germany) BND agents Heinz P. J. Felfe, Hans
Clemens, and Erwin Tiebel are arrested as Soviet
agents in a scandal which nearly destroys Reinhard
Gehlen's intelligence agency.

(Yeman) The new Soviet and Chinese consulates in
Hodeida provide cover for KGB and Chinese Secret
Service subversion against several nearby oil sheik-
doms.

(Japan) KGB agents mount a tough disinformation
campaign against the United States.

(Cuba) KGB agent-Ambassador Sergei M. Kudryavtsev participates in the secret installation of Soviet missiles. The CIA learns that Soviet missiles have been installed in Cuba and alerts government leaders.

At the end of the crisis, an American U-2 is downed while on reconnaissance over Cuba.

During the crisis, KGB *resident* in Washington Alexander Fomin negotiates with the U.S. government via ABC News correspondent-courier John Scali.

The CIA keeps tabs on the removal of Soviet missiles by analyzing the size and shape of crates on Russian freighters.

The nearly 1,300 survivors of the 1961 Bay of Pigs invasion are traded to the U.S. for several millions of dollars worth of food and drugs.

(Worldwide) Soviet reconnaissance satellites, code-named COSMOS, begin overflying the West with particular attention to the U.S.

(United States) The NSC Special Group (Augmented) is established to oversee CIA covert action against Cuba.

The FBI exposes the KGB effort to subvert Richard Flink, Republican candidate for the New York state senate.

The CIA clears pilot Francis Gary Powers of wrongdoing when he was shot down over Russia in 1960.

USN Yeoman Nelson Drummond is arrested by the FBI on charges of spying for the Soviets.

The U.S. Army Intelligence and Security Branch (AIS) is established combining the Army Intelligence Corps and Army Security Agency.

962–1963   **(France)** USAF Sergeant Robert L. Johnson delivers U.S. defense plans stolen from the Armed Forces Courier Center in Paris to the KGB.

(Laos) Thai general U Ba Thein assists the CIA in opening bases in northwestern Laos.

1962–1965   **(Syria)** Eli Cohen serves as a Mossad agent in Syria until he is caught and publicly executed.

1962–1966   **(Ghana)** KGB agents subvert and control the government of Kwane Nkrumah, employing it as a "host" for subversive activities against other African states.

1962–1968   **(Cuba)** KGB officer Aleksandr I. Shitov succeeds KGB officer Sergei N. Kudryavtsev as Russian Ambassador.

1962–1969   **(United States)** The FBI intensively monitors the background and activities of Civil Rights leader Dr. Martin L. King.

1962–1973   **(Laos)** The CIA wages a so-called "secret war in Laos" against Communist forces using the 30,000 man native *L'Armée Clandestine*, controlled by 40-50 agents with a minimum $300 million annual budget; pilots on contract to Air America fly support missions (supply and bombing) with occasional assistance from regular U.S. forces.

1963   **(USSR)** GRU Colonel Oleg Penkovsky and his British SIS contact Greville Wynne are placed on public trial for espionage; Wynne is sentenced to prison and Penkovsky to death.

The activities of the murder-kidnap section of the KGB are curtailed.

Yale professor Frederick C. Barghoorn is detained in Moscow for 16 days by the KGB; the incident results in a personal intervention by President Kennedy.

KGB agents poll the reactions of Soviet citizens to the assassination of President Kennedy.

(Britain) British SIS officer Harold "Kim" Philby defects to Russia. It is learned that he was a long-time Soviet "mole" within the English intelligence service.

In the Profumo Affair, a British defense minister is accused of sharing the favors of a call girl with a known Soviet officer.

(Sweden) Swedish police arrest Colonel Stig E. Wennerstrom on charges of passing important defense secrets to the Soviets.

(Switzerland) Two Mossad agents are caught working against the West German missile scientists employed by

Egypt. The resulting scandal leads to the resignation of Isser Harel as chief of Israeli intelligence.

(Czechoslovakia) The New China News Agency is ordered out of Prague on charges of providing a base for Chinese Secret Service espionage.

(Bulgaria) Bulgarian diplomat Asen Georgieff is tried for espionage and executed in Sofia.

(Congo) KGB agents support an unsuccessful armed rebellion.

(Iraq) Unmarked CIA contract aircraft fly supplies to the new government.

(Australia) Soviet diplomat Boris A. Skripov is expelled after being caught attempting to establish a KGB espionage network.

(Cambodia) Khmer Serai agents employing CIA-supplied transmitters begin an anti-Sihanouk campaign from posts in South Vietnam and Thailand.

(South Vietnam) The CIA is cleared of complicity in the overthrow and murder of President Diem.

(Ecuador) CIA agents gain economic and political control over the national labor movement and employ "destabilization" tactics to overthrow the government of President Carole Julio Arosemena.

(United States) The South Korean Central Intelligence Agency (KCIA) begins to monitor the activities of South Korean citizens in the U.S.

The CIA-sponsored A-11 reconnaissance aircraft becomes operational.

The CIA is criticized for not keeping track of Lee Harvey Oswald, the accused killer of President Kennedy.

1963–1968   **(USSR)** The Soviets halt the jamming of all incoming Russian-language broadcasts except those from Radio Liberty.

1964   **(USSR)** The KGB plays a background role in the downfall of Premier Nikita Khrushchev; the CIA is criticized for not forewarning the American government about the coup.

Radio Peace and Progress is created as a covert propaganda arm of the Soviet government.

(Britain) Soviet agent Konon T. Molody, alias Gordon Lonsdale, is exchanged for British agent Grenville Wynne.

(West Germany) Security agents arrest 1,104 people on charges of spying for the Soviet Union, East Germany, and other Warsaw Pact nations.

(Switzerland) Operating under cover of the New China News Agency, the Chinese Secret Service establishes its main European espionage base in Geneva.

KGB officer Yuri I. Nossenko, attached to the Soviet delegation to the Geneva Disarmament Conference, defects to the West.

(Poland) A complete electronic listening system is found in the new U.S. Embassy in Warsaw.

(Turkey) KGB-directed terrorists begin a campaign of urban guerrilla warfare.

(Sudan) Chinese Secret Service agents incite riots which bring down the government.

(Congo) The CIA supplies B-26 bombers, flown by Cuban exiles, and white mercenaries from Rhodesia and South Africa to assist the government of Joseph Mobuto to suppress a KGB-backed insurrection in Stanleyville.

(Tanzania) Czechoslovakian intelligence agents "leak" forgeries in a disinformation campaign designed to accuse the CIA of plotting a coup.

(Zanzibar) Chinese Secret Service agents support a successful coup.

(Indonesia) Czechoslovakian and KGB agents begin a

disinformation campaign to arouse native passions against the United States.

(Tonkin Gulf) Two USN destroyers on an electronic intelligence mission against North Vietnam are attacked by North Vietnamese torpedo boats.

(Brazil) The CIA proprietary labor organization AIFLD is involved in the overthrow of the Goulart regime in Brazil.

The military junta which replaces Goulart arrests and charges nine New China News Agency employees with being Chinese Secret Service officers involved in espionage.

(Chile) With the cooperation of the Agency for International Development and the State Department, the CIA secretly funnels up to $20 million into Chile to aid Eduardo Frei in a successful attempt to defeat Marxist Salvador Allende for the Presidency of the country.

(Caribbean) Two CIA-sponsored Cuban exile armed speedboats mistakenly attack and damage the Spanish freighter *Serra Aranzuzu.*

(United States) The NSC Special Group is renamed the 303 Committee.

E. Howard Hunt of the CIA's Domestic Operations Division is ordered to obtain information on Barry Goldwater and deliver it to White House aide Chester Cooper.

Czechoslovakian intelligence distributes pamphlets in America, Africa, and Asia which depict Senator Goldwater as a racist.

FBI agents monitor the activities of the Mississippi Freedom Democratic Party at the Democratic National Convention.

President Lyndon B. Johnson releases information about the A-11, redesignated the SR-71.

1964–1968 **(Africa)** Mossad agents funnel covert CIA funds to various African nations in an effort to gain support for Israel's position on Middle East issues.

(Cuba) Pro-Soviet Cubans, directed by the KGB, unsuccessfully plot the overthrow of Premier Castro's government.

1964–1969   **(China)** China claims that CIA-backed Nationalist Chinese U-2's have overflown Chinese territory and that 19 were destroyed.

1964–1973   **(West Germany)** Gerda Ostenrieder, secretary to the West German Foreign Minister, passes 500 secret documents to East Germany before she is caught.

1965   **(USSR)** U.S. salesman Newcomb Mott is arrested by the KGB after entering the USSR via the Norwegian border and later commits suicide.

Richard Sorge is posthumously awarded the title Hero of the Soviet Union for his World War II espionage work in Japan.

Soviet agent Konon T. Molody, alias Gordon Lonsdale, prepares his memoirs with the aid of the KGB; the English translation is first published in London.

(Britain) The British Defence Intelligence Staff is established in the Ministry of Defence; MI5 is renamed DI5 and MI6 becomes DI6.

Frank Bossard is convicted for selling missile designs to the Soviets.

(France) The French Air Force intercepts a U.S. reconnaissance aircraft in a prohibited area above a nuclear plant.

(Portugal) Seven CIA-owned B-26's are flown to Portugal by pilots working for the agency proprietary company Intermountain Aviation.

(Greece) The CIA station chief in Athens provides King Constantine covert funds to buy off Deputies of the Greek Center Union Party, thus assisting in the downfall of George Papandreou's Government.

(Yugoslavia) KGB agents bug the offices of Marshal Tito.

(Egypt) Mossad agents Wolfgang and Waltraund Lotz

are arrested and convicted of espionage while editor Mustafa Amin is jailed as a "tool of the CIA."

(Malawi) Chinese Secret Service agencies operating from bases in Tanzania unsuccessfully attempt to promote a coup.

(Dahomey) Chinese Secret Service agents are ordered out of the country.

(Ceylon) KGB and Chinese Secret Service agents aid different pro-Communist parties in an unsuccessful effort to influence national elections.

(Asia) U.S. Secret Service agents uncover three listening devices in hotel rooms occupied by Vice President Hubert Humphrey during his Asian tour.

(China) The CIA correctly predicts the first Chinese nuclear blast.

Chinese Secret Service agents instigate the defection of General Li Tsung-jen from Taiwan to Peking.

(Indonesia) Buoyed by a KGB-Czech disinformation campaign against the U.S., local Communists mount an unsuccessful coup.

(South Vietnam) General Edward Lansdale returns to Saigon as a personal assistant to Ambassador Henry Cabot Lodge.

Brigadier General Nguyen Ngoc Loan is appointed director general of the South Vietnamese Police and Director of the South Vietnamese Central Intelligence Organization.

(Singapore) Chinese agent Sim Siew Lim is arrested with 20 other agents and charged with plotting the assassination of government leaders.

(South America) The U.S. Department of Defense "Project Camelot," a social-science research study of possible counter-insurgency techniques in South America, is exposed.

(Dominican Republic) CIA reports and local panic lead to an armed U.S. intervention.

(**Peru**) The CIA secretly aids the government of Peru in its fight against rebel guerrilla forces by flying in arms and other equipment. CIA and Green Beret instructors help by training local troops in counter-guerrilla warfare. American support aids in crushing the insurgency.

(**United States**) Camp Hale in Colorado is closed down as a CIA training base for Tibetan guerrillas.

The Penkovskiy Papers are published in New York and become a best-seller. It is eventually learned that the CIA had much to do with their content.

USAF Sergeant Robert G. Thompson is convicted of espionage.

1965–1966   (**United States**) Admiral William Raborn serves as CIA Director.

1965–1970   (**China**) CIA-directed native intelligence-collection teams covertly enter China from bases in northern Laos.

1965–1973   (**Canada**) With CIA support, the RCMP maintains covert surveillance over U.S. draft resisters living in Canada.

1966   (**USSR**) Two Americans are expelled on charges of working for the CIA.

(**Britain**) Sir Edward M. Furnival-Jones succeeds Sir Henry Hollis as "K" of the security service DI5.

(**Netherlands**) Attempting to pass data to the West, Chinese Secret Service agent Hsu Tsu-tsai is abducted from a Dutch hospital and returned to the Chinese legation where he dies.

(**Syria**) KGB agents circulate false rumors concerning an Israeli preemptive strike.

(**Ghana**) CIA-backed revolutionaries overthrow the pro-Soviet Nkrumah government.

(**North Vietnam**) Former KGB Chairman Alexandr N.

Shelepin is sent to Hanoi for a conference on North Vietnamese war needs.

(**United States**) The U.S. expels a Soviet Embassy staff member and accuses him of attempting to purchase defense secrets. Lieutenant Colonel William Whalen (U.S. Army, Retired) is arrested by the FBI on charges of spying for the Soviets.

The U.S. Army Intelligence Corps is redesignated the Army Intelligence Command.

Czechoslovakian agents in Washington unsuccessfully attempt to install listening devices in the office of Under Secretary of State George Ball.

1966–1971   (**United States**) The CIA breaks into premises occupied by CIA employees or ex-employees and alleges that security warrants those actions.

1966–1972   (**United States**) Richard Helms serves as CIA Director.

1966–1976   (**West Germany**) While employed as a secretary in the West German Foreign Ministry, Helge Berger passes secret documents to the MfS until uncovered.

1967   (**Britain**) A London newspaper reveals that the SIS monitored private telegrams and cables sent out of Britain via the Post Office for several years.

Convicted spy George Blake escapes from Wormwood Scrubs prison and is smuggled to Moscow.

(**Belgium**) The Russians construct a Skaldia-Volga plant near Brussels to cover KGB operations against the new NATO headquarters.

(**West Germany**) Three MfS agents steal a West German air force sidewinder missile and ship it to Moscow via air freight.

(**Italy**) The arrest of masterspy Giorgio Rinaldi by Italian authorities alerts the West to a KGB espionage network in Italy, Austria, Cyprus, Japan, Spain, Greece, Tunisia, and Morocco.

(**Greece**) The CIA is implicated in the military coup

which brings Georgios Papadopoulos to power. CIA allegedly controls Papadopoulos by threatening to blackmail him by documenting his wartime collaboration with the Nazis.

(South Africa) KGB agent Yuri N. Loginov is arrested and reveals information about Soviet intelligence training procedures.

(Middle East) KGB estimates miscalculate the Israeli will to fight prior to the June war.

The KGB obtains advance knowledge of Israel's attack plans for the June war but mysteriously withholds them from the Arab nations involved.

Israel intelligence correctly chooses targets for early military action.

The CIA does not learn of the Israeli attack plans.

The U.S. intelligence ship *Liberty* is severely damaged by Israeli fighters.

KGB and Chinese Secret Service agents in the Middle East conduct a propaganda campaign against each other over responsibility for the Arab loss in the June war.

(India) The KGB releases forgeries in an effort to influence national elections.

(China) During the Cultural Revolution, CIA propaganda balloons are launched over the mainland from a secret Taiwanese base.

British engineer George Watt is arrested in Peking and sentenced to three years in prison on charges of espionage.

(Cambodia) The CIA allegedly hires members of the Khmer Serai for covert action missions against the Sihanouk government.

(South Vietnam) Ambassador William E. Colby is named chief of the U.S. pacification program.

(Bolivia) The CIA assists Bolivian soldiers in a successful effort to capture Ernesto "Che" Guevera, the Cuban revolutionary then stirring up a rebellion; Bolivian rangers execute Guevera shortly after he is taken in hand.

(**Guyana**) The CIA proprietary labor organization AIFLD is involved in the overthrow of the government of Cheddi Jagan.

(**Worldwide**) The USAF begins flying the SR-71 on strategic reconnaissance missions.

(**United States**) Stalin's daughter Svetlana Alliluyeva flees from the Soviet Union and is subjected to a severe KGB defamation campaign.

The CIA covertly funds the publication of 200 books for propaganda purposes.

Ramparts Magazine exposes the CIA-NSA subsidization of the National Student Association.

President Johnson orders the CIA to halt awarding covert research contracts and grants to American universities and private voluntary organizations.

1967–1968   (**United States**) The CIA Office of Security inserts ten agents into dissident organizations in the Washington, D.C., area to collect "information relating to plans for demonstrations, pickets, protests, or break-ins that might endanger CIA personnel facilities and information."

1967–1969   (**Nigeria**) CIA-backed mercenaries aid the Biafra secessionists in an effort to divide the country.

1967–1971   (**South Vietnam**) The Far East Division of the CIA's Clandestine Services develop a counterintelligence program codenamed "Phoenix," involving a coordinated attack by South Vietnamese and American military police and intelligence units against the Viet Cong infrastructure. "Phoenix" results in the death of 20,537 or more persons in the country before it is officially ended.

(**United States**) Army intelligence agents monitor anti-war dissidents and file data on over 18,000 people unaffiliated with the armed forces in the Continental United States (CONUS).

1967–1972   **(United States)** A special unit is established within the counterintelligence office of the CIA to examine the possibility of foreign links to American dissident elements; periodically thereafter, this group drew up reports "on the foreign aspects of the anti-war youth, and similar movements, and their links to American counterparts."

1967–1973   **(United States)** NSA monitors international cable and telephone traffic to target Americans suspected of narcotics dealings, anti-war activities, and terrorism.

1968   **(Britain)** Prepared with the assistance of the KGB, the memoirs of Harold "Kim" Philby are published in London.

(West Germany) General Gerhard Wessel succeeds retired general Reinhard Gehlen as chief of the BND.
    Respected scientist Josef Eitzenberger is arrested as an agent of Soviet Russia.

(Czechoslovakia) The CIA is faulted for failing to predict the timing of the Soviet invasion of the country, even though it provided advance warning of intense military maneuvers in the area.
    The KGB assists in the purge of the Czech government, an action which leads to the defection of several high-ranking Czech agents including Ladislav Bittman, Deputy Director of the Disinformation Department.

(Middle East) KGB residents are ordered to begin training and aiding the Palestine Liberation Organization.

(Mali) CIA-backed revolutionaries topple the government of Modibo Keita.

(North Korea) The USN intelligence ship *Pueblo* is captured by North Korean gunboats and the crew treated as spies.

(South Vietnam) Although they anticipated some show of strength, American and South Vietnamese intelligence officials fail to predict the size and timing of the Tet offensive.

(**Cuba**) Under intense economic and political pressure, Fidel Castro surrenders direction of the Cuban intelligence service to the KGB.

(**Worldwide**) Mossad agents are implicated in the disappearance of 200 metric tons of uranium ore from a tramp steamer on the high seas.

(**United States**) U.S. armed forces intelligence agencies collect data, conduct surveillance, and help protect candidates at the Democratic and Republican National Conventions.

Budget cuts eliminate a planned USAF Manned Orbiting (Reconnaissance) Laboratory.

The FBI carries out 238 surreptitious entries, called "black bag jobs," against 14 organizations since 1942.

The Defense Intelligence Agency is criticized for allowing data to go unanalyzed and is blamed for the Liberty, Pueblo, and Tet crises.

1968–1970   (**Middle East**) Employing the Egyptian-Israeli intelligence services as tools, the CIA and KGB battle test their electronic warfare systems.

1968–1971   (**United States**) The FBI counterintelligence ("Cointelpro") operation against the new left is intensified.

1968–1972   (**Canada**) The RCMP maintains a domestic intelligence file on high-ranking Canadian cabinet officials.

(**United States**) Cuban intelligence agents actively support the Weather Underground.

1968–1976   (**West Germany**) Czech spy Pavel Minarek infiltrates the offices of Radio Free Europe in Munich.

1969   (**USSR**) Department 13, the Executive Action (Covert Operations) Bureau, of the KGB's First Chief Directorate is expanded and renamed Department 5.

KGB Border Guards battle Chinese troops at

Damansk Island. KGB disinformation agents "leak" the news that the Soviet Union is planning a preemptive nuclear strike on China; the ploy leads to Sino-Soviet negotiations on their border conflict.

(Finland) The Soviet covertly-sponsored World Peace Council opens offices in Helsinki.

(Britain) Portland spies Morris Cohen and Leona Petka alias Peter and Helen Kroger are exchanged for Gerald Brooke, an Englishmen convicted of smuggling anti-Communist literature into the Soviet Union.

KGB agents spy on the Anglo-French Concorde supersonic aircraft project.

The British Department of Trade and Industry issues a pamphlet warning businessmen of potential Communist entrapment procedures in Eastern Europe.

(France) The French fold-up a Rumanian espionage net in its atomic energy program and in NATO.

KGB agents spy on the Anglo-French Concorde supersonic aircraft project.

(Netherlands) Chinese Secret Service agent Liao Ho-shu defects to the CIA in The Hague.

(West Germany) The magazine *Stern* publishes KGB forgeries showing supposed U.S. contingency plans for biological warfare.

(Lebanon) The KGB unsuccessfully plots to steal a Lebanese Air Force Mirage Interceptor.

(Egypt) An Israeli technical intelligence mission captures a complete Soviet S-12 radar unit in the Sinai.

(Japan) Indonesian exchange student Maba Odantara is arrested as a KGB agent.

(North Korea) North Korean fighters down a USN EC-121 spy plane off the coast.

(Laos) CIA-supported Meo soldiers of *L'Armée Clandestine* take the Plain of Jarres from the Pathet Lao.

(South Vietnam) An estimated 30,000 Viet Cong and North Vietnamese agents infiltrated the South Vietnamese government and armed forces—the largest spy network in history.

The CIA allegedly directs a U.S. Army Special Forces team to execute a double-agent named Thai Khae Chuyen.

(Barents Sea) The U.S. submarine *Gato* collides with a Soviet sub.

(Brazil) CIA penetration of a radical group leads to its destruction by governmental forces and the death of its leader, Carlos Marighella.

(United States) Czech agent Josef Frolik defects to the CIA revealing details of his service learned over 17 years.

The FBI begins a campaign to destroy the radical Black Panther group by creating conflict with other violence-prone organizations.

The CIA begins providing support to the government's effort to halt the flow of illegal narcotics into the U.S.

At White House direction, the FBI taps the telephones of 17 government officials in an effort to trace press leaks.

1969–1973   **(USSR)** All Russian-language foreign broadcasts into the country are once again jammed.

(United States) The Internal Revenue Service creates intelligence files on 11,000 citizens and organizations and initiates tax audits for political purposes.

1970   **(USSR)** The KGB Fifth Chief Directorate is organized to annihilate intellectual, religious, and nationalist dissent.

(West Germany) The BND openly advertises for spies.

The magazine *Stern* publishes the KGB forgery *Handbook on Nuclear Yield Requirements,* showing supposed U.S. atomic war plans.

(Middle East) The KGB begins smuggling arms to the PLO via Egypt.

(Egypt) A KGB-backed coup against the government of President Anwar Sadat is crushed.

(Zaire) KGB agents are expelled after infiltrating important branches of the government.

(Laos) Pathet Lao troops defeat the CIA's *L'Armee Clandestine* and recapture the Plain of Jarres, forcing the evacuation of 20,000 pro-government civilians and Meo irregulars.

The CIA contracts with Thai mercenaries to carry on the so-called secret war.

(Cambodia) The CIA is implicated in the overthrow of the government of Prince Sihanouk.

(Chile) Military dissidents working closely with the CIA, but not at its direction, kill General René Schneider who refused to endorse a coup against President Allende.

(Cuba) Cuban intelligence establishes its Illegal Section to train agents for sabotage and espionage efforts in the U.S.

(United States) The NSC 303 Committee is renamed the 40 Committee.

The Directors of the CIA, NSA, DIA, and FBI recommend to President Nixon an "integrated approach to the coverage of domestic unrest" which becomes known as the Huston Plan.

1970–1971 **(Mexico)** Mexican students recruited by the KGB are trained in terrorist tactics in North Korea and returned to Mexico to create difficulties.

1970–1972 **(Laos)** The CIA is accused of supporting a faction of Laotian natives engaged in the heroin trade.

(Hong Kong) KGB agents employ the city as an espionage base against China.

1970–1973   **(Chile)** The CIA tries to destabilize the government of Marxist President Salvadore Allende by funnelling over $8 million to various groups within the country opposed to the government and slipping agents into the Socialist Party to organize street demonstrations against the regime; the 1973 coup resulted in Allende's death during a military attack on the presidential palace.

(United States) The FBI collects domestic intelligence on the American feminist movement.

The CIA assists the U.S. Bureau of Narcotics and Dangerous Drugs to uncover possible corruption within that organization.

Due to a dispute, all formal liaison between the FBI and CIA is broken.

To secure access to foreign circles after the Huston Plan is rescinded, the CIA recruits some dozen informers to infiltrate U.S. dissident circles, check on foreign contacts, and maintain files; the information was eventually turned over to the FBI.

1971   **(USSR)** The Jewish Department is established within the KGB's Fifth Chief Directorate.

CIA/NSA monitoring of the telephone traffic of Soviet leaders in their Moscow limousines is exposed.

(Britain) KGB agent Oleg A. Lyalin defects to the British revealing a massive infiltration of the U.K. with operations centered in the London headquarters of the Soviet trade delegation. As a result of Lyalin's information, 105 Soviet embassy officials are expelled and accused of planning to sabotage British cities.

(Belgium) The government expels nine KGB officers engaged in covert intelligence collection.

(West Germany) The government prosecutes 47 people on charges of spying for the Russians.

(Atlantic) The Azores Fixed Acoustic Range submarine surveillance system is laid down by NATO.

(Sudan) KGB and other Eastern European agents are

expelled after attempting an unsuccessful pro-Communist coup.

(China) The USAF halts reconnaissance flights over mainland China.

(Cuba) Cuban agents under KGB direction establish connections with the Quebec Liberation Front and begin training IRA and PLO terrorists.

(Worldwide) The U.S. launches the first improved SAMOS spy sattelite, nicknamed "Big Bird."

(United States) *The New York Times* publishes the classified *Pentagon Papers*, given to it by Daniel Ellsberg; the articles document the U.S. government and intelligence involvement in Southeast Asia since the 1950s.

French External Documentation and Counterespionage Service (SDECE) officer Colonel Paul Fournier is indicted in New Jersey for conspiracy to smuggle illegal drugs into the U.S. Roger Delovette was also indicted as a "co-conspirator".

Vladimir P. Pavlichenko, Director of External Relations at the U.N. Public Information Office in New York, is exposed as a senior KGB official.

Official CIA financing of RFE and RL is discontinued.

At the request of the White House, the CIA provides a psychological profile of Dr. Daniel Ellsberg.

Former CIA agent E. Howard Hunt is named a special White House Consultant and receives technical equipment from the CIA's Technical Services Division, which he later utilizes in connection with the break-in and burglary of the office of Daniel Ellsberg's psychiatrist.

The White House "Plumber's" unit is established to halt unauthorized disclosures of government information to the press. Charles Colson and E. Howard Hunt unsuccessfully plot to show that President Kennedy was involved in the murder of Diem.

FBI agents gather covert intelligence at the Young Socialist Alliance's convention in Houston.

1971–1972   **(United States)** The CIA employs physical surveillance against five non-CIA employees, including journalist/ authors Jack Anderson, Less Whitten, Michael Getler, and Victor Marchetti, who were supposedly receiving classified information without authorization in an effort to find the sources of the leaks.

The CIA provides secret training to 50 officers of 12 U.S. city and county police organizations on the detection of wiretaps, the organization of intelligence files, and the handling of explosives.

1971–1973 **(Britain)** Soviet ships and aircraft countermeasures neutralize the U.S. early warning station at Oxford Ness.

1972 **(USSR)** KGB agents and Soviet paratroops quell a series of nationalistic demonstrations in Lithuania.

Norwegian Embassy guard Ole Martin-Høistad is compromised by Irina Pendik in Moscow and agrees to spy for the Soviets.

Rudolf Abel dies in Moscow.

(Britain) Naval officer David Bingham is convicted of passing secrets to the Soviets; during his surveillance, DI5 agents feed disinformation to the Soviets through him.

As an illustration of the dangers of undercover work in Northern Ireland, Military Reconnaissance Force agents Ted Stuart and Sarah J. Warke are attacked by IRA gunmen. Stuart was killed.

(West Germany) Former BND chief Reinhard Gehlen publishes his memoirs.

(Western Europe) Western intelligence sources estimate that 36 per cent of all Soviet officials stationed in Western European embassies are known or suspected spies.

In reprisal for the Munich Massacre, Mossad agents assassinate PLO leaders in various European capitals.

(North Vietnam) American intelligence reports Hanoi's receipt of stepped-up Chinese and Soviet aid.

(Bolivia) The government expels 69 Soviet agents caught in subversive activities.

(Colombia) Three Soviet agents caught in espionage activities are expelled.

(Chile) U.S. columnist Jack Anderson accuses the CIA of improper interference in the country's internal affairs.

(United States) Camp Perry, known as "the farm," a 10,000 acre estate in Virginia employed as a major CIA training base, is exposed.

White House consultants E. Howard Hunt and Gordon Liddy plan and execute, with the aid of Cuban exiles and certain CIA equipment, two breakins of the Democratic headquarters; one succeeds but the second is broken up leading to a scandal which eventually forces the resignation of President Nixon.

The CIA receives White House requests for information and assistance in connection with the Watergate investigations; Director Helms works to keep the agency as uninvolved as possible.

CIA agents allegedly conduct a surveillance of the Republican National Convention in Miami.

Polish agents begin an intensive disinformation campaign designed to force the U.S. Congress to ban CIA covert financing of RFE and RL.

1972–1973   **(United States)** Successive CIA directors issue internal orders banning the use of assassinations as a political weapon.

The FBI burglarizes the headquarters of the Socialist Workers Party.

1973   **(USSR)** KGB Chairman Andropov becomes the first state security official since Lavrenti Beria to gain full membership in the Politburo.

Jamming of all incoming foreign broadcasts, except those of Radio Liberty, is lifted.

(Britain) SIS chief Sir John Rennie resigns when his identity is made public during a criminal trial involving his son. Sir Maurice Oldfield becomes chief of the SIS.

(Lebanon) Mossad agents attack PLO headquarters in Beirut.

(Egypt) Prior to the Yom Kippur War, a CIA/NSA facility in Iran determines that Egypt has turned off most of her usual codes and is employing only her most sensitive one.

Despite hints such as the above, the CIA and Mossad fail to accurately predict the Arab attack on Israel.

(Hong Kong) Chinese Secret Service agents warn the British of KGB operations in the enclave and throughout the Far East.

(Guinea) The CIA is implicated in the murder of Amikan Cabral, leader of the African Party for the Independence of Guinea and the Cape Verde Islands.

(United States) The CIA proprietary airline Southern Air Transport is sold after its cover is blown.

It is revealed that the CIA has approximately 40 American journalists "working abroad on its payroll as undercover informants, some of them as full-time agents"; except for so-called "stringers," the practice is discontinued amidst a hail of public outcry.

The CIA's Directorate of Plans is redesignated Directorate of Operations.

James R. Schlesinger, former AEC boss, serves briefly as CIA Director.

CIA counterespionage chief James J. Angleton resigns following charges of agency involvement in domestic espionage.

In the first successful case of prior censorship, a federal court, at CIA insistence, bans 168 passages of the book *The CIA and the Cult of Intelligence* by Victor Marchetti and John D. Marks.

1973–1974   **(United States)** Under Directors Schlesinger and Colby, the CIA moves to terminate illegal domestic, clandestine operations.

1973–1975   **(Iraq)** CIA-backed Kurdish forces battle loyal troops.

1973–1976   **(United States)** Career officer William E. Colby succeeds James R. Schlesinger as the Director, CIA.

1973–1977   **(United States)** Korean CIA agents attempt to suborn U.S. Congressmen and other officials.

1974   **(USSR)** Dissident Alexandr Solzhenitsyn is arrested by the KGB and exiled to the West where he continues to discuss the agency's massive prison system and operations to suppress internal dissent.

(Portugal) Czech agents move to support the activities of the local Communist Party after the April coup.
The General Security Directorate is abolished one day after the coup.

(Cyprus) U.S. intelligence is unable to provide forewarning of the coup against Archbishop Makarios.

(Yemen [Aden]) KGB and MfS agents back the creation of a Ministry of State Securty.

(China) Five members of the Soviet Embassy in Peking are expelled for espionage activities.

(India) The CIA fails to predict the first Indian atomic blast.

(Pacific) The CIA/Howard Hughes *Glomar Explorer* unsuccessfully attempts to raise a sunken Soviet submarine north of Hawaii in "Operation Jennifer."

(United States) The CIA is implicated in the burglary of files from the office of Howard Hughes.
Journalist Seymour Hersh charges the CIA was involved in a massive domestic intelligence operation against anti-war dissidents during the Nixon Administration.
Having compiled 10,000 files on U.S. citizens since 1967, the CIA domestic counterintelligence program is ended.
Psychological Assessment Associates, of Washington, D.C., is exposed as a CIA proprietary company involved in secret psychological testing research.

1974–1975   **(West Germany)** BND agents mount a surveillance campaign on atomic scientist Klaus Traube.

(Portugal) Eastern European intelligence agents funnel several million dollars to the local Communist Party.

(Egypt) The U.S. installs an electronic early-warning system in the Sinai.

(Angola) The CIA is implicated in support for the FNLA movement.

(South Vietnam) CIA agents allegedly work hapazardly to replace President Thieu.

1975 **(USSR)** The KGB begins using microwaves to recharge the batteries of listening devices hidden in the American Embassy in Moscow.

(Austria) Working as a supposed CIA double agent, Nikolai Shadrin is "kidnapped" by the KGB in Vienna.

(West Germany) Former Chancellor Willy Brandt's aides Günter and Christel Guillaume are convicted of espionage.

(Italy) In a covert aid program, the CIA funnels $6 million to anti-Communist political parties and politicians; the KGB funnels funds to pro-Communist politicians, unions, and the local Communist Party.

(Portugal) The CIA is accused of covertly financing center-right political parties and unions.
   With the support of Eastern European agents, leftist elements stage an unsuccessful coup.

(Greece) After his name is published in a U.S. anti-intelligence newsletter, CIA station chief Richard Welch is murdered in Athens.

(Turkey) As a result of the Cyprus debate, Turkey suspends U.S. intelligence base operations.

(South Vietnam) CIA agents are accused of improperly preparing for the evacuation of Saigon.

(United States) President Gerald Ford creates the Commission on CIA Activities Within the United States. Release of the Rockefeller Commission report creates a public furor.

The U.S. Senate establishes a Select Committee to Study Government Operations With Respect to Intelligence Activities under Chairman Senator Frank Church.

The U.S. House of Representatives establishes a Select Committee on Intelligence under Chairman Representative Lucien Nedzie, later succeeded by Otis G. Pike.

The FBI admits placing 8,239 domestic telephone taps and 2,465 microphone bugs since 1940.

The Justice Department formally admits to electronic surveillance of foreign embassies—a common practice in many advanced nations.

Sarkis O. Paskalian is arrested by the FBI and later convicted of spying for the Soviets.

International Police Services, Inc., of Washington, D.C., is exposed as a CIA proprietary company.

1975–1976   **(Micronesia)** The CIA conducts covert surveillance operations in this U.S. administered U.N. mandate.

1976   **(USSR)** Three U.S. newsmen in Moscow are detained by the KGB on charges of spying for the CIA.

(Western Europe) Leftist newspapers in Britain, France, West Germany, Holland, Spain, and Italy publish the names of 161 Americans identified, correctly or incorrectly, as CIA agents.

(Britain) Former CIA agent Philip Agee is deported.

(France) A Paris newspaper names two Soviet diplomats as the local KGB and GRU residents.

(Austria) The KGB reports, via Soviet newspapers, that the CIA was responsible for the disappearance of spy Nikolai Shadrin who was working for the Soviets and was discovered trying to return home. The truth remains clouded.

(West Germany) The head of the Christian Democratic Party is arrested on charges of espionage.

BND agent Karl Dinhofer is arrested for giving classified documents to the press.

Renate and Lothar Lutze and Jurgen Wiegel are arrested on charges of having passed NATO defense documents to the Russians.

(**East Germany**) The MfS takes three BND agents, who are later convicted and sentenced for espionage.

(**Italy**) Italian journalists charge that Cardinal Giovanni Montini, later Pope Paul VI, was an OSS/CIA contact from 1942–1950.

(**Switzerland**) SAVAK agent Malek Mahdavi is expelled for illegal espionage activities.

(**Yugoslavia**) In the first case of its kind, a Soviet tour official is arrested on charges of espionage and later convicted.

U.S. citizen Laslo Toth is convicted of espionage, but is later released.

(**Angola**) The CIA denies charges of recruiting mercenaries to fight in the Angolan civil war.

(**Sudan**) KGB agents are implicated in a successful coup against the government.

(**Japan**) A Soviet pilot defects to the West with a top-secret MIG-25 interceptor.

Soviet newsman Alexandr Machekhin is arrested on charges of espionage, but is later released.

(**India**) The government accuses the CIA of destabilization tactics similar to those employed in Chile.

(**South Korea**) Shin Jik Soo is dismissed as director of the KCIA and is succeeded by Kim Jae Kyu.

The KCIA takes thirteen North Korean agents in Seoul.

(**Panama**) The CIA is accused of supporting a destabilization campaign against the government during the Panama Canal Treaty talks.

(**Jamaica**) The CIA is accused of undermining the government and complicity in the assassination of Prime Minister Michael Manley.

(United States) Chilean antijunta, antigovernment demonstrators accuse DINA agents, including Michael Townley, of murdering ex-ambassador Orlando Letelier in Washington, D.C.

A secret CIA national estimate of Soviet strategic capabilities and objectives is leaked to the press and causes a furor.

Former Mobil Oil Corporation executive Norman Rees commits suicide after it is disclosed that he spied for the Soviets from 1942–1972 and was an FBI double agent from 1971–1975.

The Senate Select Committee on Government Operations With Respect to Intelligence Activities completes its report after fifteen months of hearings and is disestablished.

The Senate establishes a permanent Senate Select Committee on Intelligence under the chairmanship of Senator Daniel K. Inouye (succeeded in 1978 by Senator Birch Bayh) to carry out oversight of the nation's intelligence organizations.

The House of Representatives votes to withhold public dissemination of the House Select Committee on Intelligence's final report; the report is subsequently leaked to the *Village Voice* by CBS newsman Daniel Schorr.

1976–1977   **(United States)** George Bush succeeds William Colby and serves briefly as CIA Director.

1977   **(USSR)** The KGB launches a world-wide disinformation campaign aimed at the U.S. neutron bomb.

Four leading dissidents are arrested on charges of spying for the CIA.

Dissident Anatoly Scharansky is arrested by the KGB on charges of treason and convicted of aiding the CIA.

(Britain) British newspapers report that 10 Downing Street was wiretapped by the SIS during the term of Prime Minister Harold Wilson; the charge is denied by Prime Minister James Callaghan.

(France) DST agents arrest Serge Fabiev and three

others and charge them of spying for the Soviets over a 14-year period.

(West Germany) West German Colonel Norbert Moser and two others are convicted of passing military secrets to East Germany.

Czech agent Svetozar Simko defects revealing a large Czech spy network in the Bonn area.

(Norway) Foreign Ministry official Gunvor G. Haavik is charged with spying for the Soviets.

(Switzerland) General Jean-Louis Jeanmarie is convicted of passing secrets to the Soviet Union.

KGB agents unsuccessfully attempt to blackmail U.S. UNESCO delegation member Constantine Warvariv.

(Czechoslovakia) Four BND agents are arrested and convicted of espionage.

(Greece) Five British citizens are convicted of espionage, but are later released.

(Yugoslavia) Two pro-Soviet exiles are kidnapped by Yugoslav agents abroad and returned home where they receive prison terms.

(Syria) A pair of Iraqui assassination agents are executed.

(Iran) General Ahmed Mozarrebi, convicted of passing secrets to Russia for nine years, is executed.

(Zaire) KGB agents circulate rumors that the West German company ORTAG is testing rockets for its military in this country.

(Guinea) The government withdraws permission for Soviet spy plane flights from its territory.

(Tanzania) Intelligence officer J. T. Zangira is imprisoned as a British spy.

(Australia) Prime Minister Malcolm Fraser resists calls for an investigation of alleged CIA activities.

The Prime Minister acknowledges for the first time the existence of a national foreign intelligence service and a signals intelligence organization.

Justice Robert Marsden-Hope, appointed as a one-man Royal Commission on Intelligence and Security, prepares an 8-volume report, only four volumes of which are made available to Parliament and the press.

Acting on the above report, the Australian government grants new legal powers to the Australian Secret Intelligence Service (ASIS) and the Defence Signals Division (DSD), elevating them to the status of Directorates and placing the war against subversion and terrorism in their domain.

The ASIS places ads in local newspapers seeking new recruits.

(United States) President Carter announces reorganization of the American Intelligence Community, creating a high level committee chaired by the DCI to set priorities for collecting and producing intelligence, and giving the DCI full control of budget and intelligence collection.

Admiral Stansfield Turner, USN, is appointed CIA Director and DCI. Deputy DCI Henry Knocke resigns over differences with DCI Turner.

The House of Representatives establishes a Permanent Select Committee on Intelligence under the chairmanship of Representative Edward P. Boland; this group differs from the Senate Committee on Intelligence in that it has oversight jurisdiction over the CIA but shares with several other House committees legislative oversight authority over all other intelligence agencies.

The Administration seeks additional Congressional funding for RFE, RL, and the VOA.

Various newspapers report the CIA covertly funneled large sums of cash to 16 foreign leaders since the 1950's.

President Carter releases a pessimistic CIA oil estimate which creates a furor.

Edwin G. Moore, II tosses a package of classified documents onto the lawn of the Soviet Embassy in Washington, D.C.; fearing a bomb, the Russians call in the FBI which recovers the papers and arrests Moore on charges of espionage.

Former CIA agent Philip Agee is identified as a "friend" of the Cuban intelligence service or DCI.

Soviet defector Ivan N. Rogalski is arrested as a double agent by the FBI.

Christopher J. Boyce is arrested and charged with selling sensitive electronic gear to the Soviets; Boyce claims the CIA has been manipulating Australian labor union leaders.

1977–1978   **(United States)** Over 800 CIA agents are laid off.

1978   **(USSR)** American Martha Peterson is arrested by the KGB in Moscow and charged with spying for the CIA.

The KGB arrests U.S. businessman F. Jay Crawford on charges of alleged currency crimes; Crawford is later exchanged for two Soviet spies held in the US (see below).

(Britain) A Bulgarian defector is poisoned in London by agents of the Bulgarian intelligence service.

(Italy) The KGB circulates rumors connecting the CIA to the terrorist kidnapping of former Premier Aldo Moro.

(East Germany) Three Americans imprisoned for aiding East German escapees are exchanged for a convicted KGB agent.

(South Yeman) The KGB is implicated in a plot against the government.

(Ethiopia) An anonymous spy informs the CIA that Soviet-backed Ethiopia would not attack Somalia during border disputes.

(China) Vietnam denies charges of sending spies into China.

(Afghanistan) The KGB is involved in the pro-Soviet coup against the neutralist regime of Noor Mohammad Taraki.

(Iran) SAVAK agents mount intense campaigns against dissidents as the government of the Shah nears collapse.

(Canada) A Soviet spy satellite disintegrates over Canada leading to a costly clean-up operation.

The RCMP arrests thirteen KGB agents on charges of espionage.

(United States) Soviet officials Valdik Enger and Rudolph Chernyayev are convicted of attempting to buy classified anti-submarine warfare documents.

Ronald Humphrey is convicted of passing secrets to North Vietnam. The International Communications Agency is established incorporating the functions of the USIA.

North Vietnamese U.N. diplomat Dinh Ba Thi is accused of espionage and expelled from the U.S.

Soviet U.N. diplomat A. N. Shevchenko defects and receives secret CIA funding and other favors.

Former CIA employee William Kampiles is convicted of selling the KH-11 spy satellite manual to the Russians.

President Carter signs Executive Order 12036 which reshapes the intelligence structure and provides explicit guidance on all facets of intelligence activities.

1978–1979   **(Iran)** The CIA fails to provide forewarning of Iran's Islamic revolution.

1979   **(Great Britain)** Art historian Anthony Blunt admits to spying for the Soviets in the days of Harold "Kim" Philby.

(East Germany) MfS agent Ursel Lorenzen reveals on television how she spent twelve years as a secretary spying out NATO secrets in Brussels.

(West Germany) Key MfS officer Lieutenant Werner Stiller defects to the West leading to the arrest of fourteen West German suspects on espionage charges and the flight of eighteen others.

Six West German secretaries are unmasked as MfS agents; two more escape.

(Switzerland) Western intelligence sources reveal that a number of high-ranking U.N. officials in Geneva are active KGB agents, including Luigi Cottafavi, Gely

Dneprovsky, Vladimir Lobachev, Yuri Ponomarev, and Yuri Chestnoi.

(South Africa) Certain Americans are accused of spying on local nuclear installations.

(Cuba) U.S. SR-71s monitor activities of Soviet brigade.

(Lebanon) PLO terrorist leader Abu Hassan is assassinated in Beirut by agents of the Mossad.

(Iran) The Islamic revolution topples the government of the Shah; the SAVAK is disbanded and many of its officials are executed.

CIA/NSA employees are forced to abandon the Kabkan-Behshahr listening posts in the northeast after destroying most secret electronic gear.

(United States) The SALT II treaty is signed leading to an intense debate over the ability of U.S. intelligence agencies to monitor Soviet compliance.

The KGB swaps five Soviet dissidents, including Aleksandr Ginsburg, for convicted Soviet spies Valdik Enger and Rudolph Chernyayev.

Admiral Turner faults government plans for the MX missile. The CIA takes out "help wanted" ads in large U.S. newspapers.

Mossad agents are accused of monitoring and leaking secret talks between UN Ambassador Young and PLO representatives in New York.

Principal Sources

The principal sources of the chronology are listed by entry number.

115. Seth, Ronald O. *Encyclopedia of Espionage.*

126. *Facts on File,* Editors of. *Facts on File.*

127. _____ . *News Directory.*

128. _____ . *Yearbook.*

260. Hale, Julian A. S. *Radio Power.*

427. Lisann, Maury. *Broadcasting to the Soviet Union.*

671. Dyer, Murray. *Weapon on the Wall.*

752. Handlery, George. "Propaganda and Information."

781. U.S. Congress, House, Committee on Foreign Affairs. *Radio Free Europe and Radio Liberty: Hearings.*

785. Whelan, Joseph C. *Radio Liberty.*

875. Blackstock, Paul W. *Agents of Deceit.*

925. Kahn, David. *The Codebreakers.*

1040. Klass, Philip J. *Secret Sentries in Space.*

1097. Ennes, James M., Jr. *Assault on the Liberty.*

1107. Gallery, Daniel V. *The Pueblo Incident.*

1137. Copeland, Miles. *The Real Spy World.*

1139. _____ . *Without Cloak and Dagger.*

1144. Dulles, Allen W., ed. *Great True Spy Stories.*

1162. Haswell, Chetwynd J. D. *Spies and Spymasters.*

1184. Morgan, Ted. *The Secret War.*

1213. Sweetman, David. *Spies and Spying.*

1224. Wise, David and Thomas B. Ross. *The Espionage Establishment.*

1233. McCormick, Donald. *The Chinese Secret Service.*

1235. Bittman, Ladislav. *The Deception Game.*

1244. Bullock, John. *MI5.*

1253. Kitson, Frank. *Low-Intensity Operations.*

1291. Eisenberg, Dennis, Uri Dan, and Eli Landau. *The Mossad.*

1303. McCormick, Donald. *The Israeli Secret Service.*

1330. Barron, John. *KGB.*

1395. Seth, Ronald O. *Unmasked.*

1437. Corson, William R. *The Armies of Ignorance.*

1442. Halperin, Morton H., *et al. The Lawless State.*

1453. Prouty, L. Fletcher. *The Secret Team.*

1455. Ransom, Harry H. *The Intelligence Establishment.*

1466. United States. Congress. House. Select Committee on Intelligence. *The Performance of the Intelligence Community.*

1773. _____ . _____ . Senate. Select Committee to Study Government Operations with Respect to Intelligence Activities. *The National Security Agency and Fourth Amendment Rights. (See also* 1795, 1932, 2109, 2110, 2205, 2387–2389)

1806. Jeffrey-Jones, Rhodri. *American Espionage.*

1860. Frazier, Howard, ed. *Uncloaking the CIA.*

1894. Marchetti, Victor and John D. Marks. *The CIA and the Cult of Intelligence.*

1900. Paine, Lauran B. *The CIA at Work.*

1908. Rositzke, Harry A. *The CIA's Secret Operations.*

2136. Borosage, Robert L. and John D. Marks, eds. *The CIA File.*

2206. United States. Library of Congress. Congressional Reference Service. "Reported Foreign and Domestic Covert Activities of the United States Central Intelligence Agency, 1950–1974."

2362. _____ . Commission on CIA Activities Within the United States. *Report to the President.*

2369. _____ . Congress. House. Select Committee on Intelligence. *CIA.*

2396. Agee, Philip and Louis Wolf. *Dirty Work.*

2443. Bulloch, John and Henry Miller. *Spy Ring.*

I/Reference Works

Introduction

This section first presents tools which will prove useful in updating this guide for additional research into the complexities of the secret war since 1945. Second, it cites titles which have a general impact on the topic per se or which provide background knowledge on the subject.

Current and retrospective English-language sources relative to this book can be located in the bibliographies and indexes cited in Subsection A. Quick overviews and general background information on various aspects of the topic may be found among the encyclopedias and encyclopedia articles and general histories and memoirs cited in Subsections B and E. Chronologies and other recent information can be located in the annuals in Subsection C. Terminology useful in interpreting language or concepts in some of the works cited in this guide can be found by consulting the sources in Subsection D. Users should also be certain to check the footnotes and bibliographies (where provided) in the books, scholarly journal articles, dissertations, and documents borrowed as the result of viewing titles in the sections below.

A. Bibliographies and Indexes

1. *ABS Guide to Recent Publications in the Social and Behavioral Sciences.* New York: American Behavioral Scientist, 1965.

2. _____ : *Supplements.* Beverly Hills, CA: Sage, 1966–.

3. *Abstracts of Military Bibliography.* Buenos Aires, Argentina: Navy Publications Institute, 1968–. v. 1–.

4. *America: History and Life.* Santa Barbara, CA: ABC-Clio, 1964–. v. 1–.

5. American Historical Association. *Writings on American History.* Washington, D.C.: GPO, 1948–1961.

6. _____ . _____ . Milwood, NY: Kraus, 1962–.

7. Bernan Associates. *A Checklist of Congressional Hearings and Reports.* Washington, D.C.: 1958–. v. 1–.

8. *Biography Index.* New York: H. W. Wilson, 1947–. v. 1–.

9. Blackstock, Paul W. and Frank L. Schaf. *Intelligence, Espionage, Counterespionage, and Covert Operations: A Guide to Information Sources.* International Relations Information Guide Series, v. 2. Detroit, MI: Gale Research, 1978. 255p.

10. Blum, Eleanor. *Reference Books in the Mass Media.* Urbana, IL: University of Illinois Press, 1962. 103p.

11. *Book Review Index.* New York: H. W. Wilson, 1945–.

12. "Books and Ideas." In: *Air University Review.* Maxwell AFB, AL: Air University, 1959–. v. 1–.

13. Botlorff, Robert M., ed. *Popular Periodical Index.* New York, 1973–. v. 1–.

14. Boyer, Anne. *Soviet Foreign Propaganda: An Annotated Bibliography.* Washington, D.C.: U.S. Information Agency Library, 1971. 45p.

15. Browne, Donald R. "Broadcasting in Industrially-Developed Nations: An Annotated Bibliography." *Journal of Broadcasting,* XIX (Summer 1975), 341–355.

16. Canada. Department of Public Printing and Stationery. *Canadian Government Publications.* Ottawa, 1953–. v. 1–.

17. _____ . _____ . *Government Publications: Annual Catalog.* 9 vols. Ottawa, 1943–1952.

18.   *The Christian Science Monitor Index.* Corvallis, OR: Helen M. Crop-
sey, 1960–. v. 1–.

19.   Clotfelter, James. *Communication Theory in the Study of Politics: A
Review of the Literature.* Studies in Journalism and Communications, no.
7. Chapel Hill: School of Journalism, University of North Carolina,
1968. 19p.

20.   Collison, Robert L. *Broadcasting in Britain: A Bibliography.* Cambridge, England: At the University Press, 1961.

21.   Cooling, B. Franklin, 3rd, and Alan Millett. *Doctoral Dissertations in
Military Affairs: A Bibliography.* Manhattan: Kansas State University
Library, 1972.

22.   _____ . _____ : *Update.* In: *Military Affairs.* Washington, D.C.:
American Military Institute, 1973–.

23.   *The Cumulative Book Index.* New York: H. W. Wilson, 1945–.

24.   *Current Digest of the Soviet Press.* New York: Joint Committee on
Slavic Studies, 1949–. v. 1–.

25.   DeVore, Ronald M. *Spies and All That . . . : Intelligence Agencies and
Operations, a Bibliography.* Political Issues Series, Vol. IV, no. 3. Los
Angeles, CA: Center for the Study of Armament and Disarmament,
University of California, 1977. 71p.

26.   *Dissertation Abstracts.* Ann Arbor, MI: University Microfilms,
1945–1968.

27.   *Dissertation Abstracts International: "A" Schedule.* Ann Arbor, MI:
University Microfilms, 1969–.

28.   Draughon, Donnie W., comp. *The Central Intelligence Agency's Reference Aid Series: A List.* Washington, D.C.: Document Expediting Project, Exchange and Gift Division, Library of Congress, 1979. 6p.

29.   *Forthcoming Books.* New York: R. R. Bowker, 1966–. v. 1–.

30.   Galland, Joseph S. *An Historical and Analytical Bibliography of the
Literature of Cryptology.* Northwestern University Studies in the
Humanities, no. 10. Evanston, IL: Northwestern University Press,
1945. 209p. Reprint 1970.

31.   Gardner, Mary A. "Central and South American Mass Communication: Selected Information Sources." *Journal of Broadcasting,* XXII
(Spring 1978), 217–240.

32.   Great Britain. British Museum. Department of Printed Books.
Catalog of Printed Books: Additions. London: Clewes, 1963–.

33.   Hammond, Thomas T., ed. and comp. *Soviet Foreign Relations and World Communism: A Selected, Annotated Bibliography of 7,000 Books in Thirty Languages.* Princeton, NJ: Princeton University Press, 1965. 1,240p.

34.   Harris, William R. *Intelligence and National Security: A Bibliography With Selected Annotations.* Rev. ed. Cambridge, MA: Center for International Affairs, Harvard University, 1968. 838p.

Readers should also be aware of Max Gunzenhauser's untranslated *Geschichte der Geheimen Nachrichtendienst: (Spionage, Sabotage und Abwehr): Literatur Berichte und Bibliographie* (Frankfurt, West Germany: Bernard und Graefe, 1968. 434p.).

35.   Head, Sydney W. "African Mass Communications: Selected Information Sources." *Journal of Broadcasting,* XX (Summer 1976), 381–416.

36.   Heiman, Leo. "Cloak-and-Dagger Literature Behind the Iron Curtain." *East Europe,* XIV (January 1965), 54–56.

37.   *Historical Abstracts. Part B: Twentieth Century Abstracts (1914–present).* Santa Barbara, CA: ABC-Clio, 1955–. v. 1–.

38.   Higham, Robin, ed. *A Guide to the Sources of British Military History.* Berkeley: University of California Press, 1971. 630p.

39.   _____. *A Guide to the Sources of United States Military History.* Hamden, CT: Archon Books, 1975. 559p.

40.   Holler, Frederick L., comp. *Information Sources of Political Science,* 3rd ed. Santa Barbara, CA: ABC-Clio, 1980.

41.   Hunter, David H. "The Evolution of Literature on United States Intelligence." *Armed Forces and Society,* V (Fall 1978), 31–52.

42.   *Index to the Times.* London: The Times, 1945–.

43.   *International Information Service: A Quarterly Annotated Index of Selected Materials on Current International Affairs.* Chicago: Library of International Affairs, 1963–. v. 1–.

44.   *International Relations Digest of Periodical Literature.* Berkeley, CA: Bureau of International Relations, University of California, 1950–. v. 1–.

45.   Kahn, David. "Secret Writings: Selected Works on Modern Cryptology." *Bulletin of the New York Public Library,* LXXIII (May 1969), 315–327.

46.   Lent, John A. *Asian Mass Communications: A Comprehensive Bibliography.* Philadelphia, PA: School of Communications and Theater, Temple University, 1975. 720p.

47.   _____ . "Asian Mass Communications. Selected Information Sources." *Journal of Broadcasting,* XIX (Summer 1975), 321–340.

48.   _____ . "Caribbean Mass Communications: Selected Information Sources." *Journal of Broadcasting,* XX (Winter 1976), 111–126.

49.   Little, Wendell E. "The Intelligence Bookshelf." *Air University Review,* XXX (May-June 1979), 85–91.

50.   *Masters Abstracts.* Ann Arbor, MI: University Microfilms, 1962–. v. 1–.

51.   "The Military Library." In: *Military Affairs.* Washington, D.C.: American Military Institute, 1945–. v. 8–.

52.   Miller, Lester L., Jr. *Intelligence Gathering: A Two-Part Twentieth Century Bibliography.* Report 56–52. Ft. Sill, OK: U.S. Army Field Artillery School Library, 1978. 20p.

53.   Millett, Alan, jt. author. *See* Cooling, B. Franklin, 3rd (21).

54.   Mowlana, Hamid. "Middle East Mass Communications: Selected Information Sources." *Journal of Broadcasting,* XXI (Fall 1977), 497–510.

55.   *New York Times Index.* New York: *New York Times* Company, 1945–.

56.   *Newspaper Index* [to *Chicago Tribune, Washington Pst, Los Angeles Times,* and *New Orleans Picayune*]. Wooster, OH: Bell & Howell, 1972–. v. 1–.

57.   Ney, Virgil. "Bibliography on Guerrilla Warfare." *Military Affairs,* XXIX (Fall 1960), 146–149.

58.   Paulu, Burton, "Eastern European Mass Communications: Selected Information Sources." *Journal of Broadcasting,* XXII (Winter 1978), 107–130.

59.   Powe, Marc B. "The History of American Military Intelligence: A Review of Selected Literature." *Military Affairs,* XXXIX (October 1975), 142–145.

60.   Public Affairs Information Service. *PAIS Bulletin.* New York: PAIS, 1945–.

61.   RAND Corporation. *Selected RAND Abstracts.* Santa Monica, CA: RAND Corporation, 1962–. v. 1–.

62. *Reader's Guide to Periodical Literature.* New York: H. W. Wilson, 1945–.

63. "Recent Books." In: *Naval War College Review.* Newport, RI: U.S. Naval War College, 1958–. v. 1–.

64. *Reprints From the Soviet Press.* New York: Compass Publications, 1965–.

65. Rosenberg, K. C. and J. K. *Watergate: An Annotated Bibliography.* Littleton, CO: Libraries Unlimited, 1975. 141p.

66. Schaf, F. L., jt. author. *See* Blackstock, Paul W. (9).

67. Siehl, George. "Cloak, Dust Jacket, and Dagger." *Library Journal,* XCVII (October 15, 1972), 3277–3282.

68. Slusser, Robert M. "Recent Soviet Books on the History of the Secret Service." *Slavic Review,* XXIV (March 1965), 90–98.

69. Smith, Bruce L. and Chitra M. *International Communication and Political Opinion: A Guide to the Literature.* Princeton, NJ: Published for the Bureau of Social Science Research, Washington, D.C., by Princeton University Press, 1956. 325p.

70. Smith, Myron J., Jr. *Cloak-and-Dagger Bibliography: An Annotated Guide to Spy Fiction, 1937–1975.* Metuchen, NJ: The Scarecrow Press, 1976. 225p.

71. *Social Science and Humanities Index.* New York: H. W. Wilson, 1945–.

72. *Soviet Analyst.* London: Castle Press, 1971–. v. 1–.

73. Stapleton, M. L. *The Truman and Eisenhower Years, 1945–1960: A Selective Bibliography.* Metuchen, NJ: The Scarecrow Press, 1973. 221p.

74. *Subject Guide to Books in Print.* New York: R. R. Bowker, 1957–. v. 1–.

75. Symon, Julian. "A Short History of the Spy Story." In: his *Mortal Consequences: A History—From the Detective Story to the Crime Novel.* New York: Harper & Row, 1972. Chap. XVI.

76. United States. Air Force. Academy Library. *Unconventional Warfare, Part I: Guerrilla Warfare.* Special Bibliography Series, no. 21. Colorado Springs, CO: 1962. 39p.

77. _____ . _____ . _____ . *Unconventional Warfare, Part IV: Propaganda.* Special Bibliography Series, no. 30. Colorado Springs, CO: 1964. 45p.

78. _____ . _____ . _____ . *Unconventional Warfare, Part II: Psychological Warfare.* Special Bibliography Series, no. 22. Colorado Springs, CO: 1962. 37p.

79. _____ . _____ . Air University. Library. *Air University Library Index to Military Periodicals.* Maxwell AFB, AL: 1949–. v. 1–.

80. _____ . Congress. Senate. Committee on the Judiciary, Subcommittee to Investigate the Administration of the Internal Security Act and Other Internal Security Laws. *21 Year Index: A Combined Cumulative Index, 1951–1971, to Published Hearings, Studies, and Reports.* 2 vols. Washington, D.C.: GPO, 1972.

81. _____ . Department of State. Bureau of Intelligence and Research. *Intelligence: A Bibliography of Its Functions, Methods, and Techniques.* Bibliographies, nos. 33, 331. 2 pts. Washington, D.C.: 1948–1949.

82. _____ . _____ . Division of Library and Reference Services. *Psychological Warfare in Support of Military Operations: A Bibliography of Selected Materials With Annotations.* Washington, D.C.: 1951. 25p.

83. _____ . Department of the Army. *Africa: Problems and Prospects.* Bibliographic Surveys of Strategic Areas of the World. DA PAM 550–17–1. Washington, D.C.: GPO, 1977.

84. _____ . _____ . *China.* Bibliographic Surveys of Strategic Areas of the World. DA PAM 550–1. Washington, D.C.: GPO, 1978.

85. _____ . _____ . *Latin American and the Caribbean.* Bibliographic Surveys of Strategic Areas of the World. DA PAM 550–7–1. Washington, D.C.: GPO, 1974.

86. _____ . _____ . *Middle East: The Strategic Hub.* Bibliographic Surveys of Strategic Areas of the World. DA PAM 550–16. Washington, D.C.: GPO, 1973.

87. _____ . _____ . *National Security, Military Power, and the Use of Force in International Relations.* Bibliographic Surveys of Strategic Areas of the World. DA PAM 550–19. Washington, D.C.: GPO, 1976.

88. _____ . _____ . *Scandinavia.* Bibliographic Surveys of Strategic Areas of the World. DA PAM 550–18. Washington, D.C.: GPO, 1975.

89. _____ . _____ . *South Asia and the Strategic Indian Ocean.* Bibliographic Surveys of Strategic Areas of the World. DA PAM 550–15. Washington, D.C.: GPO, 1973.

90. _____ . _____ . *U.S.S.R.* Bibliographic Surveys of Strategic Areas of the World. DA PAM 550–6–1. Washington, D.C.: GPO, 1976.

91. _____ . Library of Congress. *Library of Congress Catalog, Books, Subjects: A Cumulative List of Works Represented by Library of Congress Printed Cards.* Washington, D.C.: GPO, 1950–.

92. _____ . _____ . Congressional Research Service. *Digest of Public General Bills and Selected Resolutions, With Index.* Washington, D.C.: GPO, 1945–. v. 9–.

93. _____ . _____ . _____ . *Soviet Intelligence and Security Services: A Selected Bibliography of Soviet Publications With Some Additional Titles From Other Sources: Prepared at the Request of and Based on Materials Provided by the Subcommittee to Investigate the Administration of the Internal Security Act and Other Internal Security Laws of the Committee of the Judiciary of the United States Senate.* 2 vols. Washington, D.C.: GPO, 1972–1975.

94. _____ . National Technical Information Service. *Government Reports and Announcements.* Springfield, VA: 1946–. v. 1–.

95. _____ . Superintendent of Documents. *Monthly Catalogue of United States Government Documents.* Washington, D.C.: GPO, 1945–.

96. *The Wall Street Journal Index.* New York: Dow Jones, 1958–. v. 1–.

97. Zuehlke, Arthur A., Jr., ed. *Bibliography of Intelligence Literature: A Critical and Annotated Bibliography of Open-Source Literature.* 6th ed. Washington, D.C.: Defense Intelligence School, 1979. 68p.

B. Encyclopedias and Encyclopedia Articles

98. Blackstock, Paul W. "Espionage." In: Vol. X of the *Encyclopedia Americana.* New York: Americana Corp., 1978. pp. 584–587.

99. Callimakos, Lambros D. "Cryptology." In: Vol. VII of *Collier's Encyclopedia.* New York: Macmillan Educational Corp., 1977. pp. 519–530.

100. _____ . _____ . In: Vol. V of the *Encyclopedia Britannica.* Chicago: Encyclopedia Britannica, 1974. pp. 322–333.

101. Daugherty, William E. "Psychological Warfare." In: Vol. XIII of the *International Encyclopedia of the Social Sciences.* New York: Macmillan, 1968. pp. 46–49.

102. [Donovan, William J.] "Espionage." By W. J. Don, pseud. In: Vol. XII of the *Encyclopedia Britannica.* Chicago: Encyclopedia Britannica, 1954. pp. 459–462.

103. Dupuy, R. Ernest and Trevor N. *The Encyclopedia of Military History.* Rev. ed. New York: Harper & Row, 1976. 1,488p.

104.   Eliot, George F. "Espionage." In: Vol. IX of *Collier's Encyclopedia.* New York: Macmillan Educational Corp., 1977. pp. 312–315.

105.   Elting, John R. "Military Intelligence." In: Vol. XVI of *Collier's Encyclopedia.* New York: Macmillan Educational Corp., 1977. pp. 211–214.

106.   Giddens, Jackson A. "Propaganda." In: Vol. XXII of the *Encyclopedia Americana.* New York: Americana Corp., 1978. pp. 656–659.

107.   Hoover, J. Edgar. "Espionage and Counterespionage." In: Vol. X of the *Encyclopedia Americana.* New York: Americana Corp., 1965. pp. 504–506.

108.   Jones, David R., ed. *Military-Naval Encyclopedia of Russia and the Soviet Union.* 50 vols.+ Gulf Breeze, FL: Academic International Press, 1978–. v. 1–.

109.   Kahn, David. "Cryptology." In: Vol. VIII of the *Encyclopedia Americana.* New York: Americana Corp., 1978. pp. 276–285.

110.   Kirkpatrick, Lyman B., Jr. "Intelligence and Counterintelligence." In: Vol. II of Alexander De Conde, ed. *Encyclopedia of American Foreign Policy.* New York: Scribners, 1979. pp. 417–427.

111.   Ransom, Harry H. "Intelligence and Counterintelligence." In: Vol. IX of the *Encyclopedia Britannica.* Chicago: Encyclopedia Britannica, 1975. pp. 679–686.

112.   _____ . "Intelligence, Political and Military." In: Vol. VII of the *International Encyclopedia of the Social Sciences.* New York: Macmillan, 1968. pp. 415–421.

113.   _____ . "Intelligence, Strategic." In: Vol. XV of the *Encyclopedia Americana.* New York: Americana Corp., 1978. pp. 246–248.

114.   Sellers, Robert C., ed. *Armed Forces of the World: A Reference Handbook.* 4th ed. New York: Praeger, 1977. 288p.

115.   Seth, Ronald O. *Encyclopedia of Espionage.* Garden City, NY: Doubleday, 1974. 718p.

116.   Smith, Bruce L. "Propaganda." In: Vol. XII of the *International Encyclopedia of the Social Sciences.* New York: Macmillan, 1968. pp. 579–589.

117.   Stessin, Laurence. "Intelligence: Military, Political, and Industrial." In: Vol. XII of the *Encyclopedia Britannica.* Chicago: Encyclopedia Britannica, 1972. pp. 347–350.

118.   Wright, Charles R. "Propaganda." In: Vol. XV of the *Encyclopedia International.* New York: Grolier, 1967. pp. 97–99.

C. Annuals

119.   *Americana Corp.* Americana Annual. New York: 1946–.

120.   *The Annual Register: A Record of World Events.* New York: St. Martin's Press, 1945–.

121.   *Collier's Encyclopedia Yearbook.* New York: Crowell-Collier-Macmillan, 1945–.

122.   Congressional Information Service. *CIS Annual: Abstracts of Congressional Publications and Legislative Histories.* Washington, D.C.: 1969–. v. 1–.

123.   Congressional Quarterly, Inc. *Congressional Quarterly Almanac.* Washington, D.C.: 1945–. v. 1–.

124.   Encyclopedia Britannica. *Britannica Book of the Year.* Chicago: 1946–.

125.   *The Europa Yearbook: A World Survey and Directory of Countries and International Organizations.* London: Europa Publications, 1950–. v. 1–.

126.   *Facts on File,* Editors of. *Facts on File: A Weekly News Guide, With Cumulative Index.* New York: 1945–. v. 5–.

127.   _____. *News Directory.* New York, 1963–. v. 1–.

128.   _____. *Yearbook: The Indexed Record of World Events.* New York: 1945–. v. 4–.

129.   Institute of World Affairs. *The Yearbook of World Affairs.* London: Stevens, 1947–. v. 1–.

130.   Intelligence International, Ltd. *Intelligence Digest: A Review of World Affairs.* Cheltenham, England, 1945–. v. 8–.

131.   *The International Yearbook and Statesman's Who's Who.* London: Burke's Peerage, 1953–. v. 1–.

132.   Jones, David R., ed. *Soviet Armed Forces Review Annual.* Gulf Breeze, FL: Academic International Press, 1977–. v. 1–.

133.   *Kessing's Contemporary Archives.* London: Kessing Publications, 1945–.

134.   Royal Institute of International Affairs. *Survey of International Affairs: Post War Series, Since 1947*. London: Oxford University Press, 1952–. v. 1–.

135.   Scherer, John L., ed. *U.S.S.R. Facts and Figures Annual*. Gulf Breeze, FL: Academic International Press, 1977–. v. 1–.

136.   *The Statesman's Year-Book: Statistical and Historical Information of the States of the World for the Year* _____ . London: Macmillan, 1945–.

137.   Stockholm International Peace Research Institute. *World Armaments and Disarmament: The SIPRI Yearbook*. New York: Humanities Press, 1969–. v. 1–.

138.   United Nations. Department of Social Affairs. *Yearbook on Human Rights*. New York: 1946–. v. 1–.

139.   United States. Department of Defense. *Report of the Secretary of Defense*. Washington, D.C.: GPO, 1948–. v. 1–.

140.   *United States Political Science Documents*. Pittsburgh, PA: Publications Center, University Center for International Studies, University of Pittsburgh, 1975–. v. 1–.

D. Dictionaries and Glossaries

141.   Gale Research Company. *Acronyms and Initialisms Dictionary*. 3rd ed. Detroit, MI: 1970. 484p.

142.   Greenberg, Milton, jt. author. *See* Plano, Jack C. (147).

143.   Luttwak, Edward. *The Dictionary of Modern War*. London: Penguin Books, 1971. 224p.

144.   McCormick, Donald. "Abbreviations, Titles, and Jargon Used in Espionage in Fact and in Fiction." In: *Who's Who in Spy Fiction*. New York: Taplinger, 1977. pp. 199–215.

145.   Olton, Roy, jt. author. *See* Plano, Jack C. (148).

146.   "Picnics and Wet Stuff: A Glossary of Current Spy Terms." *Time*, XCVIII (October 11, 1971), 44.

147.   Plano, Jack C. and Milton Greenberg. *The American Political Dictionary*. 5th ed. New York: Holt, 1979. 488p.

148.   _____ , and Roy Olton. *The International Relations Dictionary*. New York: Holt, 1969. 337p.

149.   Quick, John. *Dictionary of Weapons and Military Terms.* New York: McGraw-Hill, 1973. 527p.

150.   Ruffner, Frederick G., Jr. and Robert C. Thomas, eds. *Code Names Dictionary.* Detroit, MI: Gale Research Co., 1963. 555p.

151.   Safire, William. "CIA-Ese." In: *Safire's Political Dictionary.* New York: Random House, 1979. pp. 115–118.

152.   Thomas, Robert C., jt. editor. *See* Ruffner, Frederick G., Jr. (150).

153.   United States. Air Force. *Communications-Electronics Terminology.* Washington, D.C.: 1973.

154.   _____. Army. *Dictionary of U.S. Army Terms.* Army Regulation 310–25. Washington, D.C.: 1972.

155.   _____. Central Intelligence Agency. *Data Standardization for the Intelligence Community.* Directive No. 1/5. Langley, VA: 1976.

156.   _____. _____. "Glossary of Intelligence Terms and Definitions." In: United States. Congress. House. Permanent Select Committee on Intelligence. *Annual Report.* 95th Cong., 2nd sess. Washington, D.C.: GPO, 1978. pp. 24–72.

157.   _____. Department of Defense. *Dictionary of Military and Associated Terms.* Joint Chiefs of Staff Publication, no. 1. Washington, D.C.: GPO, 1972. 350p.

158.   _____. National Security Agency. *Basic Cryptologic Glossary.* Washington, D.C.: 1971.

E. General Histories and Memoirs

159.   Acheson, Dean. *Morning and Noon: A Memoir.* Boston: Houghton Mifflin, 1965. 288p.

160.   _____. *Present at the Creation: My Years in the State Department.* New York: Norton, 1969. 798p.

161.   Adams, Sherman. *First Hand Report.* New York: Popular Library, 1962. 476p.

162.   Alsop, Stewart. *The Center: People and Politics in Political Washington.* New York: Harper & Row, 1968. 365p.

163.   Bernstein, Barton J., ed. *Politics and Policy of the Truman Administration.* Chicago: Quadrangle Books, 1970. 302p.

164.　Buncher, Judith F., ed. *Human Rights and American Diplomacy, 1975–1977.* New York: Facts on File, Inc., 1977. 271p.

165.　Cochran, Bert. *Harry Truman and the Crisis Presidency.* Freeport, NY: Funk & Wagnalls, 1973. 302p.

166.　Congressional Quarterly, Inc. *Congress and the Nation, 1945–.* Washington, D.C., 1965–. v. 1–.

167.　Donovan, Robert J. *Eisenhower: The Inside Story.* New York: Harper, 1956. 423p.

168.　Ford, Gerald R. *A Time to Heal: An Autobiography.* New York: Harper & Row, 1979. 384p.

169.　Eisenhower, Dwight D. *The White House Years.* 2 vols. Garden City, NY: Doubleday, 1963–1965.

170.　Forrestal, James V. *The Forrestal Diaries.* Edited by Walter Millis. New York: Viking Press, 1951. 581p.

171.　Grantham, Dewey W. *The United States Since 1945: The Ordeal of Power.* New York : McGraw-Hill, 1976. 298p.

172.　Great Britain. Parliament. House of Commons. *Journals.* London: H.M. Stationery Office, 1945–.

173.　Hersey, John. "The Year of the Triphammer, 1968." *Washington Post Magazine,* (October 22, 1978), 14–47.

174.　Hughes, Emmet J. *The Ordeal of Power: A Political Memoir of the Eisenhower Years.* New York: Atheneum, 1963. 372p.

175.　Johnson, Lyndon B. *The Vantage Point.* New York: Holt, 1971. 636p.

176.　Khrushchev, Nikita S. *Khrushchev Remembers.* Translated from the Russian. Boston: Little, Brown, 1970. 639p.

177.　_____ . *Khrushchev Remembers: The Last Testament.* Translated from the Russian. Boston: Little, Brown, 1974. 602p.

178.　Kissinger, Henry. *White House Years.* Boston: Little, Brown, 1979. 1,521p.

179.　Lammers, W. W. *Presidential Politics: Patterns and Prospects.* New York: Harper & Row, 1976. 310p.

180.　Leahy, William D. *I Was There: The Personal Story of the Chief-of-Staff to Presidents Roosevelt and Truman, Based on His Notes and Diaries Made at the Time.* New York: McGraw-Hill, 1950. 527p.

181. McLellan, David S. *Dean Acheson: The State Department Years.* New York: Dodd, Mead, 1976. 466p.

182. Macmillan, Harold. *Autobiography and Memoirs.* 5 vols. New York: Harper & Row, 1966–1972.

183. Mee, C. L. *Meeting at Potsdam.* New York: Evans, 1975. 370p.

184. Millis, Walter, editor. *See* Forrestal, James V. (170).

185. Mollenhoff, Clark R. *Game Plan for Disaster: An Ombudsman's Report on the Nixon Years.* New York: W. W. Norton, 1976. 384p.

186. Morris, Roger. *Uncertain Greatness: Henry Kissinger and American Foreign Policy.* New York: Harper & Row, 1977. 312p.

187. Neustadt, Richard E. *Presidential Power: The Politics of Leadership With Reflections on Johnson and Nixon.* New York: Wiley, 1976. 324p.

188. Nixon, Richard M. *R. N.: The Presidential Memoirs.* New York: Grosset & Dunlap, 1978. 1,100p.

189. Osborne, John. *The Nixon Watch.* 4 vols. New York: Liveright, 1971–1975.

190. Paper, L. J. *The Promise and the Performance: The Leadership of John F. Kennedy.* New York: Crown, 1975. 408p.

191. Schlesinger, Arthur M., Jr. *The Imperial Presidency.* New York: Popular Library, 1973. 541p.

192. _____ . *A Thousand Days: John F. Kennedy in the White House.* Boston: Houghton Mifflin, 1965. 1,087p.

193. Sorensen, Theodore C. *Decision-Making in the White House: The Olive Branch of the Arrows.* New York: Columbia University Press, 1963. 94p.

194. Spanier, John. *American Foreign Policy Since World War II.* 7th ed. New York: Praeger, 1977. 354p.

195. Stoessinger, John G. *Why Nations Go to War.* 2nd ed. New York: St. Martin's Press, 1978. 246p.

196. Taylor, Maxwell D. *Responsibility and Response.* New York: Harper & Row, 1967. 84p.

197. Thant, U. *View from the U.N.* [1961–1971]. Garden City, NY: Doubleday, 1978. 508p.

198. Trewhitt, Henry L. *McNamara.* New York: Harper & Row, 1971. 307p.

199.   Truman, Harry S. *Memoirs.* 2 vols. Garden City, NY: Doubleday, 1955–1956.

200.   _____ . *Plain Speaking: An Oral Biography of Harry S. Truman.* New York: Berkley Publishing Co., 1974. 448p.

201.   United States. Congress. *Congressional Record.* Washington, D.C.: GPO, 1945–. v. 91–.

202.   Walton, Richard J. *Cold War and Counterrevolution: The Foreign Policy of John F. Kennedy.* New York: Viking, 1972. 250p.

203.   Yergin, Daniel. *Shattered Peace: The Origins of the Cold War and the National Security State.* Boston: Houghton Mifflin, 1977. 526p.

II/Propaganda and Psychological Warfare

Introduction

Propaganda and psychological warfare were developed into fine arts of persuasion by the Allied and Axis nations during World War II. Employing new media advances, those arts have since been refined to a point where even the differences in the terms have tended to merge. Today, propaganda is usually associated with a civilian audience and "psywar" is left to the military. Regardless of how the words are viewed it is important to note that great powers and small have battled for "the minds of men" in a continuous conflict since 1945.

Propaganda and psychological warfare were a major feature of the cold war and can be found in liberal dosage under certain political circumstances even with "detente." All nations continue to feel the need to "get their stories across" to their own people and to any outsiders who will listen—hopefully to prove that certain systems, people, and circumstances are better than others.

This effort to "win the hearts and minds," as President Johnson used to say about Vietnamese peasants, employs various means. Individual citizens spread truth and rumor, or both, while national propagandists have used posters, radio and television, film, news releases, pamphlets and leaflets, magazine and newspaper articles, and other media to reach audiences at home, regionally, and world-wide. Those efforts are used today in the Sino-Soviet dispute and in the troubled areas of the Middle East and South Africa.

Psychological warfare and propaganda have been variously analyzed and labelled as the citations in Part II demonstrate. Analysts have put forward degrees of good and bad, honesty and dishonesty, as well as intention. The context of this guide provides a definition of the "color" distinctions commonly used.

Data openly attributed to actual sources is said to be "white." That openly attributed to no particular source is colored "grey." That which is deliberately and falsely attributed to a source different than the originator is covert and labelled "black."

17

Most official government information agencies and their tools deal in white and grey propaganda. The continuing British Broadcasting Corporation (BBC) and the Voice of America (VOA) broadcasts beamed to Eastern Europe contain much of this type of propaganda. Even when Radio Liberty (RL) and Radio Free Europe (RFE) were financed by the CIA they dealt mostly in white and grey data.

Black propaganda and psychological warfare are almost exclusively the product of national intelligence agencies and are often called disinformation. Examples include the famous case of Soviet forged documents. Chinese Secret Service operations in Africa, and CIA black propaganda efforts in Chile and Indochina.

The sources cited in Part II demonstrate how propaganda and psychological warfare have been employed as potent mind-bending weapons capable of obtaining specific goals when synchronized with the political, social, military, and covert efforts of any given nation or group of nations. Section A deals with the topic in general terms while Sections B and C identify sources dealing exclusively with Communist or Western sources. Part D covers nations from Albania to Vietnam, in alphabetical order.

A. General Works

204.   Alisky, Marvin, jt. author. *See* Merrill, John C. (306).

205.   Allen, George V. "The Overseas Images of American Democracy." *Annals of the American Academy of Political and Social Science,* CCCLXVI (July 1966), 60–67.

206.   *Army Times,* Editors of. *The Tangled Web: True Stories of Deception in Modern Warfare.* Washington, D.C.: Luce, 1963. 199p.

207.   Atkinson, James D. *The Edge of War.* Chicago: Regnery, 1960. 318p.

208.   Bagdikian, Benjamin H. *The Information Machines: Their Impact on Men and the Media.* New York: Harper & Row, 1971. 359p.

209.   Barclay, Cyril N. *New* [Psychological] *Warfare.* New York: Philosophical Library, 1954. 65p.

210.   Becker, Howard. "The Nature and Consequences of Black Propaganda." *American Sociological Review,* XIV (April 1949), 221–235.

211.   Belyaev, Albert. "The Technology of Lies." *Soviet Literature,* no. 7 (July 1978), 155–180.

212.   Benedict, John. "Mind Control: The Ultimate Tyranny." *American Mercury,* LXX (April 1960), 12–27.

213.   Berding, Andrew A. "Balance Sheet in the War of Ideas." *Department of State Bulletin,* XXXIX (December 15, 1958), 955–959.

214.   _____. "The Battlefield of Ideas." *Department of State Bulletin,* XXXVIII (June 23, 1958), 1043–1048.

215.   _____. "The Freedom of Ideas Versus Censorship." *Department of State Bulletin,* XXXIX (July 14, 1958), 55–61.

216.   Bingham, W. V. "Military Psychology in War and Peace." *Science,* CVI (August 22, 1947), 155–160.

217.   Bobrow, Davis. "The Transfer of Meaning Across National Boundaries." In: Richard L. Merritt, ed. *Communication in International Politics.* Urbana: University of Illinois Press, 1972. pp. 36–38.

218.   Borra, Ranjan. "The Problem of Jamming in International Broadcasting." *Journal of Broadcasting,* XI (1967), 355–368.

219.   Brown, James A. C. *Techniques of Persuasion: From Propaganda to Brainwashing.* Baltimore, MD: Penguin Books, 1963. 325p.

220.   Bryan, Carter R., jt. author. *See* Merrill, John C. (306).

221.   Buchanan, William and Hartley Cantril. *How Nations See Each Other.* Urbana: University of Illinois Press, 1953. 220p.

222.   Cantril, Hartley, jt. author. *See* Buchanan, William (221).

223.   Carlson, Oliver. *Handbook on Propaganda for the Alert Citizen.* Los Angeles, CA: Foundation for Social Research, 1953. 110p.

224.   Carr, Edward H. "Propaganda and Power." *Yale Review,* XLII (September 1952), 1–9.

225.   Casmir, Fred L., ed. *Intercultural and International Communications.* Washington, D.C.: University Press of America, 1978. 834p.

226.   Cassell, Russell N. "Psychological Warfare." *Military Review,* XXXIII (November 1953), 58–62.

227.   Cassinelli, C. W. "Totalitarianism, Ideology, and Propaganda." *Journal of Politics,* XXII (February 1960), 68–95.

228.   Catlin, George E. G. "Propaganda and the Cold War." *Yale Review,* XLIII (September 1953), 103–116.

229.   Chakotin, Serge. *The Rape of the Masses: The Psychology of Totalitarian Political Propaganda.* New York: Haskell House, 1971. 299p.

230.   Chayes, Abram, jt. author. *See* Laskin, Paul L. (289).

231.   Chkhikvadze, V. M. "Human Rights and the Ideological Struggle." *Soviet Review,* XIX (Summer 1978), 3–18.

232.   Choukas, Michael. *Propaganda Comes of Age.* New York: Public Affairs Press, 1965. 299p.

233.   Christenson, Reo M. and Robert O. McWilliams, eds. *Voice of the People: Readings in Public Opinion and Propaganda.* New York: McGraw-Hill, 1967. 632p.

234.   Christopher, Stefan C., jt. author. *See* Dodd, Stuart C. (241).

235.   Connolly, R. D. "The Principles of War and Psychological Warfare." *Military Review,* XXXVI (March 1957), 37–46.

236.   Dasbach, Anita M. "U.S.-Soviet Magazine Propaganda: *America Illustrated* and *U.S.S.R.*" *Journalism Quarterly,* XLIII (Spring 1966), 73–84.

237.   Daugherty, William E. and Morris Janowitz. *A Psychological Warfare Casebook.* Baltimore, MD: Johns Hopkins University Press, 1958. 880p.

238.   Davison, W. Phillips. *International Political Communication.* New York: Published for the Council on Foreign Relations by Praeger, 1965. 404p.

239.   _____ . "Some Trends in International Propaganda." *Annals of the American Academy of Political and Social Science,* CCCXCVIII (November 1971), 1–13.

240.   Deutsch, Karl W. *The Nerves of Government: Models of Political Communication and Control.* New York: Free Press, 1963. 316p.

241.   Dodd, Stuart C. and Stefan C. Christopher. "The Reactants Models." In: Alfred de Grazia, *et al.,* eds. *The Behavior Sciences: Essays in Honor of George A. Leindberg.* New York: Behavior Research Council, 1968. pp. 143–177.

Propaganda leaflets carried by air or balloon.

242.   Doob, Leonard W. "Propagandists vs. Propagandees." In: Alvin W. Gouldner, ed. *Studies in Leadership: Leadership and Democratic Action.* New York: Russell & Russell, 1965. pp. 439–458.

243.   _____ . *Public Opinion and Propaganda.* 2nd ed. Hamden, CT: Archon Books, 1966. 612p.

244.   _____ . "Strategies of Psychological Warfare." *Public Opinion Quarterly,* XIII (Winter 1949), 635–644.

245.   Dovring, Karin. *The Road of Propaganda: The Semantics of Biased Communication.* New York: Philosophical Library, 1959. 158p.

246.   Duke University. School of Law. *International Control of Propaganda.* Law and Contemporary Problems, v. 31, no. 3. Durham, NC: 1966. 196p.

247.   Dunn, Frederick S. *War and the Minds of Men.* New York: Published for the Council on Foreign Relations by Harper, 1950. 115p.

248.   Durieux, A. "Psychological Warfare." *Military Review,* XXXVI (February 1957), 79–87.

249.   Eckhardt, William. "War Propaganda, Welfare Values, and Political Ideologies." *Journal of Conflict Resolution,* IX (Fall 1965), 345–358.

250.   Ellul, Jacques. "International Propaganda and Myths." In: Heinz D. Fischer and John Calhoun, eds. *International and Intercultural Communications.* 2nd ed., rev. and enl. New York: Hastings House, 1976. pp. 273–279.

251.   _____ . *Propaganda: The Formation of Mens' Attitudes.* Translated from the French. New York: Knopf, 1965. 320p.

252.   Emery, Walter B. *National and International Systems of Broadcasting: Their History, Operation, and Control.* East Lansing, MI: Michigan State University Press, 1969. 752p.

253.   Ford, Joseph B. "Public Opinion and Propaganda." In: Joseph S. Roucek, ed. *Contemporary Sociology.* New York: Philosophical Library, 1958. pp. 624–641.

254.   Ford, Nick A., comp. *Language in Uniform: A Reader on Propaganda.* New York: Odyssey Press, 1967. 212p.

255.   Fraser, Lindley M. *Propaganda.* London and New York: Oxford University Press, 1957. 218p.

256.   Friedmann, Wolfgang G. "Some Impacts of Social Organization and International Law: Hostile Propaganda." *American Journal of International Law,* (July 1956), 498–500.

257.   Friedrich, Carl J. *The Pathology of Politics: Violence, Betrayal, Corruption, Secrecy, and Propaganda.* New York: Harper & Row, 1972. 287p.

258.   Goodfriend, Arthur. "The Dilemma of Cultural Propaganda." *Annals of the American Academy of Political and Social Science,* CCCXCVIII (November 1971), 104–112.

259.   Gordon, George, *et al. The Idea Invaders.* New York: Hastings House, 1963. 256p.

260.   Hale, Julian A. S. *Radio Power: Propaganda and International Broadcasting.* Philadelphia, PA: Temple University Press, 1975. 196p.

261.   Haraldsen, S. "Psychological Warfare." *Military Review,* XXIX (January 1950), 78–83.

262.   Hargreaves, Reginald. "The Fourth Arm." *Military Review,* XXXIII (September 1953), 73–81.

263.   Harter, Donald L. and John Sullivan. *The Propaganda Handbook.* Philadelphia, PA: Twentieth Century Publishing Co., 1953. 440p.

264.   Henderson, H. W. "Psychological Warfare in the Nuclear Age." *Army Quarterly,* LXXXVII (October 1963), 87–90.

265.   Hoffman, Arthur S., ed. *International Communication and the New Diplomacy.* Bloomington: Indiana University Press, 1968. 206p.

266.   Howe, Russell W. and Sarah H. Trott. *The Power Peddlers.* Garden City, NY: Doubleday, 1977. 569p.

267.   Huddleston, Sisley. *Popular Diplomacy and War.* Washington, D.C. : Smith, 1954. 285p.

268. Hummel, William C. and K. G. Huntress. *The Analysis of Propaganda.* New York: Sloane, 1949. 222p.

269. Huntress, K. G., jt. author. *See* Hummel, William C. (268).

270. Illinois, University of, Institute of Communications Research. *A Comparison of the English Language Services of the V.O.A., the B.B.C.,* [and] *Radio Moscow, From Broadcasts During December 1953: Content Analysis.* Contract S.C.C.-21437. Urbana, IL: 1954. 105p.

271. "The International Control of Propaganda." *Law and Contemporary Problems,* XXXI (Summer 1966), 439–634.

272. Irion, Frederick C. *Public Opinion and Propaganda.* New York: Crowell, 1950. 782p.

273. Janowitz, Morris, jt. author. *See* Daugherty, William E. (237).

274. Jonas, Frank H., ed. *Political Dynamiting.* Salt Lake City, UT: University of Utah Press, 1970. 281p.

275. Kalijarvi, Thorsten V. "Psychological Warfare." In: *Modern World Politics.* 2nd ed. New York: Crowell, 1945. pp. 318–338.

276. Kamins, Bernard F. *Basic Propaganda.* Los Angeles, CA: Houlgate House, 1951. 120p.

277. Katz, Daniel, ed. *Public Opinion and Propaganda: A Book of Readings.* New York: Published for the Society for the Psychological Study of Social Issues by Holt, 1962. 779p.

278. Kecskemeti, Paul. "Totalitarian Communication as a Means of Control." *Public Opinion Quarterly,* XIV (1950), 224–234.

279. Klapper, Joseph T. *The Effects of Mass Communications.* New York: Free Press, 1960. 302p.

280. Knightly, Philip. *The First Casualty, From the Crimea to Vietnam: The War Correspondent as Hero, Propagandist, and Mythmaker.* New York: Harcourt, Brace, 1975. 465p.

281. Kominsky, Morris. *The Hoaxers.* Boston: Branden Press, 1970. 735p.

282. Koop, Theodore F. *Weapon of Silence.* Chicago: University of Chicago Press, 1946. 304p.

Radio.

283. Kriesburg, Martin. "Cross-Pressures and Attitudes: A Study of the Influence of Conflicting Propaganda on Opinions Regarding American-Soviet Relations." *Public Opinion Quarterly,* XIII (Spring 1949), 5–16.

284. Kris, Ernest and Nathan Leites. "Trends in Twentieth Century Propaganda." In: Bernard Berelson and Morris Janowitz, eds. *Reader in Public Opinion and Communications.* Enl. ed. Glencoe, IL: Free Press, 1953. pp. 278–288.

285. Krugman, H. E. "The Measurement of Resistance to Propaganda." *Human Relations,* VIII (Spring 1955), 175–184.

286. Kumata, H. and Wilbur L. Schramm. *Four Working Papers on Propaganda Theory: Written in Part With the Help of the U.S. Information Agency.* Urbana, IL: Institute of Communications Research, University of Illinois, 1955. 184p.

287. Lakshmana, Rao Y. V. "Propaganda Through the Printed Media in Developing Countries." *Annals of the American Academy of Political and Social Science,* CCCXCVIII (November 1971), 93–103.

288. Larson, Arthur, jt. author. *See* Whitton, John B. (362).

289. Laskin, Paul L. and Abram Chayes. "The International Satellite Controversy: Regulating Satellites to Prevent Political Propaganda." *Society,* XIII (September 1975), 30–40.

290. Lasswell, Harold D. "The Theory of Political Propaganda." In: Bernard Berelson and Morris Janowitz, eds. *Reader in Public Opinion and Communications.* Enl. ed. Glencoe, IL: Free Press, 1953. pp. 176–180.

291. Lee, Alfred M. *How to Understand Propaganda.* New York: Rinehart, 1952. 281p.

292. Lee, John, ed. *The Diplomatic Persuaders: The New Role of the Mass Media in International Relations.* New York: Published for the Washington Journalism Center by Wiley, 1968. 205p.

293. Leighton, Alexander H. *Human Relations in a Changing World: Observations on the Use of the Social Sciences.* New York: Dutton, 1949. 354p.

Treats psychological warfare.

294. Leites, Nathan, jt. author. *See* Kris, Ernest (284).

295. Lerner, Daniel. "The Strategy of Truth: Symbol and Act in World Propaganda." In: Lyman Bryson, *et al.,* eds. *Symbols and Society.* New York: Harper, 1955. pp. 371–382.

296. _____ , ed. *Propaganda in War and Crisis.* New York: Stewart, 1951. 500p.

297. Linebarger, Paul M. A. *Psychological Warfare.* Washington, D.C.: Infantry Journal Press, 1948. 259p.

298. _____ . _____ . 2nd ed. New York: Duell, Sloan & Pearce, 1954. 318p.

299. McCormack, T. H. "The Motivation and Role of a Propagandist." *Social Forces,* XXX (May 1952), 388–394.

300. McWilliams, Robert O., jt. author. *See* Christenson, Reo M. (233).

301. Martin, Leslie J. "The Effectiveness of International Propaganda." *Annals of the American Academy of Political and Social Science,* CCCXCVIII (November 1971), 61–70.

302. _____ . _____ . In: Heinz D. Fischer and John Calhoun, eds. *International and Intercultural Communications.* 2nd ed., rev. and enl. New York: Hastings House, 1976. pp. 262–272.

303. _____ . *International Propaganda: Its Legal and Diplomatic Control.* Minneapolis: University of Minnesota Press, 1958. 283p.

304. Meaney, John W. "Propaganda as Psychical Coercion." *Review of Politics,* XIII (January 1951), 64–87.

305. Meerloo, Abraham M. "Psychological Warfare—Psychological Peacefare." In: *Aftermath of Peace: Psychological Essays.* New York: International University Press, 1946. pp. 205–218.

306. Merrill, John C., Carter R. Bryan, and Marvin Alisky. *The Foreign Press: A Survey of the World's Journalism.* Baton Rouge: Louisiana State University Press, 1970. 366p.

307. Merton, Robert K. "Mass Persuasion: The Moral Dimension." In: Bernard Berelson and Morris Janowitz, eds. *Reader in Public Opinion and Communication.* Enl. ed. Glencoe, IL: Free Press, 1953. pp. 465–468.

308. Molnar, Andrew R., *et al. Human Factors* [Psychological Warfare] *Considerations of Undergrounds in Insurgencies.* Washington, D.C.: Prepared for the U.S. Department of the Army by the Special Operations Research Office, American University, 1966. 291p.

309. Mowlana, Hamid. "Propaganda and International Relations." In: *International Communications.* Dubuque, IA: Kendall-Hart, 1971. pp. 57–67.

310. Murty, Bhagevatula S. *Propaganda and World Public Order: The Legal Regulation of the Ideological Instrument of Coercion.* New Haven, CT: Yale University Press, 1968. 310p.

311. Padover, Saul K. *Psychological Warfare.* New York: Foreign Policy Association, 1951. 62p.

312. _____ . "Psychological Warfare and Foreign Policy." *American Scholar,* XX (April 1951), 151–161.

313. Powell, Norman J. *The Anatomy of Public Opinion.* New York: Prentice-Hall, 1951. 619p.

314. "Psychological Warfare and the Soldiers." *Military Review,* XXIX (October 1949), 73–78.

315. Pye, Lucien W., ed. *Communications and Political Development.* Princeton, NJ: Princeton University Press, 1963. 381p.

316. Qualter, Terence H. *Propaganda and Psychological Warfare.* New York: Random House, 1962. 176p.

317. "Radio in the Cold War." *World Today,* X (June 1954), 245–254.

318. Richardson, John. "The Cold War of Words." In: Frank R. Barnett, ed. *Peace and War in the Modern Age: Premises, Myths, and Realities.* New York: Anchor Books, 1965. pp. 371–385.

319. Riley, J. W., Jr. "Research for Psychological Warfare." *Public Opinion Quarterly,* XXI (Spring 1957), 147–150.

320. Roberts, Arch E. *Victory Denied.* Chicago: Chas. Hallberg & Co., 1966. 306p.

321. Ronalds, Francis S., Jr. "The Future of International Broadcasting." *Annals of the American Academy of Political and Social Science,* CCCXCVIII (November 1971), 71–80.

322. Roucek, Joseph S. "The Nature of Public Opinion and Propaganda." In: *Twentieth Century Political Thought.* New York: Philosophical Library, 1946. pp. 354–382.

323. Rubin, Bernard. "International Film and Television Propaganda: Campaigns of Assistance." *Annals of the American Academy of Political and Social Science,* CCCXCVIII (November 1971), 81–92.

324. Russ, William A., Jr. "The Art of Doubletalk." *South Atlantic Quarterly,* LII (January 1953), 64–72.

325. Schramm, Wilbur L. *Mass Communication and National Development: The Role of Information in the Developing Countries.* Stanford, CA: Stanford University Press, 1964. 333p.

326. _____ , jt. author. *See* Kumata, H. (286).

327. Smith, Bruce L., *et al. Propaganda, Communication, and Public Opinion: A Comprehensive Reference Guide.* Princeton, NJ: Princeton University Press, 1946. 435p.

328. Sorensen, Richard C. "Sociological Aspects of Psychological Warfare." In: Joseph S. Roucek, ed. *Contemporary Sociology.* New York: Philosophical Library, 1958. pp. 673–695.

329. Sparke, William. *Doublespeak: Language For Sale.* New York: Harper & Row, 1975. 195p.

330. Speier, Hans. "The Future of Psychological Warfare." *Public Opinion Quarterly,* XII (Spring 1948), 5–18.

331. _____ . "International Political Communication: Elite vs. Mass." In: *Force and Folly: Essays on Foreign Affairs and the History of Ideas.* Cambridge, MA: M.I.T. Press, 1969. pp. 16–31.

332. _____ . *Social Order and the Risks of War: Papers in Political Sociology.* Cambridge, MA: M.I.T. Press, 1964. 497p.

333. Sujka, Bogumil. "International Propaganda and Information Activity." *Studies in International Relations* (Warsaw), no. 3 (March 1974), 19–37.

334. Sullivan, John, jt. author. *See* Harter, Donald L. (263).

335. Svechnikov, P. "The Training of Propagandists in Theory and Practice." *Soviet Education,* XV (November 1972), 90–106.

336. Szunyogh, Bela. *Psychological Warfare: An Introduction to Ideological Propaganda and the Techniques of Psychological Warfare.* Translated from the German. Rev. ed. New York: Pamphlet Distributing, 1955. 117p.

337. Tanaka, Yasumasa. "Psychological Factors in International Persuasion." *Annals of the American Academy of Political and Social Science,* CCCXCVIII (November 1971), 50–60.

338. Taylor, Edmund. "Political Warfare." *Reporter,* XXV (September 14, October 26, November 9, 1961), 27–31, 8+, 16+.

339. Thum, Gladys and Marcella. *The Persuaders: Propaganda in War and Peace.* New York: Atheneum, 1972. 213p.

340. "A Tried and Tested Weapon: Visual Propaganda Today." *World Marxist Review,* XVII (June 1974), 42–50.

341. Trott, Sarah H., jt. author. *See* Howe, Russell W. (266).

342.   United States. Department of the Army. *The Art and Science of Psychological Operations: Case Studies of Military Application.* DA PAM 525–7. 2 vols. Washington, D.C.: GPO, 1976.

343.   _____ . Information Agency. *External Culture and Information Programs of Selected Countries in 1974.* Washington, D.C., 1975. 61p.

344.   _____ . _____ . Office of Research and Evaluation. *International Broadcasting of All Nations: Report.* Washington, D.C., 1948–. v. 1–.

Series continued by U.S. Agency for International Information.

345.   Urban, George R. "The Concept of Propaganda in East and West." *Communist Affairs,* IV (May–June 1966), 3–6.

346.   Vallance, T. R. "Methodology in Propaganda Research." *Psychological Bulletin,* XLVIII (January 1951), 32–61.

347.   Warburg, James P. *Unwritten Treaty.* New York: Harcourt, 1946. 186p.

348.   Webb, James H., Jr. "The Cultural Attaché: Scholar, Propagandist, or Bureaucrat?" *South Atlantic Quarterly,* LXXI (Summer 1972), 352–364.

349.   Wedge, Bryant. "International Propaganda and Statecraft." *Annals of the American Academy of Political and Social Science,* CCCXCVIII (November 1971), 36–43.

350.   "What About This Psychological Warfare: A Symposium." *Reporter,* VIII (March 31, 1953), 6–7, 9–19.

351.   Whitaker, Urban G., ed. *Propaganda and International Relations.* Rev. and enl. ed. Dallas, TX: Chandler, 1962. 246p.

352.   White, John B. *The Big Lie.* New York: Crowell, 1956. 235p.

353.   White, Ralph K. "New Resistance to International Propaganda." *Public Opinion Quarterly,* XVI (Winter 1952), 539–552.

354.   _____ . "Propaganda: Morally Questionable and Morally Unquestionable Techniques." *Annals of the American Academy of Political and Social Science,* CCCXCVIII (November 1971), 26–35.

355.   Whitton, John B. "Cold War Propaganda." *American Journal of International Law,* XLV (January 1951), 151–153.

356.   _____ . "Efforts to Curb Dangerous Propaganda." *American Journal of International Law,* XLI (October 1947), 899–903.

357. _____ . "Hostile International Propaganda and International Law." *Annals of the American Academy of Political and Social Science,* CCCXCVIII (November 1971), 14–25.

358. _____ . "Propaganda in Cold Wars." *Public Opinion Quarterly,* XV (Spring 1951), 142–144.

359. _____ . "Radio Propaganda: A Modest Proposal." *American Journal of International Law,* LII (October 1958), 739–745.

360. _____ . "The United Nations Conference on Freedom of Information and the Movement Against International Propaganda." *American Journal of International Law,* XLIII (January 1949), 73–87.

361. _____ , ed. *Propaganda and the Cold War: A Princeton University Symposium.* Washington, D.C.: Public Affairs Press, 1963. 119p.

362. _____ and Arthur Larson. *Propaganda: Towards Disarmament in the War of Words.* Durham, NC: Published for the World Rule of Law Center by Duke University Press, 1964. 305p.

B. Communist

363. Alex, Robert J. "Soviet and Communist [Propaganda] Activities in Latin America." *Problems of Communism,* X (January–February 1961), 8–13.

364. Ardoin, Birthney and James L. Hall. "An Analysis of Soviet and Chinese Broadcasts Concerning U.S. Involvement in Vietnam." *Southern Quarterly,* XIII (April 1975), 175–189.

365. Boynton, John. *Aims and Means.* London: Dufour, 1964. 110p.

366. Burton, Anthony. *The Destruction of Loyalty: An Evaluation of the Threat of Propaganda and Subversion Against the Armed Forces of the West.* London: Foreign Affairs Research Institute, 1976. 63p.

367. Buzek, Anthony. *How the Communist Press Works.* New York: Praeger, 1964. 287p.

368. Clardy, J. V. "Communist Publications in the U.S. Mail." *Western Humanities Review,* XX (Winter 1966), 3–9.

369. Clews, John C. *Communist Propaganda Techniques.* New York: Praeger, 1964. 326p.

370. Coste, Brutus. "Propaganda in Eastern Europe." *Public Opinion Quarterly,* XIV (Winter 1950), 639–666.

371.   Costikyan, Simon. *Twelve Years of Communist Broadcasting, 1948–1959: A Report.* Washington, D.C.: Office of Research and Analysis, U.S. Information Agency, 1960. 79p.

372.   Dallin, Alexander. "Russia and China View the United States." *Annals of the American Academy of Political and Social Science,* CCCXLIX (September 1963), 153–162.

373.   Dasbach, Anita M. *Propaganda Behind the Wall: A Case Study in the Use of Propaganda as a Tool of Foreign Policy by Communist Governments.* Washington, D.C.: 1968. 263p.

374.   David, J. P. "How to Win Countries and Influence People." *U.N. World,* V (October 1951), 18–21.

375.   DeSola-Pool, Ithiel, jt. author. *See* Leites, Nathan (390).

376.   Eastman, Max, ed. "World War III Has Already Started." *Reader's Digest,* LXXVIII (January 1961), 36–44.

377.   Ettinger, K. E. "Foreign Propaganda in America." *Public Opinion Quarterly,* X (Fall 1946), 329–342.

378.   Evans, Frank B., ed. *Worldwide Communist Propaganda Activities.* New York: Macmillan, 1955. 222p.

379.   Flynn, John T. "Insidious Propaganda." *Vital Speeches,* XIII (December 1, 1946), 110–114.

380.   Garner, William R. "The Sino-Soviet Ideological Struggle in Latin America." *Journal of Inter-American Studies,* X (April 1968), 244–245.

381.   Gedye, G. E. K. "Broadcasting and the Iron Curtain." *Contemporary Review,* CLXXXIII (April 1953), 206–210.

382.   Grant, Natalie. *Communist Psychological Offensive: Distortions in the Translation of Official Documents.* Washington, D.C.: Research Institute of the Sino-Soviet Bloc, 1961.

383.   Hall, James L., jt. author. *See* Ardoin, Birthney (364).

384.   Hanlin, J. J. "The Big Voice Over Vienna." *Catholic World,* XVIII (January 1955), 271–277.

385.   Hunter, Edward. *Attack by Mail.* New York: Bookmailer, 1966. 252p.

386.   Kempers, F. "Communist Information Policy in Practice: The Reporting of Events in Czechoslovakia and Poland by the Party Press of Friendly Nations." *Gazette,* XIV (1968), 271–292.

387. Kirkpatrick, Evron M., ed. *Target—the World: Communist Propaganda Activities in 1955.* New York: Macmillan, 1956. 362p.

388. Kruglak, Theodore E. "The Role and Evolution of Press Agencies in the Socialist Countries." *Gazette,* XXI (1975), 1–18.

389. Labin, Suzanne. *The Unrelenting War: A Study of the Strategy and Techniques of Communist Propaganda and Infiltration.* New York: American-Asian Educational Exchange [1960?]. 47p.

390. Leites, Nathan and Ithiel DeSola-Pool. "Interaction: The Response of Communist Propaganda to Frustration." In: Harold D. Lasswell, *et al. Language of Politics: Studies in Quantitative Semantics.* New York: Stewart, 1949. pp. 344–369.

391. Markham, James W. *Voices of the Red Giants.* Ames, IA: Iowa State University Press, 1967. 513p.

392. Miller, Donald L. *Strategy For Conquest: A Study of Communist Propaganda Techniques.* New York: Public Affairs Press, 1966. 74p.

393. Morgan, Thomas B. *Among the Anti-Americans.* New York: Holt, 1967. 211p.

394. Morris, B. S. "Communist International Front Organizations: Their Nature and Function." *World Politics,* IX (October 1956), 76–87.

395. Nath Agarwala, Pran. "Communist Exploitation of Facilities in Developing Countries." *Studies on the Soviet Union,* New Series II (Fall 1963), 133–139.

396. Oliver, Robert T. "Top Communist Weapon: The Spoken Word." *Vital Speeches,* XXI (May 1, 1955), 1200–1203.

397. Paulu, Burton. *Radio and Television Broadcasting in Eastern Europe.* Minneapolis: University of Minnesota Press, 1974. 592p.

398. "Propaganda Psychology and Propaganda." *Officer,* XXXV (January 1959), 8–10+.

399. "Signed, Sealed, and Planted: Communist Forgeries." *Time,* LXXVII (February 10, 1961), 25–26.

400. United States. Central Intelligence Agency. Foreign Broadcast Information Service. *Survey of Communist Bloc Broadcasts.* 11 vols. Washington, D.C.: 1958–1967. v. 9–20.

401. _____ . _____ . _____ . *Survey of Communist Propaganda.* Washington, D.C.: 1967–. v. 20–.

402. _____ . _____ . _____ . *Survey of Far East Broadcasts.* 9 vols. Washington, D.C.: 1950–1958. v. 1–9.

403. ———. Congress. House. Committee on Un-American Activities. *The New Communist Propaganda Line on Religion: Hearings.* 90th Cong., 1st sess. Washington, D.C.: GPO, 1967. 1,029p.

404. ———. Department of Justice. *Report of the Attorney General to the Congress of the United States on the Administration of the Foreign Agents Registration Act of 1938, As Amended For the Calendar Year 1972.* Washington, D.C.: GPO, 1972. 208p.

405. ———. Information Agency. Office of Research and Intelligence. *Communist Propaganda: A Fact Book, 1957–1958.* Washington, D.C.: 1958. 192p.

406. ———. ———. ———. *Communist Propaganda Activities in the Far East, 1958: A Fact Book.* Washington, D.C.: 1959. 44p.

407. ———. ———. ———. *World-Wide Communist Propaganda Activities: O.R.I. Intelligence Summary.* Washington, D.C.: 1954–. v. 1–.

408. ———. ———. Press Service. *A Report on Communist Colonialism and International Communications.* 2 vols. Washington, D.C.: 1956.

409. ———. ———. Research and Reference Service. *Selected Communist Propaganda Activities in the Near East and South Asia, 1962.* Washington, D.C.: 1963. 101p.

410. ———. ———. ———. *Communist Propaganda Around the World: Apparatus and Activities in 1961.* Washington, D.C.: 1962. 427p.

411. "The West as Portrayed by Communist Propaganda." *World Today,* X (December 1954), 532–534.

412. Wettig, Gerhard. *Broadcasting and Detente: Eastern Policies and Their Implications For East-West Relations.* Translated from the German. New York: St. Martin's Press, 1977. 110p.

413. Whaley, Barton. *Daily Monitoring of the Western Press in the Soviet Union and Communist States.* Cambridge, MA: M.I.T. Press, 1964.

414. Wharton, David. "Poison From Red Printing Presses." *Reader's Digest,* LXXIX (November 1961), 299–303.

C. Western

415. Abshire, David M. *International Broadcasting: A New Dimension of Western Diplomacy.* Beverly Hills, CA: Published for the Center for Strategic and International Studies, Georgetown University, by Sage Publications, 1977. 92p.

416. Achard, James. "Possibilities and Well." *Military Review,* XXXVIII (July 1958), 94–98.

417. Allen, George V. "Propaganda: A Conscious Weapon of Diplomacy." *Department of State Bulletin,* XXI (December 19, 1949), 941–943.

418. Allport, F. H. "Broadcasting to An Enemy Country: What Appeals are Effective and Why." *Journal of Social Psychology,* XXIII (May 1946), 217–224.

419. Avedon, Herbert. "The Heart of the Matter." *Military Review,* XXXIV (January 1955), 59–62.

420. Bernays, Edward L. "The Engineering of Consent." *Annals of the American Academy of Political and Social Science,* CCL (March 1947), 113–120.

421. Brecker, Richard L. "Truth as a Weapon of the Free World." *Annals of the American Academy of Political and Social Science,* CCLXXVII (November 1951), 1–11.

422. Carleton, William G. "Time for a Cold War Offensive is Now." *Vital Speeches,* XXV (January 15, 1959), 209–214.

423. Carroll, Wallace. *Persuade or Perish.* Boston: Houghton Mifflin, 1948. 392p.

424. Fellers, Bonner. *The "Thought War" Against the Kremlin.* Chicago: Regnery, 1949.

425. "Foreign Lobbyists: The Hidden Pressures to Sway U.S. Policy." *Newsweek,* LX (July 30, 1962), 18–22.

426. Kelin, V. "The Battle for People's Minds." *International Affairs* (Moscow), no. 1 (January 1964), 57–61.

427. Lisann, Maury. *Broadcasting to the Soviet Union: International Politics and Radio.* New York: Praeger, 1975. 199p.

428. Luckmann, L.D. "Foreign Policy By Propaganda Leaflets." *Public Opinion Quarterly,* IX (Winter 1945), 428–429+.

429. Oliver, James H. *A Comparison of the Russian Services of the Four Major Broadcasters (V.O.A., B.B.C., D.W., R.L).* Washington, D.C.: Office of Research, U.S. Information Agency, 1975. 51p.

430. Quester, George H. "On the Identification of Real and Pretended Communist Military Doctrine." *Journal of Conflict Resolution,* X (June 1966), 172–179.

Propaganda analysis.

431. Schlesinger, Arthur M., Jr. "Psychological Warfare: Can It Sell Freedom?" *Reporter,* VIII (October 31, 1953), 9–12.

432. Skvortsov, Lev V. *The Ideology and Tactics of Anti-Communism: Myths and Reality.* Moscow: Progress Publishers, 1969. 112p.

433. Walker, R. L. "Exploiting Communist Vulnerabilities." In: Frank R. Barnett, ed. *Peace and War in the Modern Age: Premises, Myths, and Realities.* New York: Anchor Books, 1965. pp. 353–370.

434. Wilson, Thomas W. "Red Propaganda Can Be Beaten." *Reporter,* VIII (March 31, 1953), 13–15.

D. By Country

1. Albania

435. Pano, Nicholas C. "The Albanian Cultural Revolution." *Problems of Communism,* XXIV (July–August 1974), 46+.

The effects of U.S./British operations, 1949–1953.

2. Algeria

436. Bjelajac, Stavko N. "Psywar: The Lessons from Algeria." *Military Review,* XLII (December 1962), 2–7.

3. Arab Countries

437. Alexander, Yonah. *The Role of Communications in the Middle East Conflict: Ideological and Religious Aspects.* New York: Praeger, 1973. 287p.

438. Almaney, Adnan. "Government Control of the Press in the U.A.R., 1952–1970." *Journalism Quarterly,* XLIX (Summer 1972), 340–348.

439. Arsenian, Seth. "Wartime Propaganda in the Middle East." *Middle East Journal,* II (October 1948), 417–429.

The 1948 Palestine war.

440. Boyd, Douglas A. "The Development of Egypt's Radio 'Voice of the Arabs' Under Nassar." *Journalism Quarterly,* LII (Winter 1975), 645–653.

441. Browne, Donald R. "The Voices of Palestine." *Middle East Journal,* XXIX (Spring 1975), 133–150.

442. Ellis, W. S. "Nassar's Other Voice." *Harper's,* CCXXII (June 1961), 54–58.

443.   Hatim, Muhammad 'Abd al-Qadir. *Information and the Arab Cause.* London: Longmans, Green, 1974. 320p.

444.   Ibrahim, Saad E. M. "Arab Images of the United States and the Soviet Union Before and After the June War of 1967." *Journal of Conflict Resolution,* XVI (Spring 1972), 227–240.

445.   Jones, M. C. "Israel and Egypt: A Modern Myth." *Contemporary Review,* CCXXVI (January 1975), 42–44.

446.   Khan, Rais A. "Radio Cairo and Egyptian Foreign Policy, 1956–1959." Unpublished PhD Dissertation, University of Michigan, 1967.

447.   Lewis, R. G. "Israel's Rights and Arab Propaganda." *Commentary,* LX (August 1975), 38–43.

448.   Loya, A. "Radio Propaganda of the United Arab Republic: An Analysis." *Middle Eastern Affairs,* XIII (April 1962), 98–110.

449.   "Radio War." *Time,* CI (June 18, 1973), 55.

450.   Rosenthal, Alan. "Film at War." *Film Library Quarterly,* VII (Spring 1974), 7–12.

Arab-Israeli war of 1967.

451.   Schenker, Avraham. "Anti-Zionism in Arab Propaganda and the Jewish Response." *Israel Horizons,* XVIII (January 1970), 12–16.

4. Canada

452.   Canada. Justice Ministry. Committee on Hate Propaganda in Canada. *Report.* Ottawa: Queen's Printer, 1966. 327p.

5. China

453.   "Anti-Americanism in Red China's *People's Daily*: A Functional Analysis, 1959." *Journalism Quarterly,* XL (Spring 1963), 187–195.

454.   Barr, John S. "China's Use of Culture For Propaganda: An Eye-witness Account, 1949–1952." *Eastern World,* XXI (November–December 1967), 10–11.

455.   "Chinese Red Propaganda." *Newsweek,* XXXIX (May 19, 1952), 52.

456.   Chu, Godwin C. *Radical Change Through Communications in Mao's China.* Honolulu: University of Hawaii Press, 1977. 340p.

457.   Flynn, John T. *While You Slept: Our Tragedy in Asia and Who Made It.* New York: Devin-Adair, 1951. 192p.

458.   Ginsburg, Jay H. *China: Rationalizing the Demonic.* New York: Vantage Press, 1972. 153p.

459.   Hoffer, T. W. "Broadcast Blitz Against Revisionism: Radio and the Chinese Cultural Revolution." *Journalism Quarterly,* LIV (Winter 1977), 703–712.

460.   Houn, Franklin W. "Publications As a Propaganda Medium in Communist China." *Far Eastern Survey,* XXIX (December 1960), 177–186.

461.   _____ . "The Stage as a Medium of Propaganda in Communist China." *Public Opinion Quarterly,* XXII (Summer 1959), 222–235.

462._____ . *To Change a Nation: Propaganda and Indoctrination in Communist China.* New York: Crowell, 1961. 250p.

463.   Hunter, Edward. *The Black Book on China.* 5th ed. New York: Bookmailer, 1962. 136p.

464.   _____ . *Brain-Washing in Red China: The Calculated Destruction of Men's Minds.* New and enl. ed. New York: Vanguard, 1953. 341p.

The literature on brain-washing by the Chinese, especially during the Korean War, is large but except for a few samples is not analyzed here.

465.   Jan, G. P. "Radio Propaganda in Chinese Villages." *Asian Survey,* VII (May 1967), 305–315.

466.   Litvinoff, Boris. "The Psychological War Against Mao Tse-tung's Regime." *NATO's Fifteen Nations,* VIII (June-July 1963), 62–66.

467.   Liu, Alan P. L. *Communications and National Integration in Communist China.* Michigan Studies on China, no. 22. Berkeley: University of California Press, 1971. 225p.

468.   Livingstone, George D., jt. author. *See* Mohler, Jack L. (469).

469.   Mohler, Jack L. and George D. Livingstone. "The Chinese Army and Psychological Warfare: Past, Present, and Promise." *Military Review,* LV (March 1975), 58–66.

470.   Oliphant, C. A. "The Image of the United States Projected by the *Peking Review.*" *Journalism Quarterly,* XLI (Summer 1964), 416–420, 469.

471.   Pye, Lucien W. "Communications and Chinese Political Culture." *Asian Survey,* XVIII (March 1978), 221–246.

472.   Tang, Peter S. H. *Communist China as a Developmental Model For Underdeveloped Countries.* Washington, D.C.: Research Institute of the Sino-Soviet Bloc, 1960. 111p.

473.   Tsai, Chin. *Peiping's International Propaganda Activities: A United Front Plot.* Pamphlet no. 85. New Delhi, India: Asian Peoples' Anti-Communist League, 1975. 107p.

474.   Tung, Chi-ping. *The Thought Revolution.* New York: Coward-McCann, 1966. 254p.

475.   United States. Congress. House. Committee on Un-American Activities. *How the Chinese Reds Hoodwink Visiting Foreigners: Consultation With Mr. Robert Loh.* Washington, D.C.: GPO, 1960. 34p.

476.   _____ . Consulate General, Hong Kong. *Chinese Communist Propaganda Review.* Hong Kong, 1951–1953. nos. 1–45.

477.   _____ . Department of State. Office of Research and Intelligence. Division of Research for the Far East. *Chinese Communist World Outlook: Views Regarding the United States.* Intelligence Report, no. 6870-2. Washington, D.C.: 1956. 47p.

478.   _____ . Information Agency. *The External Information and Cultural Relations Programs of the P.R.C.* Washington, D.C.: 1973. 339p.

479.   Walker, R. L. "Communist China Looks at the United States." *Yale Review,* XLI (September 1951), 25–43.

480.   Yu, Frederick T. C. "Persuasive Communications During the Cultural Revolution." *Gazette,* XVI (1970), 73–87, 137–148.

481.   Yu, Te-chi. *Mass Persuasion in Communist China.* New York: Praeger, 1964. 186p.

6. Cuba

482.   Stansbury, C. M. "Castro's Radio Voice." *Popular Electronics,* XIV (March 1961), 52–54.

483.   Szulc, Tad. "Castro Tries to Export Fidelism." *New York Times Magazine,* (November 27, 1960), 19–21 +.

484.   United States. Congress. House. Committee on Un-American Activities. *Violations of State Department Regulations and Pro-Castro Propaganda Activities in the United States: Hearings.* 88th Cong., 1st and 2nd sess. 5 vols. Washington, D.C.: GPO, 1963–1964.

485.   _____ . Information Agency. *The Cuban Crisis, 1962: The U.S.I.A. in Action.* Washington, D.C.: 1963. 7p.

486.   _____ . _____ . Research Service. *Foreign Radio Listening in Cuba as Indicated by Refugee Interviews.* Washington, D.C.: 1968. 17p.

487.   "The Voice of Castro: Radio Habana Cuba." *Time,* LXXX (August 10, 1962), 22 +.

7. Czechoslovakia

488. Howell, William S. "The North America Broadcast Service of Radio Prague." *Quarterly Journal of Speech,* LV (October 1969), 247–255.

489. Kaplan, Frank L. "The Czechoslovak Press and the Reform Movement, 1963–1968." Unpublished PhD Dissertation, University of Wisconsin, 1973.

490. Koutnik, Stanislav. "Cooking the Cuban News: That Historic Week as Seen in Czechoslovakia." *New Republic,* CXLVII (December 29, 1962), 16–20; CXLVIII (January 12, 1963), 29–30.

491. Olson, K. G. "The Development of the Czechoslovak Propaganda Administration." *Public Opinion Quarterly,* XIII (Winter 1949), 607–618.

492. Reisky-Dubnic, Vladimir. *Communist Propaganda Methods: A Case Study on Czechoslovakia.* New York: Praeger, 1961. 287p.

493. Sturm, Rudolf. "Propaganda." In: Vratislav Busek and Nicholas Spulber, eds. *Czechoslovakia.* New York: Praeger, 1957. pp. 101–127.

494. United States. Information Agency. *Foreign Radio Listening in Czechoslovakia Before and After the Invasion.* Washington, D.C.: 1969. 15p.

495. Wechsberg, Joseph. *The Voices.* Garden City, NY: Doubleday, 1969. 113p.

Broadcasts during the Czech revolt of 1968.

8. France

496. Glynn, Robert B. "L'Affaire Rosenberg in France." *Political Science Quarterly,* LXX (December 1955), 498–521.

497. Zartman, I. W. "French Communist Foreign Policy, 1952–1954: A Propaganda Analysis." *Western Political Quarterly,* IX (June 1956), 344–362.

9. Germany

498. Browne, Donald R. "R.I.A.S. [East] Berlin: A Case Study of a Cold War Broadcast Operation." *Journal of Broadcasting,* X (1966), 119–135.

499. Davison, W. Phillips. "An Analysis of the Soviet-Controlled Berlin Press." *Public Opinion Quarterly,* XI (Spring 1947), 40–57.

500. Eyck, F. Günther. *External Information and Cultural Relations Programs of the Federal Republic of Germany.* Washington, D.C.: Research Service, U.S. Information Agency, 1973. 94p.

501.   Grothe, Peter. *To Win the Minds of Men: The Story of the Communist Propaganda War in East Germany.* Palo Alto, CA: Pacific Books, 1958. 241p.

502.   Joyce, Marion D. "The Vicious Estate: No Lie About the West is Taboo to 'Tabu' and Other East German Smear Sheets." *Army,* XIII (February 1963), 53–55.

503.   Paul, H. W. "Propaganda in the East German Republic." *Gazette,* V (1959), 57–86.

504.   Taylor, Edward. "R.I.A.S.: The Voice East Germany Believes." *Reporter,* IX (November 10, 1953), 28–32.

505.   United States. Information Agency. *We* [Berlin] *Vote For Freedom.* Washington, D.C.: 1961. 52p.

506.   _____ . _____ . Office of Research and Intelligence. *Soviet Reporting on the East German Uprisings of June 1953: A Case Study of Soviet Propaganda.* New Brunswick, NJ: Department of Sociology, Rutgers University, 1954. 48p.

10. Great Britain

507.   Aitken, Jonathan. *Officially Secret.* London: Weidenfeld & Nicholson, 1972.

508.   "The B.B.C.'s Russian Service." *Spectator,* CXCVIII (June 21, 1957), 803, 845; CXCIX (June 28–September 6, 1957), 15, 49, 106, 133, 161, 189, 218, 247, 274, 305.

509.   Barclay, Cyril N. *The New Warfare.* London: Clowes, 1953. 65p.

510.   Barker, Arthur J. "Propaganda." *Army Quarterly,* LXXXVII (October 1963), 53–58.

511.   Beeley, Harold. "The Changing Role of British International Propaganda." *Annals of the American Academy of Political and Social Science,* CCCXCVIII (November 1971), 124–129.

512.   Black, John B. *Organizing the Propaganda Instrument: The British Experience.* The Hague: Nijhoff, 1975. 116p.

513.   Bocca, Geoffrey. "Britain Still Rules the Waves." *Quest,* III (May 1979), 9–10.

514.   Briggs, Asa. *History of Broadcasting in the United Kingdom: Vol. IV, Sound and Fury.* London and New York: Oxford University Press, 1979.

515.   British Broadcasting Corporation. *Annual Reports and Accounts of the B.B.C.* London: H. M. Stationery Office, 1945–. v. 17–.

516. _____ . *B.B.C. Handbook.* London: H. M. Stationery Office, 1945–. v. 17–.

517. _____ . Monitoring Service. *Summary of World Broadcasts.* Caversham Park, Reading, England: 1949–. v. 1–.

518. Clark, Bennett, "The B.B.C.'s External Service." *International Affairs* (London), XXXV (April 1959), 170–180.

519. Evelegh, R. G. N. "Extra-Sensory Warfare." *Army Quarterly,* LXXXVIII (April 1964), 58–62.

520. Farago, Ladislas. "British Propaganda." *U.N. World,* II (October 1948), 22–26.

521. Gibb, H. A. R. "Anglo-Egypt Relations: An Illustration of the Influence of Propaganda." *International Affairs* (London), XXVII (October 1951), 443–445.

522. Gorham, Maurice. *Sound and Fury: Twenty-One Years in the B.B.C.* London: Percival Marshall, 1948. 248p.

523. "Information Services." *Fortnightly,* CLXXVII (May 1952), 289–290.

524. "It Can Happen Here: A Study of Communist Intrigue, With a List of Propaganda Organizations in Great Britain." *Round Table,* XLIV (September 1954), 353–362.

525. McWilliams, Carey. "Knights in Shining Buicks." *Nation,* CLXXII (January 6, 1951), 9–11.

526. Marett, Robert. *Through the Back Door: An Inside View of Britain's Overseas Information Services.* London and New York: Pergamon, 1968. 224p.

527. Morris, B. S. "War and the Psychological Services." *Fortnightly,* CLXVIII (August 1947), 112–118.

528. Ogilvy-Webb, Marjorie. *The Government Explains: A Study of the Information Services.* London: Allen and Unwin, 1965. 229p.

529. Paret, Peter. "A Total Weapon of Limited War." *Journal of the Royal United Service Institution,* CV (February 1960), 62–69.

530. Paulu, Burton. *British Broadcasting.* Minneapolis: University of Minnesota Press, 1956. 457p.

531. Stewart-Smith, Dudley G. *No Vision Here: Non-Military Warfare in Britain.* Petersham, Surrey, England: Foreign Affairs Publishing Co., 1966. 142p.

532. United States. Information Agency. Office of Research. *The American Image Among British Influentials.* Washington, D.C.: 1974. 57p.

533. Wade, William W. "How Other Nations [Britain] Tell Their Story." *Foreign Policy Bulletin,* XXXIII (September 15, 1953), 5–7.

11. India

534. Datta, Baij N. *Weapon For War, Prescription For Peace: National Security.* Bombay: India Publishing House, 1968. 288p.

535. Qutubuddin, Aziz. *Mission to Washington: An Expose of India's Intrigues in the United States of America in 1971 to Dismember Pakistan.* Karachi: Publications Division of the United Press of Pakistan, 1973. 234p.

12. Israel

536. Fancher, Michael. "Israel's Strategy of Persuasion." *Journal of the United Service Institution,* C (January–March 1970), 27–45.

537. Rubin, Ronald. "Israel's Foreign Information Program." *Gazette,* XIX (1973), 65–78.

13. Italy

538. Mendelsohn, Harold and W. J. Cahnman. "Communist Broadcasts to Italy." *Public Opinion Quarterly,* XVI (Winter 1952), 671–780.

539. United States. Department of State. Division of Radio Program Analysis. *Communist Broadcasts to Italy: A Content Analysis.* Washington, D.C.: 1953. 26p.

14. Japan

540. Nippon Hoso Kyokai. *The History of Broadcasting in Japan.* Tokyo, 1967. 423p.

540a. Peng, Sze-yen. Chinese Communist Propaganda in Japan." *Free China Review,* XV (September 1965), 25–29.

541. Wildes, H. E. "War For the Mind of Japan." *Annals of the American Academy of Political and Social Science,* CCXCIV (July 1954), 1–7.

15. Korea

542. Davison, W. Phillips. "Air Force Psychological Warfare in Korea." *Air University Quarterly Review,* IV (Summer 1951), 40–48.

543.   Gordenker, Leon. "The United Nations Use of Mass Communications in Korea, 1950–1951." *International Organization,* VIII (August 1954), 331–345.

544.   Kalisher, Peter. "We're Asking the Reds to Surrender—Please!" *Collier's,* CXXX (December 13, 1952), 15–18.

545.   "Psychological Warfare in Korea: An Interim Report." *Public Opinion Quarterly,* XV (Spring 1951), 65–75.

546.   Riley, J. W. jt. author. See Schramm, Wilbur L. (548).

547.   Sang-woo, Rhee. "A Quantity Analysis of North Korea's Unification Messages: Propaganda Messages Against South Korea 1948–1968." *East Asian Review* I (Spring 1974), 37–65.

548.   Schramm, Wilbur L. and J. W. Riley. "Communications in the Sovietized States, as Demonstrated in Korea." *American Sociological Review,* XVI (December 1951), 757–766.

549.   Simon, Sheldon W. "The *Pueblo* Incident and the South Korean Revolution in North Korea's Foreign Policy: A Propaganda Analysis." *Asian Forum,* II (Summer 1970), 201–214.

16. Nigeria

550.   Schabowska, Henryka and Ulf Himmelstrand. *Africa Reports on the Nigerian Crisis* [1967–1970]. New York: Holmes and Meier, 1979. 161 p.

17. Poland

551.   Barnett, Clifford R., *et al.* "The Diffusion and Control of Information." In: *Poland: Its People, Its Society, Its Culture.* New Haven, CT: HRAF Press, 1958. pp. 141–161.

18. Rhodesia

552.   Ranger, Terence. "The Conflict in Rhodesia: A Question of Evidence." *African Affairs,* LXXVII (January 1978), 3–5.

19. South Africa

553.   Breytenbach, W. J. *South Africa's Involvement in Africa.* Occasional paper no. 42. Pretoria: Africa Institute of South Africa, 1978. 28p.

554.   Laurence, John. *The Seeds of Disaster: A Guide to the Realities, Race Policies, and World-Wide Propaganda Campaigns of the Republic of South Africa.* New York: Taplinger, 1968. 333p.

555. McKay, Vernon. "South African Propaganda: Methods and Media." *Africa Report,* XI (February 1966), 41–46.

556. _____. "The [South African] Propaganda Battle For Zambia." *Africa Today,* (April 1966), 18–26.

557. Rogers, Barbara. "Sunny South Africa: A World-Wide Propaganda Machine." *Africa Report,* XXII (September 1977), 2+.

20. USSR

558. Andrusiak, Nicholas. "Soviet Anti-Americanism." *Ukrainian Review,* XXVI (Autumn–Winter, 1970), 270–276.

559. Araldsen, O. P. "Norway and Soviet Psychological Warfare." *Journal of the Royal United Service Institution,* CVI (November 1961), 585–588.

560. Barghoorn, Frederick C. *The Soviet Cultural Offensive.* Princeton, NJ: Princeton University Press, 1960. 329p.

561. _____. *Soviet Foreign Propaganda.* Princeton, NJ: Princeton University Press, 1964. 329p.

562. _____. *The Soviet Image of the United States: A Study in Distortion.* New Haven, CT: Published for the Institute of International Studies by Yale University Press, 1950. 297p.

563. Barkeley, Richard. "The Effect of Soviet Propaganda." *Contemporary Review,* CXCV (February 1959), 105–107.

564. Bassow, Whitman. "*Izvestia* Looks Inside the U.S.A." *Public Opinion Quarterly,* XII (Fall 1948), 430–439.

565. Benn, David W. "New Thinking in Soviet Propaganda." *Soviet Studies,* XXI (July 1970), 52–63.

566. Benton, William. *This Is the Challenge: The Benton Reports of 1956–1958 on the Nature of the Soviet Threat.* New York: Associated College Presses, 1958. 254p.

567. Bird, Robert S. "Russia's Hostile Voice." *Reader's Digest,* LII (May 1948), 62–66.

568. Boehm, E. H. "Free Germans in Soviet Psychological Propaganda." *Public Opinion Quarterly,* XIV (Summer 1950), 285–295.

569. Bolsover, G. H. "Soviet Ideology and Propaganda." *International Affairs* (London), XXIV (April 1948), 170–180.

570. Budeny, Louis F. "Packaged Thinking From Moscow." *American Mercury,* LXXX (March 1953), 93–100.

571.   Burdick, Eugene and William J. Lederer. "The Big Push in Soviet Propaganda." *Saturday Evening Post,* CCXXXIV (August 19, 1961), 13–15+.

572.   Bush, Keith. "Propaganda Considerations Impede Alleviation of Unemployment [in Russia]." *Bulletin of the Institute for the Study of the U.S.S.R.,* XIV (April 1967), 25–28.

573.   Cabot, John M. "Soviet Propaganda and International Tension." *Department of State Bulletin,* XXXI (November 8, 1954), 697–700.

574.   Caldwell, William S. "Soviet Speciality: Political Warfare." *Communist Affairs,* I (September 1963), 3–7.

575.   Chase, Stuart. "Moscow Talk." In: *The Power of Words.* New York: Harcourt, 1954. pp. 209–216.

576.   Churchill, Winston S. "Soviet Virulent Propaganda." *Vital Speeches,* XIV (November 1, 1947), 38–39.

577.   Clews, John C. "The Soviet Propaganda Apparatus." *Military Review,* XLV (July 1965), 84–90.

578.   Conquest, Robert, ed. *The Politics of Ideas in the U.S.S.R.* London: Bodley Head, 1967. 176p.

579.   Cowherd, Raymond G. "Waging the Cold War: An Analysis of Russia's Techniques." *Current History,* XV (December 1948), 334–347.

580.   Dallin, Alexander. "America Through Soviet Eyes: A Detailed Analysis of the Soviet Press in 1946—Especially *Pravda*—Reveals an Alarmingly High Proportion of Anti-United States Editorials and News." *Public Opinion Quarterly,* XI (Spring 1947), 26–39.

581.   Domenach, Jean-Marie. "Leninist Propaganda." *Public Opinion Quarterly,* XV (Summer 1951), 265–273.

582.   Drummond, Roscoe. "Moscow's Latest Propaganda Weapon, Forgery." *Reader's Digest,* LXXIII (November 1958), 29–32.

583.   Dulles, Allen W. "Brain Warfare: Russia's Secret Weapon." *US News and World Report,* XXXIV (May 8, 1953) 54+.

584.   Dunham Donald C. *Kremlin Target, U.S.A.: Conquest by Propaganda.* New York: Washburn, 1961. 274p.

585.   Gruliow, Leo. "The Soviet Press: Propagandist Agitator, Organizer." *Journal of International Affairs,* X (Summer 1956), 153–169.

586.   Grzybowski, Kazimiez. "Propaganda and the Soviet Concept of World Public Order." *Law and Contemporary Problems,* XXXI (Summer 1966), 479–505.

587.   Hazen, Baruch A. *Soviet Propaganda: A Case Study of the Middle East Conflict.* New Brunswick, NJ: Transaction Books, 1976. 293p.

588.   Hollander, Gayle D. "Communication and Social Modernization in Soviet Society." Unpublished PhD Dissertation, Massachusetts Institute of Technology, 1969.

589.   _____ . *Soviet Political Indoctrination: Developments in Mass Media and Propaganda Since Stalin.* New York: Praeger, 1972. 244p.

590.   Hopkins, Mark. *Mass Media in the Soviet Union.* New York: Pegasus, 1970. 384p.

591.   Howell, William S. "The North American Service of Radio Moscow." *Quarterly Journal of Speech,* XLVI (October 1960), 262–269.

592.   Inkeles, Alexander. "Domestic Broadcasting in the U.S.S.R." In: Paul F. Lazarsfeld and Frank N. Stanton, eds. *Communications Research 1948–1949.* New York: Harper, 1949. pp. 223–293.

593.   _____ . *Public Opinion in Soviet Russia: A Study in Mass Persuasion.* Cambridge, MA: Harvard University Press, 1951. 397p.

594.   _____ . "The Soviet Attack on the V.O.A.: A Case Study in Propaganda Warfare." *American-Slavic Review,* XII (October 1953), 319–342.

595.   _____ . "Soviet Reactions to the V.O.A." *Public Opinion Quarterly,* XVI (Winter 1952), 612–617.

596.   Jacobs, Wilbur R. and Edmond E. Masson. "History of Propaganda: Soviet Images of the American Past." *Mid America,* XLVI (April 1964), 130–144.

597.   Kecskemeti, Paul. "The Soviet Approach to International Political Communications." *Public Opinion Quarterly,* XX (Spring 1956), 299–308.

598.   Kruglah, Theodore E. *The Two Faces of Tass.* Minneapolis: University of Minnesota Press, 1962. 263p.

599.   Labin, Suzanne. *The Technique of Soviet Propaganda: A Study Prepared for the Subcommittee to Investigate the Administration of the Internal Security Act and Other Internal Security Laws of the Committee of the Judiciary of the United States Senate.* 86th Cong., 2nd sess. Washington, D.C.: GPO, 1960. 38p.

600.   Lasswell, Harold D. *The Strategy of Soviet Propaganda.* New York: Foreign Policy Association, 1951. 12p.

601.   _____ . _____ . *American Political Science Proceedings,* XXIV (January 1951), 214–226.

602.   Lederer William J., jt. author. *See* Burdick, Eugene (571).

603.   Lincoln, W. B. "Soviet Political Posters: Art and Ideas For the Masses." *History Today,* XXVI (May 1976), 302–309.

604.   Little, A. M. G. "The Soviet Propaganda Machine."*Department of State Bulletin,* XXV (September 3, 1951), 367–370.

605.   McConaughy, John B. "A Review of Soviet Psychological Warfare." *Military Review,* XL (December 1960), 3–13.

606.   Maiorov, V. V. *U.S. Aid: Weapon of the Monopolies.* Moscow: Novosti Press Agency Publishing House, 1970. 79p.

   An excellent example of Russian propaganda.

607.   Masson. Edmond E., jt author. *See* Jacobs, Wilbur R. (596).

608.   May, A. W. "Russia's Sham Weapon: East-West Trade." *U.N. World,* VII (September 1953), 47–50.

609.   Mickiewicz, Ellen. "The Modernization of Party Propaganda in the U.S.S.R." *Slavic Review,* XXX (June 1971), 257–276.

610.   Mond, G. H. "Mass Media: Mouthpiece of the Soviet Foreign Policy Between Peaceful Coexistence and Ideological Struggle." *South Atlantic Quarterly,* LXXII (Summer 1973), 374–385.

611.   Nagorski, Zygmunt, Jr. "Soviet International Propaganda: Its Role, Effectiveness, and Future." *Annals of the American Academy of Political and Social Science,* CCCXCVIII (November 1971), 130–140.

612.   Nir, Yeshayahu. "U.S. Involvement in the Middle East Conflict in Soviet Caricatures." *Journalism Quarterly,* LIV (Winter 1977), 697–702+.

613.   Padover, Saul K. "How Other Nations [U.S.S.R.] Tell Their Story." *Foreign Policy Bulletin,* XXXIII (September 15, 1953), 4–5.

614.   Powell, David E. *Anti-Religious Propaganda in the Soviet Union: A Study in Mass Persuasion.* Cambridge, MA: M.I.T. Press, 1975. 206p.

615.   _____ . "The Effectiveness of Soviet Anti-Religious Propaganda." *Public Opinion Quarterly,* XXXI (Fall 1967), 366–380.

616. Rastvorov, Yuri A. "Red Fraud and Intrigue in the Far East." *Life*, XXXVII (December 6, 1954), 174–176+.

617. Reiners, Wilfred O. *Soviet Indoctrination of German War Prisoners, 1941–1956*. Cambridge, MA: Center for International Studies, Massachusetts Institute of Technology, 1959. 80p.

618. Rudzinski, A. W. "Peace in Soviet Mass Propaganda." *International Conciliation*, CDXC (April 1953), 210–215.

619. Sager, Peter. *Moscow's Hand in India: An Analysis of Soviet Propaganda*. Berne, Switzerland: Swiss Eastern Institute, 1966. 224p.

620. Sites, James N. "Special Report: Some First-Hand Observations on Soviet Propaganda." *Public Relations Journal*, XIX (June 1963), 6–12.

621. Smith, Don P. "Some Effects of Radio Moscow's North American Broadcasts." *Public Opinion Quarterly*, XXXIV (Winter 1970–1971), 539–551.

622. "Soviet Radio Propaganda in the Far East." *World Today*, VI (October 1950), 434–441.

623. Speier, Hans. "Soviet Atomic Blackmail and the North Atlantic Alliance." *World Politics*, IX (April 1957), 307–328.

624. Stanford, Neal. "Anti-American Propaganda in Russia." *American Mercury*, LXIII (November 1946), 517–524.

625. Strakhovsky, Leonid I. "The Nature of Soviet Propaganda in the Near East." In: Richard N. Frye, ed. *The Near East and the Great Powers*. Cambridge, MA: Harvard University Press, 1951. pp. 65–69.

626. Strausz-Hupé, Robert. "Soviet Psychological Strategy." *US Naval Institute Proceedings*, LXXXVII (June 1961), 22–28.

627. Szalay, Lorand D. "Soviet Domestic Propaganda and Liberalization." *Orbis*, XI (Spring 1967), 210–218.

628. Taylor, Edmond. "How the Russians Wage Political Warfare." *Reporter*, XXVI (May 10, 1962), 16–20.

629. United States. Central Intelligence Agency. "Russia's Massive Campaign to Blacken the U.S. Image: A C.I.A. Report." *U.S. News and World Report*, LXXXV (August 7, 1978), 42–43.

630. _____ . _____ . "The Soviet and Communist Bloc Defamation Campaign." *Congressional Record*, CXI (September 28, 1965), 25391–25393.

631. _____ . _____ . "Soviet Use of the Media." In: U.S. Congress. House. Permanent Select Committee on Intelligence. *The C.I.A. and the Media: Hearings.* 95th Cong., 1st sess. Washington, D.C.: GPO, 1978. pp. 531–559.

632. _____ . _____ . Foreign Broadcast Information Service. *A Survey of Soviet Union Radio Broadcasts.* Washington, D.C.: 1947. 1v.

633. _____ . _____ . _____ . *A Survey of U.S.S.R. Radio Broadcasts.* 3 vols. Washington, D.C.: 1947–1950. v. 1–3.

634. _____ . _____ . _____ . *Survey of U.S.S.R. Broadcasts.* 8 vols. Washington, D.C.: 1950–1958. v. 3–11.

635. _____ . Congress. Senate. Committee on the Judiciary. Subcommittee to Investigate the Administration of the Internal Security Act and Other Internal Security Laws. *Soviet Disarmament Propaganda and the Strange Case of Marshal* [A.A.] *Grechko: A Staff Study.* 93rd Cong., 2nd sess. Washington, D.C.: GPO, 1974. 108p.

636. _____ . Department of State. Office of Intelligence Research and Analysis Division of Research for the U.S.S.R. and Eastern Europe. *Soviet Propaganda Facilities Continue Expansion.* Report 7592. Washington, D.C.: 1957. 18p.

637. _____ . Information Agency. Office of Research and Intelligence. *The Image of the V.O.A. as Drawn in Soviet Media.* New Brunswick, NJ: Department of Sociology, Rutgers University, 1954. 34p.

638. _____ . _____ . Research Service. *The External Information and Cultural Relations Programs of the U.S.S.R.* Washington, D.C.: 1973. 153p.

639. Voronitsyn, S. "The Modernization of Soviet Propaganda." *Institute for the Study of the U.S.S.R. Bulletin,* XII (October 1965), 32–39.

640. Waples, Douglas. "Publicity Versus Diplomacy: Notes on the [Soviet] Reporting of the 'Summit' Conferences." *Public Opinion Quarterly,* XX (Spring 1956), 308–314.

641. Whaley, Barton. *Soviet Clandestine Communications Nets.* Cambridge, MA: Center for International Studies, M.I.T., 1969. 199p.

Emphasis on the Far East and Southeast Asia.

642. White, J. A. "As the Russians Saw Our China Policy." *Pacific Historical Review,* XXVI (May 1957), 147–160.

643. "Who is Dean Reed?: An American Singer as a [Soviet] Propaganda Tool." *Time,* CXII (November 27, 1978), 46.

644. Willetts, H. T. "Pavlov or Khrushchev?: Soviet Methods in Political Warfare." *World Today,* XVI (October 1960), 426–435.

645.   Williams, Richard. "The Soviet Philosophy of Broadcasting." *Journal of Broadcasting,* VI (Winter 1961), 3–10.

646.   Zoul, Louis. *The Soviet Inferno: A Validation of the Soviet Manual of Materialistic Broadcasting Known in Communist Jargon as the Manual of Instructions on Psychological Warfare.* Long Island City, NY: Public Opinion Box, 1966. 144p.

21. United States

a. General Works

647.   Allen, George V. "Telling Our Side of the Story." *Department of State Bulletin,* XX (January 30, 1949), 142–143.

648.   _____ . "The U.S. Information Program." *Vital Speeches,* XIV (September 1, 1948), 702–704.

649.   Anisimov, Oleg. "A New Policy For American Psychological Warfare." *Russian Review,* XIV (July 1955), 175–183.

650.   Barnard, Thomas L. "Truth Propaganda and the U.S. Information Program." *Department of State Bulletin,* XXV (November 26, 1951), 851–854.

651.   Barrett, Edward W. *Truth is Our Weapon.* New York: Funk & Wagnalls, 1953. 355p.

652.   _____ . "U.S. Information Aims in the Cold War." *Department of State Bulletin,* XXII (June 19, 1950), 992–995.

653.   Bernays, Edward L., ed. *The Case For Reappraisal of U.S. Overseas Information Policies and Programs.* New York: Praeger, 1971. 316p.

654.   Bunge, Walter. "Johnson's Information Strategy For Vietnam: An Evaluation." *Journalism Quarterly,* XLV (Autumn 1968), 419–425.

655.   Campbell, John F. "The Intelligence and Propaganda Complexes." In: *The Foreign Affairs Fudge Factory.* New York: Basic Books, 1971. pp. 147–177.

656.   Castle, Eugene W. *Billions, Blunders, and Baloney: The Fantastic Story of How Uncle Sam is Squandering Your Money Overseas.* New York: Devin-Adair, 1955. 278p.

657.   Chittick, William O. "American Foreign Policy Elites: Attitudes Toward Secrecy and Publicity." *Journalism Quarterly,* XLVII (Winter 1970), 689–695.

658.   Clay, George. "Balloons For a Captive Audience." *Reporter,* XI (November 18, 1954), 28–31.

659.   Compton, Wilson M. "The Crusade of Ideas." *Department of State Bulletin,* XXVII (September 8, 1952), 343–348.

660.   _____ . "Information and U.S. Foreign Policy." *Department of State Bulletin,* XXVIII (February 16, 1953), 252–256.

661.   Cowles, Fleur. "Our Propaganda in Asia." *Atlantic,* CXCI (February 1953), 60–62.

662.   Crabb, Cecil V., Jr. "Psychological Warfare." In: *American Foreign Policy in the Nuclear Age.* 2nd ed. New York: Harper, 1965. pp. 338–358.

663.   Crane, Robert D. "Psychostrategy: A New Concept." In: John Erickson, ed. *The Military-Technical Revolution: Its Impact on Strategy and Foreign Policy.* New York: Published for the Institute for the Study of the U.S.S.R. by Praeger, 1966. pp. 229–238.

664.   Daugherty, William E. "The Role of Intelligence, Research, and Analysis in Psychological Warfare." In: *A Psychological Warfare Casebook.* Baltimore, MD: Johns Hopkins University Press, 1958. pp. 425–549.

665.   Davies, R. T. "The American Commitment to Public Propaganda." *Law and Contemporary Problems,* XXXI (Summer 1966), 452–457.

666.   Davison, W. Phillips. "Political Communication as an Instrument of Foreign Policy." *Public Opinion Quarterly,* XXVII (Spring 1963), 28–36.

667.   _____ . "Voices of America." In: Lester Market, *et al. Public Opinion and Foreign Policy.* New York: Published for the Council on Foreign Relations by Harper, 1949. pp. 156–179.

668.   Doob, Leonard W. "What's Wrong With U.S. Propaganda?" *U.N. World,* V (November 1951), 29–31.

669.   Dulles, Allen W. "Reds Plan to Use Freedom to Destroy the Free." *U.S. News and World Report,* XL (May 25, 1956), 132–134+.

670.   _____ . "The Weaknesses of the Communist Dictatorship: An Address." *Department of State Bulletin,* XXXV (December 3, 1956), 874–879.

671.   Dyer, Murray. *Weapon on the Wall: Rethinking Psychological Warfare.* Baltimore, MD: Johns Hopkins University Press, 1960. 269p.

672.   Falk, Irving A., jt. author. *See* Gordon, George N. (681).

673.   Farrell, J. T. "P[eople to] P[eople] P[rogram] Incorporated." *Antioch Review,* XVII (Spring 1957), 82–93.

674.   Freed, Darryl W. *Psychological Warfare: A Case of Credibility.* Maxwell AFB, AL: Air Command and Staff College, Air University, 1971. 41p.

675.   Fuller, John F. C. "Subverting the Red Threat." *Ordnance,* XLVII (January–February 1963), 414–417.

676.   Gallup, George H. "One War We are Losing." *National Municipal Review,* XL (January 1951), 12–16+.

677.   _____ . "Why We are Doing So Badly in the Ideological War." *Vital Speeches,* XVIII (June 1, 1952), 501-504.

678.   Gessner, Peter. "Films From the Vietnam Congress." *Nation,* CCII (January 24, 1966), 110–111.

679.   Glaser, William. "Semantics of the Cold War." *Public Opinion Quarterly,* XX (Winter 1957), 691–716.

680.   Gleason, Robert L. "Psychological Operations and Air Power: Its Hits and Misses." *Air University Review,* XXII (March–April 1971), 34–46.

681.   Gordon, George N. and Irving A. Falk. *The War of Ideas: America's International Identity Crisis.* New York: Hastings House, 1974. 362p.

682.   Greene, Felix. *A Curtain of Ignorance: How the American Public Has Been Misinformed About China.* Garden City, NY: Doubleday, 1964. 340p.

683.   Hall, Donald F. "Psychological Warfare Training." *Army Information Digest,* VI (January 1951), 40–46.

684.   Harris, Elliot. *The Un-American Weapon: Psychological Warfare.* New York: Lads, 1968. 211p.

685.   Hohenberg, John L. *Between Two Worlds: Policy, Press, and Public Opinion in Asian-American Relations.* New York: Praeger, 1967.

686.   Holsinger, William. "One Lawyer and Fourth Dimension Warfare: An Address." *Vital Speeches,* XXVI (September 15, 1960), 713–716.

687.   Holt, Robert T. and Robert W. Van de Velde. *Strategic Psychological Operations and American Foreign Policy.* Chicago: University of Chicago Press, 1960. 243p.

688.   Huppert, Harry. "Bullets Alone Won't Win." *Infantry,* LIV (July–August 1964), 38–42.

689.   Joyce, Walter. *The Propaganda Gap.* New York: Harper, 1963. 144p.

690.   Kehn, H. D. "The Methods and Functions of Military Psychological Warfare." *Military Review,* XXVI (January 1947), 2–15.

691. _____ . "Organization for Military Psychological Warfare." *Military Review,* XXVI (February 1947), 10–15.

692.   Kelly, George A. "Revolutionary War and Psychological Action." *Military Review,* XL (October 1960), 4–13.

693.   Linebarger, Paul M. A. *A Syllabus of Psychological Warfare.* Washington, D.C.: Propaganda Branch, Intelligence Division, U.S. War Department, 1946. 45p.

694.   McClure, Robert A. "Psychological Strategy as a Preventative of Large War: An Interview." *U.S. News and World Report,* XXXIV (January 2, 1953), 60–69.

695.   McGranahan, D. V. "U.S. Psychological Warfare Policy." *Public Opinion Quarterly,* X (Fall 1946), 446–450.

696.   Macmahon, Arthur W. *Memorandum on the Postwar International Information Program of the United States.* Publication 2438. Washington, D.C.: Department of State, 1945. 135p.

697.   Marshall, Samuel L. A. "Stress and Recovery." *Army,* VIII (September 1957), 22–23.

698.   Meyerhoff, Arthur E. *The Strategy of Persuasion: The Use of Advertising Skills in Fighting the Cold War.* New York: Coward-McCann, 1965. 191p.

699.   Moore, Preston J. "We Must Learn to Fight a New King of War." *American Legion Magazine,* LXVII (August 1959), 16–17+.

700.   Newman, W. J. "Propaganda and the American Intellectual." *20th Century,* CLIII (January 1953), 30–35.

701.   Philipps, Mrs. R. Hart. "The Future of American Propaganda in Latin America." *Public Opinion Quarterly,* IX (Fall 1945), 305–312.

702.   Pollard, J. A. "Words are Cheaper Than Blood: The Overseas O[ffice of] W[ar] I[nformation] and the Need For a Permanent Propaganda Agency." *Public Opinion Quarterly,* IX (Fall 1945), 283–304.

703.   "Propaganda: What We Say and How." *Newsweek,* LXXIX (May 15, 1972), 60+.

704.   Randel, William. "The American Search For an Image Abroad." *Mississippi Quarterly,* XVI (Winter 1963), 15–22.

705.   Rorty, James. "What are Our Propagandists Up To?" *National Review,* XIII (October 23, 1962), 309–310.

706. Rowan, Carl T. "We're Helping the Communists Win the Propaganda War." *Reader's Digest,* LXXXIX 87 (November 1966), 106–110.

707. Shakespeare, Frank. "Who's Winning the Propaganda War: An Interview." *U.S. News and World Report,* LXXII (May 1, 1972), 48–52.

708. Sharp, Erwin A. "On the Psychological Front." *All Hands,* no. 517 (February 1960), 14–17.

709. Sondern, Frederick, Jr. "Balloons Over the Iron Curtain." *Catholic World,* CLXXX (November 1954), 126–131.

710. Sorensen, Thomas C. *The World War: The Story of American Propaganda.* New York: Harper & Row, 1968. 337p.

711. Sparks, Kenneth R. "Selling Uncle Sam in the Seventies." *Annals of the American Academy of Political and Social Science,* CCCXCVIII (November 1971), 113–123.

712. Speier, Hans. "Psychological Warfare Reconsidered." In: Daniel Lerner and Harold D. Lasswell, eds. *The Policy Sciences: Recent Developments in Scope and Method.* Stanford, CA: Stanford University Press, 1951. pp. 252–270.

713. Spelman, Franz. "What the Hungarians Say About Western Propaganda." *Harper's,* CCXIV (April 1957), 70–74.

714. Spitzer, H. M. "Presenting America in American Propaganda." In: Steuart H. Britt, ed. *Selected Readings in Social Psychology.* New York: Rinehart, 1950. pp. 452–459.

715. Staton, Thomas F. "Airpower's Fourth Dimension." *Air Power Historian,* VII (January 1960), 53–58.

716. _____ . "The Psycho-Social Instrument of National Policy." *Air Power Historian,* VIII (October 1961), 207–219.

717. Straubel, James H. "The Gap in Our Strategy: How Airpower Can Fight the Psychological War." *Air Force,* XXXV (February 1952), 22–25+.

718. Summers, Robert E., ed. *America's Weapons of Psychological Warfare.* Reference Shelf, v. 23, no. 4. New York: H. W. Wilson, 1951. 206p.

719. Thompson, Lewis S. "The Psychological Impact of Airpower." *Annals of the American Academy of Political and Social Science,* CCXCIX (May 1955), 58–66.

720. Thomson, Charles A. *The Overseas Information Service of the United States Government.* Washington, D.C.: Brookings Institution, 1948. 397p.

721.   United States. Army. *Psychological Operations: Techniques and Procedures.* FM 33-5. Ft. Bragg, NC: 1974.

722. _____ . _____ . *Psychological Operations: U.S. Army Doctrine.* FM 33-1. Ft. Bragg, NC: 1971.

723. _____ . _____ . Special Forces. *Special Forces Psychological Operations.* Army Subject Schedule 31-42. Ft. Bragg, NC: 1966.

724. _____ . Congress. House. Committee on Foreign Affairs, Subcommittee on International Organizations and Movements. *Winning the Cold War, the U.S. Ideological Offensive: Hearings.* 9 pts. 88th Cong., 1st sess.–89th Cong., 1st sess. Washington, D.C.: GPO, 1963–1965.

725.   Urban, George R., ed. *Scaling the Wall: Talking to Eastern Europe.* Detroit, MI: Wayne State University Press, 1964. 303p.

726.   Van de Velde, Robert W., jt. author. *See* Holt, Robert T. (687).

727.   Veandry, Wallace F. "A New Look at Psychological Warfare." *Army,* XV (August 1964), 57–61.

728.   "The Voices of America." *Newsweek,* LXXXIX (April 11, 1977), 30.

729.   "The Voices of Freedom." *U.S. Army Talks,* IV (September 16, 1945), 1–31.

730.   Walker, Fred W. "Psyop is a Nasty Term—Too Bad!" *Air University Review,* XXVIII (September–October 1977), 71–76.

731.   "The War We're Losing." *Printer's Ink,* CCLXXX (September 14, 1962), 27–72.

732.   Wechsler, James A. "A Study of Suppression: Propaganda in the Press." *Progressive,* XXVII (August 1963), 10–14.

733.   Williams, Frederick W. "Psychological Warfare and Strategic Intelligence Research: Policy and Planning Considerations." In: John C. Flanagan, *et al. Current Trends: Psychology in the World Emergency.* Pittsburgh, PA: University of Pittsburgh Press, 1952. pp. 137–159.

734.   Wychoff, Don P. "Bloodless Weapon." *U.S. Naval Institute Proceedings,* XCV (September 1969), 64–69.

735.   Zacharias, Ellis M. "What Should the New Administration Do About Psychological Warfare?" *Foreign Policy Bulletin,* XXXII (March 15, 1953), 4–6.

b. International Communications Agency

736. Carter, Jimmy. "New Communications Agency Proposed: Message to Congress, October 11, 1977." *Department of State Bulletin,* LXXCII (November 14, 1977), 683–685.

737. "International Communications Agency." In: U.S. Office of the Federal Register, National Archives and Record Service, General Services Administration. *U.S. Government Manual, 1978–1979.* Washington, D.C.: GPO, 1978. pp. 573–578.

The U.S.I.A. was merged into this organization in 1978.

c. Foreign Broadcast Information Service (CIA)

738. United States. Central Intelligence Agency. Foreign Broadcast Information Service. *Broadcasting Stations of the World.* Washington, D.C.: 1948–. v. 1–.

739. _____ . _____ . _____ . *Daily Report: Foreign Radio Broadcasts.* Washington, D.C.: 1948–. v. 1–.

740. _____ . _____ . _____ . *F.B.I.S. in Retrospect: 30 Years of the Foreign Broadcast Information Service, 1941–1971.* Washington, D.C.: 1971. 56p.

741. _____ . _____ . _____ . *Long, Medium, and Short Wave Broadcasting Stations of the World According to Country and City.* Washington, D.C.: 1949. 209p.

742. _____ . _____ . _____ . *Long and Medium Wave Broadcasting Stations of the World According to Frequency.* Washington, D.C.: 1948–. v. 1–.

743. _____ . Central Intelligence Group. Foreign Broadcast Intelligence Group, Far Eastern Section. *Daily Report: Foreign Radio Broadcasts.* 44 vols. Washington, D.C.: 1946–1947. nos. 1–296.

Similar reports were also prepared by the European and Latin American Sections.

744. Weinstein, Walter W., comp. *Preliminary Inventory of the Records of the Foreign Broadcast Intelligence Service (Record Group 262).* Preliminary Inventories, no. 115. Washington, D.C.: National Archives and Records Service, General Services Administration, 1959. 53p.

d. Radio Free Europe/Radio Liberty (CIA)

745. Bezymensky, Lev. "The Radio Subversion Continues." *New Times* (Moscow), no. 7 (February 1976), 10–11.

746.   Brown, Thomas H. "Radio Free Europe: Its Audience and Its Policies." *N.A.E.B. Journal*, XIX (July–August 1960), 82–88.

747.   Buckley, James L. "Disinformation—Will It Destroy Radio Free Europe and Radio Liberty?" *Congressional Record*, CXXI (May 19, 1975). 14939–14945.

748.   *CIA Radio Saboteurs.* Moscow: Publishing House of the Soviet Committee for the Maintenance of Cultural Ties With Fellow Countrymen Abroad, 1972. 112p.

749.   Copp, Deweitt S. "The Radio Free Europe Story." *Human Events*, XXXIII (May 5, 1973), 16+.

750.   Dewhirst, Martin and Robert Ferrell. *The Soviet Censorship.* Metuchen, NJ: Published in Co-operation with the Radio Liberty Committee, New York, by the Scarecrow Press, 1973. 177p.

751.   Ferrell, Robert, jt. author. *See* Dewhirst, Martin (750).

752.   Handlery, George. "Propaganda and Information: The Case of U.S. Broadcasts to Eastern Europe." *Eastern European Quarterly*, VIII (January 1975), 391–412.

753.   Heffner, Linda J. "Radio Free Europe Gets Secret Aid From the CIA, [Senator Clifford] Case Says—Asks Control: Reprinted from the *Philadelphia Bulletin*, January 24, 1971." *Congressional Record*, CXVII (February 25, 1971), 3994–3995.

754.   "Hidden CIA Financing: Reprinted from the Des Moines *Register*, February 3, 1971." *Congressional Record*, CXVII (February 24, 1971), 3718–3719.

755.   Holt, Robert. *Radio Free Europe.* Minneapolis: University of Minnesota Press, 1958. 249p.

756.   Kneitel, Tom. " 'Radio Swan,' the Thorn in Castro's Side." *Popular Electronics*, XIV (March 1961), 52–53+.

757.   Kurchatov, A. "U.S. Radio: Propaganda and Espionage." *International Affairs* (Moscow), no. 10 (October 1971), 73–78.

758.   Michie, Allan A. *Voices Through the Iron Curtain: The Radio Free Europe Story.* New York: Dodd, Mead, 1963. 304p.

759.   Price, James R. *Radio Free Europe: A Survey and Analysis.* Washington, D.C.: Congressional Research Service, Library of Congress, 1972.

760.   Radio Free Europe. *America or Russia?: 3,200 East European Respondents Select the "Most Influential Country in the World."* Munich, West Germany: Audience Research Department, Radio Free Europe, 1965. 7p.

761.   _____ . Audience and Public Opinion Research Department. *Central Europeans and Communications Appeal: An Experiment in Communications Research With Poles, Hungarians, and Czechs/Slovaks.* New York, 1969. 52p.

762.   _____ . _____ . *East European Attitudes to the Vietnam Conflict: A Study in Radio Effectiveness.* Munich, West Germany, 1967. 9p.

763.   _____ . _____ . *The Effectiveness of Radio Free Europe.* Munich, West Germany, [1965?] 37p.

764.   _____ . _____ . *Flight Motivations of Refugees From Four Soviet Bloc Countries.* Munich, West Germany, 1963. 47p.

765.   _____ . _____ . *Radio Free Europe's Coverage on the Death of a President.* New York, 1963. 8p.

766.   _____ . _____ . *The Sino-Soviet Conflict (As Seen by 4,093 Respondents From Czechoslovakia, Hungary, Poland, and Rumania).* Munich, West Germany, 1964. 47p.

767.   _____ . Free Europe Committee. *Mao Tse-Tung: His Rise and His Role.* Special Report, no. 68. New York, 1953. 21p.

768.   _____ . _____ . *Party and Police Control of the Soviet Army.* Special Report, no. 84. New York, 1954. 22p.

769.   _____ . _____ . *Uprisings Against Communist Rule.* New York, 1957. 6p.

769a.   "Radio Free Europe 'Financed by the CIA': Reprinted from the San Francisco *Examiner,* January 24, 1971." *Congressional Record,* CXVII (February 25, 1971), 3996.

770.   [Radio Liberty Committee]. *The Beleagured Fortress: A Survey of the Present Status of Religion in the U.S.S.R.* New York: American Committee for Liberation, 1963. 40p.

771.   _____ . *Electoral and Parliamentary Practices in the U.S.S.R. and Poland.* New York: American Committee for Liberation, 1957. 44p.

772.   _____ . *Pravda as a Mirror of Recent Soviet Policy: The United States and China.* New York, 1967. 9p.

773. _____ . *Red Star Over Islam.* New York: American Committee for Liberation, 1961. 24p.

774. _____ . *Sparks Into the Soviet Union: The Story of Radio Liberation.* New York: American Committee for Liberation, 1957. 47p.

775. _____ . Audience and Program Evaluation Division. *Radio Liberty's Audience in the U.S.S.R.* Washington, D.C., 1973. 15p.

776. *Radio Stations of the Cold War.* Moscow: Novosti Press Agency Publishing House, 1973. 55p.

777. Rusk, Kenneth. "[State] Department Urges Continued Government Support of Radio Free Europe and Radio Liberty." *Department of State Bulletin,* LXIX (July 9, 1973), 72–77.

778. "South Vietnam Capitulation: A Comparison of Radio Free Europe and Radio Liberty Coverage With Soviet and East European Media Coverage." In: U.S. Congress. Senate. Committee on Foreign Relations. *Foreign Relations Authorization, FY 1976 and FY 1977: Hearings.* 94th Cong., 1st sess. Washington, D.C.: GPO, 1975. pp. 128–132.

779. Ulsamer, Edgar. "Moscow's Misinformation Pays Off." *Air Force Magazine,* LXI (November 1978), 88–90.

780. United States. Congress. House. Committee on Foreign Affairs. *Radio Free Europe and Radio Liberty: Hearings.* 92nd Cong., 1st sess. Washington, D.C.: GPO, 1971. 131p.

781. _____ . _____ . Senate. Committee on Foreign Relations. *Funding of Radio Free Europe and Radio Liberty: Hearings.* 92nd Cong., 2nd sess. Washington, D.C.: GPO, 1972. 83p.

782. _____ . _____ . _____ . _____ . *Financing of Radio Free Europe and Radio Liberty: Hearings.* 92nd Cong., 1st sess. Washington, D.C.: GPO, 1971. 175p.

783. Wallach, John P. "Senator Case Asks Overseas Radio CIA Funding Cut-off: Reprinted from the Baltimore *News-American,* January 24, 1971." *Congressional Record,* CXVII (February 25, 1971), 3995–3996.

784. "War of Words." *Newsweek,* LVIII (July 24, 1961), 47.

785. Whelan, Joseph C. *Radio Liberty: A Study of Its Origins, Structure, Policy, Programming, and Effectiveness.* Washington, D.C.: Congressional Research Service, Library of Congress, 1972.

e. U.S. Information Agency/Voice of America (Department of State)

786. "Ads That Pierce the Iron Curtain: The USIA Magazine [*America Illustrated*]." *Business Week,* (July 18, 1970), 30+.

787.   Akers, Robert W. "An Indispensable Diplomacy." In: John Lee, ed. *Diplomatic Persuaders: The New Role of the Mass Media in International Relations.* New York: Wiley, 1969. pp. 1–13.

788.   Barghoorn, Frederick C. "To Meet the Propaganda Challenge." *New York Times Magazine,* (January 19, 1964), 13+.

789.   Begg, J. M. "An American Idea: Package It For Export." *Department of State Bulletin,* XXIV (March 12, 1951), 409–412.

790.   Bellquist, Eric C. "The Overseas Information and Cultural Relations of the Department of State." *Institute of World Affairs Proceedings,* XXIII (1946), 100–109.

791.   Bermel, Albert. "The Split Personality of the USIA." *Harper's,* CCXXXI (November 1965), 116–124.

792.   Black, Robert B., Jr., jt. author. *See* Esterline, John (804).

793.   Bogart, Leo. *Premises For Propaganda: The United States Information Agency's Operating Assumptions in the Cold War.* Riverside, NJ: Free Press, 1976. 250p.

794.   _____ . "Measuring the Effectiveness of an Overseas Information Campaign: A Case Study." *Public Opinion Quarterly,* XXI (Winter 1958), 475–498.

795.   _____ . "Projecting America." *Society,* XII (September 1975), 57–61.

796.   _____ . "A Study of the Operating Assumptions of the U.S. Information Agency." *Public Opinion Quarterly,* XIX (Winter 1956), 369–379.

797.   Chancellor, John W. "How the U.S. Tells Its Story to the World: An Interview." *U.S. News and World Report,* LXII (February 20, 1967), 76–79.

798.   _____ . "International Broadcasting and the Changing World Audience." *Annals of the American Academy of Political and Social Science,* CCCLXXII (July 1967), 72–79.

799.   Coleman, W. A. "TV, Radio: The VOA in Ceylon." *America,* LXXXIX (April 18, 1953), 89–91.

800.   Compton, Wilson M. "VOA at the Water's Edge." *Department of State Bulletin,* XXVI (June 2, 1952), 864–867.

801.   Deakin, David. "And Now A Few Words From Comrade Ivan Serov." *New York Times Magazine,* (January 21, 1962), 59–60.

802.   Dizard, Wilson P. *The Strategy of Truth: The Story of the USIA.* Washington, D.C.: Public Affairs Press, 1961. 213p.

803.   Elder, Robert E. *The Information Machine.* Syracuse, NY: Syracuse University Press, 1968.

804.   Esterline, John and Robert B. Black. "USIA." In: *Inside Foreign Policy: The Department of State Political System and Its Subsystems.* Palo Alto, CA: Mayfield Publishing Co., 1975. pp. 106–169.

805.   Goodfield, Arthur. *The Twisted Image.* New York: St. Martin's Press, 1963. 264p.

806.   Griswold, Wesley S. "How We Fight With Words." *Popular Science,* CLX (May 1952), 148–152+.

807.   Henderson, John W. *The United States Information Agency.* New York: Praeger, 1969. 324p.

808.   Hessman, James D. "The Voice of America: Small Voice." *Sea Power,* XX (February 1977), 11–16.

809.   "His Master's Voice: White House Censorship of [VOA] News Broadcasts." *Newsweek,* LXV (June 7, 1965), 16–17.

810.   Keogh, James. "How a Troubled America Puts Its Best Foot Forward Abroad: An Interview." *U.S. News and World Report,* LXXVII (September 30, 1974), 37–40.

811.   Kohler, Floyd D. "The VOA: Spokesman of the Free World." *American Political Science Proceedings,* XXIV (January 1951), 240–247.

812.   Kretzmann, E. M. J. "VOA's Counterattack on the Siren Voice of Moscow." *Department of State Bulletin,* XXVI (February 18, 1952), 249–251.

813.   Lawson, Murray G., *et al. The United States Information Agency During the Johnson Administration, 1963–1968.* Washington, D.C.: USIA, 1968.

814.   Lippmann, Walter. "Why the VOA Should Be Abolished." *Reader's Digest,* LXIII (August 1953), 41–43.

815.   "Lowering the Voice [of America]: Handling the Watergate Story." *Newsweek,* LXXXII (July 9, 1973), 60–61.

816.   Lyons, Eugene. "How Good is the VOA?" *Reader's Digest,* LXIV (June 1954), 87–92.

817.   McCormick, John M. "The United States Information Service." *Kenyon Review,* XXIV (Spring 1962), 330–350.

818. Murrow, Edward R. "An Address." *National Education Association Proceedings,* CI (1963), 34–40.

819. _____. "Our Educational Image Abroad." *NEA Journal,* LI (March 1962), 8–11.

820. _____. "The USIA." *Reporter,* XXVIII (May 9, 1963), 6+.

821. "The Muted VOA." *Time,* CIV (December 16, 1974), 80+.

822. Nash, Henry T. "The United States Information Agency." In: *American Foreign Policy: Response to a Sense of Threat.* Homewood, IL: Dorsey Press, 1973. pp. 79–82.

823. Percy, Charles H. and John M. Slack, Jr. "Should the VOA Be Made an Independent Agency?" *American Legion Magazine,* CII (April 1977), 32–33.

824. Pirsein, Robert W. "The VOA: A History of the International Broadcasting Activities of the United States Government, 1940–1962." Unpublished PhD Dissertation, Northwestern University, 1970.

825. Poli, Kenneth. "Photography U.S.A.: A USIA Show." *Popular Photography,* LXXVI (March 1975), 82–91.+.

826. Raffaele, John A. "United States Propaganda Abroad: Notes on the U.S. Information Service in Italy." *Social Research,* XXVII (Fall 1960), 277–294.

827. Ronalds, Francis S., Jr. "Latin America and VOA." In: *International Broadcasting.* Washington, D.C.: Association For Professional Broadcasting Education, 1971. pp. 69–79.

828. Rowan, Carl T. "USIA: Building Bridges For Peace in a Changing World." *Department of State Bulletin,* LI (February 28, 1964), 906–912.

829. Rubin, Ronald I. *The Objectives of the U.S. Information Agency.* New York: Praeger, 1966. 251p.

830. "The Shakespeare Era." *Newsweek,* LXXV (January 12, 1970), 20+.

831. Slack, John M., Jr., jt. author. *See* Percy, Charles H. (823).

832. Squires, Leslie A. "USIA: Mechanism vs. Function." *Foreign Service Journal,* LI (May 1974), 17–29.

833. Stephens, Oren. *Facts to a Candid World: America's Overseas Information Program.* Stanford, CA: Stanford University Press, 1955. 164p.

834. Sundstrom, Harold W. "The United States Information Agency." *Vital Speeches,* XXIX (December 1, 1962), 120–123.

835. United States. Congress. House. Committee on Foreign Affairs. Subcommittee on State Department Organization and Foreign Operations. *U.S. Information Agency Operations: Hearings.* 2 pts. 91st Cong., 1st and 2nd sess. Washington, D.C.: GPO, 1972–1973.

836. _____ . _____ . _____ . Committee on Government Operations. Subcommittee on Government Information and Individual Rights. *Oversight of the U.S. Information Agency: Hearings.* 94th Cong., 1st sess. Washington, D.C.: GPO, 1975. 90p.

837. _____ . Information Agency. *The Agency in Brief, 1971.* Washington, D.C.: 1971. 49p.

838. _____ . _____ . Books, Exhibits, and Cultural Activities in the *Overseas Information Program.* Washington, D.C.: GPO, 1956. 13p.

839. _____ . _____ . *Facts About USIA.* Washington, D.C.: 1974.

840. _____ . _____ . *The Film Program of the USIA: Motion Pictures in the Overseas Information Program.* Washington, D.C.: 1956. 15p.

　　　　Until very late in its operations, USIA films could not be viewed by American audiences in the United States.

841. _____ . _____ . *The Overseas Information Program.* Washington, D.C.: 1960. 13p.

842. _____ . _____ . *Report to Congress.* Washington, D.C.: 1953–1977. v. 1–24.

843. _____ . _____ . *Review of Operations.* Washington, D.C.: 1953–1977. v. 1–24.

844. _____ . _____ . *The Voice of America Broadcasts: In 41 Languages, Over a Network of 78 Transmitters, Around the Clock, Around the Globe.* Washington, D.C.: 1956. 12p.

845. _____ . _____ . Broadcasting Service. *Catalog of Selected VOA Programs.* Washington, D.C.: 1963. 187p.

846. _____ . _____ . International Press Service. *So the World May Understand: The Story of the International Press Activities of the U.S. Information Agency.* Washington, D.C.: GPO, 1956. 9p.

847. _____ . _____ . Office of Public Information. *The Radio Broadcasting System of the United States Information Agency.* Washington, D.C.: 1974.

848. _____ . _____ . Office of Research. *External Cultural and Information Programs of Selected Non-Communist Countries in 1976*. Washington, D.C.: 1977. 37p.

849. _____ . _____ . *VOA and Radio Havana Audiences in Central America*. Washington, D.C.: 1973. 40p.

850. "USIA: Beginning of the End?" *Time*, CV (March 24, 1975), 74.

851. Vetter, Charles T., Jr. "United States Information Service." *Vital Speeches*, XXVIII (February 1, 1962), 250–256.

852. Walton, Richard J. "Voice of America." *Nation*, CCV (August 28, September 25, 1967), 135–138, 258+.

853. Wilhoit, Grover C. "USIA's Television Service." *NAEB Journal*, XXI (September–October 1962), 62–72.

22. Vietnam

854. Bain, Chester A. "Charlie's Line." *Army*, XVIII (October 1968), 18–25.

855. _____ . "Viet Cong Propaganda Abroad." *Foreign Service Journal*, XLV (October 1968), 18–21.

856. Bjelajac, Stavko N. "A Design for Psychological Operations in Vietnam." *Orbis*, X (Spring 1966), 126–137.

857. Herz, M. F. "VC/NVA Propaganda Leaflets Addressed to U.S. Troops: Some Reflections." *Orbis*, XXI (Winter 1978), 913–926.

858. Johnson, Keith B. *Psychological Warfare* [in Vietnam]: *A Neglected Weapon*. Professional Study. Maxwell AFB, AL: Air War College, Air University, 1971. 15p.

859. Labin, Suzanne. "Killing Our Ally: A Disclosure of Communist Methods Used to Discredit and Undermine the Government of South Vietnam." *Military Review*, XLII (May 1962), 28–38.

860. Mahoney, Tom. "The War of the Leaflets." *American Legion Magazine*, LXXX (May 1966), 18–21+.

861. Nathan, Reuben S. "Psychological Warfare: Key to Success in Vietnam." *Orbis*, XI (Spring 1967), 182–193.

862. Nguyen, To-thi. "A Content Analysis of VOA News Broadcasts to Vietnam." Unpublished PhD Dissertation, Ohio State University, 1977.

863. Nighswonger, William A. "Propaganda and Information Media and Programs." In: *Rural Pacification in Vietnam*. New York: Praeger, 1966. pp. 154–159.

864. Offer, Thomas W. "Nguyen Van Be as Propaganda Hero of the North and South Vietnamese Governments: A Case Study of Mass Media Conflict." *Southern Speech-Communication Journal*, XL (Fall 1974), 63–80.

865. Rolph, Hammond, jt author. *See* Swearington, Roger (869).

866. "Saigon Follies?: Newsmen Accuse USIS of Withholding News." *Newsweek*, LXVIII (August 15, 1966), 54+.

867. "Sticks and Stones: Saigon, USIA." *Newsweek*, LIX (June 18, 1962), 44.

868. Swanson, John. "New Psychological Approach: Vietnam." *National Review*, XXVII (February 14, 1975), 161–162.

869. Swearington, Roger and Hammond Rolph. *Communism in Vietnam: A Documentary Study of Theory, Strategy, and Operational Practices*. New York: American Bar Association, 1967. 195p.

870. United States. Information Agency. *At Stake—The Cause of Freedom: The Eleven Years Since the Geneva Accords on Vietnam*. Washington, D.C., 1965. 25p.

871. _____ . Information Service, Saigon. *An Analysis: National Liberation Front Propaganda*. Maxwell AFB, AL: Warfare Systems School, Air University, 1962. 13p.

872. White, Ralph K. "The [Vietnam] Conflict as Seen by the Communists." *Journal of Social Issues*, XXII (July 1966), 44–64.

III/Intelligence, Espionage, and Covert Operations

Introduction

Intelligence, for our purposes, means "a body of evidence and the conclusions drawn therefrom which is acquired and furnished in response to the known or perceived requirements of customers."[1] This information, drawn from a variety of sources, is sifted and evaluated in a cyclical process known as the Intelligence Cycle[2] and offered to policymakers for consideration in the planning and implementation of state objectives.

Since World War II, intelligence has generally come to be classified into three categories: 1) national-strategic; 2) combat-tactical; and 3) counterintelligence. With the advent of sophisticated collection and decision-making arrangements, the first two have tended to merge.

National-strategic intelligence seeks to give insight into the intentions and capabilities of another state. Combat-tactical intelligence provides data on opposing military forces valuable in planning or mounting campaigns, battles, or interventions. Counterintelligence, largely a police function, revolves around an "activity, with its resultant product, intended to detect, counteract, and/or prevent espionage and other clandestine intelligence activities, sabotage, international terrorist activities, or assassinations conducted for or on behalf of foreign powers, organizations, or persons."[3] Occasionally, counterintelligence can be a positive factor in revealing intelligence about a foe or potential foe.

The materials covered in this section treat intelligence generally, with emphasis on works describing the national-strategic concept. Many of these titles are classics of serious analysis, such as those by Sherman Kent and Harold Wilensky. There is a fall-out and the other forms of intelligence mentioned receive varying degrees of attention.

Notes

1. U.S. Central Intelligence Agency. "Glossary of Intelligence Terms and Definitions." In: U.S. Congress. House. Permanent Select Committee on Intelligence, *Annual Report* (95th Cong., 2nd sess. Washington, D.C.: GPO, 1978), p. 40.
2. See Chart I.
3. U.S. Central Intelligence Agency, *op cit.*, pp. 37–38.

A. Intelligence—General Works

873. Amnesty International. *Report on Torture.* New York: Farrar, Straus, and Giroux, 1975. 285p.

With comments on various government secret services.

874. Ayer, Frederick, Jr. "Intelligence Services." *Vital Speeches,* XXIV (February 1, 1958), 247–251.

875. Blackstock, Paul W. *Agents of Deceit: Frauds, Forgeries, and Political Intrigue Among Nations.* New York and Chicago: Quadrangle, 1966. 315p.

876. _____ . *The Strategy of Subversion: Manipulating the Politics of Other Nations.* New York and Chicago: Quadrangle Books, 1964. 351p.

877. Bose, Nikhilesh. "Strategic Intelligence and National Security." *United Service Institution of India Journal,* XCVI (January–March 1966), 1–14+.

878. Burns, Arthur L. "The International Consequences of Expecting Surprise [Attack]." *World Politics,* X (July 1958), 512–536.

879. Colby, William E. "Modern Intelligence, Myth and Reality: Reprinted from the *New York Times,* September, 1975." *Congressional Record,* CXXI (September 25, 1975), 30369–30370.

880. Copeland, Miles. "The Functioning of Strategic Intelligence." *Defense and Foreign Affairs Digest,* nos. 2–4 (1977), 29–32, 36–38+, 32–35+.

881. Couloumbis, Theodore A. and James H. Wolfe. "Political Warfare and Intelligence." In: *Introduction to International Relations: Power and Justice.* Englewood Cliffs, NJ: Prentice-Hall, 1978. pp. 136–152.

882. Dulles, Allen W. *The Craft of Intelligence.* New York: Harper, 1963. 277p.

883. _____ . _____ . *Harper's,* CCXXVI (April 1963), 128–174.

884. _____ . "Free World Defense Against Communist Subversion: An Address, October 3, 1955." *Department of State Bulletin,* XXXIII (October 17, 1955), 600–604.

885. _____ . "The Role of Intelligence in the Cold War." In: Frank R. Barnett, ed. *Peace and War in the Modern Age: Premises, Myths, and Realities.* New York: Anchor Books, 1965. pp. 205–221.

886. Dyer, George B. "An Introduction to Strategic Intelligence, With A Classification System for Strategic Intelligence Source Materials." Unpublished PhD Dissertation, University of Pennsylvania, 1950.

887. Gwynne-Jones, Alan. "The World Nation-State Structure Makes Intelligence Essential: Reprinted from the *New York Times*, February 15, 1976." In: George Wittman, ed. *The Role of the American Intelligence Organizations.* Reference Shelf, v. 48, no. 5. New York: H. W. Wilson, 1976. pp. 91–95.

888. Hartmann, Frederick H. "Espionage and Intelligence." In: *The Relations of Nations.* 4th ed. New York: Macmillan, 1973. pp. 171–173.

889. Ingersoll, Ralph. *Top Secret.* New York: Harcourt, 1946. 373p.

890. Jervis, Robert. "Hypotheses on Misperception." *World Politics,* XX (April 1968), 454–479.

891. Kendall, Willmoore. "The Function of Intelligence." *World Politics,* I (July 1949), 542–552.

892. Kent, Sherman. "Intelligence Is Knowledge." In: George Wittman, ed. *The Role of American Intelligence Organizations.* Reference Shelf, v. 48, no. 5. New York: H. W. Wilson, 1976. pp. 12–20.

893. McDouglas, Myres. "The Intelligence Function and World Public Order." *Temple Law Quarterly,* XLVI (Spring 1973), 365+.

894. McGovern, William M. *Strategic Intelligence and the Shape of Tomorrow.* Chicago: Published in Cooperation with the Foundation for Foreign Affairs by Regnery, 1961. 191p.

895. Platt, Washington. *Strategic Intelligence Production: Basic Principles.* New York: Praeger, 1957. 302p.

896. Ransom, Harry H. *Strategic Intelligence* [A Learning Module]. Morristown, NJ: General Learning Press, 1973. 20p.

897. Roberts, John W., Jr. "Toward a Theory of Intelligence: Testing For Correlates of Forecasting." Unpublished M.A. Thesis, University of Georgia, 1973.

898. Schaf, Frank L. *The Evolution of Modern Strategic Intelligence.* Research Study. Carlisle Barracks, PA: U.S. Army War College, 1965. 698p.

899. Scott, John. "Intelligence." In: his *Political Warfare: A Guide to Competitive Co-existence.* New York: John Day, 1955. pp. 139–157.

900. Walter, Georg. "Secret Intelligence Services." *Military Review,* XLIV (August 1964), 91–98.

901. Wilensky, Harold L. *Organizational Intelligence: Knowledge and Policy in Government and Industry.* New York: Basic Books, 1967. 226p.

902. Wolfe, James H., jt. author. *See* Couloumbis, Theodore A. (881).

B. Communications-Electronic Intelligence—General Works

Introduction

The American intelligence community has labelled communications intelligence as "Comint" and electronic intelligence as "Elint." Together they form signals intelligence or "Sigint." These methods of gathering data became very important during the Second World War ("Magic" and "Ultra") and have grown steadily more important ever since.

Communications intelligence is defined as "technical and intelligence information derived from intercept of foreign communications by other than the intended recipients."[1] Electronic intelligence is defined as "technical and intelligence information derived from foreign noncommunications electromagnetic radiations emanating from other than atomic detonation or radioactive sources."[2] Signals intelligence is defined as "intelligence information comprising either individually or in combination all communications intelligence, electronics intelligence, and foreign instrumentation signals intelligence, however transmitted."[3] All of this means simply an ability to gather data by "listening" to various emissions with a variety of sophisticated instruments.

One of the oldest elements of communications intelligence is cryptology, the "science of producing signals intelligence and maintaining signals security."[4] This phase concerns codes and their application and analysis. It is often difficult, even with the use of computers, to crack certain codes as a reading of the following sources will demonstrate.

Electronic intelligence is important. By using radar, radio intercept, direction finding, voiceprinting, and analyzing signal traffic and communications networks valuable data is often obtained.

Complex security systems can usually be found in use by most advanced and a few less-advanced nations to safeguard "Sigint" operations. Signals security ("Sigsec") is defined as "communications security and electronics security . . . which encompasses measures intended to deny or counter hostile exploitation of electronic emissions."[5] This security is systematically examined to ascertain its adequacy, provide information, and improve its operation.

The citations in this section provide information on a rather secretive part of the intelligence collection process. The material is weighted in favor of cryptology, although the other forms defined above are discussed. These sources should be employed in conjunction with certain titles in the next subsection as well as in the subsection dealing with the National Security Agency.

Notes

1. U.S. Central Intelligence Agency. "Glossary of Intelligence Terms and Definitions." In: U.S. Congress. House. Permanent Select Committee on Intelligence, *Annual Report* (95th Cong., 2nd sess. Washington, D.C.: GPO, 1978), p. 31.
2. *Ibid.,* p. 36.
3. *Ibid.,* p. 50.
4. *Ibid.,* p. 33.
5. *Ibid.,* p. 50.

903.   Ablett, Charles B. "Electronic Warfare: A Modern Weapons System." *Military Review,* XLVI (November 1966), 3–11.

904.   American Cryptogram Association. *Practical Cryptanalysis.* 5 vols. New York, 1960–1967.

Vol. I: *Digraphic Substitutes,* by William H. Bowers (1960);

Vol. II: *The Bifid Cipher,* by William M. Bowers (1960);

Vol. III: *The Trifid Cipher,* by William M. Bowers (1960);

Vol. IV–Vol. V: *Cryptographic ABC's,* by W. G. Bryan (1967).

905.   *Aviation Week and Space Technology,* Editors of. "Electronic Countermeasures Symposium: A Special Report." *Aviation Week and Space Technology,* XCVI (February 21, 1972), 33–40+.

906.   _____ . "Special Report on Electronic Warfare." *Aviation Week and Space Technology,* XCIX (January 27, 1975), 41–144.

907.   Bond, Raymond T., ed. *Famous Stories of Code and Cipher.* New York: Collier Books, 1965. 383p.

908.   Campbell, Duncan. "Facts and Figures on Phone Tapping [in Britain]." *New Statesman and Nation,* XCVII (February 9, 1979), 183.

909.   _____ . "Global Boom in Eavesdropping: Signals Intelligence." *Atlas,* XXVI (May 1979), 26–28.

910.   _____ . "Secret Security Computers [in Britain]." *New Statesman and Nation,* XCVI (December 1, 1978), 732.

911.   _____ . "The Threat of the Electronic Spies." *New Statesman and Nation,* XCVII (February 2, 1979), 142–145.

912.   Carroll, John M. *Secrets of Electronic Espionage.* New York: E. P. Dutton, 1966. 224p.

913.   "Computers Aid Intelligence Data Retrieval." *Aviation Week and Space Technology,* CI (July 15, 1974), 189+.

914. Dickerson, Paul and John Rothchild. "The Electronic Battlefield: Wiring Down the [Vietnam] War." *Washington Monthly,* (May 1971), 6–14.

915. Friedman, William F. *Advanced Military Cryptography.* Rev. ed. Laguna Hills, CA: Aegean Park Press, 1976.

916. _____ . *Elementary Military Cryptography.* Rev. ed. Laguna Hills, CA: Aegean Park Press, 1976.

917. _____ . *Elements of Cryptanalysis.* Laguna Hills, CA: Aegean Park Press, 1976.

918. Goulden, Joseph C. *Truth is the First Casualty.* Chicago: Rand McNally, 1969. 285p.

See Part II for electronic espionage.

919. Gwynne, Peter. "The Heat-Wave Spies." *Newsweek,* XC (February 23, 1976), 57.

920. Haldane, Robert L. *The Hidden World.* New York: St. Martin's Press, 1976. 207p.

921. Hendrickson, James L. *Joint Army-Air Force Planning and Employment of Electronic-Countermeasures.* Ft. Leavenworth, KA: U.S. Army Command and Staff College, 1978. 168p.

922. Hezlet, Arthur. *Electronics and Sea Power.* New York: Stein and Day, 1976. 319p.

923. Inman, Bobby R. "The NSA Perspective on Telecommunications Protection in the Nongovernmental Sector." *Signal,* XXXIII (March 1979), 6–9+.

924. Kahn, David. "The Code Battle." *Playboy,* XXII (December 1975), 132+.

925. _____ . *The Codebreakers: The Story of Secret Writing.* New York: Macmillan, 1967. 1,164p.

926. _____ . "Modern Cryptology." *Scientific American,* CCXV (July 1966), 38–46.

927. Keegan, Kenneth. "Bugs in the System: Soviet Interception of U.S. Phone Calls." *New Republic,* CLXXVII (August 6, 1977), 14–16.

928. Kempster, Norman. "Spying Has Come a Long Way Since the Microphone in the Eagle: Reprinted from the *Washington Star,* July 16, 1975." In: U.S. Congress. Senate. Committee on the Judiciary. Subcommittee on Constitutional Rights. *Surveillance Technology, 1976.* 94th Cong., 2nd sess. Washington, D.C.: GPO, 1976. pp. 1023–1026.

929.   Kirchhofer, Kirk H. "Cryptology." *International Defense Review,* IX (April–August 1976), 281–286, 389–394, 585–590.

930.   Lysing, Henry. *Secret Writing: An Introduction to Cryptograms, Ciphers, and Codes.* New York: Dover Books, 1974. 117p.

931.   Meunier, Patrick. "High Speed Intelligence For the Divisional Commander." *NATO's Fifteen Nations,* XXII (October–November 1977), 90–91+.

932.   Moore, Frederick L. "Radio Countermeasures." *Air University Quarterly Review,* II (Fall 1948), 57–66.

933.   O'Ballance, Edgar. *The Electronic War in the Middle East, 1968–1970.* Hamden, CT: Archon Books, 1974. 148p.

934.   Price, Alfred. *Instruments of Darkness: The History of Electronic Warfare.* Rev. ed. London: Macdonalds & Janes, 1977. 284p.

935.   Rolya, William I. "Intelligence, Security, and Electronic Warfare." *Signal,* XXXII (March 1978), 15–17.

936.   Rothchild, John, jt. author. *See* Dickerson, Paul (914).

937.   Saville, Gordon P. "Electronics in Air Defense." *Signal,* IV (September–October 1949), 5–7.

938.   Shannon, Calude E. "Communication Theory of Secret Systems." *Bell System Technical Journal,* XXVIII (1949), 656–715.

939.   Sinkov, Abraham. *Elementary Cryptanalysis: A Mathematical Approach.* New York: Random House, 1968. 189p.

940.   Smith, Lawrence D. *Cryptography: The Science of Secret Writing.* New York: Dover Books, 1955. 164p.

941.   Stone, Jeremy J. "New Worry—Is the Soviet Listening in?: Reprinted From the *Washington Star,* July 23, 1975." In: U.S. Congress. Senate. Committee on the Judiciary. Subcommittee on Constitutional Rights. *Surveillance Technology, 1976.* 94th Cong., 2nd sess. Washington, D.C.: GPO, 1976. pp. 1026–1033.

942.   United States. Congress. Senate. Committee on Commerce, Science, and Transportation. *Microwave Irradiation of the U.S. Embassy in Moscow: Committee Print.* 96th Cong., 1st sess. Washington, D.C.: GPO, 1979. 26p.

943.   _____ . _____ . _____ . Committee on Foreign Relations. *Early Warning System in the Sinai: Hearings.* 94th Cong., 1st sess. Washington, D.C.: GPO, 1975. 264p.

944.   Weizenbaum, Joseph. "Incomprehensible Programs." In: *Computer Power and Human Reason: From Judgement to Calculation*. San Francisco, CA: W. H. Freeman and Co., 1978. pp. 228–258.

C. Scientific-Technical Intelligence

Introduction

Scientific and technical (S&T) intelligence is defined as intelligence "concerning foreign developments in basic and applied scientific and technical research and development, including engineering and production techniques, new technology, and weapons systems and their capabilities and characteristics."[1] This field of intelligence became a separate aspect of the national information-collection process during World War II. Since 1945, S&T intelligence has advanced like communications and electronics intelligence and is now a regular feature of the intelligence cycle.

Not much has been written about modern S&T intelligence and the extant literature often tends to blur into general discussions of non-personnel aspects of data collection, verification, and other forms of "national technical means." For that reason, various titles in this section reflect the main topic as well as the more general approach. The reader should employ these citations in conjunction with those in the previous section.

In addition, this section features three subsections dealing with the means by which the more technical non-personnel forms of intelligence are gathered: 1) reconnaissance aircraft; 2) reconnaissance satellites; and 3) reconnaissance ships. These means have frequently been in the news during the past two decades, especially when their operations have gone astray.

Note

1. U.S. Central Intelligence Agency. "Glossary of Intelligence Terms and Definitions." In: U.S. Congress. House. Permanent Select Committee on Intelligence, *Annual Report* (95th Cong., 2nd sess. Washington, D.C.: GPO, 1978) p. 48.

1. General Works

945.   Aspin, Les. "Verification of the SALT II Agreement." *Scientific American*, CXL (February 1979), 38–45.

946. Barnet, Richard J. "Inspection, Shadow and Substance." In: Richard J. Barnet and Richard A. Falk, eds. *Security in Disarmament.* Princeton, NJ: Princeton University Press, 1965. pp. 15–36.

947. Brandenberger, Arthur J. "What Can Photos Tell Us?" *International Science and Technology,* LXIX (September 1967), 56–62, 65–66.

948. Butler, David. "Monitoring Moscow's ICBMs: The Key SALT Issue." *Newsweek,* XCIII (April 23, 1979), 46, 51.

949. Drew, H. A. W. "The Verification of Strategic Arms Agreements." *Hawk,* no. 35 (February 1974), 45–50.

950. Dunlap, Orrin E. *Radar: What It Is and How It Works.* New York: Harper, 1948. 268p.

951. Glenn, John. "Some Pepper For SALT: John Glenn's Verification Criticism." *Time,* CXIII (April 23, 1979), 20–21.

952. Harvey, Mose L. and Vladimir Prokofiefe. *Science and Technology as an Instrument of Soviet Foreign Policy.* Miami, FL: Center For International Studies, University of Miami, 1972. 219p.

953. Henderson, Wallace D. "Surveillance and Warning." *Signal,* XXXIII (November–December 1978), 39–40+.

954. "If Moscow Cheats on SALT: The Verification Issue." *Time,* CXIII (April 30, 1979), 21.

955. Institute for Defense Analysis. *Verification and Response in Disarmament Agreements.* 2 vols. Washington, D.C.: GPO, 1962.

956. _____. _____ : *Excerpts. Bulletin of the Atomic Scientists,* XIX (April 1963), 44–48.

957. Karkoszka, Andrzej. *Strategic Disarmament: Verification and National Security.* New York: Published for the Stockholm International Peace Research Institute by Crane, Russak, 1977. 174p.

958. Katz, Amrom H. "Hiders and Finders: An Approach to Inspection and Evasion Technology." In: Ernest W. Lefever, ed. *Arms and Arms Control* New York: Praeger, 1962. pp. 199–207.

959. Lall, Betty G. "Information in Arms Control Verification." *Bulletin of the Atomic Scientists,* XX (October 1964), 43–45.

960. _____ . "Perspectives on Inspection for Arms Control." *Bulletin of the Atomic Scientists,* XXI (March 1965), 51–53.

961. McGuire, Martin C. *Secrecy and the Arms Race: A Theory of the Accumulation of Strategic Weapons and How Secrecy Affects It.* Harvard Economic Studies, v. 125. Cambridge, MA: Harvard University Press, 1965. 249p.

962. Mann, Martin. "Our Secret Radar War With Russia." *Popular Science,* CLXXVIII (January 1961), 66–69+.

963. Miller, Barry. "Soviet Radar." *Aviation Week and Space Technology,* XCIV (February 15–22, 1971), 14–16, 42–50.

964. Paszek, Lawrence J., jt. editor. *See* Wright, Monte D. (976).

965. Piggott, Francis J. C. "Verification: Intelligence or Inspection.' *Disarmament,* VI (June 1965), 18–20.

966. Prokofiefe, Vladimir, jt. author. *See* Harvey, Mose L. (952).

967. Rowan, Ford. *Technospies.* New York: Putnam, 1978.

968. "Satellites, Planes, Ships: America's Network of Spies." *U.S. News and World Report,* LXXVII (September 16, 1974), 33.

969. Scoville, Herbert, Jr. "Verification of Nuclear Arms Limitations: An Analysis." *Bulletin of the Atomic Scientists,* XXVI (October 1970), 6–12.

970. Stockholm International Peace Institute. "Non-Seismic Detection of Underground Nuclear Tests." In: *World Armaments and Disarmament: SIPRI Yearbook, 1972.* New York: Humanities Press, 1972. pp. 437–460.

971. "Surveillance: How It Gets Done." *Business Week,* (April 28, 1969), 523–524.

972. Thurmond, Strom. "The Growth of Reconnaissance and Surveillance in Political Decisions." *Data,* XII (April 1967), 11–12.

973. United States. Arms Control and Disarmament Agency. *Verification: The Critical Element of Arms Control.* Publication no. 85. Washington, D.C.: GPO, 1976.

974. _____ . Department of the Army, Office of the Adjutant General. *Technical Intelligence.* FM 30–6. Washington, D.C.: GPO, 1966. 76p.

975. Vance, Robert T. "Inspection: Essential Element of Arms Control and Disarmament." Unpublished PhD Dissertation, George Washington University, 1965.

976.   Wright, Monte D. and Lawrence J. Paszek, eds. *Science, Technology, and Warfare: Proceedings of the Third Military History Symposium Held at the USAF Academy, 8–9 May 1969.* Washington, D.C.: GPO, 1971. 221p.

977.   Young, Wayland. "Verification." *Disarmament and Arms gcontrol,* II (Summer 1964), 342–352.

2. Spy Planes

978.   "Aerial Reconnaissance." *Data,* X (April 1965), 7–41.

979.   Bulban, Erwin J. "Techniques Used on the RB–57F." *Aviation Week and Space Technology,* LXXXI (July 20, 1964), 51–53, 56–57.

980.   Carroll, Raymond. "Spy in the Sky Flap." *Newsweek,* XCIII (April 23, 1979), 45.

      U.S. operations over South Africa.

981.   Cornelius, George. "Air Reconnaissance: Great Silent Weapon." *U.S. Naval Institute Proceedings,* LXXXV (July 1959), 35–42.

982.   "The Cuban Pictures That Spurred Us to Act." *Life,* LIII (November 2, 1962), 38–41.

983.   Ecevit, Bulent. "Turkey and the U-2: An Interview." *Newsweek,* XCIII (June 25, 1979), 59–60.

984   Elmhurst, Thomas. "Air Reconnaissance: Its Purpose and Value." *Journal of the Royal United Service Institution,* XCVII (February 1952), 84–86.

985.   "Gallery of Soviet Aerospace Weapons: Reconnaissance, ECM, and Early Warning Aircraft." *Air Force Magazine,* LXI (March 1978), 100–101.

986.   "Gallery of USAF Weapons: Reconnaissance and Special-Duty Aircraft." *Air Force Magazine,* LXI (March 1978), 118–119.

987.   "The Gamble Goes On: Intelligence-Gathering by EC-121." *Time,* XCIII (May 16, 1969), 23.

988.   Gaskin, Robert. "Flying the U-2." *Air Force Magazine,* LX (April 1977), 66–71.

989.   George, James A. "Where the High Flyers Go." *Airman,* XXII (September 1978), 22–31.

990.   Goddard, George W. *Overview: A Life-Long Adventure in Aerial Photography.* Garden City, NY: Doubleday, 1969, 415p.

991.   Helman, Grover. *Aerial Photography: The Story of Aerial Mapping Reconnaissance.* New York: Macmillan, 1972. 180p.

992.   Infield, Glenn B. *Unarmed and Unafraid.* New York: Macmillan, 1970. 292p.

993.   Jarvinen, Philip L. "Everything You've Always Wanted to Know About a U-2 Navigator." *Navigator,* XXV (Spring 1978), 5–9.

994.   Laurence, William L. "On Inspection and Control." In: *The Hell Bomb.* New York: Knopf, 1951. pp. 149–198.

995.   Lawrence, David. "The Right of Defensive Surveillance—No Legal Ban on Watch Flights Found in International Agreements: Reprinted from the *Washington Star,* June 7, 1960." *Congressional Record,* CVI (June 8, 1960), 12088–12089.

996.   Levison, Walter J. "Capabilities and Limitations of Aerial Inspection." In: Seymour Melman, ed. *Inspection For Disarmament.* New York: Columbia University Press, 1958. pp. 59–74.

997.   "Low-Level Photos Pinpoint Cuban Missile Sites." *Aviation Week and Space Technology,* LXXVII (November 5, 1962), 54–55.

998.   Mondey, David, jt. author. *See* Taylor, John W. R.

999.   Nechayuk, L. "Comments on U.S. Strategic Reconnaissance Aircraft [U-2 and SR-71]: Reprinted from *Kryl'ya Rodiny,* November 1978." *Translations on U.S.S.R Military Affairs,* no. 1427 (April 9, 1979), 5–9.

1000.   Nelson, David C. "History of the 67th Tactical Reconnaissance Wing." *Tactical Air Reconnaissance Digest,* II (February and May, 1968), 22–26, 6–11.

1002.   Nielsen, Milton. "[Mission] 'Busy Observer I.' " *Navigator,* XXV (Winter 1978), 20–22.

1003.   "The Spy Planes [EC-121]: What They Do and Why." *Time,* XCIII (April 25, 1969), 17.

1004.   Sturm, Ted R. "The Lonely Ones." *Space World,* III (July 1962), 42–44.

1005.   Taylor, John W. R. "Reconnaissance 1972." *Royal Air Forces Quarterly,* XII (Spring 1972), 7–14.

1006.   _____ and David Mondey. *Spies in the Sky.* New York: Scribner, 1972. 128p.

1007.   "U-2 Developmental and Operational Chronology." *Congressional Record,* CVI (June 7, 1960), 11977–11978.

1008.   Whitehouse, Arthur G. J. "Arch." *Spies With Wings.* New York: Putnam, 1967. 156p.

1009.   "Why Spy Planes are Necessary." *U.S. News and World Report,* LXVI (April 28, 1969), 27.

1010.   Winchester, James H. "Aerial Reconnaissance in Peace and War." *NATO's Fifteen Nations,* VIII (August–September, October–November, 1963), 98–100+, 90–94+.

3. Spy Satellites

1011.   Bates, E. Asa. "National Technical Means of Verification." *Journal of the Royal United Service Institution for Defence Studies,* CXXIII (June 1978), 64–72.

1012.   Beecher, William. "Spy Satellites Will Monitor [SALT] Pacts." *Sea Power,* XV (July–August 1972), 20–24.

1013.   Bradsher, Henry S. "In Focus—Spy Satellites Getting Priority in Soviet Space Program: Reprinted From the *Washington Star,* May 12, 1976." In: U.S. Congress. Senate. Committee on the Judiciary. Subcommittee on Constitutional Rights. *Surveillance Technology, 1976.* 94th Cong., 2nd sess. Washington, D.C.: GPO, 1976. pp. 1121–1124.

1014.   Brown, Neville. "Reconnaissance From Space." *World Today,* XXVII (February 1971), 68–76.

1015.   Butz, J. S. "New Vistas in Reconnaissance From Space." *Air Force and Space Digest,* LI (March 1968), 46–56.

1016.   Coates, G. P. "Reconnaissance Satellites." *Spaceflight,* III (May 1961), 100–104.

1017.   Cox, Donald W. "Overflight by Satellite." *Nation,* CXC (June 4, 1960), 486–489.

1018.   Davies, Merton E. and Bruce C. Murray. "Inspection of Earth From Orbit." In: *The View From Space.* New York: Columbia University Press, 1971. pp. 9–33.

1019.   "Detection of ICBM's Key in MOL Approval." *Aviation Week and Space Technology,* LXXXII (September 27, 1965), 26–27.

1020.   De Weerd, Harvey A. "Verifying the SALT Agreements." *Army,* XXVIII (August 1978), 15–18.

1021.   Donnelly, Christopher, jt. author. *See* Vigor, Peter H. (1085).

1022.   "Eyes in the Sky." *Time,* XCI (June 7, 1978), 36+.

1023. Friedmann, Wolfgang. "The U-2 and Outer Space Control" *Foreign Policy Bulletin,* XXXIX (January 1, 1960), 157–159.

1024. Fusca, J. A. "Space Surveillance." *Space/Aeronautics,* XLI (June 1964), 92–103.

1025. Galloway, Alec. "A Decade of U.S. Reconnaissance Satellites." *Interavia,* XXVII (April 1972), 376–380.

1026. _____. _____. *International Defense Review,* V (June 1972), 249–253.

1027. Gatland, Kenneth W. "Espionage From Orbit." *Flight International,* XCV (April 10–17, 1969), 604, 642.

1028. Goldhammer, J. S. "An Integrated Photographic Reconnaissance System." *Interavia,* XVII (March 1962), 304–307.

1029. Greenwood, Ted. "Reconnaissance and Arms Control." *Scientific American,* CCXXVIII (February 1973), 14–25.

1030. _____. *Reconnaissance, Surveillance, and Arms Control.* Adelphi Papers, no. 88. London: International Institute for Strategic Studies, 1972. 31p.

1031. Heaps, Leo. *Operation Morning Light: Terror in the Skies, the True Story of Cosmos 954.* New York: Paddington Press, 1978. 208p.

1032. Hockman, Sandra and Sybil Wong. *Satellite Spies: The Frightening Impact of a New Technology, an Investigation.* Indianapolis, IN: Bobbs-Merrill, 1976. 212p.

1033. Jasani, Bhupendra. "Verification Using Reconnaissance Satellites." In: Stockholm International Peace Research Institute. *SIPRI Yearbook of World Armament and Disarmament, 1973.* New York: Humanities Press, 1973. pp. 60–101.

1034. Jensen, Neils. *Optical and Photographic Reconnaissance Systems.* New York: Wiley, 1968. 211p.

1035. Katz, Amrom H. "Observation Satellites: Problems and Prospects." *Astronautics,* V (June–October 1960), 26–29+, 30+, 32–33+, 36–37+.

1036. _____. _____. RAND Paper P-1707. Santa Monica, CA: RAND Corporation, 1959. 128p.

1037. Klass, Philip J. "Keeping the Nuclear Peace: Spies in the Sky." *New York Times Magazine,* (September 3, 1972), 6–7, 31–32, 35–36.

1038. _____ . "Lack of Infrared Data Hampers Midas." *Aviation Week and Space Technology,* LXXVII (September 24, 1962), 54–55+.

1039. _____ . "Reconnaissance Satellite Assumes Dual Role." *Aviation Week and Space Technology,* XCV (August 30, 1971), 12–13.

1040. _____ . *Secret Sentries in Space.* New York: Random House, 1971. 236p.

1041. _____ . "USAF Boosts Reconnaissance Satellite Lifetimes." *Aviation Week and Space Technology,* CIII (July 7, 1974), 21–22.

1042. Kolcum, Edward H. "Operational Russian Satellites Scan U.S." *Aviation Week and Space Technology,* LXXXII (February 22, 1965), 22.

1043. Kroeck, Patricia, jt. author. *See* Ossenbeck, Frederick J. (1053).

1044. Latour, Charles. "Ocean Reconnaissance From the Sky." *NATO's Fifteen Nations,* XIX (October–November 1974), 34–43.

1045. Lord, Carnes. "Verification and the Future of Arms Control." *Strategic Review,* VI (Spring 1978), 24–32.

1046. Marriott, John. "[Spy] Satellites." *Army Quarterly,* CVII (July 1977), 291–297.

1047. Meeker, Leonard C. "Observation in Space." *Department of State Bulletin,* XLVIII (May 13, 1963), 746–751.

1048. Moore, Otis C. "No Hiding Place in Space." *Air Force Magazine,* LVII (August 1974), 43–48.

1049. "More Spies in the Sky: How the U.S. and Russia Watch Each Other." *U.S. News and World Report,* LXXV (August 13, 1973), 27–28.

1050. Morrison, Philip. "The Role of Reconnaissance Satellites in the Arms Race." *Scientific American,* CCXXV (September 1971), 229–230+.

1051. Murray, Bruce C., jt. author. *See* Davies, Merton E. (1018).

1052. "Now, Instant Warning if the U.S. is Attacked." *U.S. News and World Report,* LXXIII (November 15, 1971), 108–109.

1053. Ossenbeck, Frederick J. and Patricia C. Kroeck. *Open Space and Peace: A Symposium on the Effects of Observation.* Stanford, CA: Stanford University Press, 1964. 227p.

1054. O'Toole, Thomas. "Cloak and Dagger Cameras." *Science Digest,* XLIX (February 1961), 9–12.

1055.   Passony, Stefan T. "Open Skies, Arms Control, and Peace." *Air Force and Space Digest*, XLVII (March 1964), 71–72.

1056.   Perry, Geoffrey C. "Cosmos Observation." *Flight International*, XCVII (July 1, 1971), 29–32.

1057.   _____ . "The Cosmos Programme." *Flight International*, XCIV (December 26, 1968), 1077–1079; XCV (May 8, 1969), 773–776.

1058.   _____ . "Reconnaissance Aspects of 8-Day Cosmos Satellites." *Spaceflight*, X (June 1968), 204–206.

1059.   _____ . "Recoverable Cosmos Satellites for Military Reconnaissance." In: U.S. Library of Congress. Science Policy Research Division, Congressional Research Service. *Soviet Space Programs, 1971–1975.* 2 vols. Washington, D.C.: GPO, 1976. I, 457–478.

1060.   _____ . "Russian Ocean Surveillance Satellites." *Royal Air Forces Quarterly*, XVIII (Spring 1978), 60–67.

1061.   "Playing Russian Roulette With Missiles: Monitoring by Soviet Reconnaissance Satellites." *Newsweek*, XCIII (May 7, 1979), 29.

1062.   Porter, Richard W. *The Versatile Satellite.* New York and London: Oxford University Press, 1977. 173p.

1063.   Pursglove, S. David. "Electronics Expands the Vision of Sky Spies." *Electronic Design*, XIII (October 11, 1965), 26–33.

1064.   "Reconnaissance Satellites." *Interavia*, XX (January 1965), 104–107.

1065.   _____ . In: R.U.S.I. and Brassey's, *Defence Yearbook, 1974.* New York: Praeger, 1974. pp. 263–270.

1066.   _____ . In: R.U.S.I. and Brassey's, *Defence Yearbook, 1975/76.* Boulder, CO: Westview Press, 1975. pp. 304–311.

1067.   _____ . In: R.U.S.I. and Brassey's, *Defence Yearbook, 1976/77.* Boulder, CO: Westview Press, 1976. pp. 283–287.

1068.   _____ . In: R.U.S.I. and Brassey's, *Defence Yearbook, 1977/78.* Boulder, CO: Westview Press, 1977. pp. 371–378.

1069.   Rochlin, Robert S. "Observation Satellites for Arms Control Inspection." *Journal of Arms Control*, I (1963), 224–227.

1070.   Sandefur, K. L. "Space Reconnaissance." *Aerospace Engineering*, XIX (November 1960), 28–31+.

1071. Sheldon, Charles S., 2nd. "Program Details of Unmanned Flights: The Cosmos Program, Military Observation Recoverable Satellites." In: U.S. Library of Congress. Science Policy Research Division and Foreign Affairs Division, Congressional Research Service. *Soviet Space Programs, 1966–1970: A Staff Report.* Washington, D.C.: GPO, 1971. pp. 180–186.

1072. _____ . "Soviet Military Space Activities." In: U.S. Library of Congress. Science Policy Research Division, Congressional Research Service. *Soviet Space Programs, 1971–75.* 2 vols. Washington, D.C.: GPO, 1976. I, 12–15.

1073. Sorahan, Joseph R. "Reconnaissance Satellites: Legal Characteristics and Possible Utilization for Peacekeeping." *McGill Law Journal,* XIII (Fall 1967), 458–493.

1074. "Space Patrol: How the U.S. Watches the Russians." *U.S. News and World Report,* LXVII (November 24, 1969), 32–33.

1075. "Spies Above." *Time,* XCVIII (August 30, 1971), 20+.

1076. "Spies in Space: They Make an Open Book of Russia." *U.S. News and World Report,* LXV (September 9, 1968), 69–72.

1077. Spurr, Robert. "Sky Spies." *Far Eastern Economic Review,* XCV (February 25, 1977), 24–28.

1078. "Spy Race in the Sky." *U.S. News and World Report,* LXIX (October 12, 1970), 24–26.

1079. "Spying and Space." *New Republic,* CXLII (May 30, 1960), 3–4.

1080. Steeg, George F. "The Military Characteristics of Reconnaissance and Surveillance." *Electronic Warfare,* VIII (September–October 1976), 71+.

1081. Strother, Robert S. "Space Cameras on Peace Patrol." *Popular Science,* CLXXX (January 1962), 76–79+.

1082. Taubenfeld, Howard J. "Surveillance From Space: The American Case For Peace-Keeping and Self-Defense." *Air Force and Space Digest,* XLVI (October 1963), 54+.

1083. "USAF Reconnaissance Satellites." *Aviation Week and Space Technology,* LXXXVI (March 6, 1967), 116.

1084. Vayrynen, Raimo. "Military Uses of Satellite Communication." *Instant Research on Peace and Violence,* II (Winter 1973), 44–49.

1085. Vigor, Peter H. and Christopher Donnelly. "Soviet Reconnaissance." *Journal of the Royal United Service Institution for Defence Studies,* CXX (December 1975), 41–45; CXXI (March 1976), 68–75.

1086. "Watch From Space: The Midas Satellite." *Newsweek,* LV (June 6, 1960), 39–40.

1087. White, Peter T. "The Camera Keeps Watch on the World." *New York Times Magazine,* (April 3, 1966), 26+.

1088. Wong, Sybil, jt. author. *See* Hochman, Sandra (1032).

1089. Wu, Yuan-li. "Solving the Red Chinese Puzzle From Space." *Air Force and Space Digest,* XLVII (February 1964), 59–62.

4. Spy Ships

a. General Works

1090. Coyle, Robert E. "Surveillance From the Seas." *Military Law Review,* LX (Spring 1973), 75–97.

1091. "The Ferret Fleets." *Time,* XCII (February 2, 1968), 15.

1092. "Fishing Vessels, or Fishy Ones: The Flotilla of Soviet and Polish Trawlers off the Atlantic Coast." *Newsweek,* LXXIII (February 24, 1969), 26.

1093. Goulding, Philip G. *Confirm or Deny: Informing the People on National Security.* New York: Harper & Row, 1970. 369p.

1094. "How the Russians Use Ships to Snoop." *U.S. News and World Report,* XXXVI (April 30, 1954), 35–36.

1095. Rowan, Carl T. "Why We Need Spy Ships and Planes." *Reader's Digest,* XCV (September 1969), 122–126.

1096. "Spy Business as Usual For U.S. Spook Fleet: The Navy's Task Force 71 in the Sea of Japan." *Business Week,* (April 26, 1969), 54+.

b. Liberty *Incident (1967)*

1097. Ennes, James M., Jr. *Assault on the Liberty: The True Story of the Israeli Attack on an American Intelligence Ship.* New York: Random House, 1980. 288p.

1098. Lentini, Joseph C. "I Was on Board the *Liberty.*" *U.S. Naval Institute Proceedings,* CIII (December 1977), 108–109.

1099. "New Light on the *Liberty:* Reprinted From the *Washington Post,* September 19, 1977." *U.S. Naval Institute Proceedings,* CIII (December 1977), 108.

1100. Pearson, Anthony. *Conspiracy of Silence.* New York: Horizon Press, 1978. 179p.

1101. "When U.S. Ship was the Victim of a Shoot-First Policy." *U.S. News and World Report,* LXIV (May 13, 1968), 12.

c. Pueblo *Affair (1968)*

1102. Armbrister, Trevor. *A Matter of Accountability: The True Story of the Pueblo Affair.* New York: Coward, McCann, 1970. 408p.

1103. _____. "The *Pueblo* Crisis and Public Opinion." *Naval War College Review,* XXIV (March 1971), 84–110.

1104. Bucher, Lloyd M. "*Pueblo* Captain Tells His Story of Capture and Captivity: Excerpts From a News Conference, December 23, 1968." *U.S. News and World Report,* LXVI (January 6, 1969), 30–31.

1105. _____, and Mark Rasovich. *Bucher: My Story.* Garden City, NY: Doubleday, 1970. 447p.

1106. Chang, Henry S. "In the Wake of the *Pueblo.*" *Far Eastern Economic Review,* LIV (March 14, 1968), 454–456.

1107. Gallery, Daniel V. *The Pueblo Incident.* Garden City, NY: Doubleday, 1970. 174p.

1108. "How the Communists Capured a U.S. Warship." *U.S. News and World Report,* LXIV (February 5, 1968), 24–25.

1109. "How U.S. Ship Spied on the Russians." *U.S. News and World Report,* LXV (September 23, 1968), 11+.

1110. Koh, B. C. "The *Pueblo* Incident in Perspective." *Asian Survey,* IX (April 1969), 264–280.

1111. Kopkind, Andrew. "Significance of the *Pueblo.*" *New Statesman and Nation,* LXXV (February 2, 1968), 131–132.

1112. Lentner, Howard H. "The *Pueblo* Affair: Anatomy of a Crisis." *Military Review,* XLIX (July 1969), 55–66.

1113. Marshall, Samuel L. A. "The *Pueblo* Affair: Ignoring Murphy's Law." *New Leader,* LI (February 12, 1968), 3–8.

1114. _____. "The *Pueblo* and the [Geneva Convention] Code." *New Leader,* LII (April 14, 1969), 10–11.

1115. "More on the Strange Story of the *Pueblo.*" *U.S. News and World Report,* LXVI (February 10, 1969), 33–34.

1116. "*Pueblo* Surrender: Who Made the Mistakes?" *U.S. News and World Report,* LXVI (February 24, 1969), 58–59.

1117. Rasovich, Mark, jt. author. *See* Bucher, Lloyd M. (1105).

1118.   "Remembering the *Pueblo*." *Newsweek,* LXXV (June 8, 1970), 16.

1119.   Schratz, Paul R. "A Commentary on the *Pueblo* Affair." *Military Review,* XXXV (October 1971), 93–94.

1120.   Schumacher, F. Carl and George C. Wilson. *Bridge of No Return: The Ordeal of the U.S.S. Pueblo.* New York: Harcourt, Brace, 1971. 242p.

1121.   "Snoopers: Looking and Listening." *Newsweek,* LXXIII (February 5, 1968), 16–21.

1122.   United States. Congress. House. Committee on Armed Services. Special Subcommittee on U.S.S. *Pueblo. Inquiry into the U.S.S. Pueblo and EC-121 Plane Incidents: Hearings.* 91st Congress, 1st sess. Washington, D.C.: GPO, 1969. 547p.

1123.   _____ . _____ . _____ . _____ . _____ . *Report.* 91st Cong., 1st sess. Washington, D.C.: GPO, 1969. 77p.

1124.   Wilson, George C., jt. author. *See* Schumacher, F. Carl (1120).

1125.   Wise, David. "When Spies Get Caught: Perspectives on the *Pueblo*." *New Republic*, CLVIII (February 10, 1968), 9–10.

D. Espionage—General Works

Introduction

Espionage is often called the world's second oldest profession and has been a part of the intelligence function longer than any other. Espionage conducted by secret agents, as opposed to that done by radar or satellite, is the most glamorous aspect of the intelligence cycle, but it is the least important factor in the American and certain other advanced national collection processes. Spies are far out-weighed in importance by the massive and organized study conducted by intelligence organizations of overt sources such as books, journals, newspapers, documents, etc., and by the recent advances in "Sigint" and S&T intelligence.

Secret agents (who are often paid traitors) do, however, still operate and a few are caught each year. Fiction and the movies, however, often overvalue their importance because their individual stories make rattling good reading with some gems of instruction for the uninitiated. Even the CIA definition of espionage is glamorous: "intelligence activity directed toward the acquisition of information through clandestine means and proscribed by the laws of the country against which it is committed."[1] In the 1970's and 1980's *agents provocateurs* have and will continue to stir up political unrest. Other agents will implement disinformation gambits as well as help their countries to understand the political attitudes of foreign populations and leaders.

The national antidote to espionage is counterintelligence. Such work, often done by regular police forces, has broken most of the big postwar spy networks in this country and abroad. For example, massive counter-intelligence operations in Russia and China combined with the regulation of their otherwise closed societies have thwarted Western attempts to infiltrate and maintain agents within those countries since 1945.

The serious and analytical literature of espionage and counterespionage since World War II is limited. Much of what has been published appears in the form of general works or memoirs. Even then, one cannot be sure how much of the data in various works is factual and how much is disinformation inspired by "ghosts" assisting the authors. A good rule of thumb is to get the same facts from at least two different sources.

The citations in this section are general. They are amplified by those in the two previous sections dealing with more technical forms and by those in the next section which treat the work of national intelligence agencies, and by the general and specific biographies and autobiographies in Part IV.

Notes

1. U.S. Central Intelligence Agency. "Glossary of Intelligence Terms and Definitions." In: U.S. Congress. House. Permanent Select Committee on Intelligence, *Annual Report* (95th Cong., 2nd sess. Washington, D.C.: GPO, 1978), p. 37.

1126.   "Action Behind the [Canadian] Spy Scare: Espionage by All Major Nations." *U.S. News and World Report,* XX (March 1, 1946), 15–16.

1127.   Altavilla, Enrico. *The Art of Spying: The Truth Behind the International Espionage Networks.* Translated from the Italian. Englewood Cliffs, NJ: Prentice-Hall, 1965. 199p.

1128.   "Battle Order of World Espionage." *U.N. World,* III (June–July 1949), 28–30, 31–33.

1129.   Bergier, Jacques. *Secret Armies: The Growth of Corporate and Industrial Espionage.* Translated from the French. Indianapolis, IN: Bobbs-Merrill, 1975. 268p.

1130.   _____ . *Secret Weapons—Secret Agents.* Translated from the French. London: Hurst & Blackett, 1956. 184p.

1131.   Burkholtz, Herbert, jt. author. *See* Irving, Clifford (1169).

1132.   Cecil, Robert. "Legends Spies Tell." *Encounter,* L (April 1978), 9–17.

1133.   Clark, Ronald W. *Great Moments in Espionage.* New York: Roy, 1964. 126p.

1134.   Cohen, Daniel. *The Art of Spying.* New York: McGraw-Hill, 1977. 112p.

1135.   Colby, William E. "Why the Spy War Seems to be Heating Up: An Interview." *U.S. News and World Report,* LXXXIV (July 3, 1978), 39+.

1136.   Cookridge, E. H., pseud. *See* Spiro, Edward (1209).

1137.   Copeland, Miles. *The Real Spy World.* London: Weidenfeld and Nicholson, 1974. 351p. Reprint 1978.

1138.   _____ . "Without Cloak and Dagger: A Report on Spies in the Seventies." *Cosmopolitan,* CLXXVIII (January 1975), 90+.

1139.   _____ . *Without Cloak and Dagger: The Truth About the New Espionage.* New York: Simon and Schuster, 1974. 351p.

1140.   De Gramont, Sanche, pseud. *See* Morgan, Ted (1184).

1141.   Deindorfer, Robert G., ed. *The Spies.* Greenwich, CT: Fawcett Books, 1969. 240p.

1142.   _____ , jt. author. *See* Rowan, Richard W. (1196).

1143.   Donovan, James B. "Why We Must Spy." *America,* CIII (May 28, 1960), 307–309.

1144.   Dulles, Allen W., ed. *Great True Spy Stories.* New York: Harper & Row, 1968. 393p.

1145.   _____ , and Ian Fleming. "Redbook Dialogue." *Redbook,* CXXIII (June 1964), 44–45+.

1146.   Dunlop, Robert. "This Business of Spying." *Popular Mechanics,* CXIV (September 1960), 94–100+.

1147.   Edmondson, Leslie S. "Espionage in Transnational Law." *Vanderbilt Journal of Transnational Law,* V (Spring 1972), 434–458.

1148.   Elliott-Bateman, Michael. *Intelligence, Subversion, Resistance.* Vol. I of *The Fourth Dimension of Warfare.* New York: Praeger, 1970. 181p.

1149. Epstein, Edward J. "War of the Moles: An Interview." *New York Magazine*, XI (February 27–March 13, 1978), 28–33+, 55–59, 12–13.

1150. "Espionage/U.S.A.: A Symposium." *Society*, XII (March 1975), 7–8, 26–80.

1151. Fairfield, Cecily E. *The New Meaning of Treason.* By Rebecca West, pseud. New York: Viking Press, 1964. 374p.

1152. Farago, Ladislas. *The War of Wits: The Anatomy of Espionage and Intelligence.* New York: Funk and Wagnalls, 1954. 379p.

1153. Felix, Christopher, pseud. *A Short Course in the Secret War.* New York: E. P. Dutton, 1963. 314p.

1154. FitzGibbon, Constantine. *Secret Intelligence in the Twentieth Century.* London: Hart-Davis, 1976. 350p.

1155. Fleming, Ian, jt. author. *See* Dulles, Allen W. (1145).

1156. French, Scott R. *The Big Brother Game.* London: Stuart, 1976.

1157. Frewin, Leslie R., comp. *The Spy Trade: An Anthology of International Espionage in Fact and Fiction.* London: Frewin, 1966. 248p.

1158. Gelb, Norman. *Enemy in the Shadows: The World of Spies and Spying.* New York: Hippocrene Books, 1976. 157p.

1159. Gibson, Walter B., ed. *The Fine Art of Spying.* New York: Grosset and Dunlap, 1965. 236p.

1160. Gribble, Leonard R. *Famous Feats of Espionage.* London: Barker, 1972. 153p.

1161. Halacy, Daniel S., ed. *The Master Spy.* New York: McGraw-Hill, 1968. 192p.

1162. Haswell, Chetwynd J. D. *Spies and Spymasters: A Concise History of Intelligence.* London: Thames and Hudson, 1977. 176p.

1163. Hill, John. *The Man From UNCLE's ABC's of Espionage.* New York: Signet Books, 1966. 128p.

1164. Hinchley, Vernon. *Spy Mysteries Unveiled.* New York: Dodd, Mead, 1963. 254p.

1165. Hoar, William P. "Secret Police: Watching the KGB and CIA." *American Opinion*, XVIII (April 1975), 27–31+.

1166. Horowitz, Irving L. "Spying and Security." *Current*, CLXXIII (May 1975), 3–6.

1167.   Hughes, V. W. "Intelligence Work Requires Behavior Outside the Norm: Reprinted From the Fort Worth *Star-Telegram,* October 5, 1975." *Congressional Rcord,* CXXI (October 9, 1975), 32941.

1168.   Ind, Allison. *A Short History of Espionage.* New York: McKay, 1963. 337p.

1169.   Irving, Clifford and Herbert Burkholtz. *Spy: The Story of Modern Espionage.* New York: Macmillan, 1969. 206p.

1170.   Joesten, Joachim. *The Call It Intelligence: Spies and Spy Techniques Since World War II.* New York: Abelard-Schuman, 1963. 314p.

1171.   Johnson, Brian D. G. *The Secret War.* New York and London: Methuen, 1978. 352p.

1172.   Kent, Graeme. *Espionage.* London: Batsford, 1974. 96p.

1173.   Knorr, Klaus E. *Foreign Intelligence and the Social Sciences.* Resident Monograph, no. 17. Princeton, NJ: Center of International Studies, Princeton University, 1964. 58p.

1174.   Komroff, Manuel. *True Adventures of Spies.* Boston: Little, Brown, 1954. 220p.

1175.   Laird, Melvin R. "Why We Need Spies." *Reader's Digest,* CXIV (March 1979), 87–99.

1176.   Lane, Shedlon, comp. *The Spying Game.* London: Mayflower, 1967. 144p.

1177.   Liston, Robert A. *The Dangerous World of Spies and Spying.* New York: Platt and Monk Co., 1967. 274p.

1178.   Lowry, R. P. "Secrecy and Spying." *Sociological Quarterly,* XIX (Winter 1978), 152–160.

1179.   McCormick, Donald. *The Master Book of Spies: The World of Espionage, Master Spies, Tortures, Interrogations, Spy Equipment, Escapes, Codes, and How You Can Become a Spy.* New York: Watts, 1974. 190p.

1180.   Mackenzie, Compton. "Spy Circus." *Nation,* CLXXXIX (December 5, 1959), 411–414.

1181.   Marshall, Stephen. "The Man in the Gray Flannel Cloak." *Chicago,* XXIV (October 1975), 177–183.

1182.   Meyer, Karl E. and Waverly Root. "Other Democracies Do Their Spying in Different Ways—In Britain, They Keep Quiet—In France, They Pay Openly: Reprinted From the *Washington Post,* February 26, 1967." *Congressional Record,* CXIII (February 26, 1967), 4671.

1183.   Micoleau, Charles J. "The 'Secret War': Myths, Morals, and Misconceptions." *School of Advanced International Studies* (SAS) *Review,* IX (Summer 1965), 21–28.

1184.   Morgan, Ted. *The Secret War: The Story of International Espionage Since World War II.* By Sanche De Gramont, pseud. New York: Putnam, 1962. 515p.

1185.   Murphy, Brian M. *The Business of Spying.* London: Milton House Books, 1973. 208p.

1186.   "New Espionage, American Style." *Newsweek,* LXXVIII (November 22, 1971), 28–32+.

1187.   Newman, Bernard. *Epics of Espionage.* New York: Philosophical Library, 1951. 270p.

1187a.   Newman, Bernard. *The World of Espionage.* New York: Ryerson Press, 1962. 245p.

1188.   Palmer, Raymond. *Undercover: The Making of a Spy.* London: Aldus Books, 1977. 144p.

1189.   "Peacetime Spying—Is It a Must?: Pro and Con Discussion." *Senior Scholastic,* LXXVII (September 14, 1960), 14–16+.

1190.   Perles, Alfred, ed. *Great True Spy Adventures.* New York: Arco, 1957. 210p.

1191.   "Regarding Men: 'Send Thou Men That They May Search Out the Land.'" *Newsweek,* LVI (August 22, 1960), 28–29.

1192.   Root, Waverly, jt. author. *See* Meyer, Karl E. (1182).

1193.   Ross, Thomas B., jt. author. *See* Wise, David (1224).

1194.   Rowan, Carl T. "We Have to Stay in the Dirty Business of Spying: Reprinted From the *Washington Evening Star,* October 1, 1971." *Congressional Record,* CXVII (October 12, 1971), 35924–35925.

1195.   Rowan, Richard W. *Spy Secrets.* New York: Buse Publications, 1946. 112p.

1196.   _____ , and Robert G. Deindorfer. *Secret Service: 33 Centuries of Espionage.* New and rev. ed. New York: Hawthorn Books, 1967. 786p.

1197.   Scoville, Herbert, Jr. "Is Espionage Necessary For Our Security?" *Foreign Affairs,* LIV (April 1976), 357–368.

1198.   Seth, Ronald. *The Art of Spying.* New York: Philosophical Library, 1957. 183p.

1199.   _____ . *How Spies Work.* New York: Farrar, Straus, 1957. 175p.

1200.   _____ . *Spies at Work: A History of Espionage.* New York: Philosophical Library, 1955. 234p.

1201.   _____ . *True Book About the Secret Service.* London: Muller, 1953. 142p.

1202.   Singer, Kurt D. *More Spy Stories.* London: Allen & Unwin, 1955. 224p.

1203.   _____ . *Spy Stories From Asia.* New York: Funk and Wagnalls, 1955. 336p.

1204.   _____ , ed. *Three Thousand Years of Espionage: An Anthology of the World's Greatest Spy Stories.* New York: Prentice-Hall, 1948. 384p.

1205.   _____ . *The World's Best Spy Stories: Fact and Fiction.* New York: Ryerson, 1954. 342p.

1206.   "Spies and Morality." *America,* CIII (May 28, 1960), 303–304.

1207.   "Spies: A Symposium." *Esquire,* LXV (May 1966), 77–105+.

1208.   "Spies: Footsoldiers in an Endless War." *Time,* XCVIII (October 11, 1971), 41–42+.

1209.   Spiro, Edward. *The Spy Trade.* By E. H. Cookridge, pseud. London: Hodder and Stoughton, 1971. 288p.

1210.   "The Spy Business Keeps on Booming." *U.S. News and World Report,* XL (May 25, 1956), 51–54.

1211.   "Spying: Opposing View Points." *Skeptic,* VII (May–June 1975), 1+.

1212.   Stanger, Roland J., ed. *Essays in Espionage and International Law.* A Merchon Center Publication. Columbus, OH: Ohio State Univeristy Press, 1963. 101p.

1213.   Sweetman, David. *Spies and Spying.* London: Wayland, 1978. 96p.

1214.   Taylor, Edmond. "The Cult of the Secret Agent." *Horizon,* XVII (Spring 1975), 4–13.

1215.   Tregenza, Michael. *Espionage.* London and New York: Hamlyn, 1974. 127p.

1216. United States. National Foreign Intelligence Board. *National Foreign Intelligence Plan For Human Resources.* Directive 27.7/5. Washington, D.C.: 1977.

1217. Vladimirov, Ye. "Imperialist Intelligence and Propaganda." *International Affairs* (Moscow), no. 9 (September 1971), 42–45.

1218. Walker, Warren S. "Spying: The Second Oldest Profession." *Saturday Review of Literature,* XLVI (May 25, 1963), 30–31+.

1219. West, Rebecca, pseud. *See* Fairfield, Cecily I.

1220. "When the Spy Business Gets in the News." *U.S. News and World Report,* LIX (November 15, 1965), 70–71.

1221. "Who Is Spying and Why." *U.S. News and World Report,* XLIX (August 8, 1960), 46–48+.

1222. "Who's Spying For Whom?" *U.S. News and World Report,* LV (July 29, 1963), 54–55.

1223. Wilhelm, John L. "The Murky World of Espionage." Philadelphia *Enquirer Magazine,* (January 29, 1978), 24–29.

1224. Wise, David and Thomas B. Ross. *The Espionage Establishment.* New York: Random House, 1967. 308p.

Britain, China, U.S.S.R., U.S.A.

1225. _____ . _____ . *Saturday Evening Post,* CCXL (October 21–November 18, 1967), 29–31+, 50–53+, 76–80+.

1226. "The World's Big Spy Game." *U.S. News and World Report,* XLVIII (May 23, 1960), 46–48+.

E. National Intelligence Agencies

Introduction

References to Soviet intelligence, Israeli intelligence, British intelligence, American intelligence and so forth usually employ a sort of code-word to address all of the security and intelligence agencies of a given nation.

Most advanced countries—and some not so advanced—maintain complicated intelligence structures often comprised of several agencies, each with specific duties and responsibilities.

For example, Soviet intelligence agencies include the Committee for State Security (KGB), and its subservient military counterpart, the

Chief Intelligence Directorate of the General Staff (GRU). Within each agency, component departments and divisions contribute specific functions to the operation as a whole (see Chart II). Incidentally, chiefs and deputies of foreign intelligence agencies serve terms often determined as much by political events as orderly process. The KGB (see Chart III) had an unusually high turnover in its formative and near-formative years, however, it has been stable since the assignment of Chairman Andropov in 1967. Andropov became the first KGB boss elevated to the Politburo in 1973 but one wonders what his fate will be in the post-Brezhnev era.

This section cites works which examine the history and roles of national intelligence organizations per se. References to many component agencies within foreign intelligence structures are often scarce in English so those citations are listed under national headings, e.g., Australia. In all, fifteen foreign organizations are covered in alphabetical order. As with citations to U.S. material, references to foreign agencies are often rich in biographical and operational information.

Because the United States is the country of publication of this guide and the source of a vast literature, it is the final nation to have its intelligence organizations examined in this subsection. The subsection on the United States begins with an overview of the American Intelligence Community, followed by citations dealing with economic, political, military estimates and the role of intelligence in U.S. foreign policy, and a review of the work of agencies which have an independent body of literature. The review ends with citations to Congressional oversight and the various administrative reforms of the intelligence organization as a whole.

By Presidential Executive Order no. 12036 of January 26, 1978, Jimmy Carter assigned the Director of Central Intelligence the responsibility to act as the primary adviser to the President and the National Security Council on national foreign intelligence. To discharge this and other assigned duties, the Director became the appointed head of both the Central Intelligence Agency and the American Intelligence Community. These relationships and the mechanisms established to sustain them can best be seen by addressing these little known organizations: the National Security Council (NSC), the Policy Review Committee (PRC), the Special Coordination Committee (SCC), the Intelligence Oversight Board (IOB), and finally, the intelligence community as a whole. Bear in mind that the Congress also plays a role in overseeing intelligence through the Senate Select Committee on Intelligence and the House Permanent Select Committee on Intelligence (see Chart IV).

The NSC was established by the National Security Act of 1947 which also created the Central Intelligence Agency. The NSC is charged to advise the President with respect to the integration of domestic, foreign, military policies relating to the national security. The NSC is the highest Executive Branch entity providing review of, guidance for, and direction to the conduct of all national foreign intelligence and counterintelligence activities. The statutory members of the NSC are the President, Vice President, the Secretary of State, and the Secretary of Defense. The Director of Central Intelligence and the Chairman of the Joint Chiefs of Staff participate as advisors. Other Executive Branch intelligence officials may be called upon for information from time to time.

The Policy Review Committee of the NSC is composed of the Vice President, the Secretaries of State, Treasury, and Defense, the Assistant to the President for National Security Affairs, the Chairman of the Joint Chiefs of Staff, and other senior officials as appropriate. The PRC chairman varies according to the meeting agenda, e.g., the Director of Central Intelligence is chairman when the body addresses intelligence matters. PRC duties in connection with national foreign intelligence require that it establish requirements and priorities, relate these requirements to budget proposals and resource allocations, review and evaluate the quality of intelligence products, and report annually on its activities to the NSC.

The Special Coordination Committee of the NSC is chaired by the Assistant to the President for National Security Affairs and is composed of the statutory members of the NSC and other senior officials as appropriate. The SCC deals with cross-cutting issues requiring coordination in the development of options and the implementation of Presidential decisions. Regarding intelligence issues, the SCC is required to consider and submit to the President policy recommendations on special activities; review and approve proposals for sensitive foreign intelligence collection operations; develop policy, standards, and doctrine for approved U.S. counterintelligence activities; and submit annually to the President an assessment of the relative threat to U.S. interests posed by the intelligence and security services of foreign powers and international terrorist activities.

The President's Intelligence Oversight Board functions within the White House. The IOB consists of three members from outside government appointed by the President. The duties of the IOB include reviewing the practices and procedures of the Inspectors General and General Counsels with responsibilities for agencies within the intelligence community; discovering and reporting to the IOB intelligence activities that raise questions of legality or propriety; reporting to the President any intelligence activities that raise serious questions of legality; and forwarding to the Attorney General reports on activities that raise questions of legality. This board is intended to prevent many of the difficulties brought to public light during the Congressional investigations of 1975–1976.

The Director of Central Intelligence is head of the CIA, and at the same time serves as the leader of the American Intelligence Community (AIC) of which the CIA is but one component. The AIC refers in the aggregate to those Executive Branch agencies and organizations that conduct the variety of intelligence activities which comprise the total U.S. national intelligence effort. The Community (see Chart V) includes the Central Intelligence Agency; the intelligence units of the Defense Department (Defense Intelligence Agency, National Security Agency, Army, Navy, and Air Force Intelligence, and Offices for Collection of Specialized National Foreign Intelligence); the Federal Bureau of Investigation; the State Department's Bureau of Intelligence and Research; the Department of the Treasury; the Department of Energy; the Drug Enforcement Administration; and staff elements of the Office of the Director of Central Intelligence. Members of the community advise the Director of Central Intelligence through their representation on a number of specialized committees that deal with intelligence matters of common concern. Among these groups is the National Foreign Intelligence Board which the Director of Central Intelligence chairs and which includes the Assistant to the President for National Security Affairs as an observer.

The Central Intelligence Agency created in 1947 by the National Security Act of 1947 and strengthened by law several times since enjoyed almost total public support until the Vietnam War era. The Indochina conflict, Watergate, and growing national outrage over secret intelligence operations such as the Bay of Pigs and the intervention in Chile brought the CIA, and other intelligence agencies, notably the FBI and NSA, under close investigation and oversight. The presidential reorganizations like that imposed by President Ford were designed to ensure that such "irregularities" do not occur again. The CIA, now mostly out of the covert operations business, has begun to openly emphasize its intelligence gathering and refinement process, so it is possible to purchase some of the CIA documents cited in Subsection 16:b. See Chart VI.

When Admiral Stansfield Turner, USN, was sworn in as the twelfth Director of Central Intelligence on March 9, 1977 his command responsibilities (Chart VII) were different from those of his predecessors. His principal deputies reflected the tight relationship between the CIA and the rest of the American Intelligence Community.

The major deputies of the Director of Central Intelligence (DCI) are the Deputy Director of Central Intelligence (DDCI), Ambassador Frank C. Carlucci; the Deputy to the Director of Central Intelligence for National Intelligence (D/DCI/NI), Robert R. Bowie; the Deputy to the Director of Central Intelligence for Collection Tasking (D/DCI/CT), Lieutenant General Frank A. Camm, USA (Ret.); the Deputy to the Director of Central Intelligence for Resource Management

(D/DCI/RM), a new position under John E. Koehler; the Deputy to the Director of Central Intelligence for Administration (DDA), Don I. Wortman; the Deputy to the Director of Central Intelligence for Operations (DDO) whose name, for security reasons, is not publicized; and the Deputy to the Director of Central Intelligence for Science and Technology (DDS&T). Chart VIII shows the organization of deputies and briefly discusses their duties under the terms of the Carter reorganization plan.

Incidentally, American CIA chiefs and their deputies, like their Soviet counterparts, have often had their terms of service influenced by political events. Allen Dulles bowed out as a result of the Bay of Pigs fiasco while William E. Colby was a victim of the so-called 1975 "year of intelligence." Chart IX lists the Directors of the CIA from 1946 to 1980.

The references in this section are supplemented by additional citations detailing operational and biographical details in Sections A, D, and F and in Part IV.

1. Australia

1227. Australia. Royal Commission on Intelligence and Security. *Report.* 4 vols. Canberra: Australian Government Printing Office, 1977.

The first public acknowledgement in print of an Australian foreign intelligence apparatus.

2. Canada

1228. Elliot, S. R. "The Canadian Intelligence Corps." *Canadian Army Journal,* XVII (April 1963), 122–127.

3. China

1229. Deacon, Richard, pseud. *See* McCormick, Donald (1233).

1230. Hai-po, Wang. "An Analysis of the Chinese Communists' Secret Service Organizations." *Freedom Front* (Hong Kong), XV (July 17, 1953), 17+.

1231. Han-po, Ch'en. *I Was in the Service of Mao Tse-tung's Secret Agents.* Translated from the Chinese. Hong Kong, 1952. 131p.

1232. Harvey, David. "CCIS (Chinese Communist Intelligence Service)." *Defense and Foreign Affairs Digest,* nos. 11–12 (1975–1976), 14–16+, 16–17+.

1233. McCormick, Donald. *The Chinese Secret Service.* By Richard Deacon, pseud. New York: Taplinger, 1974. 523p.

1234.   Wise, David and Thomas B. Ross. "Communist China." In: *The Intelligence Establishment.* New York: Random House, 1967. pp. 176–201.

4. Czechoslovakia

1235.   Bittman, Ladislav. *The Deception Game: Czechoslovak Intelligence in Soviet Political Warfare.* Syracuse, NY: Syracuse University Press, 1972. 246p.

1236.   Buzek, Antonin. "Diplomacy and Espionage." *Military Review,* XLIII (January 1963), 85–88.

1237.   FitzGibbon, Constantine. "Spies, Spies, Spies." *Encounter,* XLV (August 1975), 69–75.

1238.   "If We Sent a Spy, Here are Some to Be Sent: Red Agents From Czechoslovakia, Too." *U.S. News and World Report,* XLVIII (May 23, 1960), 58–59.

1239.   Noyes, Arthur. "They Bite Our Helping Hand: Refugees From Red Czechoslovakia." *Saturday Evening Post,* CCXXV (July 12, 1952), 32–33+.

5. France

1240.   "Lo, the Poor Spy: The Financial Aspirations of French Spies." *Newsweek,* LXVI (September 27, 1965), 50–51.

1241.   Stead, Philip J. *Second Bureau.* London: Evans, 1959. 212p.

6. Germany

1242.   "Not So Secret Service." *German International,* XV (April 1971), 23–26.

7. Great Britain

1243.   Andrew, Christopher. "Whitehall, Washington, and the Intelligence Services." *International Affairs* (London), LIII (July 1977), 390–404.

1244.   Bullock, John. *MI 5: The Origin and History of the British Counterespionage Service.* London: Barker, 1963. 206p.

1245.   Busch, Tristan, pseud. *See* Schuetz, Arthur (1264).

1246.   Chernyavskiy, V. "Espionage, the Tories' Ace in the Hole." *New Times* (Moscow), no. 42 (October 1971), 29–30.

1247.   Courtiour, Roger, jt. author. *See* Stuart-Pemrose, Barrie (1267).

1248.   Deacon, Richard, pseud. *See* McCormick, Donald (1257).

1249.   Grunbaum, W. F. "The British Security Program, 1948–1958." *Western Political Quarterly,* XIII (September 1960), 764–779.

1250.   Haswell, Chetwynd J. D. *British Military Intelligence.* London: Weidenfeld and Nicholson, 1973. 262p.

1251.   Holland, Mary. "Special Branch's Specialty." *New Statesman and Nation,* LXXXIX (April 26, 1974), 568–569.

1252.   Hovarth, Patrick, ed. *Special Operations.* London: Routledge, 1955. 239p.

1253.   Kitson, Frank. *Low-Intensity Operations: Subversion, Insurgency, Peace-Keeping.* Hamden, CT: Archon Books, 1974. 208p.

1254.   Lejeune, Anthony. "MI5 Charged With Bugging 10 Downing Street." *Human Events,* XXXVII (September 17, 1977), 7.

1255.   Lewis, David. "On Her Majesty's Sexual Service." *Penthouse,* VII (March 1976), 55+.

1256.   Lockhart, John B. "The Relationship Between Secret Services and Government in a Modern State." *Journal of the Royal United Service Institution for Defence Studies,* CXIX (June 1974), 3–8.

1257.   McCormick, Donald. *A History of the British Secret Service.* By Richard Deacon, pseud. New York: Taplinger, 1970. 440p.

1258.   McLachlan, Donald. "Will Europe Unite Its Intelligence?" *Round Table,* LIX (October 1969), 357–359+.

1259.   Muggeridge, Malcolm. "Public Thoughts on a Secret Service." *New Statesman and Nation,* LXII (August 25, 1961), 238–240.

1260.   Nicolson, Harold. "East Chair: Intelligence Services, Their Use and Misuse." *Harper's,* CCXV (November 1957), 12+.

1261.   Ransom, Harry H. "The British Intelligence System." In: *The Intelligence Establishment.* Cambridge, MA: Harvard University Press, 1970. pp. 180–207.

1262.   _____ . "Great Britain's Secret Secret Service." *Midway,* VIII (June 1967), 19–35.

1263.   Ross, Thomas B., jt. author. *See* Wise, David (1270).

1264. Schuetz, Arthur. *Secret Service Unmasked.* By Tristan Busch, pseud. Translated from the German. London: Hutchinson, 1950. 272p.

1265. Scotland, Alexander P. *London Cage.* London: Evans, 1957. 203p.

1266. Smith, Adrian. "*New Statesman* Editor in Pay of British Security Services." *New Statesman and Nation*, XCVI (December 22–29, 1978), 861–862.

1267. Stuart-Pemrose, Barrie and Roger Courtiour. *The Pencourt File.* New York: Harper & Row, 1978. 423p.

1268. "Under the Table: British Security Procedures." *Time*, LXXXV (May 21, 1965), 38–39.

1269. Whitwell, John, pseud. *British Agent.* London: Kimber, 1966. 224p.

1269a. Williams, David. *Not in the Public Interest.* London: Hutchison, 1965.

1270. Wise, David and Thomas B. Ross. "Great Britain." In: *The Espionage Establishment.* New York: Random House, 1967. pp. 78–131.

8. Hungary

1271. United States. Congress. House. Committee on Armed Services. Special Subcommittee on the Central Intelligence Agency. *Statement of Laszio Szabo: Hearings.* 89th Cong., 2nd sess. Washington, D.C.: GPO, 1966. 46p.

9. Iran

1272. Baraheni, Reza. "The Shah's Executioner." *Index on Censorship*, V (Spring 1976), 13–20.

1273. _____ . "Terror in Iran." *New York Review of Books*, XXIII (October 28, 1976), 21–25.

1274. CBS News. "SAVAK [Sazemane Etelaat va Aminiate Kechvar]." Transcript of "60 Minutes," IX, no. 24 (March 6, 1977).

1275. Rose, G. F. "The Shah's Secret Police are Here: SAVAK Agents." *New York Magazine*, XI (September 18, 1978), 45–51.

1276. "SAVAK: 'Like the CIA.' " *Time*, CXIII (February 19, 1979), 32.

1277. "The Shah's Secret Police." *Atlas*, XXIV (January 1977), 18+.

1278.   Shearer, Lloyd. "The Shah and SAVAK." *Parade,* (March 11, 1979), 24.

1279.   "Torture as Policy: The Network of Evil." *Time,* CX (August 16, 1976), 31–34.

10. Israel

1280.   Ben-Porath, Y. "The Secret Warriors." *Israel Magazine,* (January 1973), 37–42.

1281.   Brecker, Michael. *Decisions in Israel's Foreign Policy.* New Haven, CT: Yale University Press, 1975. 639p.

1282.   Broder, Jonathan D. "The War of the Innocents." *Oui,* IV (August 1975), 54+.

1283.   Bushinsky, Jay. "Spies and Spooks." *Present Tense,* IV (Spring 1977), 21–24.

1284.   Christensen, Dag, jt. author. *See* Tinnin, David B. (1313).

1285.   Cookridge, E. H., pseud. *See* Spiro, Edward (1309).

1286.   Dan, Uri, jt. author. *See* Eisenberg, Dennis (1291).

1287.   _____ , jt. author. *See* Zion, Sidney (1315).

1288.   Deacon, Richard, pseud. *See* McCormick, Donald (1303).

1289.   Dehel, Efraim. *Shai: The Exploits of Hagana Intelligence.* New York: Yoselof, 1959. 369p.

1290.   Eisenberg, Dennis. *Operation Uranium Ship: A True Story.* New York: New American Library, 1978.

1291.   _____ , Uri Dan, and Eli Landau. *The Mossad—Inside Stories: Israel's Secret Intelligence Service.* New York: Paddington Press, 1978. 272p.

1292.   Fialka, John J. "How Israel Got the Bomb: The Question of Missing Uranium From the Nuclear Materials and Equipment Corporation." *Washington Monthly,* X (January 1979), 50–58.

1293.   Golan, Aviezer. *Operation Susannah.* Translated from the Hebrew. New York: Harper & Row, 1978. 283p.

1294.   Hacohen, David. "Smuggling Arms For the Haganah." *Jerusalem Quarterly,* XXX (Fall 1978), 55–63.

1295.   Hareven, Adolph. "Disturbed Hierarchy: Israeli Intelligence in 1954 and 1973." *Jerusalem Quarterly,* XXX (Fall 1978), 3–19.

1296.   Heiman, Leo. "All's Fair." *Marine Corps Gazette*, XLVIII (June 1964), 37–40.

1297.   _____ . "Israeli Military Intelligence." *Military Review*, XLIII (January 1963), 79–84.

1298.   Hotz, Robert. "Classic Example: The Failure of Israeli Intelligence." *Aviation Week and Space Technology*, CII (March 31, 1975), 7+.

1299.   "Institute Strikes Again: The Work of the Mossad." *Time*, CVI (July 14, 1975), 31–32.

1300.   Jacobs, Paul. "Israel's Early-Warning System in the Arab World." *New York Times Magazine*, (February 8, 1970), 23–25+.

1301.   Kohn, Howard and Barbara Newman. "How Israel Got the Nuclear Bomb." *Rolling Stone*, CCLIII (December 1, 1977), 38–40.

1302.   Landau, Eli, jt. author. *See* Eisenberg, Dennis (1291).

1303.   McCormick, Donald. *The Israeli Secret Service*. By Richard Deacon, pseud. New York: Taplinger, 1978. 318p.

1304.   Millar, Lauritz. *Operation Godiva*. Rutland, VT: Tuttle, 1971. 221p.

1305.   "New Ghosts: Shin Bet's Secret Deal With Moslem Morocco." *Newsweek*, LXIX (March 6, 1967), 49.

1306.   Newman, Barbara, jt. author. *See* Kohn, Howard (1301).

1307.   O'Ballance, Edgar. "Israeli Counter-Guerrilla Measures." *Journal of the Royal United Service Institution for Defence Studies*, CXVII (March 1972), 47–52.

1308.   Slater, Leonard. *The Pledge*. New York: Simon and Schuster, 1970. 350p.

1309.   Spiro, Edward. "The Middle East's Master Spies: Israeli Agents Star in a Deadly Web of Intrigue." By E. H. Cookridge, pseud. *Atlas*, XXIII (October 1976), 9–13.

1310.   Stevenson, William. *Zanek: A Chronicle of the Israeli Air Force*. New York: Viking Press, 1971. 344p.

1311.   Tadmor, Joshua. *The Silent Warriors*. Translated from the Hebrew. New York: Macmillan, 1969. 189p.

1312.   Tinnin, David B. "The Wrath of God." *Playboy*, XXIII (August 1976), 71+.

1313. _____ and Dag Christensen. *The Hit Team.* New York: Dell, 1977. 240p.

1314. "Uranium: Israel's Connection." *Time,* CIX (May 30, 1977), 32–34.

1315. Zion, Sidney and Uri Dan. "The Untold Story of the Mideast Talks." *New York Times Magazine,* (January 21, 1979), 20–22, 46–53.

11. Japan

1316. Seth, Ronald. *Secret Servants: A History of Japanese Espionage.* New York: Farrar, Straus, 1957. 278p. Reprint 1978.

12. Korea

1317. Marks, John D. "From Korea With Love." *Washington Monthly,* V (February 1974), 55–61.

1318. "Spooks on the Namsan: The Korean Central Intelligence Agency." *Newsweek,* LXXXII (October 22, 1973), 96.

1319. Szulc, Tad. "Inside South Korea's CIA." *New York Times Magazine,* (March 6, 1977), 41–42+.

13. Poland

1320. "Mr. X," pseud., with Bruce E. Henderson. *Double Eagle: The Autobiography of a Polish Spy Who Defected to the West.* Indianapolis, IN: Bobbs-Merrill, 1979. 227p.

1321. United States. Congress. House. Committee on Un-American Activities. *Testimony of Wladyslaw Tykocinski: Hearings.* 89th Cong, 2nd sess. Washington, D.C.: GPO, 1966. 58p.

1322. _____ . _____ . Senate. Committee on the Judiciary. Sub-committee to Investigate the Administration of the Internal Security Act and Other Internal Security Laws. *Soviet Espionage Through Poland: Hearings, and Testimony of Pawel Monat.* 86th Cong., 2nd sess. Washington, D.C.: GPO, 1960. 41p.

14. South Africa

1323. "The View From BOSS." *Newsweek,* LXXXVIII (October 25, 1976), 53–54.

15. USSR

1324. Alexinsky, Gregoire. "The Evolution of a Police State." *Military Review,* XLII (April 1962), 79–85.

1325.   Artemiev, Vyacheslav. "OKR: State Security in the Soviet Armed Forces." *Military Review,* XLIII (September 1963), 21–31.

1326.   Bailey, Geoffrey. *The Conspirators.* New York: Harper, 1960. 306p.

1327.   Barron, John. "Espionage, the Dark Side of Detente: KGB Agents." *Reader's Digest,* CXII (January 1978), 78–82.

1328.   _____ . The GRU: Soviet Military Intelligence." In: *KGB: The Secret Work of Soviet Secret Agents.* New York: Reader's Digest Press; dist. by E. P. Dutton, 1973. pp. 343–345.

1329.   _____ . "The KGB." *Reader's Digest,* XCVII (August 1970), 201–215+.

1330.   _____ . *KGB: The Secret Work of Soviet Secret Agents.* New York: Reader's Digest Press; dist. by E. P. Dutton, 1973. 462p.

1331.   _____ . "The Plot to Steal a Fighter Plane." *Reader's Digest,* XCVIII (February 1971), 69–74.

1332.   _____ . "The Schooling of a Soviet Spy." *Reader's Digest,* XCVI (April–May 1970), 225–228+, 217–222+.

1333.   Barry, Donald D. and Carol B. *Contemporary Soviet Politics: An Introduction.* Englewood Cliffs, NJ: Prentice-Hall, 1978. 406p.

1334.   Benjamin, M. R. "Inside the KGB." *Newsweek,* LXXXIX (June 27, 1977), 16.

1335.   "Beyond Britain: What Red Spies are Doing All Over the World." *U.S. News and World Report,* LXXI (October 11, 1971), 25–26.

1336.   Conquest, Robert. *Power and Policy in the U.S.S.R.: The Study of Soviet Dynastics.* New York: St. Martin's Press, 1961. 485p.

1337.   _____ . "Russia's KGB Continues on an Absolutely Enormous Scale: An Interview." *U.S. News and World Report,* LXXVIII (February 24, 1975), 44–46.

1338.   _____ . *The Soviet Police System.* New York: Praeger, 1968. 103p.

1339.   Cookridge, E. H., pseud. *See* Spiro, Edward (1404).

1340.   Cowherd, Raymond G. "Waging the Cold War: An Analysis of Russia's Techniques." *Current History,* XV (December 1948), 334–347.

1341.   Crankshaw, Edward. "Big Brother is Still Watching." *New York Times Magazine,* (December 29, 1963), 8+.

1342.   Crozier, Brian. "New Light on Soviet Subversion." *Soviet Analyst*, III (April 11, 1974), 1–3.

1343.   Dallin, David J. *Soviet Espionage.* New Haven, CT: Yale University Press, 1956. 558p.

1344.   Deacon, Richard, pseud. *See* McCormick, Donald (1377).

1345.   Deriabin, Petr S. *Watchdogs of Terror: Russian Bodyguards From the Tsars to the Commissars.* New Rochelle, NY: Arlington House, 1972. 448p.

1346.   _____ , and Frank Gilney. "Kremlin Intrigue and Debauchery." *Life*, XLVI (March 30, 1959), 80–85+.

1347.   "Despite Detente, Soviet Spying is on the Increase Around the World." *U.S. News and World Report*, LXXXIII (October 17, 1973), 89–91.

1348.   DeWar, Hugo. *Assassins at Large.* London: Wingate, 1951. 203p.

1349.   _____ . "Spies Unlimited." *Problems of Communism*, XV (July 1966), 54–57.

1350.   Dulles, Allen W. "The Secret Challenge." *Department of State Bulletin*, XXXVIII (March 8, 1958), 338–343.

1351.   Evans, Medford. "Conspiracy: The New World Order Isn't New." *American Opinion*, XVII (December 1974), 47–52+.

1352.   Garthoff, Raymond L. "Prediction, Intelligence, and Reconnaissance." In: *Soviet Military Doctrine.* Glencoe, IL: Free Press, 1953. pp. 265–277.

1353.   _____ . "The Soviet Intelligence Services." In: Basil H. Liddell-Hart, ed. *The Red Army.* New York: Harcourt, Brace, 1956. pp. 265–274.

1354.   Gess, K. N. "Timetable For Spies." *U.N. World*, V (July 1951), 17–20.

1355.   Gilney, Frank, jt. author. *See* Deriabin, Petr S. (1346).

1356.   Gottlieb, Jeff. "The KGB." In: David Wallechinsky and Irving Wallace. *The People's Almanac 2.* New York: Morrow, 1978. pp. 1312–1314.

1357.   Guillaume, Augustin L. *Soviet Arms and Soviet Power: The Secrets of Russia's Might.* Washington, D.C.: Infantry Journal Press, 1949. 212p.

1358.   Heilbrunn, Otto. *The Soviet Secret Services.* New York: Praeger, 1956. 216p.

1359.   Hingley, Ronald. "The KGB." In: *The Russian Secret Police: Muscovite, Imperial Russian and Soviet Political Security Operations, 1565–1970.* London: Hutchinson, 1970. pp. 224–264.

1360.   Hirsch, Richard. *The Soviet Spies.* New York: Duell, 1947.

1361.   "How Russia Spies: A New Game, the KGB Network." *Newsweek,* LXXVIII (October 11, 1971), 31–32+.

1362.   Hutton, Joseph B. *School For Spies: The ABC's of How Russia's Secret Service Operates.* New York: Coward-McCann, 1962. 222p.

1363.   _____. *Struggle in the Dark: How Russian and Other Iron Curtain Spies Operate.* London: Harrap, 1969. 208p.

1364.   Israels, Josef, 2nd, jt author. *See* Timakhov, Nicholas (1407).

1365.   Jelagin, Juri, "New Year's Eve in the Kremlin: NKVD." *New Yorker,* XXIV (October 9, 1948), 113–116+.

1366.   Jones, C. A. "The World's Most Professional Machine: The Soviet Intelligence Network." *Military Review,* LIV (February 1974), 74–81.

1367.   "The KGB: Russia's Old Boychiks." *Time,* CXI (February 6, 1978), 25–26.

1368.   Khokhlov, Nicholas E. "Cold-Blooded Murder is Part of Russia's Cold War in the West: Testimony Before the Senate Internal Security Committee." *American Mercury,* LXXIX (September 1974), 144–157.

1369.   Kirkpatrick, Lyman B., Jr. *Russian Espionage: Communist and Imperialist.* New York: National Strategy Information Center, 1970.

1370.   _____, and Howland H. Sargeant. *Soviet Political Warfare Techniques: Espionage and Propaganda in the 1970's.* Strategy paper, no. 11. New York: National Strategy Information Center, 1972. 82p.

1371.   Krammer, Arnold P. "Russian Counterfeit Dollars: A Case of Early Soviet Espionage." *Slavic Review,* XXX (1971), 762–773.

1372.   Lee, Asher. "Soviet Intelligence Problems." In: James L. Moulton, ed. *Brassey's Annual: The Armed Forces Yearbook.* New York: Praeger, 1966. pp. 167–174.

1373.   Levytsky, Boris. "The KGB." In: *The Soviet Secret Police, 1917–1970.* New York: Coward, McCann, 1972. pp. 130–155, 227–276.

1374.   Lewis, Anthony M. "The Blind Spot of U.S. Foreign Intelligence." *Communication Quarterly,* XXVI (Winter 1976), 44–55.

1375.   Lewis, David. "The [KGB] Assault on NATO." *Penthouse,* VII (February 1976), 5+.

1376.   _____ . *Sexpionage: The Exploitation of Sex by Soviet Intelligence.* New York: Harcourt, Brace, 1976. 174p.

1377.   McCormick, Donald. *A History of the Russian Secret Service.* By Richard Deacon, pseud. New York: Taplinger, 1972. 568p.

1378.   Matthews, Mervyn. *Privilege in the Soviet Union: A Study of Elite Life-Styles Under Communism.* London: Allen and Unwin, 1978. 192p.

1379.   Metzel, Lothar. "Reflections on the Soviet Police and Intelligence Services." *Orbis,* XVIII (Fall 1974), 917–930.

1380.   Moore, Barrington, Jr. *Terror and Progress in the U.S.S.R.: Some Sources of Change and Stability in the Soviet Dictatorship.* Cambridge, MA: Harvard University Press, 1954. 261p.

1381.   National Strategy Committee. "The Goals of the KGB." In: *Peace and Freedom Through Cold War History.* Chicago: American Security Council Press, 1964. pp. 115–119.

1382.   Noel-Baker, Francis E. *Spy Web.* New York: Vanguard, 1955. 242p.

1383.   Nolin, Simon. "The KGB." In: *The Soviet Secret Police.* New York: Praeger, 1957. pp. 28–29, 60–61, 152–154, 158–172.

1384.   Orlov, Alexander. *Handbook of Intelligence and Guerrilla Warfare.* Translated from the Russian. Ann Arbor: University of Michigan Press, 1963. 187p.

1385.   "The Other Side of the Story—What the Red's are Doing: Methods of the KGB." *U.S. News and World Report,* LXII (March 13, 1967), 96–98.

1386.   RAND Corporation, Social Sciences Division. *Soviet Military Intelligence: Comments on the Book "Handbook for Spies."* RAND Memorandum RM-207a. Santa Monica, CA, 1949. 30p.

Alexander Foote's title is cited in Vol. I of this series, no. 2175.

1387.   Reddaway, Peter. "The Relentless KGB." *New York Review of Books,* XXIII (February 5, 1976), 18.

1388.   Reitz, James T. *Soviet Defense: Associated Activities Outside the Ministry of Defense.* McLean, VA: Research Analysis Corp., 1969.

1389.   Reshetar, John S., Jr. *The Soviety Polity: Government and Politics in the U.S.S.R.* 2nd ed. New York: Harper & Row, 1978. 413p.

1390. Rositzke, Harry. "The KGB's Broadening Horizons." *Problems of Communism,* XXIV (May 1975), 43–45.

1391. Ross, Thomas B., jt. author. *See* Wise, David (1421).

1392. Sargeant, Howland H., jt. author. *See* Kirkpatrick, Lyman B., Jr.

1393. Set, Alan. "Top Secret: The Red Police." *American Mercury,* LXXIX (October 1954), 81–86.

1394. Seth, Ronald O. *The Executioners: The Story of SMERSH.* New York: Hawthorn Books, 1967. 199p.

1395. _____. *Unmasked: The Story of Soviet Espionage.* New York: Hawthorn Books, 1965. 306p.

1396. Sinevirskii, Nikolai. *SMERSH.* Translated from the Russian. New York: Holt, 1950. 253p.

1397. Slusser, Robert M., jt author. *See* Wolin, Simon (1422).

1398. Smith, Edward E. *The Okhrana: The Russian Department of Police.* Stanford, CA: Hoover Institution of War and Peace, 1967. 280p.

1399 Smith, Truman. "The Infamous Record of Soviet Espionage." *Reader's Digest,* LXXVII (August 1960), 36–42.

1400. Smith, W. B. "Why the Russian People Don't Rebel." *Saturday Evening Post,* CCXXII (November 26, 1949), 22–23+.

1401. Sorokin, V. "Activities Aboard a [KGB-Controlled] Border Patrol Ship: Reprinted from *Sovetskiy Patriot,* November 7, 1978." *Translations of U.S.S.R. Military Affairs,* no. 1404 (December 21, 1978), 24–27.

1402. *Soviet Spies in the Scientific and Technical Fields.* Wavre, Belgium: Ligue de la Liberté, 1968.

1403. *Soviet Spies in the Shadow of the U.N.* Wavre, Belgium: Ligue de la Liberté, 1968.

1404. Spiro, Edward. "How the Soviet Spy Network Covers the World." By E. H. Cookridge, pseud. *U.S. News and World Report,* XXXIX (August 19, 1955), 114–155.

1405. _____. *Net That Covers the World.* By E. H. Cookridge, pseud. New York: Holt, 1955. 315p.

1406. Taylor, Henry J. "Columnist Recalls Soviet Intrigues— Espionage is a Tricky Business: Reprinted from the *Columbia* (SC) *State,* September 26, 1967." *Congressional Record,* CXIII (September 27, 1967), 27050–27051.

1407.   Timakhov, Nicholas and Josef Israels, 2nd. "How Russia Uses White Slaves as Red Spies." *Coronet,* XXVI (May 1949), 44–50.

1408.   Tsinev, G. "Military Counterintelligence History Reviewed: Reprinted from *Kommunist Vooruzhennyke Sil,* December 1978." *Translations of U.S.S.R. Military Affairs,* no. 1421 (March 20, 1979), 1–9.

1409.   Ulsamer, Edgar. "The Soviet [Intelligence] Juggernaut: Racing Faster Than Ever." *Air Force Magazine,* LIX (March 1976), 56–58+.

1410.   United States. Central Intelligence Agency. "International Communist Front Organizations." In : U.S. Congress. House. Permanent Select Committee on Intelligence. *The CIA and the Media: Hearings.* 95th Cong., 1st and 2nd sess. Washington, D.C.: GPO, 1978. pp. 560–625.

1411.   _____ . Congress. House. Committee on Un-American Activities. *The Kremlin's Espionage and Terror Organizations: Hearings, With the Testimony of Petr S. Deriabin, Former Officer of the U.S.S.R.'s Committee of State Security (KGB).* 86th Cong., 1st sess. Washington, D.C.: GPO, 1959. 16p.

1412.   _____ . _____ . _____ . _____ . *Patterns of Communist Espionage: Report.* 85th Cong., 2nd sess. Washington, D.C.: GPO, 1958. 81p.

1413.   _____ . _____ . _____ . _____ . *The Soviet Union, From Lenin to Khrushchev.* Vol. II of *Facts on Communism: A Staff Study.* 87th Cong., 1st sess. Washington, D.C.: GPO, 1961. 367p.

1414.   _____ . _____ . Senate. Committee on the Judiciary. Subcommittee to Investigate the Administration of the Internal Security Act and Other Internal Security Laws. *Murder International, Inc.— Murder and Kidnapping as an Instrument of Soviet Policy: Hearings.* 89th Cong., 1st sess. Washington, D.C.: GPO, 1965. 176p.

1415.   Van Cleave, William R. and Seymour Weiss. "National Intelligence and the U.S.S.R." *National Review,* XXX (June 23, 1978), 777–780.

1416.   Walker, Gordon W. "Russia's Busiest Spy Nest." *Collier's,* CXXVI (December 2, 1950), 18–19+.

1417.   Weiss, Seymour, jt. author. *See* Van Cleave, William R. (1415).

1418.   Wesson, Robert G. *Communism and Communist Systems.* Englewood Cliffs, NJ: Prentice-Hall, 1978. 227p.

1419.   White, John B. *Pattern of Conquest.* London: Hale, 1956. 223p.

1420.   Willenson, Kenneth. "Terror International." *Newsweek,* XCI (May 22, 1978), 36–37.

1421. Wise, David and Thomas B. Ross. "The Soviet Union." In: *The Intelligence Establishment.* New York: Random House, 1967. pp. 7–77.

1422. Wolin, Simon and Robert M. Slusser, eds. *The Soviet Secret Police.* New York: Praeger, 1957. 408p.

16. United States

a. The American Intelligence Community—General Works

1423. Agee, Philip. "The American Security Services: Where Do We Go From Here?" *Journal of Contemporary Asia,* VII (Spring 1977), 251–259.

1424. Allison, Graham T., jt. author. *See* Szanton, Peter (1463).

1425. Baldwin, Hanson W. "The Future of Intelligence." *Strategic Review,* IV (Summer 1976), 6–24.

1426. ———. "The Growing Risks of Bureaucratic Intelligence." *Reporter,* XXIX (August 15, 1963), 48–50, 53.

1427. ———. *The Price of Power.* New York: Harper, 1948. 361p.

1428. Bauer, Theodore W., jt. author. *See* Falk, Stanley L. (1441).

1429. Bird, Robert S., jt. author. *See* Reid, Ogden R. (1456).

1430. Blackstock, Paul W. *CIA and the Intelligence Community: Their Roles, Organization, and Functions.* St. Louis, MO: Forum Press, 1974. 14p.

1431. ———. "The Intelligence Community Under the Nixon Administration." *Armed Forces and Society,* I (February 1975), 231–250.

1432. "Blueprint For a Super-Secret Police: FBI, CIA, DIA, and NSA." *Newsweek,* LXXXI (June 4, 1973), 18–19.

1433. Borosage, Robert L. "Para-Legal Authority and Its Perils." *Law and Contemporary Problems,* XL (Summer 1976), 168–188.

1434. Branyan, Robert L. and Lawrence H. Larsen. "The Intelligence Community." In: *The Eisenhower Administration, 1953–1961: A Documentary History.* New York: Random House, 1971. pp. 1208–1280.

1435. Chase, Michael T. "All-Source Intelligence: A New Name For an Old Thoroughbred." *Military Review,* LVI (July 1976), 43–49.

1436. "CIA: Only a Part of the Big U.S. Intelligence Network." *U.S. News and World Report,* LXII (March 6, 1967), 29+.

1437. Corson, William R. *The Armies of Ignorance: The Rise of the American Intelligence Empire.* New York: Dial Press, 1977. 640p.

1438.   Dawson, Raymond H., jt. author. *See* Scott, Andrew M. (1460).

1439.   Fain, Tyrus G., comp. *The Intelligence Community: History, Organization, and Issues.* New York: R. R. Bowker, 1977. 1,036p.

1440.   Falk, Stanley L. "The Intelligence Community." In: *The National Security Structure.* Washington, D.C.: Industrial College of the Armed Forces, 1967. pp. 97–115.

1441.   _____ and Theodore W. Bauer. "The Intelligence Community." In: *The National Security Structure.* Rev. ed. Washington, D.C.: Industrial College of the Armed Forces, 1972. pp. 115–136.

1442.   Halperin, Morton H., *et al. The Lawless State: The Crimes of the U.S. Intelligence Agencies.* London: Penguin Books, 1976. 328p.

1443.   Kirkpatrick, Lyman B., Jr. "Is United States Intelligence Answering the Red Challenge?: An Address, November 21, 1960, With Questions and Answers." *Vital Speeches,* XXVII (January 15, 1961), 206–210.

1444.   _____ . *The U.S. Intelligence Community: Foreign Policy and Domestic Activities.* New York: Hill and Wang, 1973. 212p.

1445.   Larsen, Lawrence H., jt. author. *See* Branyan, Robert L. (1434).

1446.   Larson, Janet K. "The Shadow Knows: The CIA and Other U.S. Intelligence Agencies." *Christian Century,* XCIII (March 10, 1976), 211–213.

1447.   MacCloskey, Monro. *The American Intelligence Community.* New York: R. Rosen Press, 1967. 190p.

1448.   McGarvey, Patrick J. "Of Spooks and Spies and Cloaks and Daggers: The U.S. Intelligence Community." *Government Executive,* III (August 1970), 19+.

1449.   Marks, John D. "How to Spot a Spook." *Washington Monthly,* VI (November 1974), 5–11.

1450.   "The Organization and Functions of the Intelligence Community." *Department of State Bulletin,* LXXVII (September 5, 1977), 306–308.

1451.   Possony, Stefan T. "U.S. Intelligence at the Crossroads." *Orbis,* IX (Fall 1965), 587–612.

1452.   Prouty, L. Fletcher. "The Secret Team and the Games They Play." *Washington Monthly,* II (May 1970), 11–19.

1453. _____ . *The Secret Team: The CIA and Its Allies in Control of the United States and the World.* Englewood Cliffs, NJ: Prentice-Hall, 1973. 496p.

1454. Ransom, Harry H. *Can American Democracy Survive Cold War?* Garden City, NY: Doubleday, 1963. 262p.

1455. _____ . *The Intelligence Establishment.* Rev. ed. Cambridge, MA: Harvard University Press, 1970. 309p.

1456. Reid, Ogden R. and Robert S. Bird. "Are We Inviting Disaster: Reprinted From the *Hartford Courant,* August 2, 1950." *Congressional Record Appendix,* (August 8, 1950), A 5623–A 5624.

1457. Rosenberg, Bernard. "CIA, DIA, FBI, and 50 More!" *Dissent,* XXII (Fall 1975), 311–315.

1458. Ross, Thomas B., jt. author. *See* Wise, David (1469).

1459. Schemmer, Benjamin F. "The Slow Murder of the American Intelligence Community." *Armed Forces Journal International,* CXVI (March 1979), 50–54.

1460. Scott, Andrew M. and Raymond H. Dawson. "The Intelligence Community." In: *Readings in the Making of American Foreign Policy.* New York: Macmillan, 1965. pp. 431–467.

1461. Sitton, Ray B. "The Intelligence Community: An Address." *Vital Speeches,* XLII (December 1, 1975), 125–128.

1462. Stephens, Thomas W. "Bureaucracy, Intelligence, and Technology: A Reappraisal." *World Affairs,* CXXXIX (Winter 1977), 231–243.

1463. Szanton, Peter and Graham Allison. "Intelligence: Seizing the Opportunity." *Foreign Policy,* XXII (Spring 1976), 183–214.

1464. Theoharis, Athan G. "Public or Private Papers?: The Arrogance of the Intelligence Community." *Intellect,* CVI (October 1977), 118–120.

1465. "U.S. Intelligence: Is It Good Enough?" *U.S. News and World Report,* LV (September 9, 1963), 66–67.

1466. United States. Congress. House. Select Committee on Intelligence. *The Performance of the Intelligence Community: Hearings.* 94th Cong., 1st sess. Washington, D.C.: GPO, 1975. 306p.

1467. _____ . _____ . Senate. Select Committee to Study Government Operations With Respect to Intelligence Activities. *Supplementary Reports on Intelligence Activities.* 94th Cong., 2nd sess. Washington, D.C.: GPO, 1976. 368p.

A history of the intelligence community.

1468. Vladimirov, Ye. "Spotlight on the U.S. Intelligence Services." *U.S.A.: Economics, Politics, Ideology* (Moscow), no. 2 (February 1971), 84–88.

1469. Wise, David and Thomas B. Ross. *The Invisible Government.* New York: Random House, 1964. 375p.

1470. _____ . "The U.S.A." In: *The Intelligence Establishment.* New York: Random House, 1967. pp. 132–175.

1471. Wittman, George, ed. *The Role of American Intelligence Organizations.* Reference Shelf, v. 48, no. 5. New York: H. W. Wilson, 1976. 160p.

1472. Zlotnick, Jack. *National Intelligence.* Rev. ed. Washington, D.C.: Industrial College of the Armed Forces, 1964. 75p.

b. Economic/Political/Military Estimates and the Role of Intelligence in U.S. Foreign Policy—General Works

1473. Ambrose, Stephen E. *The Rise to Globalism: American Foreign Policy, 1938–1976. Pelican History of the United States,* v. 8. Rev. ed. New York: Pelican Books, 1976. 390p.

1474. Ashman, Harold L. "Intelligence and Foreign Policy: A Functional Analysis." Unpublished PhD Dissertation, University of Utah, 1973.

1475. Babcock, James H. "Intelligence and National Security." *Signal,* XXXIII (November–December 1978), 16–18+.

1476. Barnds, William J. "Intelligence and Foreign Policy: Dilemmas of a Democracy." *Foreign Affairs,* XLVII (January 1969), 281–295.

1477. Belden, Thomas G. "Indications, Warnings, and Crisis Operations." *International Studies Quarterly,* XXI (March 1977), 181–198.

1478. Berkowitz, Morton, *et al. The Politics of American Foreign Policy: The Social Context of Decisions.* Englewood Cliffs, NJ: Prentice-Hall, 1977. 310p.

1479. Betts, Richard K. "Analysis, War, and Decision: Why Intelligence Failures are Inevitable." *World Politics,* XXXI (October 1978), 61–90.

1480. Birnbaum, Norman. "The Failure of Intelligence." *Nation,* CCXXVIII (January 20, 1979), 40–43.

1481. Black, Robert B., jt. author. *See* Esterline, John H. (1502).

1482. Blackman, Morris J. "The Stupidity of Intelligence." In: Morton Halperin and Arnold Kanter, eds. *Readings in American Foreign Policy.* Boston: Little, Brown, 1973. pp. 328–334.

1483. Bobrow, Davis B. "Analysis and Foreign Policy Choice." *Policy Sciences,* IV (1975), 437–451.

1484. Brownlow, Cecil. "CIA Threat-Juggling Confirmed." *Aviation Week and Space Technology,* CIV (May 3, 1976), 14–15.

1485. Buncher, Judith F., ed. *The CIA and the Security Debate, 1975– 1976.* New York: Facts on File, Inc., 1977. 240p.

1486. Cabell, C. P. "What the CIA Has Learned About the Communist Threat: Reprinted from *U.S. News and World Report,* August 21, 1959." *Congressional Record,* CV (September 9, 1959), 18861–18863.

1487. Campbell, John F. "The Intelligence and Propaganda Complexes." In: *The Foreign Affairs Fudge Factory.* New York: Basic Books, 1971. pp. 147–171.

1488. "The CIA's Goof in Assessing the Soviets: The Agency Seriously Miscalculated How Defense Fits Into the Russian Economy." *Business Week,* (February 28, 1977), 96–98.

1489. Chan, Steve. "The Intelligence of Stupidity: Understanding Failures in Strategic Warning." *American Political Science Review,* LXXIII (March 1979), 171–180.

1490. Clark, K. C. and L. J. Legere, eds. *The President and the Management of National Security.* New York: Praeger, 1969. 274p.

1491. Cline, Ray S. "Policy Without Intelligence." *Foreign Policy,* XVII (Winter 1975), 121–135.

1492. Cox, Arthur M. "Making Better Global Guesses: Reprinted Fom the *Washington Post,* November 2, 1975." *Congressional Record,* CXXI (November 4, 1975), 35003–35004.

1493. Crangle, Robert D. "Spying, the CIA, and the New Technology." *Ripon Forum,* VI (February 1970), 7–14.

1494. Cutler, Robert. "The Development of the National Security Council." *Foreign Affairs,* XXXIV (April 1956), 441–458.

1495. Dale, Edwin L., Jr. "Soviet Has Trade Surplus With the West, CIA Reports: Reprinted From the *New York Times,* April 8, 1975." *Congressional Record,* CXXI (April 10, 1975), 9929.

1496. De Poix, Vincent P. "Security and Intelligence." *National Defense,* LIX (July–August 1974), 34–39.

1497. Destler, I. M. *Presidents, Bureaucrats, and Foreign Policy.* Princeton, NJ: Princeton University Press, 1974. 355p.

1498. Dulles, Allen W. "Intelligence Estimating and National Security: An Address, January 26, 1960." *Department of State Bulletin,* XLII (March 14, 1960), 411–417.

1499. _____ . _____ . *U.S. News and World Report,* XLVIII (February 8, 1960), 102–103.

1500. Enthoven, Alain C. and K. Wayne Smith. "What Forces For NATO? . . . And From Whom?" *Foreign Affairs,* XLVIII (October 1969), 80–89.

1501. Estace, Harry F. "Changing Intelligence Priorities." *Electronic Warfare/Defense Electronics,* X (November 1978), 35+.

1502. Esterline, John H. and Robert B. Black. "The Intelligence Community: An Advisory Role." In: *Inside Foreign Policy: The Department of State Political System and Its Subsystems.* Palo Alto, CA: Mayfield Publishing Co., 1975. pp. 33–38.

1503. Evans, Allan. "Intelligence and Policy Formation." *World Politics,* XII (October 1959), 84–91.

1504. Falk, Stanley M. "The National Security Council Under Truman, Eisenhower, and Kennedy." *Political Science Quarterly,* LXXIX (September 1964), 403–434.

1505. Freedman, Lawrence. *U.S. Intelligence and the Soviet Strategic Threat.* Boulder, CO: Westview Press, 1978. 235p.

1506. George, Alexander L. "The Case for Multiple Advocacy in the Making of Foreign Policy." *American Political Science Review,* LXVI (1972), 751–785.

1507. Graff, Henry F. *The Tuesday Cabinet: Deliberations and Decisions on Peace and War Under Lyndon B. Johnson.* Englewood Cliffs, NJ: Prentice-Hall, 1970. 200p.

1508. Groth, Alexander J. "On the Intelligence Aspects of Personal Diplomacy." *Orbis,* VII (Winter 1964), 833–848.

1509.   Hammond, P. Y. "The National Security Council as a Device For Interdepartmental Co-ordination: An Interpretation and Appraisal." *American Political Science Review*, LIV (1960), 899–910.

1510.   Hanson, Philip. "Estimating Soviet Defence Expenditure." *Soviet Studies*, XXX (July 1978), 403–410.

1511.   Hermann, Charles F. "International Crisis as a Situation Variable." In: James N. Rosenau, ed. *International Politics and Foreign Policy*. New York: Free Press, 1969. pp. 409–421.

1512.   Heuer, Richard J., Jr. *Quantitative Approaches to Political Intelligence: The CIA Approach*. Boulder, CO: Westview Press, 1978.

1513.   Hilsman, Roger. "Intelligence and Policy-Making in Foreign Affairs." *World Politics*, V (October 1952), 1–45.

1514.   _____. _____. In: Andrew M. Scott and Raymond H. Dawson, eds. *Readings in the Making of Foreign Policy*. New York: Macmillan, 1965. pp. 447–456.

1515.   _____. "The Intelligence Process." In: Andrew M. Scott and Raymond H. Dawson, eds. *Readings in the Making of Foreign Policy*. New York: Macmillan, 1965. pp. 456–466.

1516.   _____. "Intelligence Through the Eyes of the Policy-Maker." In: Richard H. Blum, ed. *Surveillance and Espionage in a Free Society*. New York: Praeger, 1972.

1517.   _____. *The Politics of Policy-Making in Defense and Foreign Affairs*. New York: Harper and Row, 1971. 198p.

1518.   _____. *Strategic Intelligence and National Decisions*. New York: Free Press, 1956. 187p.

1519.   _____. *To Govern America: Politics, Power, and Policy-Making*. New York: Harper and Row, 1978. 598p.

1520.   Hoeksema, Renze L. "The President's Role in Insuring Efficient, Economical, and Responsible Intelligence Services." *Presidential Studies Quarterly*, VIII (Spring 1978), 187–198.

1521.   Hook, Sidney. "Intelligence, Morality, and Foreign Policy." *Freedom at Issue*, no. 25 (March–April 1976), 3–7.

1522.   _____. "The Strategy of Political Warfare." In: *Political Power and Personal Freedom: Critical Studies in Democracy, Communism, and Civil Rights*. New York: Criterion Books, 1959. pp. 389–401.

1523.   Howard, John R. *Fourteen Decisions For Undeclared War*. Washington, D.C.: University Press of America, 1978. 165p.

1524.   Hughes, Thomas L. *The Fate of Facts in a World of Men: Foreign Policy and Intelligence-Making.* Headline Series, no. 233. New York: Foreign Policy Association, 1976. 62p.

1525.   Jackson, Henry M., ed. *The National Security Council: Jackson Subcommittee Papers on Policy-Making at the Presidential Level.* New York: Praeger, 1965. 311p.

1526.   Janis, Irving L. *Victims of Groupthink: A Psychological Study of Foreign Policy Decisions and Fiascos.* Boston: Houghton Mifflin, 1972. 277p.

1527.   Jervis, Robert. "Hypothesis on Misperception." In: Morton Halperin and Arnold Kanter, eds. *Readings in American Foreign Policy.* Boston: Little, Brown, 1971. pp. 113–138.

1528.   Johnson, Robert H. "The National Security Council: The Relevance of Its Past to Its Future." *Orbis,* XIII (Fall 1969), 709–735.

1529.   Kent, Sherman. "Estimates and Influence: Some Reflections on What Should Make Intelligence Persuasive in Policy Deliberations." *Foreign Service Journal,* (April 1969), 16–18, 45.

1530.   ———. *Strategic Intelligence For American World Power.* 3rd ed. Hamden, CT: Archon Books, 1965. 226p.

1531.   Lasswell, Harold D. "Policy and the Intelligence Function: Ideological Intelligence." In: *The Analysis of Political Behavior.* London: Routledge and Kegan Paul, 1951. pp. 55–68.

1532.   Lee, William T. *The Estimation of Soviet Defense Expenditures, 1955–1975: An Unconventional Approach.* New York: Praeger, 1977. 358p.

1533.   ———. *Understanding the Soviet Military Threat: How the CIA Estimates Went Astray.* New York: Published for the National Strategy Information Center, by Crane, Russak, 1977. 73p.

1534.   Legere, L. J., jt. editor. *See* Clark, K. C. (1490).

1535.   Millikan, Max F. "Inquiry and Policy: The Relationship of Knowledge to Action." In: Daniel Lerner, ed. *The Human Meaning of the Social Sciences.* New York: Meridian Press, 1959. pp. 158–180.

1536.   Moor, R. Carl, Jr. "Strategic Economic Intelligence: A Systems Approach." *Military Review,* LVI (October 1976), 47–51.

1537.   Nash, Henry T. "Intelligence and Foreign Policy." In: *American Foreign Policy: Response to a Sense of Threat.* Homewood, IL: Dorsey Press, 1973. pp. 130–152.

1538. Nathan, James A. and James K. Oliver. *United States Foreign Policy and World Order.* Boston, MA: Little, Brown, 1976. 598p.

1539. Navrozov, Lev. "What the CIA Knows About Russia, With Discussion." *Commentary,* LXVI (September, November 1978), 51–58, 4+.

1540. Nitze, Paul H. "National Policymaking Techniques." *SAIS Review,* III (Spring 1959), 3–8.

1541. Oliver, James K., jt. author. *See* Nathan, James A. (1538).

1542. Pearson, Drew. "Ike Angered By His CIA Chief: Reprinted From the *Washington Post,* February 8, 1960." *Congressional Record,* CVI (February 8, 1960), 2164–2165.

CIA and Soviet missile strength estimates.

1543. Pinkerton, Roy H. "The Role of Intelligence in Policy-Making." *Military Review,* XLVI (July 1966), 40–51.

1544. Platt, Washington. *National Character in Action: Intelligence Factors in Foreign Relations.* New Brunswick, NJ: Rutgers University Press, 1961. 250p.

1545. Poteat, George H. "The Intelligence Gap: Hypotheses on the Process of Surprise." *International Studies Notes,* III (Fall 1976), 15+.

1546. Quandt, William B. *Domestic Influences on U.S. Foreign Policy in the Middle East: The View From Washington.* RAND Paper P-4309. Santa Monica, CA: RAND Corporation, 1970.

1547. Radway, Laurence T. "The Intelligence Community." In: *Foreign Policy and National Defense.* Atlanta, GA: Scott, Foresman, and Co., 1969. pp. 69–74.

1548. Ransom, Harry H. "Strategic Intelligence and Foreign Policy." *World Politics,* XXVII (October 1974), 131–146.

1549. Sapin, Burton M. "Intelligence Planning and Policy Analysis." In: *The Making of United States Foreign Policy.* New York: Published for the Brookings Institution by Praeger, 1966. pp. 287–328.

1550. ———. "The Organization and Procedures of the National Security Mechanism." In: Bernard C. Cohen, ed. *Foreign Policy in American Government.* Boston: Little, Brown, 1965. pp. 89–110.

1551. Smith, K. Wayne, jt. author. *See* Enthoven, Alain C. (1500).

The following CIA-NFAC citations are selected to demonstrate the kinds of economic, political, and military intelligence which is gathered and analyzed.

1552.   United States. Central Intelligence Agency. National Foreign Assessment Center. *Atlas Issues in the Middle East.* Washington, D.C.: GPO, 1973. 40p.

1553. _____ . _____ . _____ . *Average Annual Money Earnings in Soviet Industry, 1940–1960.* Washington, D.C.: 1960. 11p.

1554. _____ . _____ . _____ . *Average Annual Money Earnings of Workers and Staff in Communist China, 1949–1960.* Washington, D.C.: 1960. 11p.

1555. _____ . _____ . _____ . *Average Annual Money Earnings of Wage-Workers in Soviet Industry, 1928–1961.* Washington, D.C.: 1963. 17p.

1556. _____ . _____ . _____ . *Biological and Environmental Factors Affecting Soviet Grain Quality.* Washington, D.C.: 1978.

1557. _____ . _____ . _____ . *The C.P.S.U. Under Brezhnev.* Research Aid. Washington, D.C.: 1976. 77p.

1558. _____ . _____ . _____ . *China: Agricultural Performance, 1975.* Washington, D.C.: 1976. 25p.

1559. _____ . _____ . _____ . *China: Economic Indicators.* Reference Aid. Washington, D.C.: 1977. 58p.

1560. _____ . _____ . _____ . *China: Gross Value of Industrial Output, 1965–1977.* A Research Paper. Washington, D.C.: 1978. 69p.

1561. _____ . _____ . _____ . *China: International Trade, 1976–1977.* A Research Paper. Washington, D.C.: 1977. 25p.

1562. _____ . _____ . _____ . *China: 1977 Midyear Grain Outlook.* Washington, D.C.: 1977. 9p.

1563. _____ . _____ . _____ . *China: The Coal Industry.* Research Aid. Washington, D.C.: 1976. 23p.

1564. _____ . _____ . _____ . *China's Economy.* A Research Paper. Washington, D.C.: 1977. 14p.

1565. _____ . _____ . _____ . *Communist Aid to the Less Developed Countries of the Free World, 1976.* Washington, D.C.: 1977. 37p.

1566. _____ . _____ . _____ . *A Comparison of Capital Investment in the U.S. and U.S.S.R., 1950–1959.* Washington, D.C.: 1961. 57p.

1567. _____ . _____ . _____ . *A Comparison of Consumption in the U.S.S.R. and U.S.* Washington, D.C.: 1964. 70p.

1568. _____ . _____ . _____ . _____ . *Supplement.* Washington, D.C.: 1964. 184p.

1569. _____ . _____ . _____ . *A Comparison of U.S. and Soviet Professional Manpower.* Washington, D.C.: 1963. 47p.

1570. _____ . _____ . _____ . "Communist Military and Economic Aid to North Vietnam, 1970–1974." *Congressional Record,* CXXI (March 7, 1975), 5767–5768.

1571. _____ . _____ . _____ . *The Cuban Economy: A Statistical View, 1968–1976.* Research Aid. Washington, D.C.: 1976. 17p.

1572. _____ . _____ . _____ . *Directory of Soviet Research Organizations.* Reference Aid. Washington, D.C.: 1976. 237p.

1573. _____ . _____ . _____ . _____ . Washington, D.C.: 1978. 290p.

1574. _____ . _____ . _____ . *Directory of U.S.S.R. Foreign Trade Organizations and Officials.* Reference Aid. Washington, D.C.: 1974. 74p.

1575. _____ . _____ . _____ . *A Dollar Comparison of Soviet and U.S. Defense Activities, 1965–1975.* Washington, D.C.: 1976. 8p.

1576. _____ . _____ . _____ . *A Dollar Cost Comparison of Soviet and U.S. Defense Activites, 1966–1976.* Washington, D.C.: 1977. 15p.

1577. _____ . _____ . _____ . *Estimated Soviet Defense Spending in Rubles, 1970–1975.* Washington, D.C.: 1976. 17p.

1578. _____ . _____ . _____ . *Estimated Soviet Defense Spending: Trends and Prospects.* Washington, D.C.: 1978. 14p.

1579. _____ . _____ . _____ . *Export Refining Centers of the World.* Washington, D.C.: 1975. 31p.

1580. _____ . _____ . _____ . *Foreign Trade of the East European Countries, 1960–1970.* Research Aid. Washington, D.C.: 1972. 44p.

1581. _____ . _____ . _____ . *Free World Oil Refineries.* Research Aid. Washington, D.C.: 1975. 59p.

1582. _____ . _____ . _____ . *Handbook of Economic Statistics, 1975.* Research Aid. Washington, D.C.: 1975. 163p.

1583. _____ . _____ . _____ . *International Energy Biweekly Statistical Review.* Washington, D.C.: 1977–. v. 1–.

1584. _____ . _____ . _____ . *The International Energy Situation: Outlook to 1985.* Washington, D.C.: 1977. 18p.

1585. _____ . _____ . _____ . *Korea: The Economic Race Between the North and the South.* Research Paper. Washington, D.C.: 1978. 21p.

1586. _____ . _____ . _____ . *The Least-Developed Countries: Economic Characteristics and Stake in the North-South Issues.* Research Paper. Washington, D.C.: 1978. 52p.

1587. _____ . _____ . _____ . *Major Oil and Gas Fields of the Free World.* Research Aid. Washington, D.C.: 1976. 30p.

1588. _____ . _____ . _____ . *Major Petroleum Refining Centers for Export.* Washington, D.C.: 1977. 38p.

1589. _____ . _____ . _____ . *Methods of Constructing Economic Indexes From Incomplete Data.* Research Aid. Washington, D.C.: 1974. 22p.

1590. _____ . _____ . _____ . *National Basic Intelligence Factbook.* Washington, D.C.: GPO, 1979. Annual.

1591. _____ . _____ . _____ . *Natural Gas.* Research Aid. Washington, D.C.: 1977. 43p.

1592. _____ . _____ . _____ . *Nuclear Energy.* Washington, D.C.: 1977. 65p.

1593. _____ . _____ . _____ . *The OPEC Countries: Current Account Trends, 1975–1976.* Research Aid. Langley, VA: 1976. 21p.

1594. _____ . _____ . _____ . *Organization and Management in the Soviet Economy: The Ceaseless Search for Panaceas.* Research Paper. Washington, D.C.: 1977. 30p.

1595. _____ . _____ . _____ . *P[eople's] R[epublic of] C[hina]: Estimating Yuan Value of Foreign Trade in Machinery and Equipment, 1951–1973.* Washington, D.C.: 1976. 20p.

1596. _____ . _____ . _____ . *PRC: Foreign Trade in Machinery and Equipment Since 1952.* Research Aid. Washington, D.C.: 1975. 34p.

1597. _____ . _____ . _____ . *PRC: Handbook of Economic Indicators.* Research Aid. Washington, D.C.: 1976. 34p.

1598. _____ . _____ . _____ . *PRC: International Trade Handbook.* Washington, D.C.: 1972–. v. 1–.

1599. _____ . _____ . _____ . *Profile of Violence: An Analytical Model.* Research Project. Washington, D.C.: 1976. 55p.

1600. _____ . _____ . _____ . *The Problem of Water Conservancy in Communist China, 1949–1961.* Washington, D.C.: 1962. 49p.

1601. _____ . _____ . _____ . *Prospects For Soviet Oil Production.* Washington, D.C.: 1977. 35p.

1602. _____ . _____ . _____ . *Recent Developments in Soviet Agriculture.* Washington, D.C.: 1962. 31p.

1603. _____ . _____ . _____ . *Recent Developments in Soviet Hard Currency Trade.* Research Aid. Washington, D.C.: 1976. 22p.

1604. _____ . _____ . _____ . *Recent Trends in the Economy of Poland.* Washington, D.C.: 1960. 19p.

1605. _____ . _____ . _____ . *Soviet Commercial Operations in the West.* Washington, D.C.: 1977. 29p.

1606. _____ . _____ . _____ . *The Soviet Economy in 1973: Performance, Plans, and Implications.* Research Aid. Washington, D.C.: 1974. 27p.

1607. _____ . _____ . _____ . *The Soviet Economy: 1974 Results and 1975 Prospects.* Research Aid. Washington, D.C.: 1975. 25p.

1608. _____ . _____ . _____ . *The Soviet Economy in 1976–1977 and Outlook for 1978.* Research Paper. Washington, D.C.: 1978. 20p.

1609. _____ . _____ . _____ . *Soviet Economic Plans For 1976–1980: A First Look.* Research Aid. Washington, D.C.: 1976. 37p.

1610. _____ . _____ . _____ . *Soviet Long-Range Energy Forecasts.* Washington, D.C.: 1975. 27p.

1611. _____ . _____ . _____ . *The Soviet State Budget Since 1965.* Research Paper. Washington, D.C.: 1977. 40p.

1612. _____ . _____ . _____ . *The Soviet Tin Industry: Recent Developments and Prospects Through 1980.* Research Aid. Washington, D.C.: 1977. 20p.

1613. _____ . _____ . _____ . *Survey of Soviet Economists and Economic Research Organizations.* Washington, D.C.: 1960. 30p.

1614. _____ . _____ . _____ . *Taxation in Communist China, 1950–1959.* Washington, D.C.: 1961. 117p.

1615. _____ . _____ . _____ . *U.S.S.R. Agriculture Atlas.* Washington, D.C.: 1974. 59p.

1616. _____ . _____ . _____ . *U.S.S.R. Foreign Trade.* 5 vols. in 11. Washington, D.C.: 1970.

1617. _____ . _____ . _____ . *U.S.S.R.: Gross National Product Accounts, 1970.* Research Aid. Washington, D.C.: 1975. 93p.

1618. _____ . _____ . _____ . *U.S.S.R.: Some Implications of Demographic Trends For Economic Policies.* Research Aid. Washington, D.C.: 1977. 20p.

1619. _____ . _____ . _____ . *U.S.S.R.: The Impact of Recent Climate Change on Grain Production.* Research Aid. Washington, D.C.: 1976. 35p.

1620. _____ . _____ . _____ . *Value Added by Work Brigades in Railway and Highway Construction in China, 1952–1957.* Research Aid. Washington, D.C.: 1975. 11p.

1621. _____ . _____ . _____ . *World Oil Refineries.* Research Aid. Washington, D.C.: 1975. 46p.

1622. _____ . _____ . _____ . *World Shipbuilding: Facing Up to Overcapacity.* Research Aid. Washington, D.C.: 1977. 11p.

1623. _____ . _____ . _____ . *World Steel Market: Continued Trouble Ahead.* Washington, D.C.: 1977. 11p.

1624. _____ . _____ . Office of Economic Research. *Economic Indicators.* Washington, D.C.: 1976. v. 1–.

1625. _____ . _____ . _____ . *International Oil Developments: A Statistical Survey.* Washington, D.C.: 1976–. v. 1–.

1626. _____ . _____ . Office of Political Research. *Appearances and Activities of Leading Personalities of the People's Republic of China.* Reference Aid. Washington, D.C.: 1972–. v. 1–.

1627. _____ . _____ . _____ . *Appearances of Soviet Leaders.* Reference Aid. Washington, D.C.: 1972–. v. 1–.

1628. _____ . _____ . _____ . *Chiefs of State and Cabinet Members of Foreign Governments.* Washington, D.C.: 1972–. v. 1–.

1629. _____ . _____ . _____ . *Chinese Communist Party Provincial Leaders.* Reference Aid. Washington, D.C.: 1973. 117p.

1630. _____ . _____ . _____ . *Communist China: Revolutionary Government in the Provinces.* Washington, D.C.: 1968. 93p.

1631. _____ . _____ . _____ . *Council of Ministers of the Socialist Republic of Vietnam.* Reference Aid. Washington, D.C.: 1977. 103p.

1632. _____ . _____ . _____ . *Directory of Czechoslovak Officials.* Reference Aid. Washington, D.C.: 1972–. v. 1–.

1633. _____ . _____ . _____ . *Directory of East German Officials.* Reference Aid. Washington, D.C.: 1972–. v. 1–.

1634. _____ . _____ . _____ . *Directory of Soviet Officials.* Reference Aid. Washington, D.C.: 1972–. v. 1–.

1635. _____ . _____ . _____ . *Directory of U.S.S.R. Ministry of Defense and Armed Forces Officials.* Reference Aid. Washington, D.C.: 1972–. v. 1–.

1636. _____ . _____ . _____ . *Directory of U.S.S.R. Ministry of Foreign Affairs Officials.* Reference Aid. Washington, D.C.: 1974–. v. 1–.

1637. _____ . _____ . _____ . *Issues in the Middle East: Atlas.* Washington, D.C.: 1973. 40p.

1638. _____ . _____ . _____ . *Potential Implications of Trends in World Population, Food Production, and Climate.* Washington, D.C.: 1974. 51p.

1639. _____ . _____ . _____ . _____ . In: U.S. Congress. House. Committee on Interstate and Foreign Commerce. *Middle- and Long-Term Energy Policies and Alternatives, Part 4: Hearings.* 94th Cong., 2nd sess. Washington, D.C.: GPO, 1976. pp. 225–283.

Many of the above documents are available from the Document Expediting Service of the Library of Congress Exchange and Gift Division or from the National Technical Information Service.

1640. _____ . Commission on the Organization of the Government For the Conduct of Foreign Policy. *Report.* Washington, D.C.: GPO, 1975. 278p.

See Chap. 7 for intelligence data in this Murphy Report.

1641. _____ . Congress. Joint Economic Committee. *The Soviet Economy in a New Perspective: A Compendium of Papers.* 94th Cong., 2nd sess. Washington, D.C.: GPO, 1976. 821p.

1642. _____ . _____ . _____ . Subcommittee on Economic Statistics. *A Comparison of the United States and Soviet Economies: Supplemental Statistics on Costs and Benefits to the Soviet Union of Its Bloc and Pact System, Prepared by the CIA.* Washington, D.C.: GPO, 1960. 50p.

1643. _____ . _____ . _____ . Subcommittee on Priorities and Economy in Government. *Allocation of Resources in the Soviet Union and China, 1978: Hearings.* 95th Cong., 1st sess. 4 pts. Washington, D.C.: GPO, 1977.

1644. _____ . _____ . Senate. Committee on Foreign Relations. *Intelligence and the ABM: Hearings.* 91st Cong., 1st sess. Washington, D.C.: GPO, 1969. 76p.

1645. _____ . _____ . _____ . Committee on Government Operations. Subcommittee on United States National Security Organizations. *Organizing For National Security: Hearings.* 3 vols. 86th Cong., 2nd sess. Washington, D.C.: GPO, 1960.

1646. _____ . _____ . _____ . Select Committee on Intelligence. *The National Intelligence Estimates, A–B. Team Episode Concerning Soviet Strategic Capability and Objectives.* 95th Cong., 2nd sess. Washington, D.C.: GPO, 1978.

1647. _____ . _____ . _____ . *The Soviet Oil Situation, an Evaluation of CIA Analyses of Soviet Oil Production: A Staff Report.* 95th Cong., 2nd sess. Washington, D.C.: GPO, 1978. 15p.

1648. _____ . National Security Council. *Foreign Intelligence Production.* Intelligence Directive, no. 3. Washington, D.C.: 1972.

1649. _____ . Department of State. Bureau of Intelligence and Research. *Africa: 1941–1961.* Part XIII of *OSS/State Department Intelligence and Research Reports.* 10 reels, 35mm microfilm. Washington, D.C.: University Publications of America, 1979.

1650. _____ . _____ . _____ . *China and India* [to 1950]. Part III of *OSS/State Department Intelligence and Research Reports.* 16 reels, 35mm microfilm. Washington, D.C.: University Publications of America, 1976–1977.

1651. _____ . _____ . _____ . *China and India: 1940–1961.* Part IX of *OSS/State Department Intelligence and Research Reports.* 5 reels, 35mm microfilm. Washington, D.C.: University Publications of America, 1979.

1652. _____ . _____ . _____ . *Europe: 1950–1961.* Part X of *OSS/State Department Intelligence and Research Reports.* 11 reels, 35 mm microfilm. Washington, D.C.: University Publications of America, 1979.

1653. _____ . _____ . _____ . *Japan . . .* [to 1950]. Part I of *OSS/State Department Intelligence and Research Reports.* 16 reels, 35mm microfilm. Washington, D.C.: University Publications of America, 1976–1977.

1654. _____ . _____ . _____ . *Japan, Korea, Southeast Asia, and the Far East, Generally: 1950–1961.* Part VIII of *OSS/State Department Intelligence and Research Reports.* 7 reels, 35mm microfilm. Washington, D.C.: University Publications of America, 1979.

1655. _____ . _____ . _____ . *Latin America: 1941–1961.* Part XIV of *OSS/State Department Intelligence and Research Reports.* 10 reels, 35mm microfilm. Washington, D.C.: Umiversity Publications of America, 1979.

1656. _____ . _____ . _____ . *The Middle East* [to 1950]. Part VII of *OSS/State Department Intelligence and Research Reports.* 3 reels, 35mm microfilm. Washington, D.C.: University Publications of America, 1976–1977.

1657. _____ . _____ . _____ . *The Middle East: 1950–1961.* Part XII of *OSS/State Department Intelligence and Research Reports.* 3 reels, 35mm microfilm. Washington, D.C.: University Publications of America, 1979.

1658. _____ . _____ . _____ . *Postwar Europe.* Part V of *OSS/State Department Intelligence and Research Reports.* 10 reels, 35mm microfilm. Washington, D.C.: University Publications of America, 1977.

1659. _____ . _____ . _____ . *Postwar Japan, Korea, and Southeast Asia.* Part II of *OSS/State Department Intelligence and Research Reports.* 6 reels, 35mm microfilm. Washington, D.C.: University Publications of America, 1976–1977.

1660. _____ . _____ . _____ . *The Sino-Soviet Economic Offensive Through 1960.* Intelligence Report, no. 8426. Washington, D.C.: 1961. 34p.

1661. _____ . _____ . _____ . *The Soviet Union* [to 1950]. Part VI of *OSS/State Department Intelligence and Research Reports.* 8 reels, 35mm microfilm. Washington, D.C.: University Publications of America, 1976–1977.

1662. _____ . _____ . _____ . *The Soviet Union: 1950–1961.* Part XI of *OSS/State Department Intelligence and Research Reports.* 6 reels, 35mm microfilm. Washington, D.C.: University Publications of America, 1979.

1663. _____ . _____ . Division of Research for the U.S.S.R. and Eastern Europe. *Soviet World Outlook: A Handbook of Communist Statements.* Prepared for the Co-ordinator of Psychological Warfare, U.S. Information Agency. Rev. ed. Washington, D.C.: 1954. 434p.

1664. _____ . _____ . Office of Intelligence and Research. *The World Strength of the Communist Party Organizations.* Washington, D.C.: 1956. 77p.

1665. _____ . _____ . _____ . External Research Staff. *The Soviet Union as Reported by Former Soviet Citizens: Interview Reports.* Washington, D.C.: 1951–1961. v. 1–10.

1666. Walton, Robert. *Cold War and Counterrevolution: The Foreign Policy of John F. Kennedy.* Baltimore, MD: Pelican Books, 1973. 250p.

1667. Wasserman, Benno. "The Failure of Intelligence Predictions." *Political Studies*, VIII (June 1960), 156–169.

1668. Westwood, James T. "A Contemporary Political Dilemma: The Impact of Intelligence Operations on Foreign Policy." *Naval War College Review*, XXIX (Spring 1977), 86–92.

1669. Wilensky, Harold L. "Intelligence, Crises, and Foreign Policy: Reflections on the Limits of Rationality." In: Richard H. Blum, ed. *Surveillance and Espionage in a Free Society*. New York: Praeger, 1972. pp. 236–266.

1670. Williams, Philip. "Intelligence Failures in National Security." *Royal Air Forces Quarterly*, XIII (Autumn 1973), 223–227.

1671. Wohlstetter, Roberta. "Intelligence and Decision-Making." In: Andrew M. Scott and Raymond H. Dawson, eds. *Readings in the Making of American Foreign Policy*. New York: Macmillan, 1965. pp. 431–447.

c. Military Intelligence

(1) GENERAL WORKS

1672. Andregg, Charles H. *The Management of Defense Intelligence.* Washington, D.C.: Industrial College of the Armed Forces, 1968. 52p.

1673. Banfill, C. Y. "Military Intelligence and Command." *Infantry Journal*, LXII (February 1948), 28–30.

1674. Borden, William L. *There Will Be No Time: The Revolution in Strategy.* New York: Macmillan, 1946. 225p.

1675. Ellsworth, Robert F. "Military Intelligence—Streamlined, Centralized, Civilianized: An Interview." *Air Force Magazine*, LIX (August 1976), 26–30.

1676. Fulbright, James W. *The Pentagon Propaganda Machine.* New York: Liveright, 1970. 166p.

1677. Graham, Daniel O. "The Intelligence Mythology of Washington." *Strategic Review*, IV (Summer 1976), 59–66.

1678. Haswell, Jock. "The Need To Know." *Military Review*, LVI (September 1976), 45–55.

1679. Laughlin, Mike. "Eyes and Ears Around the World." *Profile*, XXI (February 1978), 4–6.

1680. McDonald, L. P. "A Talk With MG George Keegan on Defense." *American Opinion*, XX (September 1977), 1–4+.

1681. Matsulenko, V. "Surprise: How It Is Achieved and Its Role." *Soviet Military Review,* nos. 5–6 (May–June 1972), 37–39, 37–39.

A Russian view.

1682. Neumann, Robert G. "Political Intelligence and Its Relation to Military Government." In: Carl J. Friedrich, *et al.,* eds. *The American Experience in Military Government in World War II.* New York: Rinehart, 1948. pp. 70–85.

1683. Powe, Marc B. "Which Way For Tactical Intelligence After Vietnam?" *Military Review,* LIV (September 1974), 48–56.

1684. ———, jt. author. *See* Spirito, Leonard A. (1686).

1685. "The Significance and Effects of Surprise in Modern War." *History, Numbers, and War,* I (Spring 1977), 3–15.

1686. Spirito, Leonard A. and Marc B. Powe. "Military Intelligence: A Fight For Identity." *Army,* XXVI (May 1976), 14–21.

1687. Szulc, Tad. "Freezing Out the CIA: The Ascendant Pentagon." *New Republic,* CLXXV (July 24, 1976), 12–14.

1688. United States. Armed Forces Staff College. *Intelligence For Joint Forces.* AFSC Pubn., no. 5. Rev. ed. Norfolk, VA., 1967. 96p.

1689. Vagts, Alfred. "Diplomacy, Military Intelligence, and Espionage." In: his *Defense and Diplomacy.* New York: Kings Crown Press, 1956. pp. 61–77.

1690. ——— . *The Military Attaché.* Princeton, NJ: Princeton University Press, 1967. 408p.

1691. Vecchiotti, Robert A. *Training in Utilization of Surveillance and Reconnaissance By Combat Arms Officers.* Report ARI-TP-325. St. Louis, MO: McDonnell-Douglas Corp., 1978. 69p.

(2) Defense Intelligence Agency

1692. Graham, Daniel O. "DIA: The Unglamorous But Crucial Role of Satisfying the Foreign Military Intelligence Requirements of the D[epartment] O[f] D[efense]." *Commander's Digest,* XVII (April 24, 1975), 1–20.

1693. ——— . "Estimating the Threat: A Soldier's Job." *Army,* XXIII (April 1973), 14–18.

1694. McGarvey, Patrick J. "DIA: Intelligence to Please." In: Morton Halperin and Arnold Kanter, eds. *Readings in American Foreign Policy.* Boston: Little, Brown, 1973. pp. 318–328.

1695.   United States. Defense Intelligence Agency. *Defense Intelligence Collection Requirements Manual.* Washington, D.C.: 1975.

1696.   ———. ———. *Handbook on the Chinese Armed Forces.* DDI-2680-32-6. Washington, D.C.: 1976. 255p.

1696a.   ———. ———. *Handbook on the Soviet Armed Forces.* DDB-2680-40-78. Washington, D.C.: 1979. 235p.

1697.   ———. Office of the Federal Register, National Archives and Record Service, General Services Administration. "Defense Intelligence Agency." In: *United States Government Manual 1978/79.* Washington, D.C.: GPO, 1978. pp. 232–233.

(3) ARMY INTELLIGENCE

1698.   "Army Counterintelligence: Fact Vs. Fiction." *Army Information Digest,* XVIII (November 1973), 29–31.

1699.   Baldwin, Hanson W. "Battlefield Intelligence." *Combat Forces,* III (February 1953), 30–41.

1700.   Bidwell, Bruce W. "History of the Military Intelligence Division, Department of the Army General Staff, Part I." Unpublished paper, Files of the U.S. Army Center of Military History Library, 1954.

1701.   Booth, Walter B. "War By 'Other Means.' " *Army,* XXV (January 1975), 21–24.

1702.   Brown, Dallas C., Jr. "Combat Intelligence Today." *Armor,* LXXIII (September–October 1964), 20–23.

1703.   Chandler, Stedman, *et al. Front-Line Intelligence.* Washington, D.C.: Infantry Journal Press, 1946.

1704.   Churchill, Marlborough. "The Military Intelligence Division, General Staff." *Journal of the United States Artillery,* LIV (April 1970), 293–315.

1705.   Daniel, Charles D. "Status and Needs of Army Intelligence, Surveillance, and Target Acquisition." *Electronic Warfare/Defense Electronics,* X (September 1978), 57+.

1706.   Davidson, Philip B. and Robert R. Glass. *Intelligence is For Commanders.* 2nd ed. Harrisburg, PA: Military Publishing Co., 1952. 184p.

1707.   "Diplomats in Uniform." *New Republic,* CXLIX (November 2, 1963), 13–15.

1708.   Doleman, Edgar C. "The Army Intelligence and Security [Branch]: A Progress Report." *Army Information Digest,* XIX (April 1964), 16–19.

1709.   Duncan, Harry N. "Combat Intelligence For Modern War." *Army Information Digest,* XVII (June 1962), 24–31.

1710.   Fitch, Alva R. "Intelligence and Security: The Army's Newest Basic Branch." *Army Information Digest,* XVII (August 1962), 2–8.

1711.   Fletcher, John. "Intelligence: A Principle of War." *Military Review,* L (August 1970), 42–57.

1712.   Glass, Robert R., jt. author. *See* Davidson, Philip B. (1706).

1713.   Halpin, Stanley M. *A Validation of the Structure of Combat Intelligence Ratings.* Report ARI-TP-302. Alexandria, VA: U.S. Army Institute for the Behavioral and Social Sciences, 1978. 51p.

1714.   Heymont, Irving. *Combat Intelligence in Modern Warfare.* Harrisburg, PA: Stackpole Books, 1960. 244p.

1715.   "Intelligence: Yesterday, Today, Tomorrow." *Journal of the U.S. Army Intelligence and Security Command,* I (October 1977), 6–16.

1716.   James, Charles D. "Combat Intelligence For [Army] Aviation." *U.S. Army Aviation Digest,* XVI (January 1970), 15–18.

1717.   Jorgenson, Conrad A., jt. author. *See* Layne, Donald Q. (1718).

1718.   Layne, Donald Q. and Conrad A. Jorgenson. "Combat Intelligence." *Marine Corps Gazette,* LVIII (March 1974), 29–36.

The Marines are entered here as land forces instead of under Naval Intelligence as amphibious forces.

1719.   Liberti, Joseph C. "Counterintelligence in Direct Support." *Infantry,* LXIV (March–April 1974), 39–43.

1720.   Nelson, Otto L., Jr. *National Security and the General Staff: A Study of Organization and Administration.* Washington, D.C.: Infantry Journal Press, 1946. 608p.

1721.   "Oak Leaf," pseud. "A Look at G-2." *Infantry Journal,* LVIII (April 1946), 19–21.

1722.   Powe, Marc B. and Edward E. Wilson. "The Evolution of American Military Intelligence." Unpublished paper, Files of the U.S. Army Intelligence Center, Ft. Huachua, AZ: 1973.

1723.   Rolya, William I. "INSCOM: Who Are We? Where Have We Been? Where are We Going?: An Interview." *Journal of the U.S. Army Intelligence and Security Command,* II (October–November 1978), 15–19.

1724.   Townsend, Elias C. *Risks: The Key to Combat Intelligence.* Harrisburg, PA: Military Service Publishing Co., 1955. 82p.

1725. United States. Army. Intelligence and Security Command School. *Combat Intelligence.* FM-30-5. Arlington, VA: 1973.

1726. _____ . _____ . _____ . *Counterintelligence Operations.* FM 30-17. Arlington, VA: 1972.

1727. _____ . _____ . _____ . *Counterintelligence Special Operations (U.).* FM 30–17A. Arlington, VA: 1973.

1728. _____ . _____ . _____ . *Intelligence Collection Operations (U.).* FM 30–18. Arlington, VA: 1973.

1729. _____ . _____ . _____ . *Intelligence Interrogation.* FM–15. Arlington, VA: 1973.

1730. _____ . _____ . _____ . *Military Intelligence Organizations.* FM 30–9. Arlington, VA: 1973.

1731. _____ . _____ . _____ . *Opposing Forces: Europe.* FM 30–102. Arlington, VA: 1977.

1732. _____ . _____ . _____ . *Tactical Counterintelligence.* Training Circular 30–24. Arlington, VA: 1977.

1733. _____ . _____ . _____ . *Technical Intelligence.* FM–30–16. Arlington, VA: 1972.

1734. _____ . _____ . Office of the Adjutant General. *Combat Intelligence.* FM 30–5.Washington, D.C.: 1971. 205p.

1735. _____ . Marine Corps. *Intelligence.* Washington, D.C.: 1967. 425p.

1736. Whitehouse, Arthur G. J. "Arch." *Espionage and Counterespionage: Adventures in Military Intelligence.* Garden City, NY: Doubleday, 1964. 298p.

1737. Williams, Robert W. "Commanders and Intelligence: The Growing Gap." *Army,* XXII (December 1972), 21–24.

1738. Wilson, Edward E., jt. author. *See* Powe, Marc B. (1722).

(4) NAVAL INTELLIGENCE

1739. Deacon, Richard, pseud. *See* McCormick, Donald (1741).

1740. Homes, Wilfred J. *Double-Edged Secrets.* Annapolis, MD: U.S. Naval Institute, 1979. 231p.

1741. McCormick, Donald. *The Silent War: A History of Western Naval Intelligence.* By Richard Deacon, pseud. New York: Hippocrene Books, 1978. 288p.

(5) AIR FORCE INTELLIGENCE

1742. Barber, Charles H. "Some Problems of Air Intelligence." *Military Review,* XXVI (August 1946), 76–78.

1743. Cohen, Victor H. *The Development of the Intelligence Function in the U.S.A.F., 1917–1950.* Special Studies Report. Maxwell AFB, AL: Research Studies Institute, Air University, 1957.

1744. James, Peter N. *The Air Force Mafia.* New Rochelle, NY: Arlington House, 1975. 347p.

1745. Kalisch, Robert B. "Air Force Technical Intelligence." *Air University Review,* XXII (July–August 1971), 2–11.

1746. Kaufmann, David. "The Foreign Technology Division: Unlocking the Secrets of Foreign Aerospace Technology." *Contact,* XXVI (May–June 1972), 2–5.

1747. Koch, R. W. "The CIA's Death Valley Albatross." *Air Classics,* XV (April 1979), 68–73, 98.

The USAF 580th, 581st, and 582nd Air Resupply and Communications Wings, under CIA control, were commissioned to drop agents in the Far East, Europe, and Africa.

1748. MacCloskey, Monro. *Alert the Fifth Force: Counterinsurgency, Unconventional Warfare, and Psychological Operations of the United States Air Force in Special Air Warfare.* New York: R. Rosen, 1969. 190p.

1749. Warner, R. G. M. "The Joint Photographic Intelligence Centre." *Roundel,* XV (October 1963), 22–26.

(6) NATIONAL SECURITY AGENCY

1750. "The CIA's Big Sister." *Time,* XC (November 3, 1967), 22.

1751. Dash, Samuel, *et al. Eavesdroppers.* New Brunswick, NJ: Rutgers University Press, 1960. 484p.

1752. Davy, John and Andrew Wilson. "The Secret World War of the Antennae." *Atlas,* XV (March 1968), 17–19.

1753. "Eavesdropper." *Newsweek,* LXV (May 31, 1965), 21.

1754. Gaines, J. R. "'Project Minaret': Investigating NSA's Communications Interception Program." *Newsweek,* LXXXVI (November 10, 1975), 31+.

1755. Griswold, Wesley S. "Secrets of the Electronic Snoopers." *Popular Science,* CLXXI (October 1957), 126–130+.

1756. Halperin, Morton H. "Most Secret Agents." *New Republic,* CLXXIII (July 26, 1975), 12–13.

1757. Inman, Bobby R. "Intelligence Chief Seeks Dialogue With Academics." *Science,* CCII (October 6, 1978), 42.

1758. Kahn, David. "Big Ear or Big Brother?" *New York Times Magazine,* May 16, 1976), 13+.

Also consult Kahn's *The Codebreakers* no. 924.

1759. _____ . "Did They Unlock Secrets or Plain Rot?: The Codes Battle." *Playboy,* XXII (December 1975), 132+.

1760. _____ . "Lgen Otuu Wllwgh Wi Etfown." *New York Times Magazine,* (November 13, 1960), 71+.

1761. _____ . "Top-Secret Language." *Reader's Digest,* LXXIX (August 1961), 164–165+.

1762. "NSA: Inside the Puzzle Palace." *Time,* CXVI (November 10, 1975), 14.

1763. Norman, Lawrence. "Tapping K[hruschev]'s Top Secrets." *Newsweek,* LV (February 8, 1960), 36–38.

1764. Ransom, Harry H. "Other Principal Members." In: *The Intelligence Establishment.* Cambridge, MA: Harvard University Press, 1970. pp. 126–133.

1765. Shaul, W. Dennis, jt. author. *See* Stearns, Richard G. (1766).

1766. Stearns, Richard G. and W. Dennis Shaul. "Modern Dilemma: Two Views of the NSA-CIA Crisis by Present and Former NSA Officers." *Mademoiselle,* LXV (August 1967), 232–233+.

1767. Szulc, Tad. "The NSA—America's $10 Billion Frankenstein." *Penthouse,* VII (November 1975), 55–56, 70–72, 184–195.

1768. Toffler, Al. "Washington's Electronic Eavesdroppers." *Coronet,* XLV (January 1959), 88–93.

1769. Tully, Andrew. *The Super Spies: More Secret, More Powerful Than the CIA.* London: Barker, 1970. 256p.

1770. "U.S. Electronic Espionage, a Memoir: An Interview With a Former NSA Analyst." *Ramparts,* XI (August 1972), 35–50.

1771. "The U.S. Is Doing Better Than Is Generally Known." *U.S. News and World Report,* XLIX (September 19, 1960), 42–43.

1772.   United States. Congress. House. Committee on Un-American Activities. *Amending the Internal Security Act of 1950 to Provide For Maximum Personnel Security in the National Security Agency: Report.* 87th Cong., 2nd sess. Washington, D.C.: GPO, 1962. 62p.

1773.   _____ . _____ . Senate. Select Committee to Study Government Operations with Respect to Intelligence Activities. *The National Security Agency and Fourth Amendment Rights: Hearings.* 94th Cong., 1st sess. Washington, D.C.: GPO, 1976. 165p.

1774.   _____ . _____ . _____ . Select Committee on Intelligence. *Unclassified Summary, Involvement of NSA in the Development of the Data Encryption Standard: A Staff Report.* Washington, D.C.: GPO, 1978. 4p.

1775.   _____ . Office of the Federal Register, National Archives and Record Service, General Services Administration. "National Security Agency/Central Security Service." In: *United States Government Manual, 1978/79.* Washington, D.C.: GPO, 1978. p. 242.

1776.   Watson, Robert. "No Place to Hide: NSA's Eavesdropping Technology." *Newsweek,* LXXXVI (September 8, 1975), 19–21.

1777.   Wilson, Andrew, jt. author. *See* Davy, John (1752).

d. Department of State, Bureau of Intelligence and Research

1778.   Evans, Allan. *Research in Action: The Department of State's Bureau of Intelligence and Research.* Publication 7964. Rev. ed. Washington, D.C.: 1968. 27p.

1779.   _____ and R. D. Gatewood. "Intelligence and Research: Sentinel and Scholar in Foreign Affairs." *Department of State Bulletin,* XLII (June 1960), 1023–1027.

1780.   Gatewood, R. D., jt. author. *See* Evans, Allan (1778).

1781.   Leacacos, John P. "Intelligence: The Raw Material of Diplomatists." In: his *Fires in the In-Basket: The ABC's of the State Department.* Cleveland, OH: World Publishing Co., 1968. pp. 468–537.

1782.   United States. Department of State. Bureau of Intelligence and Research. *INR: Intelligence and Research in the Department of State.* Document no. 0–496–792. Washington, D.C.: GPO, 1973. 19p.

e. Federal Bureau of Investigation

1783.   Brown, Bill, jt. author. *See* Sullivan, William C.

1784.   Collins, Frederick L. *The FBI in Peace and War.* Rev. and enl. New York: Ace Books, 1962. 320p.

1785. "The FBI's Black-Bag Boys." *Newsweek,* LXXXVI (July 28, 1975), 24–25.

1786. Felt, Mark. *The FBI Pyramid: From the Inside.* New York: G. P. Putnam, 1979. 351p.

1787. Gillers, Stephen, jt. author. *See* Watters, Pat (1796).

1788. Navasky, Victor. *Kennedy Justice.* New York: Atheneum, 1971. 482p.

1789. Schlesinger, Arthur M., Jr. *Robert Kennedy and His Times.* Boston: Houghton, Mifflin, 1978. 1,066p.

Includes material on the FBI and other intelligence agencies.

1790. Schott, Joseph L. *No Left Turns: The FBI in Peace and War.* New York: Praeger, 1975. 214p.

1791. Sullivan, William C. and Bill Brown. *The Bureau: My Thirty Years in Hoover's FBI.* New York: W. W. Norton, 1979. 286p.

1792. Turner, William W. *Hoover's FBI: The Man and the Myth.* Los Angeles, CA: Sherbourne Press, 1970. 352p.

1793. Ungar, Sanford J. *FBI.* Boston: Little, Brown, 1975. 682p.

1794. United States. Congress. House. Committee on the Judiciary. Subcommittee on Civil and Constitutional Rights. *FBI Oversight: Hearings.* 95th Cong., 1st and 2nd sess. Washington, D.C.: GPO, 1978. 391p.

1795. _____ . _____ . Senate. Select Committee to Study Government Operations With Respect to Intelligence Activities. *The Federal Bureau of Investigation: Hearings.* 94th Cong., 1st sess. Washington, D.C.: GPO, 1976. 1,000p.

1796. Watters, Pat and Stephen Gillers, eds. *Investigating the FBI.* Garden City, NY: Doubleday, 1973. 518p.

1797. Wright, Richard O., ed. *Whose FBI?* New York: Open Court Publishing Co., 1974. 405p.

f. Central Intelligence Agency

(1) OSS, CENTRAL INTELLIGENCE GROUP, AND THE NATIONAL SECURITY ACT

1798. Andrews, Robert H. "How the CIA Was Born." *Mankind,* V (April 1975), 14–15, 68.

1799. Braden, Tom. "The Birth of the CIA." *American Heritage,* XXVIII (February 1977), 4–13.

1800.   Bruce, David K. E. "The National Intelligence Authority." *Virginia Quarterly Review,* XXII (Summer 1946), 355–369.

1801.   Chamberlain, John. "The OSS." *Life,* XVI (November 19, 1945), 119–130.

1802.   Dondero, George A. "The Deadly Parallel." *Congressional Record,* XCIII (July 22, 1947), 9768–9770.

1803.   Donovan, William J. "Intelligence: Key to Defense." *Life,* XVII (September 30, 1946), 108–120.

1804.   Dulles, Allen W. "Views on Central Intelligence [1947]." In: Harry H. Ransom. *The Intelligence Establishment.* Cambridge, MA: Harvard University Press, 1970. pp. 257–263.

1805.   Gervasi, Frank. "What's Wrong With Our Spy System?" *Collier's,* CXIX (November 6, 1946), 13+; CXXII (January 1949), 37–39+.

1806.   Jeffrey-Jones, Rhodri. *American Espionage: From Secret Service to CIA.* New York: Free Press, 1977. 276p.

1807.   Johnson, Thomas. "America Has to Know: A Good Intelligence Service is Indispensable in Peace as Well as War." *Reader's Digest,* XLVIII (May 1946), 53–59.

1808.   Kellis, James G. "The Development of U.S. National Intelligence, 1941–1961." Unpublished PhD Dissertation, Georgetown University, 1963.

1809.   Langer, William L. "Scholarship and the Intelligence Problem." *American Philosophical Society Proceedings,* XCII (March 1948), 43–45.

1810.   McCone, John A. "Why the CIA was Created." In: George Wittman, ed. *The Role of the American Intelligence Organizations.* Reference Shelf, v. 48, no. 5. New York: H. W. Wilson, 1976. pp. 41–47.

1811.   Patterson, James T. "The Intelligence System: Reprinted From the *Washington Post,* May 3, 1947." *Congressional Record,* XCIII (1947), A2139.

1812.   Pettee, George S. *The Future of American Secret Intelligence.* Washington, D.C.: Infantry Journal Press, 1946. 120p.

1813.   Pratt, Fletcher. "How Not to Run a Spy System." *Harper's* CXCV (September 1947), 241–246.

1814.   Sanders, Alfred D. "Truman and the National Security Council, 1945–1947." *Journal of American History,* LIX (September 1972), 369+.

1815.   Smith, Richard H. *OSS: The Secret History of America's First Central Intelligence Agency.* Berkeley: University of California Press, 1972. 458p.

1816.   Trager, Frank N. "The National Security Act of 1947: Its 30th Anniversary." *Air University Review,* XXIX (November–December 1977), 2–15.

1817.   Truman, Harry. "Harry Truman on the Role of the CIA." *Oklahoma Observer,* VII (March 10, 1975), 11.

1818.   United States. Bureau of the Budget. *Intelligence and Security Activities of the Government: A Report to the President.* Washington, D.C.: 1945.

1819.   _____ . Congress. Senate. Committee on Armed Services. *Central Intelligence.* Part III of *National Defense Establishment: Hearings.* 80th Cong., 1st sess. 3 pts. Washington, D.C.: GPO, 1947.

1820.   _____ . Office of Strategic Services. Assessment Staff. *The Assessment of Men.* New York: Rinehart, 1947. 541p.

1821.   Van de Water, Marjorie. "Selecting Secret Agents for OSS Service." *Science News Letter,* XLIX (January 12, 1946), 26–27.

RESEARCH NOTE

Additional references to the O.S.S. will be found in the first volume of *The Secret Wars: Intelligence, Propaganda, and Psychological Warfare, Resistance Movements, and Secret Operations, 1939–1945.*

(2) CIA—GENERAL WORKS

1822.   Agee, Philip. *Inside the Company: A CIA Diary.* New York: Stonehill Publishing Co.; dist. by Braziller, 1975. 639p.

1823.   Alsop, Stewart. "CIA: The Battle For Secret Power." *Saturday Evening Post,* CCXXXVI (July 27, 1963), 17–21.

1824.   _____ . "CIA" Triumph of the Prudent Professionals." In: *The Center: People in Power in Political Washington.* New York: Harper & Row, 1968. pp. 213+.

1825.   "The Anomalous CIA." *Nation,* CCII (May 16, 1966), 570–571.

1826.   Attwood, William. "A Former Ambassador Says a Few Kind Words For the CIA." *Look,* XXXI (April 18, 1967), 70–71.

1827.   Bagdikian, Benjamin H. "An Unsecretive Report on the CIA." *New York Times Magazine,* (October 27, 1963), 18+.

1828.   Baldwin, Hanson W. *New York Times* Intelligence Series, by date: 1)"Intelligence—One of the Weakest Links in Our Security Survey Shows Omissions, Duplications." *New York Times,* (July 20, 1948), p. 6; 2)"Older Agencies Resent a Successor and Try to Restrict Its Scope of Action." *New York Times,* (July 22, 1948), p. 2; 3)"Intelligence Ill: Errors in Collecting Data Held Exceeded by Evaluation Weakness." *New York Times,* (July 23, 1948), p. 5; 4)"Competent Personnel Held Key to Success—Reform Suggested." *New York Times,* (July 24, 1948), p. 5; 5)"Broader Control Set-Up is Held Needed With a 'Watch-Dog' Committee for Congress." *New York Times,* (July 25, 1948), p. 15.

Baldwin's series is so important that it is entered here despite the fact that it has not been reprinted in an anthology.

1829.   Bedell-Smith, Walter. "Of Spies and Counterspies." *U.S. News and World Report,* XXXIII (October 10, 1952), 47–49.

1830.   Blackstock, Paul W. "CIA: A Non-Inside Report," *Worldview,* IX (May 1966), 10–13.

1831.   Boeth, Robert. "Backstage at the CIA." *Newsweek,* XC (September 12, 1977), 27–28.

1832.   Bonafede, Dom. "The CIA Under [Stansfield] Turner." *National Journal,* IX (December 17, 1977), 1948–1954.

1833.   Borosage, Robert L. "The Central Intelligence Agency: The King's Men and the Constitutional Order." In: Robert L. Borosage and John D. Marks, eds. *The CIA File.* New York: Grossman, 1976. pp. 125–141.

1834.   Braden, Thomas W. "Speaking Out: I'm Glad the CIA is Immoral." *Saturday Evening Post,* CCXL (May 20, 1967), 10+.

1835.   Branch, Taylor and John D. Marks. "Tracing the CIA." *Harper's Weekly,* no. 3109 (January 24, 1975), 1+.

1836.   Brandon, Henry. "New Tools For the CIA." *Saturday Review of Literature,* XLVIII (May 22, 1965), 16+.

1837.   "Brightening the Image." *Parade,* (December 18, 1977), 5.

1838.   Brower, Brock. "Why People Like You Joined the CIA." *Washington Monthly,* VIII (November 1976), 50–60.

1839.   Buckley, William F., Jr. "Second-Class Citizens." *National Review,* XXVII (November 21, 1975), 1312–1313.

1840.   Cannon, J. M. "CIA: How Super are the Sleuths?" *Newsweek,* LVII (May 8, 1961), 29–30+.

1841.   Capell, Frank A. "No Intelligence—A Worried Look at the CIA: Reprinted From *American Opinion,* January 1971." *Congressional Record,* CXVII (May 24, 1971), 16551–16557.

1842.   Carter, Jimmy. "Central Intelligence Agency: Remarks to Employees, August 16, 1978." *Weekly Compilation of Presidential Documents,* XIV (August 21, 1978), 1434–1436.

1843.   "CIA: The Best in the World." *U.S. News and World Report,* LXXIX (August 25, 1975), 39+.

1844.   "CIA: How Badly Hurt?" *Newsweek,* XCI (February 6, 1978), 18–19+.

1845.   "CIA: The Human Side." *New Republic,* CXLV (July 3, 1961), 4–5.

1846.   "CIA: No Comment on Anything." *Fortune,* XLVIII (July 1953), 36+.

1847.   "CIA Not Playing Cricket—Cold War No Game: Reprinted From the *Detroit News,* February 19, 1967." *Congressional Record,* CXIII (March 2, 1967), 5239.

1848.   Church, Frank and William E. Colby. "Pacem in Terris IV: The CIA." *Center Magazine,* IX (March 1976), 21–38.

1849.   Clifford, George. "Listening in With the CIA." *Argosy,* CCLXXXI (September 1975), 34+.

1850.   Colby, William E., jt. author. *See* Church, Frank (1848).

1851.   Collins, Frederic W. "In Defence of the CIA." *Round Table,* LVII (January 1967), 115–121.

1852.   Cook, Fred J. "The CIA." *Nation,* CXCII (June 24, 1961), 529–572.

1853.   Cooper, Chester L. "The CIA and Decision-Making." *Foreign Affairs,* L (February 1972), 223–236.

1845.   Copeland, Miles. *Beyond Cloak-and-Dagger: Inside the CIA.* New York: Pinnacle Books, 1975. 379p.

1855.   "Crippled CIA—As the U.S. Seeks Critical Answers." *U.S. News and World Report,* LXXVIII (April 7, 1975), 22–23.

1856.   Davis, Ivor. "The Spies Who Came in From the Sun." *Los Angeles Magazine,* XXII (June 1977), 100+.

1857.   Donovan, Robert J. "The CIA." In: *Conflict and Crisis: The Presidency of Harry S. Truman, 1945–1948.* New York: W. W. Norton, 1977. pp. 305–312.

1858.   Epstein, Edward J. "The War Within the CIA." *Commentary,* LXVI (August 1978), 35–39.

1859.   Felix, Christopher, pseud. "The Unknowable CIA." *Reporter,* (April 6, 1967), 20–24.

1860.   Frazier, Howard, ed. *Uncloaking the CIA: Presentations Made at the Conference on the CIA and World Peace, Held at Yale University on April 5, 1975.* New York: Free Press, 1978. 288p.

1861.   Getlein, Frank. "Lies, Damned Lies, and Intelligence." *Commonweal,* CV (January 20, 1978), 36–38.

1862.   Godfrey, E. Drexel, Jr. "Ethics and Intelligence, With Reply." *Foreign Affairs,* LVI (April, July 1978), 624–642, 867–875.

1863.   Goldman, Peter. "The Great Mole Hunt: Alleged CIA Infiltration of the Executive." *Newsweek,* LXXXVI (July 21, 1975), 16–17.

1864.   Gottlieb, Jeff. "The CIA." In: David Wallechinsky and Irving Wallace. *The People's Almanac 2.* New York: Morrow, 1978. pp. 1310–1312.

1865.   Gunther, John. "Inside the CIA." *Reader's Digest,* LXI (October 1952), 129–133.

1866.   Harkness, Richard and Gladys. "The Mysterious Doings of CIA." *Saturday Evening Post,* CCXXVII (October 30–November 13, 1954), 19–21+, 34–35+, 30+.

1867.   Harris, Richard E. "Reflections." *New Yorker,* LIV (April 10, 1978), 44–48+.

1868.   "Have We an Intelligence Service?" *Atlantic,* CLXXXI (April 1948), 66–70.

1869.   Higgins, James. "Lunch With Mr. So-and-CIA: Flunking Out of the Network." *Nation,* CCXXVI (January 21, 1978), 48–50.

1870.   Hilsman, Roger. "President Kennedy and the CIA." In: *To Move a Nation: The Politics of Foreign Policy in the Administration of John F. Kennedy.* Garden City, NY: Doubleday, 1967. pp. 63–91.

1871.   Hobbing, Enno. "CIA: Hottest Role in the Cold War." *Esquire,* LVII (September 1957), 31–34.

1872. Holford, D. J. "I Want to Be a Spy Mr. CIA-Man." *Popular Electronics,* XXXI (August 1969), 51–52.

1873. "Hot-Cold War Team." *U.S. News and World Report,* XXXIV (February 6, 1953), 42–45.

1874. "How [Oversight] Troubles Will Change the CIA." *U.S. News and World Report,* LXXVIII (January 13, 1975), 18+.

1875. "The Invisible Government." *Newsweek,* LXXXV (February 3, 1975), 17–18.

1876. Jerrold, Elbert S. "Why Do We Need the CIA?: The Story of Our 'Spy Agency's' Many-Sided Mission." *American Legion Magazine,* LXXXII (June 1967), 6–11+.

1877. Karalekas, Anne. *History of the Central Intelligence Agency.* Laguna Hills, CA: Aegean Park Press, 1977. 295p.

1878. Karnow, Stanley. "CIA in Flux." *New Republic,* CLXIX (December 8, 1973), 13–17.

1879. Kelly, S., *et al.* "Is the Worst Over For the CIA?: With an Interview With Stansfield Turner." *U.S. News and World Report,* LXXXVI (May 7, 1979), 26–32.

1880. Kim, Young H., comp. *The Central Intelligence Agency: Problems of Security in a Democracy.* Boston: D. C. Heath, 1970. 113p.

1881. Kirkpatrick, Lyman B., Jr. "CIA." *U.S. News and World Report,* LXXIV (October 11, 1971), 46–51.

1882. ———. *The Real CIA.* New York: Macmillan, 1968. 312p.

1883. ———, jt. author. *See* Marchetti, Vincent (1893).

1884. Kondracke, M. "The Days of Derring-Don't." *New Republic,* CLXXX (March 10, 1979), 13–16.

1885. Laird, Melvin R. "Let's Stop Undermining the CIA." *Reader's Digest,* CVIII (May 1976), 101–105.

1886. "The Leaky Ship." *Newsweek,* LXVI (December 27, 1965), 25–26.

1887. Lindsay, John V. "Inquiry Into the Darkness of the Cloak and the Sharpness of the Dagger." *Esquire,* LXI (March 1964), 106–107+.

1888. Lovell, Stanley P. "Cloak-and-Dagger Behind-the-Scenes." *Saturday Evening Post,* CCXXXV (March 3, 1962), 30+.

1889.   McCone, John A. "Why We Need the CIA." *TV Guide*, XXIV (January 10, 1976), 6+.

1890.   McGarvey, Patrick J. *CIA: The Myth and the Madness*. New York: Saturday Review Press, 1972. 240p.

1891.   Mailer, Norman. "A Harlot High and Low: Reconnoitering Through the Secret Government." *New York Magazine*, IX (August 16, 1976), 22+.

1892.   Marchetti, Victor. "CIA: The President's Loyal Tool." *Nation*, CCXIX (April 3, 1972), 430–433.

1893.   _____ and Lyman B. Kirkpatrick. "CIA: An Attack and a Reply." *U.S. News and World Report*, LXXI (October 11, 1978), 78–82+.

1894.   _____ and John D. Marks. *The CIA and the Cult of Intelligence*. New York: Knopf, 1974. 398p.

1895.   Marks, John D., jt. author. *See* Branch, Taylor (1835).

1896.   _____ , jt. author. *See* Marchetti, Victor (1892).

1897.   Morris, Roger. "The 'Company'—Banality of Power: Reprinted From the *New Republic*, October 4, 1975." *Congressional Record*, CXXI (October 9, 1975), 32916–32917.

1898.   "Multinational CIA: Ties With Foreign Intelligence Agencies." *Nation*, CCXXIII (November 13, 1976), 482–484.

1899.   O'Donnell, John P. "CIA: Intelligence or Ignorance?" *American Mercury*, LXXXV (July 1957), 118–120.

1900.   Paine, Lauran B. *The CIA at Work*. London: Hale, 1977. 192p.

Distributed in the U.S. in 1978 by the Levittown firm of Transatlantic.

1901.   "A Peek in the CIA's Closet." *Newsweek*, LXXXV (January 27, 1975), 28–30.

1902.   Raborn, William F. *Meet the Press: Guest, William F. Raborn, Former Director, CIA*. Washington, D.C.: Merkle Press, 1966. 9p.

Television interview, July 19, 1966.

1903.   _____ . "What's 'CIA'?: An Interview." *U.S. News and World Report*, LXI (July 18, 1966), 74–80.

1904.   Ransom, Harry H. "CIA's Statutory Functions." In: George Wittman, ed. *The Role of the American Intelligence Organizations*. Reference Shelf, v. 48, no. 5. New York: H. W. Wilson, 1976. pp. 48–53.

1905.   Reilly, John E., ed. *American Public Opinion and U.S. Foreign Policy, 1979.* Chicago: Chicago Council on Foreign Relations, 1979. 30p.

Shows a slight rise in public confidence in CIA.

1906.   Robinson, Donald B. "Our Comic-Opera Spy Set-Up: Reprinted From *American Legion Magazine,* February 1951." *Congressional Record,* CXVI (1950), A953–A955.

1907.   _____ . "They Fight the Cold War Under Cover." *Saturday Evening Post,* CCXXI (November 20, 1948), 30+.

1980.   Rositzke, Harry A. *The CIA's Secret Operations: Espionage, Counterespionage, and Covert Action.* New York: Reader's Digest Press; dist. by Crowell, 1977. 286p.

1909.   Schechter, Dan, *et al.* "CIA as an Equal Opportunity Employer." *Ramparts,* VII (June 1969), 25–33.

1910.   "Shake-Up at CIA." *Newsweek,* LXVII (June 27, 1966), 31–32.

1911.   Sherrill, Robert. "No Success Like Failure." *Playboy,* XXI (July 1974), 49+.

1912.   Sidey, Hugh. "Another Look at the CIA." *Time,* CV (January 20, 1975), 72.

1913.   "The Silent Service." *Time,* LXXXIX (February 25, 1967), 13–17.

1914.   Singer, Peter. "Forswearing Secrecy." *Nation,* CCXXVIII (May 5, 1979), 488–491.

1915.   Slocum, Bill. "It Could Be CIA is Doing a Good Job: Reprinted From the New York *World-Journal Tribune,* February 23, 1967." *Congressional Record,* CXIII (February 28, 1967), A960.

1916.   Smith, Joseph B. "Life Without Badges: The Cost of Cover in the CIA." *Washington Monthly,* X (May 1978), 44–48.

1917.   Sofokidis, Jeanette. "A Close Look at the CIA." *American Education,* IV (May 1968), 2–4.

1918.   Szulc, Tad. "Staying Spooked." *Penthouse,* VIII (January 1977), 56+.

1919.   Talbot, S. "Toward Restoring the Necessary CIA: A *Time* Essay." *Time,* CVI (September 29, 1975), 24+.

1920.   "Tantalizing Bits of Evidence: Efficiency, Low; Momentum, Low; Morale, Low." *Time,* CVI (August 4, 1975), 8–10.

1921. Taylor, Michael D. "The Exposed Flank of National Security." *Orbis,* XVIII (Winter 1975), 1011–1022.

1922. Taylor, Telford. "To Improve Our Intelligence System." *New York Times Magazine,* (May 27, 1951), 12+.

1923. Thimmesch, Nick. "CIA." *Saturday Evening Post,* CCXLVII (May 1975), 10+.

1924. Tully, Andrew. *CIA: The Inside Story.* New York: Morrow, 1962. 276p.

1925. United States. Central Intelligence Agency. *The Central Intelligence Agency.* Washington, D.C.: 1974.

1926. _____ . _____ . "Organizational History: March 1975." In: U.S. Congress. Senate. Select Committee to Study Government Operations With Respect to Intelligence Activities. *Intelligence Costs and Fiscal Procedures, Part I: Hearings.* 94th Cong., 1st sess. Washington, D.C.: GPO, 1975. pp. 537–544.

1927. _____ . Congress. *Act to Provide For the Administration of the CIA . . . and Other Purposes.* Public Law 110. 80th Cong., 1st sess. 1949. 63 Stat. 208.

1928. _____ . _____ . *National Security Act of 1947.* Public Law 253. 80th Cong., 1st sess. 1947. 61 Stat. 495; 50 USC Supp. 403.

1929. _____ . _____ . House. Committee on Armed Services. *Amending the Central Intelligence Act of 1949: Report.* 89th Cong., 2nd sess. Washington, D.C.: GPO, 1966.

1930. _____ . _____ . _____ . Committee on Un-American Activities. *Testimony of General Walter Bedell-Smith: Hearings.* 82nd Cong., 2nd sess. Washington, D.C.: GPO, 1952. 15p.

1931. _____ . _____ . Senate. Committee on Foreign Relations. *CIA Foreign and Domestic Activities: Hearings.* 94th Cong., 1st sess. Washington, D.C.: GPO, 1975. 39p.

1932. _____ . _____ . _____ . Select Committee to Study Government Operations With Respect to Intelligence. *Foreign and Military Intelligence.* 94th Cong., 2nd sess. Washington, D.C.: GPO, 1976. 651p.

1933. _____ . Office of the Federal Register, National Archives and Records Service, General Services Administration. "Central Intelligence Agency." In: *United States Government Manual, 1978/79.* Washington, D.C.: GPO, 1978. pp. 98–99.

1934. "The Visible CIA." *Nation,* CXCVIII (June 22, 1964), 613–614.

1935.   Walden, Jerrold L. "The CIA: A Study in the Arrogation of Administrative Powers." *George Washington Law Review,* XXXIX (1970), 66, 82–84.

1936.   Warner, E. "Strengthening the CIA: A *Time* Essay." *Time,* CXIII (April 30, 1979), 95–96.

1937.   Wicker, Tom. "Dealing With CIA." *Current,* CLXX (February 1975), 11–12.

1938.   _____ , *et al.* "*New York Times* Responsibility Reports on CIA: Reprinted From the *New York Times,* April 25–29, 1966." *Congressional Record,* CXII (May 3, 1966), 9566–9581.

Contents with dates: "CIA: Maker of Policy, or Tool? (April 25, 1966)"; "How CIA Put 'Instant Air Force' Into the Congo (April 26, 1966)"; "CIA Spies From 100 Miles Up: Satellite Probes Secret of Soviets (April 27, 1966)"; CIA Operations: A Plot Scuttled (April 28, 1966)"; "CIA: Qualities of Director (April 29, 1966)."

1939.   Wills, Garry. "The CIA From Beginning to End." *New York Review of Books,* XXII (January 22, 1976), 23+.

1940.   Wolfe, Alan. "Behind the CIA: The Emergence of the Dual State." *Nation,* CCXX (March 29, 1975), 363–369.

1941.   Wrong, D. H. "After the Cuban Crisis." *Commentary,* XXXV (January 1963), 29–33.

(3) CIA AND ACADEMIA

1942.   Austin, C. G. "Credibility Gap." *Journal of Higher Education,* XXXVIII (May 1967), 278–280.

1943.   Bates, William. "The UC [University of California]-CIA Connection: Dishonorable Schoolboys." *New West,* III (March 13, 1978), 56+.

1944.   Boyce, Allen. "Covert Scholarship: The Market For Potted Expertise—Activities of Operations and Policy Research Incorporated." *Nation,* CCXXVII (November 11, 1978), 489+.

1945.   Bush, George. "The Central Intelligence Agency and the Intellectual Community: A Banquet Address, June 9, 1976." *Signal,* XXX (August 1976), 36–37+.

1946.   Carter, Elton S., jt. author. *See* Clauser, James K. (1948).

1947.   "CIA and the Kiddies." *Newsweek,* LXIX (February 27, 1967), 25–28.

1948.   Clauser, James K. and Elton S. Carter. *The Design of an Intelligence Education: Assessment of Intelligence Educational and Training Requirements.* State College, PA: H.R.B.-Singer, Inc., 1965.

1949.   Collins, Frederick W. "In Defence of the CIA: Too Much Pious Hypocrisy." *Round Table,* CCXXV (1967), 115–121.

1950.   Divale, William T., with James Joseph. *I Lived Inside the Campus Revolution.* New York: Cowles Book Co., 1970.

1951.   Fitzgerald, Frances. "The CIA Campus Tapes." *New Leader,* VI (January 23, 1976), 37+.

1952.   Flippo, Chet. "Can the CIA Turn Students Into Spies?" *Rolling Stone,* no. 208 (March 11, 1976), 28+.

1953.   Harwood, Richard. "CIA Subsidies Study Reaches No Decision: Reprinted From the *Washington Post,* December 19, 1967." *Congressional Record,* CXIV (February 20, 1968), 3467.

1954.   Howell, Leon. "Growing Up in the U.S.A.: The CIA Debacle." *Christianity and Crisis,* XXVII (March 20, 1967), 49–52.

1955.   Hunt, Richard M. "The CIA Exposures: End of an Affair." *Virginia Quarterly Review,* XLV (Spring 1969), 211–229.

1956.   Kopkind, Andrew. "CIA: The Great Corrupter." *New Statesman and Nation,* LXXIII (February 24, 1967), 249–250.

1957.   Larson, Janet K. "Cloak, Dagger, and Gown: The CIA in Academe." *Christian Century,* XCIV (October 19, 1977), 931–933.

1958.   Lawrence, David. "The CIA Issue in Simplest Form: Reprinted From the Washington *Evening-Star,* February 21, 1967." *Congressional Record,* CXIII (February 23, 1967), 4335.

1959.   Lerner, Max. "International Student Activity Due Open Aid: Reprinted From the Washington *Evening-Star,* February 22, 1967." *Congressional Record,* CXIII (February 28, 1967), 4681–4682.

1960.   Lippmann, Walter. "Intelligence and Dirty Tricks: Reprinted From the *Washington Post,* February 23, 1967." *Congressional Record,* CXIII (March 8, 1967), 5917–5918.

1961.   Noyes, Crosby S. "CIA Flap Hardly as Shocking as All That: Reprinted From the Washington *Evening-Star,* February 21, 1967." *Congressional Record,* CXIII (February 23, 1967), 4334–4335.

1962.   _____ . "What are We Trying to Do to the CIA?: Reprinted From the Washington *Sunday-Star,* February 19, 1967." *Congressional Record,* CXIII (February 23, 1967), 4334.

1963. Phelps, Robert H. "Panel on CIA Subsidies Divided Over Alternatives: Reprinted From the *New York Times,* December 18, 1967." *Congressional Record,* CXIV (February 20, 1968), 3466–3467.

1964. "Preventing Subversion: Reprinted From the *Washington Post,* February 21, 1967." *Congressional Record,* CXIII (February 27, 1967), 4503–4504.

1965. Radosh, Ronald. "The CIA and the Academy." *Change,* VIII (August 1976), 38+.

1966. Raymont, Henry. "*Look,* in a Signed Editorial, Supports CIA Subsidies For Students' Organizations: Reprinted From the *New York Times,* April 4, 1967." *Congressional Record,* CXIII (April 6, 1967), A1633–A1634.

1967. "Report on CIA Secret Subsidies, 1967." *Department of State Bulletin,* LXIII (April 24, 1967), 665–668.

1968. "A Report on the U.S. National Student Association." *Congressional Record,* CXV (March 3, 1969), 5012–5019.

1969. Reston, James. "How Corrupt is America?: Reprinted From the *New York Times,* February 26, 1967." *Congressional Record,* CXIII (February 27, 1967), 4661.

1970. _____ . "Washington—The CIA and the Unanswered Question: Reprinted From the *New York Times,* February 22, 1967." *Congressional Record,* CXIII (February 23, 1967), 4405–4406.

1971. Rowan, Carl T. "In Defense of the CIA's Undercover 'Links': Reprinted From the Washington *Evening-Star,* February 26, 1967." *Congressional Record,* CXIII (February 28, 1967), 4670–4671.

1972. Shearer, Lloyd. "The CIA in Academe." *Parade,* (December 24, 1978), 33.

1973. Sherrill, Robert G. "The Professor and the CIA: Operations and Policy Research, Inc., Funds." *Nation,* CCIV (February 27, 1961), 258–260.

1974. Stern, Sol. "A Short Account of International Student Politics and the Cold War, With Particular Reference to NSA, CIA, etc." *Ramparts,* VII (January 25, 1967), 87–97.

This article set off much of the newspaper commentary cited in this section and was reprinted in the *Congressional Record,* CXIII (March 9, 1967), 6154–6159.

1975. White, William S. "Mobism at Large—Need We Apologize For the CIA Effort?: Reprinted From the *Washington Post,* February 22, 1967), 4387–4388.

1976. Wicker, Tom. "In the Nation—Vive le Difference: Reprinted from the *New York Times*, March 7, 1967." *Congressional Record,* CXIII (March 8, 1967), 5918.

1977. Wolfson, Lewis S. "The CIA Scandal—a Test of Democracy: Reprinted From the *Providence Sunday-Journal*, February 26, 1967." *Congressional Record,* CXIII (March 8, 1967), 5915–5917.

(4) CIA FUNDING AND PROPRIETARY COMPANIES

1978. "The CIA's Secret Funding and the Constitution." *Yale Law Review,* LXXXIV (January 1975), 608–636.

1979. "Cloak and Ledger: Is CIA Funding Constitutional?" *Hastings Constitutional Law Quarterly,* II (Summer 1975), 717–755.

1980. "COPE–and–Dagger Stories: Accusations of CIA Ties." *Time,* CVI (August 11, 1975), 61–62.

1981. DeLong, Edward K. "The Activities of the Central Intelligence Agency, at Six Billion Dollars a Year." *Computers and Automation,* XXI (February 1972), 38–40.

1982. "Don't Ask: CIA Funding." *New Republic,* CLXIV (February 6, 1971), 13–14.

1983. Farago, Ladislas. "Secrets of the Secret Service." *Saturday Review of Literature,* L (November 18, 1967), 31–32.

1984. Fisher, Louis. "Covert Financing." In: *Presidential Spending Power.* Englewood Cliffs, NJ: Prentice-Hall, 1975. pp. 202–229.

1985. Grabowicz, Peter and John Kotkin. "CIA Puts Its Money Where Its Friends Are: Schroders Limited." *New Times,* XI (November 27, 1978), 24–25.

1986. Harrington, Michael J. "Should the CIA Budget Be Disclosed?" *American Legion Magazine,* CV (October 1978), 10+.

1987. "House of Glass: Funneling Money Through a Maze of Philanthropic Funds." *Newsweek,* LXIX (March 6, 1967), 28+.

1988. Kotkin, John, jt. author. *See* Grabowicz, Peter (1985).

1989. Kozicharow, Edward. "Aircraft Firm Seeks Damages From CIA: General Aircraft Corp." *Aviation Week and Space Technology,* CV (October 18, 1976), 22–23.

1990. _____ . "Assets of Air America Totaled $50 Million During Peak Years." *Aviation Week and Space Technology,* CIV (May 3, 1976), 15–16.

1991. Lens, Sidney. "Partners: Labor and the CIA." *Progressive,* XXXIX (February 1975), 35–39.

1992. Luce, Phillip A. "Fly Away With the CIA: Reprinted From the *New Guard,* April 1967." *Congressional Record,* CXV (March 3, 1969), 5019–5020.

1993. Marks, John D. "A Kafka Story, But It's True." *Playboy,* XXII (August 1975), 54+.

1994. Robbins, Christopher. *Air America.* New York: Putnam, 1979. 314p.

1995. Schwartzman, Robert B. "Fiscal Oversight of the Central Intelligence Agency: Can Accountability and Confidentiality Co-exist?" *New York University Journal of International Law and Politics,* VII (Winter 1974), 493–544.

1996. Scott, Peter D. "The Vietnam War and the CIA Financial Establishment." In: Mark Selden, ed. *Remaking Asia: Essays on the American Uses of Power.* Asia Library. New York: Pantheon Books, 1974. pp. 91–154.

1997. Sherrill, Richard G. "Foundation Pipe Lines: The Beneficient CIA Funneling of Money to Shape Foreign Policy." *Nation,* CCII (May 9, 1966), 542–544+.

1998. Tsulc, Tad. "Money Changer: The Customers of Deak and Company." *New Republic,* CLXXIV (April 10, 1976), 10–13.

1999. United States. Congress. House. Select Committee on Intelligence. *Intelligence Costs and Fiscal Procedures: Hearings.* 94th Cong., 1st sess. Washington, D.C.: GPO, 1975. 630p.

2000. _____ . _____ . Senate. Select Committee on Intelligence. *Whether Disclosure of Funds Authorized For Intelligence Activities is in the Public Interest: Hearings.* 95th Cong., 1st sess. Washington, D.C.: GPO, 1977. 475p.

2001. _____ . _____ . _____ . Select Committee on Small Business. Subcommittee on Monopoly. *The Decline of Supplemental Air Carriers in the United States: Hearings.* 2 pts. 94th Cong., 2nd sess.–95th Cong., 1st sess. Washington, D.C.: GPO, 1976–1977.

(5) CIA Media Connection and Censorship

2002. Alpern, David M. "The Question of Leakage: Publication of CIA Report in the *Village Voice.*" *Newsweek,* LXXXVII (February 23, 1976), 12–13.

2003. "Banned in McLean." *New Republic,* CLXIX (October 6, 1973), 9–10. Marchetti and Marks.

2004. Barbosa, Roberto. "The CIA and the Press: Foreign Reaction to Disclosures of Media Manipulation." *Atlas,* XXV (March 1978), 22–25.

2005. Bernstein, Carl. "The CIA and the Media: How America's Most Powerful News Media [CBS] Worked Hand-in-Glove With the CIA and Why the Church Committee Covered It Up." *Rolling Stone,* (October 20, 1977), 55–67.

2006. Bernstein, Robert L. "Censoring the Whistleblowers: *The Decent Interval* Case." *Encore,* VII (April 3, 1978), 36–37.

2007. Bethell, Tom. "The [Norman] Mailer–CIA Connection." *Washington Monthly,* VIII (October 1976), 54–59.

2008. Branch, Taylor. "The Censors of Bumbledom." *Harper's,* CCL (January 1974), 56–63.

CIA vs. Marchetti and Marks.

2009. Bray, Howard. "Journalists as Spooks: The CIA Use of Newsmen on Intelligence Operations." *Progressive,* XLI (February 1977), 9–10.

2010. Buchanan, Patrick. "Regarding the Ethics and Veracity of Daniel Schorr." *TV Guide,* XXIV (March 13, 1976), A3+.

2011. "CIA Admits Help From 25 in U.S. Media, But Won't Give Any Names." *Broadcasting,* XC (May 3, 1976), 32–33.

2012. "CIAntics: U.S. Journalists Abroad as Undercover Agents." *New Republic,* CLXIX (December 15, 1973), 7–8.

2013. "CIA, FBI, and the Media: Excerpts From the Senate Report on Intelligence Activities." *Columbia Journalism Review,* XV (July 1976), 37–42.

2014. "The CIA in Wonderland: The Controversy as Reflected in the Media." *National Review,* XXVII (January 31, 1975), 88+.

2015. Chittick, William O. "American Foreign Policy Elites: Attitudes Toward Secrecy and Publicity." *Journalism Quarterly,* XLVII (Winter 1970), 689–696.

2016. Clifford, George. "The Plumbers Plot to 'Get' Jack Anderson." *Argosy,* CCLXXXI (January 1975), 14+.

2017. Colby, William E. "How Can the Government Keep a Secret?" *TV Guide,* XXV (February 12, 1977), 2+.

2018.   Crock, Stan. "[CIA Director James] Schlesinger Says Leaks Curb CIA: Reprinted From the *Washington Post,* August 3, 1975." *Congressional Record,* CXXI (October 28, 1975), 33896.

2019.   "*Counterspy:* Exposing the Identities of CIA Agents." *Newsweek,* LXXXVII (January 5, 1976), 41.

2020.   Crile, George, 3rd. "The Fourth Estate: A Good Word For the CIA." *Harper's,* CCLII (January 1976), 28–30+.

2021.   Cuneo, Ernest. "What's the Story Behind the CIA and Newsmen Abroad?" *Human Events,* XXXIII (December 22, 1973), 8+.

2022.   Drummond, William J. "Agents as Authors: The Influence of the CIA on American Foreign Correspondents." *Nation,* CCXXVII (September 23, 1978), 260–262.

2023.   Edgar, Harold and Benno C. Schmidt, Jr. "The Espionage Statutes and Publication of Defense Information." *Columbia Law Review,* LXXIII (May 1973), 929–1087.

2024.   Futterman, Stanley N. "Controlling Secrecy in Foreign Affairs." In: Francis O. Wilcox and Richard A. Frank, eds. *The Constitution and the Conduct of Foreign Policy: An Inquiry by a Panel of the American Society of International Law.* New York: Praeger, 1976. pp. 6–58.

2025.   Gelb, Leslie H. "The CIA and the Press: Bearing Out Seymour Hersh." *New Republic,* CLXXII (March 22, 1975), 13–16.

2026.   Goulding, Philip G. *Confirm or Deny: Informing the Public on National Security.* New York: Harper & Row, 1970. 361p.

2027.   Guidry, Vernon A., Jr. "CIA Goal—Drug, Not Kill, [Jack] Anderson: Reprinted From the Washington *Evening-Star,* June 9, 1976." In: U.S. Congress. House. Permanent Select Committee on Intelligence, Subcommittee on Oversight. *CIA and the Media: Hearings.* 95th Cong., 1st and 2nd sess. Washington, D.C.: GPO, 1978. p. 353.

2028.   Halperin, Morton H. " 'CIA News Management' and 'How CIA Managed the News After Agent's Murder in '75': Reprinted From the *Washington Post* and Washington *Sunday-Times,* January 23, 1977." In: U.S. Congress. House. Permanent Select Committee on Intelligence. Subcommittee on Oversight. *CIA and the Media: Hearings.* 95th Cong., 1st and 2nd sess. Washington, D.C.: GPO, 1978. pp. 441–442.

2029.   _____ and Daniel Hoffman. *Top Secret: National Security and the Right to Know.* New York: Simon and Schuster, 1977. 158p.

2030.   Hoffman, Daniel, jt. author. *See* Halperin, Morton H. (2029).

2031. "If You Print My Name, I May Be Killed." *More*, VI (January 1976), 14–15.

The activities of *Counterspy* magazine.

2032. Ignatius, David. "Dan Schorr: The Secret Sharer." *Washington Monthly*, VIII (April 1976), 6–20.

2033. Johnson, M. B. *Government Secrecy Controversy: A Dispute Involving the Government and the Press in the Eisenhower, Kennedy, and Johnson Administrations*. New York: Vantage Press, 1967. 136p.

2034. Johnson, Oswald. "Journalists Doubling as CIA Contacts: Reprinted From the Washington *Star-News*, November 30, 1973." In: U.S. Congress. House. Select Committee on Intelligence. *U.S. Intelligence Agencies and Activities, Risks and Control of Foreign Intelligence: Hearings.* 94th Cong., 1st sess. Washington, D.C.: GPO, 1975. pp. 1965–1968.

2035. Karnow, Stanley. "Associating With the Agency." *Newsweek*, XCI (October 10, 1977), 11.

2036. Kondracke, Morton. "*Penthouse* Interview: Vincent Marchetti." *Penthouse*, VI (January 1975), 60+.

2037. Lawrence, David. "The CIA and American Interests: Reprinted From the Washington *Evening-Star*, May 3, 1966." *Congressional Record*, CXII (May 5, 1966), 9882–9883.

Comments on the *New York Times* articles by Tom Wicker, *et al.*, published in April 1966.

2038. Ledeen, Michael A. "Scoop-and-Dagger." *Harper's*, CCLVIII (January 1979), 91–94.

2039. Loory, Stuart H. "The CIA Use of the Press." *Columbia Journalism Review*, XIII (September–October 1974), 9–18.

2040. Marchetti, Vincent. "Spooking the Spooks: An Interview." *Ramparts*, XI (December 1972), 8+.

2041. Marks, John D. "On Being Censored." *Foreign Policy*, XV (Summer 1974), 93–107.

2042. Muggeridge, Malcom. "Books: The CIA Cultural Penetration." *Esquire*, LXVIII (September 1967), 12+.

2043. Nathan, James. "Did Kissinger Leak the Big One?" *Washington Monthly*, VI (July 1974), 25–27.

2044. "No Newsmen in CIA's Future, But the Past Still Haunts Some." *Broadcasting*, XC (February 16, 1976), 22–24.

2045. Nufer, Harold F. "Four Momentous Events in 1971–72: Catalysts For Reform of the National Security Classification System." *Air University Review*, XXVIII (July–August 1977), 56–64.

Pentagon Papers and "scoops" by Jack Anderson.

2046. Nwuneli, Emmanuel O. "The Rise and Fall of *Transition* Magazine." Unpublished M.A. thesis, University of Wisconsin, 1970. CIA front journal in Uganda.

2047. Pincus, William. "Covering Intelligence: *New York Times* Coverage of Central Intellegence Agency Operations." *New Republic*, CLXXII (February 1, 1975), 10–12.

2048. "Rising Criticism of the Leaks: The Final Report of the House Intelligence Committee." *Time*, CVII (February 9, 1976), 18+.

2049. Rogers, J. N. " 'The Selling of the Pentagon': Was CBS the Fulbright Propaganda Machine?" *Quarterly Journal of Speech*, LVII (October 1971), 266–273.

No direct CIA tie-in.

2050. Roman, Dave, jt. author. *See* Trenton, Joe (2066).

2051. Rosenfeld, Stephen S. "An Ex-Moscow Correspondent's CIA Footnote: Reprinted from the *Washington Post*, April 30, 1976." In: U.S. Congress. House. Permanent Select Committee on Intelligence. Subcommittee on Oversight. *CIA and the Media: Hearings.* 95th Cong., 1st and 2nd sess. Washington, D.C.: GPO, 1978. p. 357.

Establishes that *The Penkovskiy Papers* was written by the CIA.

2052. Rourke, Francis E. *Secrecy and Publicity: Dilemma of Democracy.* Baltimore, MD: Johns Hopkins University Press, 1961. 236p.

2053. Schmidt, Benno C., jt. author. *See* Edgar, Harold (2023).

2054. Schorr, Daniel. "Are CIA Assets a Press Liability?" *More*, VIII (February 1978), 18–23.

2055. _____ . "Behind the Lines With Daniel Schorr: An Interview." *Christianity and Crisis*, XXXVI (April 26, 1976), 93–98.

2056. _____ . "The CIA at CBS: Cloak-and-Camera at Black Rock." *New York Magazine*, X (September 26, 1977), 40+.

2057. _____ . *Clearing the Air.* Boston: Houghton, Mifflin, 1977. 333p.

2058. _____ . "The FBI and Me." *Columbia Journalism Review*, XIII (November 1974), 8–14.

2059. _____ . "My Eighteen Months on the CIA Watch: A Backstage Journal." *Rolling Stone,* no. 210 (April 8, 1976), 32+.

2060. "Schorr Statement on the House CIA Report." In: Robert A. Diamond, ed. *Historic Documents of 1976.* Washington, D.C.: Congressional Quarterly, Inc., 1977. pp. 683–687.

2061. "Schorr Strikes Back," *More,* VII (September 1977), 48+.

2062. Seib, Charles B. "The Press/Spy Affair—Cozy and Still Murky: Reprinted From the *Washington Post,* October 11, 1977." In: U.S. Congress. House. Permanent Select Committee on Intelligence. Subcommittee on Oversight. *CIA and the Media: Hearings.* 95th Cong., 1st and 2nd sess. Washington, D.C.: GPO, 1978. p. 338.

Comments on Carl Bernstein's *Rolling Stone* article cited above.

2063. Stern, Laurence. "The Daniel Schorr Affair, With Reply by Daniel Schorr." *Columbia Journalism Review,* XV (May, July 1976), 20–25, 48–49.

2064. Stone, Isidor F. "The Schorr Case: The Real Dangers." *New York Review of Books,* XXIII (April 1, 1976), 6–11.

2065. "Tinker, Tailor, Newsman, Spy?" *Broadcasting,* XC (February 2, 1976), 33+.

2066. Trenton, Joe and Dave Roman. "The Spies Who Came In From the Newsroom." *Penthouse,* VIII (August 1977), 44+.

2067. "Trying to Expose the CIA." *Time,* CIII (April 22, 1974). 22+.

Marchetti and Marks.

2068. United States. Congress. House. Committee on Interstate and Foreign Commerce. *Network News Documentary Practices; CBS "Project Nassau": Hearings.* 91st Cong., 1st and 2nd sess. Washington, D.C.: GPO, 1978. 487p.

TV news program looks at a group determined to invade Haiti; for contacts between CIA, FBI, and CBS, see pp. 128–147.

2069. _____ . _____ . _____ . _____ . *Network News Documentary Practices; CBS "Project Nassau": Report.* 91st Cong., 2nd sess. Washington, D.C.: GPO, 1970. 154p.

2070. _____ . _____ . _____ . Committee on Government Operations. Subcommittee on Foreign Operations and Government Information. *Security Classification Reform: Hearings.* 93rd Cong., 2nd sess. Washington, D.C.: GPO, 1974. 756p.

2071. _____ . _____ . Senate. Permanent Select Committee on Intelligence. Subcommittee on Oversight. *The CIA and the Media: Hearings.* 95th Cong., 1st and 2nd sess. Washington, D.C.: GPO, 1978. 627p.

2072. _____ . _____ . _____ . Committee on Armed Services. *Unauthorized Disclosures and Transmittal of Classified Documents: Report.* 93rd Cong., 2nd sess. Washington, D.C.: GPO, 1974. 11p.

2073. "United States v. Marchetti and Alfred A. Knopf, Inc. v. Colby (509 F 2nd 1362): Secrecy 2—First Amendment 0." *Hastings Constitutional Law Quarterly,* III (Fall 1976), 1073–1105.

2074. Werth, Alexander. "Literary Bay of Pigs: [CIA] Subsidies to Cultural Freedom Publications." *Nation,* CCIV (June 5, 1967), 710–711.

2075. "When Spies Talk Shop." *Nation,* CCXXIV (April 16, 1977), 452–453.

2076. Wicker, Tom. "Secrecy Triumphant: Reprinted From the *New York Times,* June 24, 1975." *Congressional Record,* CXXI (June 25, 1975), 20925.

2077. Wise, David. "Hidden Hands in Publishing." *New Republic,* CLVII (October 21, 1967), 17–18.

2077a. Zahn, Gordon C. "One Man's Files." *America,* CXXXV (December 18, 1976), 438–442.

    (6) Cia and Science: Hardware, Animals, Poisons,
        Weather, and Behavior Modification

2078. A.B.C. News *A.B.C. News Closeup—Mission: Mind Control; Transcript of a TV Broadcast, January 30, 1979.* New York, 1979.

2079. "The Beep, Blink and Thrum of Spy Gadgetry." *Newsweek,* LXXXV (November 22, 1971), 38.

2080. Buckman, John. "Brainwashing, LSD, and the CIA: Historical and Ethical Perspectives." *Journal of Social Psychology,* XXIII (Spring 1977), 8–19.

2081. Caldwell, Carol. "Beyond ESP: The Work of Russell Targ and Harold Puthoff." *New Times,* X (April 3, 1978), 42–50.

2082. Caplan, Peter. "Weather Modification and War." *Bulletin of the Concerned Asian Scholars,* VI (January–March 1974), 28–31.

2083. "CIA Climate Report: Assessing the Impact." *Science News,* CIX (May 15, 1976), 310–311.

2084. Clark, Edward. "How Business Bolsters Our Intelligence Defenses." *Nation's Business,* LX (August 1972), 54–56+.

2085. Crangle, Robert D. "Spying, the CIA, and the New Technology." *Ripon Forum*, VI (February 1970), 7–14.

2086. "ESP: Another of CIA's Secret Weapons?" *Psychic World*, VII (May 1976), 19–20.

2087. Gaines, J. R. "The CIA's Show-and-Tell: Toxic Weapons Stockpile." *Newsweek*, LXXXVI (September 29, 1975), 42+.

2088. Getlein, Frank. "Mind Controllers." *Commonweal*, CIV (September 2, 1977), 548–549.

2089. Greenwood, Michael. "Dolphins: Deadly Underwater Weapon." *Argosy*, CCCLXXXIV (October 1976), 24–28.

2090. Lardner, George, Jr. "CIA Said to Keep Poisons: Reprinted From the *Washington Post*, September 9, 1975." *Congressional Record*, CXXI (October 28, 1975), 33902–33903.

2091. Lubow, Robert E. *The War Animals*. Garden City, NY: Doubleday, 1977. 255p.

2092. McLean, Donald B. *The Plumber's Kitchen: The Secret Story of American Spy Weapons*. Wickenburg, AZ: Normount Technical Publications, 1975. 282p.

2093. Marks, John D. *The Search For the Manchurian Candidate: The CIA and Mind Control*. New York: Times Books, 1979. 320p.

2094. _____. "Sex, Drugs, and the CIA: The Shocking Search For an 'Ultimate Weapon.'" *Saturday Review*, VI (February 3, 1979), 12–17.

2095. Milin, Sergei. "Porpoises in CIA Employ." *New Times* (Moscow), no. 28 (July 1978), 38–30.

2096. "Mind-Bending Disclosures: Drug Testing." *Time*, CX (August 15, 1977), 22+.

2097. Minnery, John and J. D. Truby. *Improvised Modified Firearms*. Boulder, CO: Paladin Press, 1975. 140p.

2098. "The Motto is 'Think Big, Think Dirty.'" *Time* CXI (February 6, 1978), 12–13.

Secret supplies and equipment.

2099. Orth, Maureen. "Memoirs of a CIA Psychologist." *New Times*, VI (June 25, 1976), 18+.

2100. Osmond, Humphrey. "Science and Secrecy." *20th Century*, CLVI (October 1954), 320–328.

2101.   Packard, Vance. *The People Shapers.* Boston: Little, Brown, 1977.

2102.   Paine, Lauren B. *The Technology of Espionage.* London, Hale, 1978. 191p.

2103.   Scoville, Herbert, Jr. "The Technology of Surveillance." *Society,* XII (March 1975), 58–63.

Other references on technology and surveillance are cited under Covert Operations—North America—United States and National Security Agency.

2104.   Szulc, Tad. "The CIA's Electric Kool-Aid Acid Test: LSD Experimentation." *Psychology Today,* XI (November 1977), 92–94+.

2105.   "Toxin Tocsin: The CIA Stockpile of Toxin Weapons." *Time,* CVI (September 22, 1975), 31.

2106.   United States. Central Intelligence Agency. "CIA-Fort Detrich Army Biological Laboratory Joint Biological Weapons Testing Activities, 1953–1970: Declassified Summary Report, 1975." In: U.S. Congress. Senate. Committee on Human Resources. *Biological Testing Involving Human Subjects by the Department of Defense: Hearings.* 95th Cong., 1st sess. Washington, D.C.: GPO, 1977. pp. 244–256.

2107.   _____ . _____ . Office of Research and Development. *A Study of Climatological Research as It Pertains to Intelligence Problems.* Washington, D.C.: 1974. 36p.

2108.   _____ . Congress. Senate. Committee on Human Resources. *Biological Testing Involving Human Subjects by the Department of Defense: Hearings.* 95th Cong., 1st sess. Washington, D.C.: GPO, 1977.

2109.   _____ . _____ . _____ . Select Committee on Intelligence and Committee on Human Resources, Subcommittee on Health and Scientific Research. *Project MKultra, the CIA's Program of Research in Behavior Modification* [1953–1964]: *Joint Hearings.* 95th Cong., 1st sess. Washington, D.C.: GPO, 1977. 171p.

2110.   _____ . _____ . _____ . Select Committee to Study Government Operations With Respect to Intelligence Activities. *Unauthorized Storage of Toxic Agents: Hearings.* 94th Cong., 1st sess. Washington, D.C.: GPO, 1976. 245p.

2111.   Waldron, Helen J. *The Acquisition of Special Materials and Symposia, With Notes on Intelligence Materials.* RAND Paper P-3175. Santa Monica, CA: RAND Corporation, 1965. 39p.

2112.   Wall, Patrick D. "Scientists and the CIA, With Discussions." *Science,* CXXXVI (April 13 and June 8, 1962), 173+, 914+; CXXXVII (August 24, 1962), 573.

2113.   Watson, Peter. *War on the Mind: The Military Uses and Abuses of Psychology.* New York: Basic Books, 1978. 534p.

(7) COVERT OPERATIONS—GENERAL WORKS

2114.   Africa Research Group. *Intelligence and Foreign Policy* [The Bissell Remarks]. Cambridge, MA: [1972?] 38p.

2115.   Alpern, David M. "CIA: Assassination Politics." *Newsweek,* LXXXV (June 30, 1975), 16–17.

2116.   _____ . "The CIA's Hit List." *Newsweek,* LXXXVI (December 1, 1975), 28–32+.

2117.   _____ . "How the CIA Does Business." *Newsweek,* LXXXV (May 19, 1975), 25+.

2118.   _____ . "A Tale of Assassination." *Newsweek,* LXXXV (October 4, 1975), 54+.

2119.   "American Militarism: CIA-Directed Paramilitary Operations." *New Republic,* CLX (April 12, 1969), 7–9.

2120.   Anderson, Jack. "CIA Teaches Terrorism to Its Friends: Reprinted From the *Washington Post,* October 8, 1973." In: U.S. Congress. House. Permanent Select Committee on Intelligence. Subcommittee on Oversight. *CIA and the Media: Hearings.* 95th Cong., 1st and 2nd sess. Washington, D.C.: GPO, 1978. p. 352.

2121.   Anson, Robert S. "The CIA and the Mafia." *New Times,* IV (May 20, 1975), 34+.

2122.   Ashman, Charles. *The CIA-Mafia Link.* New York: Manor Books, 1975.

2123.   Bach, C. L. "The CIA and the Funny Men." *America,* CXXXVII (September 17, 1977), 142–145.

2124.   Barnet, Richard J. "The CIA's New Cover." *New York Review of Books,* (December 30, 1971), 6–8.

2125.   _____ . "Dirty Tricks and the Intelligence Underworld." *Society,* XII (March–April 1975), 52–57.

2126.   _____ . "The 'Dirty-Tricks Gap.'" In: Robert L. Borosage and John D. Marks, eds. *The CIA File.* New York: Grossman, 1976. pp. 214–288.

2127.   _____ . *Intervention and Revolution: America's Confrontation With Insurgent Movements Around the World.* Cleveland, OH: World Publishing Co., 1968. 302p.

2128.   Beilenson, L.W. *Power Through Subversion*. Washington, D.C.: Public Affairs Press, 1972. 310p.

2129.   Berger, Marilyn. "Dirty Tricks Have Had a Long History: Reprinted From the *Washington Post*, May 28, 1973." *Congressional Record*, CXIX (May 29, 1973), 17056–17058.

2130.   Bevilacqua, A. C. "Intelligence and Insurgency." *Marine Corps Gazette*, LX (January 1976), 40–46.

2131.   Bissell, Richard M., Jr. "The Bissell Philosophy: Minutes of the 1968 'Bissell Meeting' at the Council on Foreign Relations as Reprinted by the African Research Group." In: Victor Marchetti and John D. Marks. *The CIA and the Cult of Intelligence*. New York: Knopf, 1974. pp. 379–398.

2132.   "Bits and Pieces: Assassination Plots." *Nation*, CCXXI (July 5, 1975), 4–5.

2133.   Blackstock, Paul W. *Agents of Deceit: Frauds, Forgeries, and Political Intrigue Among Nations*. New York: Quadrangle Books, 1966. 315p.

2134.   _____. *Intelligence and Covert Operations: Changing Doctrine and Practice*. Columbia, SC: Department of Government and International Studies, University of South Carolina, 1973. 125p.

2135.   _____. *The Strategy of Subversion: Manipulating the Politics of Other Nations*. New York: Quadrangle Books, 1964. 351p.

2136.   Borosage, Robert L. and John D. Marks, eds. *The CIA File: Proceedings and Papers Presented at a Conference, "The CIA and Covert Action," Held in Washington, D.C., September 1974, Sponsored by the Center for National Security Studies*. New York: Grossman, 1976. 236p.

2137.   Branch, Tom. "Raising a Glass to Beau Geste." *Esquire*, LXXXVI (August 1976), 30–33.

2138.   "Brutal Intelligence: The CIA's Assassination Plots Against Foreign Leaders." *New Republic*, CLXXIII (December 6, 1975), 5–6.

2139.   Burroughs, William S. "The Time of the Assassins." *Crawdaddy*, (October 1975), 12+.

2140.   "The CIA and Assassination Plots: The Rockefeller Report Stirs a Furor." *U.S. News and World Report*, LXXVIII (June 16, 1975), 33+.

2141.   "CIA Murder Plots: Weighing the Damage to the U.S." *U.S. News and World Report*, LXXIX (December 1, 1975), 13–16.

2142.   Camellion, Richard. *Assassination: Theory and Practice*. Boulder, CO: Paladin Press, 1977. 161p.

2143.   Church, Frank. "Covert Action: The Swampland of American Foreign Policy." *Bulletin of the Atomic Scientists,* XXXII (February 1976), 7–11.

2144.   _____ . "The Covert Operations." *Center Magazine,* IX (March–April 1976), 21–25.

2145.   Cohen, Eliot A. *Commandos and Politicians: Elite Military Units in Modern Democracies.* Studies in International Affairs, no. 40. Cambridge, MA: Center for International Affairs, Harvard University, 1978. 136p.

2146.   Colby, William E. "CIA's Covert Actions." *Center Magazine,* VIII (March 1975), 71–80.

2147.   _____ . "The View From Langley." In: Robert L. Borosage and John D. Marks, eds. *The CIA File.* New York, Grossman, 1976. pp. 181–187.

2148.   Cottam, Richard W. *Competitive Interference and 20th Century Democracy.* Pittsburgh, PA: University of Pittsburgh Press, 1967. 243p.

Important because of one statement: "If the CIA is to be effective in the more clandestine aspects of diplomacy, it must be granted a good deal of freedom to interpret and improvise upon stated general policy."

2149.   Donner, Frank J. "Intelligence on the Attack: The Terrorist as Scapegoat." *Nation,* CCXXVI (May 20, 1978), 590–594.

2150.   Draper, Theodore. *Abuse of Power.* New York: Viking, 1967.

2151.   Dulles, Allen W. "Problems of Freedom in Newly-Emerging States: Remarks, October 15, 1958." *Department of State Bulletin,* XXXIX (November 24, 1958), 827–830.

2152.   Eisenhower, David. "The White House Killers: Reprinted From the *Wall Street Journal,* December 4, 1975." *Congressional Record,* CXXI (December 19, 1975), 42085–42086.

2153.   Evans, Medford. "Fit to Kill: The Presidency and Political Assassination." *American Opinion,* XVII (May 1974), 35–37+.

2154.   Falk, Richard A. "CIA Covert Action and International Law." *Society,* XII (March–April 1975), 39–44.

2155.   _____ . "President Gerald Ford, CIA Covert Operations, and the Status of International Law." *American Journal of International Law,* LXIX (April 1975), 354–358.

2156.   Fallows, James. "Crazies By the Tail: Bay of Pigs, Diem, and [Gordon] Liddy." *Washington Monthly,* VI (July 1974), 50–58.

2157. _____ . "Murder By the Book." *Washington Monthly*, VIII (April 1976), 22–24.

2158. Ford, Harold P. "Piety and Wit: The Bad Effects of Covert CIA Activity." *America*, CXXXII (January 11, 1975), 10–11.

2159. "Foreign Watergates: Collaboration Between the CIA and American Multi-National Corporations in Foreign Intrigue." *Nation*, CCXXI (August 16, 1975), 98–99.

2160. Frank, Elke, jt author. *See* Irish, Marian (2169).

2161. Friedrich, Carl J. *The Pathology of Politics: Violence, Betrayal, Corruption, Secrecy, and Propaganda*. New York: Harper & Row, 1972. 287p.

2162. Gelb, Leslie H. "Should We Play Dirty Tricks in the World." *New York Times Magazine*, (December 21, 1975), 10–11 +.

2163. George, Alexander L. *The Limits of Coercive Diplomacy*. Boston: Little, Brown, 1971.

2164. Halperin, Morton H. "Activists at the CIA: The Cult of Incompetence." *New Republic*, CLXXIII (November 8, 1975), 11–12 +.

2165. _____ . "Covert Operations: Effects of Secrecy on Decision-Making." In: Robert L. Borosage and John D. Marks, eds. *The CIA File*. New York: Grossman, 1976. pp. 159–177.

2166. _____ . "Decision-Making For Covert Operations." *Society*, XII (March–April 1975), 45–51.

2167. _____ and Jeremy J. Stone. "Secrecy and Covert Intelligence Collection and Operations." *Congressional Record*, CXX (September 19, 1974), 31791–31799.

2168. Hoffman, Kenneth, *et al*. "Should Our Foreign Policy Include Covert Action By the CIA?" In: Pamela W. Barry, ed. *A Teacher's Guide to "The Advocates."* Boston: WGBH Educational Foundation, 1979. pp. 3–6.

2169. Irish, Marian and Elke Frank. "Intelligence and Covert Operations." In: *U.S. Foreign Policy: Context, Conduct, and Content*. New York: Harcourt, Brace, 1975. pp. 482–492.

2170. Jackson, Robert L. "CIA-Mafia Links Confirmed: Reprinted From the *Washington Post*, July 10, 1975." *Congressional Record*, CXXI (October 28, 1975), 33897.

2171. Jacobs, Arthur L. "Should the U.S. Use Covert Action in the Conduct of Foreign Policy?" *Freedom at Issue*, XXXV (1976), 13–19.

2172.   Kennedy, Robert F., Jr. "Politics and Assassinations: Reprinted From the *Wall Street Journal,* December 6, 1975." *Congressional Record,* CXXI (December 19, 1975), 42086–42087.

A reply to the piece by David Eisenhower (2152).

2173.   Kirkpatrick, Lyman B., Jr. "Overseas Operations." In: *The U.S. Intelligence Community: Foreign Policy and Domestic Activities.* New York: Hill and Wang, 1973. Chpt. V.

2174.   Kohn, Howard. "Strange Bedfellows: The Hughes, Nixon, Lansky Connection—the Secret Alliances of the CIA From World War II to Watergate." *Rolling Stone,* no. 213 (May 20, 1976), 40+.

2175.   Kondracke, Morton. "The CIA and Our Conspiracy." *More,* V (May 1975), 10–12.

2176.   Latham, Aaron. "Orchids For Mother: Behind the CIA Cover Stories." *New York Magazine,* VIII (April 7, 1975), 27+.

2177.   McCarthy, Eugene. "Speaking Out: The CIA is Getting Out of Hand and Meddles in Foreign Policy." *Saturday Evening Post,* CCXXXVII (January 4, 1964), 6+.

2178.   Marchetti, Victor and John D. Marks. "Inside the CIA: The Clandestine Mentality." *Ramparts,* XII (July 1974), 21–25+.

2179.   Marks, John D., jt author. *See* Marchetti, Victor (2178).

2180.   _____ , jt. editor. *See* Borosage, Robert L. (2136).

2181.   Masters, Barrie P. "The Ethics of Intelligence Activities." *National Security Affairs Forum,* no. 24 (Spring–Summer 1976), 39–47.

2182.   Mauzy, Richard, jt. author. *See* Morris, Roger P. (2184).

2183.   "Militarism and the Impact of CIA." *Current,* CVIII (June 1969), 55–58.

2184.   Morris, Roger P. and Richard Mauzy. "Following the Scenario: Reflections on Five Case Histories in the Mode and Aftermath of CIA Intervention." In: Robert L. Borosage and John D. Marks, eds. *The CIA File.* New York: Grossman, 1976. pp. 28–45.

2185.   "Murder, Inc." *Commonweal,* CII (July 18, 1975), 259–260.

2186.   Murphy, Charles J. V. "Assassination Plot that Failed: The CIA's Alleged Plots." *Time,* CV (June 30, 1975), 28–29.

2187.   Osborn, Kenneth B. "The CIA Scapel Cut Deep."*Playboy,* XXII (August 1975), 58+.

2188.   Rositzke, Harry. "America's Secret Operations: A Perspective." *Foreign Affairs,* LIII (January 1975), 334–351.

2189.   _____ . *The CIA's Secret Operations: Espionage, Counterespionage, and Covert Action.* New York: Reader's Digest Press; dist. by Crowell, 1977. 286p.

2190.   Russell, Charles A. and Robert E. Hildner. "Intelligence and Information Processing in Counterinsurgency." *Air University Review,* XXIV (July–August 1973), 46–56.

2192.   Salisbury, Harrison E. "The Gentlemen Killers of the CIA." *Penthouse,* VI (May 1975), 47+.

2192.   Schorr, Daniel. "The Assassins." *New York Review of Books,* XXIV (October 13, 1977), 14+.

2193.   Scott, Andrew M. *The Revolution in Statecraft: Informal Penetration.* New York: Random House, 1965. 194p.

2194.   *Should the CIA Engage in Covert Operations: Transcript of a Debate on "The Advocates," February 11, 1979.* Boston: WGBH Educational Foundation, 1979. 35p.

2195.   Simonyan, R. "CIA: The Back-Stage Manager." *Soviet Military Review,* no. 8 (August 1976), 44–47.

2196.   Stone, Jeremy J., jt. author. *See* Halperin, Morton H. (2167).

2197.   Szulc. Tad. "Exporting Revolution." *New Republic,* CLXXI (September 21, 1974), 7–9.

2198.   _____ . *The Illusion of Peace: Foreign Policy in the Nixon Years.* New York: Viking Press, 1978. 822p.

Covers covert operations, especially in South America.

2199.   _____ . "Murder By Proxy." *Penthouse,* VI (August 1975), 44+.

2200.   Taylor, Maxwell D. *Swords and Plowshares.* New York: Norton, 1972. 434p.

2201.   United States. Army. Special Forces. *Clandestine and Intelligence Operations (U.).* Army Subject Schedule (c.) 31–22. Ft. Bragg, NC, 1967.

2202.   _____ . _____ . _____ . *Sabotage (U.).* Army Subject Schedule (c.) 31–28. Ft. Bragg, NC, 1967.

2203.   _____ . Central Intelligence Agency. *Co-ordination of U.S. Clandestine Foreign Intelligence and Activities Abroad.* Directive, no. 5/1. Langley, VA: 1976.

2204. _____. _____. *The Defector Program Abroad.* Directive, no. 4/2. Langley, VA, 1976.

2205. _____. Congress. Senate. Select Committee to Study Government Operations With Respect to Intelligence Activities. *Alleged Assassination Plots Involving Foreign Leaders: An Interim Report.* 94th Cong., 1st sess. Washington, D.C.: GPO, 1975. 349p.

2206. _____. Library of Congress. Congressional Reference Service. "Reported Foreign and Domestic Covert Activities of the United States Central Intelligence Agency, 1950–1974: CRS Study 75–50F." *Congressional Record,* CXXI (September 30, 1975), 31023–31025.

2207. Walden, Jerrold L. "Proselytes For Espionage: The CIA and Domestic Fronts." *Journal of Public Law,* XIX (1970), 179+.

2208. Watching the CIA at Work Around the World." *U.S. News and World Report,* LXII (March 6, 1961), 28–30.

2209. Westerfield, H. Bradford. "Methods and Lessons of Nonmilitary Intervention." In: *The Instruments of America's Foreign Policy.* New York: Crowell, 1963. pp. 443–455.

2210. Wise, David. "Covert Operations Abroad: An Overview." In: Robert L. Borosage and John D. Marks, eds. *The CIA File.* New York: Grossman, 1976. pp. 3–27.

2211. Wolpin, Miles D. "Egalitarian Reformism in the Third World vs. the Military: A Profile of Failure." *Journal of Peace Research,* XV (Spring 1978), 89–107.

g. Congressional Oversight and Administrative Reform

2212. Adam, Corinna. "CIA Under the Bed." *New Statesman and Nation,* LXXXVII (February 1, 1974), 138+.

2213. Adler, Renata. "Reflections on a Political Scandal." *New York Review of Books,* XXIV (December 8, 1977), 20–33.

2214. Agee, Philip. "How to Neutralize the CIA." *Skeptic,* no. 7 (May–June 1975), 50–51.

2215. Alpern, David M. "Ford's CIA Shake-up." *Newsweek,* LXXXVII (March 1, 1976), 18–19.

2216. _____. "Going Public." *Newsweek,* LXXXV (May 26, 1975), 32+.

2217. _____. "Inquest on Intelligence: Final Report of the Senate Select Committee." *Newsweek,* LXXXVII (May 10, 1976), 40+.

2218. _____ . "Is the CIA Hobbled?" *Newsweek,* XCIII (March 5, 1979), 41–44.

2219. _____ . "Now You See It [Rockefeller Commission], Now You Don't." *Newsweek,* LXXXV (June 16, 1975), 18+

2220. _____ . "Who's Watching Whom?" *Newsweek,* LXXXV (June 23, 1975), 19–22+.

2221. "As Pressure on CIA Builds Up, With an Interview With Robert Conquest." *U.S. News and World Report,* LXXVIII (February 24, 1975), 44–46.

2222. Association of the Bar of the City of New York. *The Central Intelligence Agency: Oversight and Accountability.* New York, 1975. 46p.

2223. "Backlash Over All Those Leaks: The Reform of Intelligence Agencies." *Time,* CVII (February 23, 1976), 11–12.

2224. Ball, George. *Diplomacy For a Crowded World: An American Foreign Policy.* Boston: Little, Brown, 1976. 356p.

See Part III for reform recommendations.

2225. Barnet, Richard J. "The Next Move is Up to Congress: Oversight of Intelligence Operations, A Statement, February 23, 1976." *Nation,* CCXXII (March 13, 1976), 299–301.

2226. Berman, Jerry J. and Morton H. Halperin. "Fight Over Oversight: The Proposed Senate Committee to Oversee Intelligence Agencies." *New Republic,* CLXXIV (May 8, 1976), 11–14.

2227. _____ , *et al. A Comparison of Proposals For Reforming the Intelligence Agencies.* Washington, D.C.: Center for National Security Studies, Georgetown University, 1978. 71p.

2228. "Big Changes Ahead For the CIA After a Damaging [Rockefeller Commission] Review." *U.S. News and World Report,* LXXVIII (June 23, 1975), 17–19.

2229. "The Big Shake-up in a Gentleman's Club." *Time,* CI (April 30, 1973), 18–19.

2230. "Blue-Ribbon [Rockefeller Commission] Treatment For the CIA." *Newsweek,* LXXXV (January 13, 1975), 24–26.

2231. Borosage, Robert L. "[President] Ford's Blueprint For Arrogance: The Program to Overhaul the Intelligence Agencies." *Nation,* CCXXII (March 13, 1976), 296–299.

2232. Braden, Tom. "What's Wrong With the CIA?" *Saturday Review,* II (April 5, 1975), 14–18.

2233. Branch, Taylor. "The Scandal-Maker Stakes." *More*, V (March 1975), 18–21.

2234. _____ . "The Trial of the CIA." *New York Times Magazine*, (September 12, 1976), 35+.

2235. "Breaking Up CIA." *New Republic*, CXLIV (June 19–26, 1961), 1+.

2236. Buckley, William F., Jr. "The Assault on the CIA." *National Review*, XXVII (March 14, 1975), 302.

2237. _____ . "The CIA on the Defensive." *National Review*, XXVII (February 28, 1975), 240–241.

2238. _____ . "Intelligence Notes." *National Review*, XXX (September 15, 1978), 1164–1165.

2239. _____ . "The [Senate] Intelligence Committee." *National Review*, XXVIII (July 9, 1976), 750–751.

2240. Carter, Jimmy. "The Intelligence Community: Announcement of the President's Decision on the Organization and Functions of the Community, August 4, 1977." *Weekly Compilation of Presidential Documents*, XIII (August 8, 1977), 1175–1177.

2241. _____ . "United States Intelligence Activities: Executive Order 12036." *Federal Register*, XLIII (January 26, 1978), Appendix III, 3675–3680.

2242. "The Central Intelligence Agency: Present Authority and Proposed Legislative Change." *Virginia Law Review*, LXII (March 1976), 332–382.

2243. "Checking the CIA." *New Republic*, CLXXII (January 4, 1975), 7–8.

2244. Cherne, Leo. "Intelligence Cannot Help a Nation Find Soul: It is Indispensable, However, to Help Preserve That Nation's Safety While It Continues the Search." *Freedom at Issue*, XXXV (1976), 6–11.

2245. "The CIA Must Be Salvaged: Reprinted From the *San Diego Union*, June 13, 1975." *Congressional Record*, CXXI (June 19, 1975), 19891–19892.

2246. "The CIA Scandal—and the Backlash." *U.S. News and World Report*, LXXVIII (January 6, 1975), 51–52.

2247. "CIA Target of Overkill: Reprinted from the *Aiken* [South Carolina] *Standard*, September 2, 1975." *Congressional Record*, CXXI (September 16, 1975), 28871–28872.

2248. "CIA: Time To Come in From the Cold." *Time,* CIV (September 30, 1974), 16–24.

2249. Colby, William E. "After Investigating U.S. Intelligence." In: George Wittman, ed. *The Role of the American Intelligence Organizations.* Reference Shelf, v. 48, no. 5. New York: H. W. Wilson, 1976. pp. 133–135.

2250. _____ . "Colby Report on the CIA." In: Robert E. Cuthriell, ed. *Historical Documents of 1975.* Washington, D.C.: Congressional Quarterly, Inc., 1976. pp. 523–529.

2251. _____ . "It's Maddening and Frustrating: An Interview." *Time,* CVII (January 19, 1976), 14+.

2252. "A New Law to Guard National Secrets?: An Interview." *U.S. News and World Report,* LXXIX (August 18, 1977), 37–38.

2253. _____ , et al. "Reorganizing the CIA: Who and How." *Foreign Policy,* (Summer 1976), 53–63.

2254. Commager, Henry S. "Intelligence: The Constitution Betrayed." *New York Review of Books,* XXIII (September 30, 1976), 32–37.

2255. "Commonsense Proposals [by Senator Walter Mondale] on Intelligence: Reprinted from the *Minneapolis Tribune,* October 9, 1975." *Congressional Record,* CXXI (October 9, 1975), 32873–32874.

2256. "Congress and Intelligence." *New Republic,* CLXXII (May 10, 1975), 5–6.

2257. "Congress and the CIA." *Nation,* CCXIII (November 29, 1971), 548–549.

2258. Costa, John and Gary L. Evans. *Legislation Introduced Relative to the Activities of the Intelligence Agencies, 1947–1972.* UB-250-U.S.A.-73-22F. Washington, D.C.: Congressional Research Service, Library of Congress, 1973. 63p.

2259. Cotter, R. D. "Notes Towards a Definition of National Security." *Washington Monthly,* VII (December 1975), 4–16.

2260. Crouse, Timothy. "Beware of Spooks Bearing Gifts." *Esquire,* LXXXV (January 1976), 38+.

2261. "Curbing the Spooks: Hearings on the National Intelligence Reorganization and Reform Act of 1978." *Progressive,* XLII (November 1978), 10–11.

2262. Day, Bonner. "The Battle Over U.S. Intelligence." *Air Force Magazine,* LXI (May 1978), 42–47.

2263.   Dedijer, Stevan. "Watching the Watchmen: Parliaments and National Intelligence Services." *Bulletin of the Atomic Scientists,* XXXIV (June 1978), 40–43.

2264.   Dellums, Robert V. "Probing the Intelligence Community." *Ebony,* XXXI (March 1976), 42+.

2265.   Donner, Frank J. "Investigating the FBI and the CIA." *Current,* CLXXII (April 1975), 31–37.

2266.   Donovan, Thomas A. "Asking the Unthinkable." *Commonweal,* CII (June 20, 1975), 196–198.

2267.   _____ . "The CIA Investigation." *Foreign Service Journal,* LII (October 1975), 19–20.

2268.   Eisenhower, David and Robert F. Kennedy, Jr. "Another Generation Heard From: Investigations of Executive Responsibilities." *Saturday Evening Post,* CCXLVIII (April 1976), 18+.

2269.   Eliff, John T. *The Reform of FBI Intelligence Activities.* Princeton, NJ: Princeton University Press, 1979. 248p.

2270.   Evans, Gary L., jt author. *See* Costa, John (2258).

2271.   "Examining the Examiners." *Time,* CV (January 20, 1975), 31–32.

2272.   Fallows, James. "Putting the Wisdom Back Into Intelligence." *Washington Monthly,* V (April 1973), 6–17.

2273.   Ford, Gerald R. "Ford's Intelligence Reorganization." In: Robert A. Daniel, ed. *Historical Documents of 1976.* Washington, D.C.: Congressional Quarterly, Inc., 1977. pp. 125–143.

2274.   _____ . "President Ford Announces Plans For Reorganization of the Intelligence Community: Opening Statement From News Conference, With Text of Message to Congress, February 18, 1976." *Department of State Bulletin,* LXXIV (March 8, 1976), 292–294.

2275.   _____ . "The President's News Conference of February 17, 1976." *Weekly Compilation of Presidential Documents,* XII (February 23, 1976), 227–232.

2276.   _____ . "United States Foreign Intelligence Activities: Executive Order 11905, February 18, 1976." *Weekly Compilation of Presidential Documents,* XII (February 23, 1976), 234–243.

2277.   "Ford's Plan to Rein in the CIA: Its Impact." *U.S. News and World Report,* LXXX (March 1, 1976), 18+.

2278.   Fritchey, Clayton. "The CIA Under Fire." *Harper's,* CCXXXIII (October 1966), 37–38+.

2279.   Fromm, John. "Reform of the CIA: What It Really Boils Down To." *U.S. News and World Report,* LXXX (May 10, 1976), 23–24.

2280.   Futterman, Stanley N. "Toward Legislative Control of the CIA." *New York University Journal of International Law and Politics,* IV (Winter 1971), 431–458.

2281.   Gaines, J. R. "The Wounded CIA." *Newsweek,* LXXXVI (November 17, 1975), 47+.

2282.   Gelb, Leslie H. "Spy Inquiries, Begun in Outrage, End in Indifference: Reprinted From the *New York Times,* May 12, 1976." In: George Wittman, ed. *The Role of the American Intelligence Organizations.* Reference Shelf, v. 48, no. 5. New York: H. W. Wilson, 1976. pp. 114–121.

2283.   Godfrey, E. Drexell, Jr. and Arthur L. Jacobs. "Ethics and Intelligence." *Foreign Affairs,* LVI (April, July 1978), 624–642, 867–875.

2284.   Gray, Robert C. "Reforming the CIA." *Intellect,* CIV (March 1976), 426–428.

2285.   Greenfield, Meg. "Why We Don't Know Anything." *Newsweek,* XCII (December 18, 1978), 112.

2286.   Griswold, Lawrence. "The Congress and Intelligence." *Sea Power,* XIX (June 1976), 31–34.

2287.   Gruenstein, Peter. "Congress' Consistent Failure: Reprinted From the Valparaiso [Indiana] *Vidette-Messenger,* April 2, 1975." *Congressional Record,* CXXI (April 22, 1975), 11304–11305.

2288.   Halperin, Morton H. "CIA: Denying What's Not in Writing." *New Republic,* CLXXIII (October 4, 1975), 11–12.

2289.   ———. "Removing Kissinger's Cover." *Playboy,* XXIII (October 1976), 45+.

2290.   ———, jt. author. *See* Berman, Jerry J. (2226).

2291.   Hamilton, Andrew. "The CIA's Dirty Tricks Under Fire at Last." *Progressive,* XXXVII (September 1973), 14–22.

2292.   Harrington, Michael J. "Congress' CIA Cover-up: Getting Out the Truth." *New Republic,* CLXXIII (July 26, 1975), 14–17.

2293. Hersh, Seymour M. "Watching the Watchdogs: Revelations." *Commonweal,* CI (January 17, 1975), 318–320.

2294. Horrock, Nicholas M. "A Few in Congress Could See What the Spooks Were Doing: Reprinted From the *New York Times,* February 1, 1976." In: George Wittman, ed. *The Role of the American Intelligence Organizations.* Reference Shelf, v. 48, no. 5. New York: H. W. Wilson, 1976. pp. 84–88.

2295. _____. "Ford Aides Seek to Modify Laws on Spying Methods: Reprinted From the *New York Times,* October 15, 1975." *Congressional Record,* CXXI (October 28, 1975), 33900–33901.

2296. Hunt, Richard M. "CIA Exposures: End of an Affair." *Virginia Quarterly Review,* XLV (Spring 1969), 211–229.

2297. "Intelligence and Horse Sense." *Nation,* CCXXII (April 3, 1976), 386–388.

2298. "Intelligence Agencies and the Constitution: Reprinted From the *Washington Post,* January 14, 1975." *Congressional Record,* CXXI (January 17, 1975), 800–801.

2299. Jacobs, Arthur L., jt. author. *See* Godfrey, E. Drexell, Jr. (2283).

2300. Kaiser, Frederick M. *Congressional Oversight of Intelligence: Status and Recommendations.* Washington, D.C.: Congressional Research Service, Library of Congress, 1976. 50p.

2301. Kissinger, Henry A. "Congress and the U.S. Intelligence Community: A Statement, February 5, 1976." *Department of State Bulletin,* LXXIV (March 1, 1976), 274–277.

2302. Kraft, Joseph. "Recasting Intelligence: Reprinted From the *Washington Post,* November 9, 1971." *Congressional Record,* CXVII (November 10, 1971), 40284–40285.

2303. Labreche, John. "The CIA Affair: A Bad Trip Revisited." *Maclean's,* XCII (February 12, 1979), 18–20.

2304. Lardner, George, Jr. "Clash in Congress Over the Honorable Schoolboy: Hearings on the National Intelligence Act." *Nation,* CCXXVII (September 2, 1978), 168–171.

2305. _____. "The Intelligence Investigations: Congress Cops Out." *Progressive,* XL (July 1976), 13–17.

2306. Larson, Janet K. "Watch List For Intelligence Reform." *Christian Century,* XCIV (August 3, 1977), 688–691.

2307. "Leashing Up the CIA." *New Republic,* CXLIV (May 8, 1961), 3–5.

2308. Lewis, Anthony. "Laws, Men, and the CIA: Reprinted From the *New York Times,* February 23, 1976." In: George Wittman, ed. *The Role of the American Intelligence Organizations.* Reference Shelf, v. 48, no. 5. New York: H. W. Wilson, 1976. pp. 78–80.

2309. Ligonien, John. "Will CIA Survive This Anti-Intelligence Mania?" *Human Events,* (January 11, 1975), 1+.

2310. "A Little Help From Some Friends." *Time,* CVI (December 1, 1975), 30+.

2311. Long, Wayne E. "Reorganization: The Revolution in Intelligence." *Military Review,* LVII (October 1977), 25–31.

2312. McGhee, George C. "CIA Reform: How Much is Enough?" *Saturday Review,* III (May 29, 1976), 5+.

2313. "Major Intelligence Shift Set." *Aviation Week and Space Technology,* CVII (August 8, 1977), 14–17.

2314. Maxfield, David M. and Pat Towell. "Divided [Senate] Intelligence Panel Issues Final Report." *Congressional Quarterly Weekly Report,* XXXIV (February 21, 1976), 1019–1025.

2315. Mondale, Walter F. "The American Intelligence Community and the Future of U.S. Foreign Policy: A Speech Delivered at Denison University, Reprinted." *Congressional Record,* CXXI (October 9, 1975), 32871–32873.

2316. Murphy, Charles J. V. "Uncloaking the CIA." *Fortune,* XCI (June 1975), 88–91+.

2317. National Association of Pro-America. "Urge Protection of Internal Security Organizations: A Resolution, Reprinted." *Congressional Record,* CXXI (December 19, 1975), 42304–42305.

2318. "New Policemen to Battle Abuses: The Overhaul of the Intelligence Agencies." *Time,* CVII (March 1, 1976), 11–12.

2319. Nichols, W. Thomas. "Before Reforming the 'Intelligence Community,' What Questions Must Be Asked?" *Freedom at Issue,* XXXV (1976), 20–23.

2320. Nixon, Richard M. "U.S. Foreign Intelligence Community Reorganized by President Nixon: White House Announcement, November 5, 1971." *Department of State Bulletin,* LXV (December 6, 1971), 658–659.

2321. "Nobody Asked 'Is It Moral?': The Final Report of the Senate Select Committee on Intelligence." *Time,* CVII (May 10, 1976), 32+.

2322. O'Connell, B. J. "Doing Away With Covert Operations." *America,* CXXXIV (March 13, 1976), 204–206.

2323. Osborne, John. "CIA Screw Up." *New Republic,* CLXXII (June 21, 1975), 4–7.

2324. _____ . "Carter and Spyland." *New Republic,* CLXXVI (June 11, 1977), 9–11.

2325. _____ . "Happenings: Government Reorganization [of Intelligence]." *New Republic,* CLXXVII (December 17, 1977), 9–12.

2326. "Laundering the Spies." *New Republic,* CLXXIV (March 6, 1976), 7–9.

2327. Paper, L. J. "Congress and the CIA." *Progressive,* XL (May 1976), 8–9.

2328. Peck, Winslow. "The AFL-CIA." In: Howard Frazier, ed. *Uncloaking the CIA.* New York: Free Press, 1978. pp. 225–265.

2329. Pell, Robert. "American Intelligence: A Second Look." *America,* CV (May 27, 1961), 371–373.

2330. Pepper, Thomas. "Revamping the Spy Game—Can the Old Mold Be Broken?: Reprinted From the *Baltimore Sun,* October 19, 1975." *Congressional Record,* CXXI (November 13, 1975), 36477–36478.

2331. Pike, Otis G. "Exposing CIA—Does the Nation Suffer?: An Interview." *U.S. News and World Report,* LXXX (January 12, 1976), 21–22.

2332. _____ . "Otis Pike and the CIA: An Interview." *New Republic,* CLXXIV (April 3, 1976), 8–12.

2333. "Playing Games With the CIA." *Nation,* CCXX (January 11, 1975), 2–3.

2334. "Probing the CIA: Investigators Under Fire." *U.S. News and World Report,* LXXVIII (January 20, 1975), 22–23.

2335. Railford, William. *Legislation Introduced Relative to the Activities of U.S. Intelligence Agencies, 1973–1974.* M-75-76F. Washington, D.C.: Congressional Research Service, Library of Congress, 1975. 21p.

2336. Ransom, Harry H. "Congress and the Intelligence Agencies." *Academy of Political Science Proceedings,* XXXII (1975), 153–166.

2337. _____. "Containing Central Intelligence." *New Republic,* CLIII (December 11, 1965), 12–15; CLIV (February 5, 1966), 37–38.

2338. _____. "Secret Intelligence Agencies and Congress." *Society,* XII (March–April 1975), 33–38.

2339. _____. "Surveillance by Congress." In: *The Intelligence Establishment.* Cambridge, MA: Harvard University Press, 1970. pp. 159–180.

2340. _____. "The Uses (and Abuses) of Secret Power: Toward Re-Shaping the Intelligence Community." *Worldview,* XVIII (May 1975), 11–18.

2341. Raskin, Marcus G. and Robert L. Borosage. "National Security and Official Accountability: Can We Return to a Government Ruled by Law?" *Vital Issues,* XXIII (September 1973), 1–4.

2342. Roberts, Adam. "The CIA: Reform is Not Enough." *Millennium,* VI (Spring 1977), 64–72.

2343. Robison, Olin. "The CIA and the Tar Baby: Reprinted From the *Maine News,* January 24, 1975." *Congressional Record,* CXXI (February 5, 1975), 2546–2547.

2344. "Rocky's Probe: Bringing the CIA to Heel." *Time,* CV (June 23, 1975), 6–10+.

2345. Rovere, Richard H. "Letter From Washington." *New Yorker,* LI (November 3, 1975), 165–170.

2346. Rushford, George G. "Making Enemies: The Pike Committee's Struggle to Get the Facts." *Washington Monthly,* VIII (July–August 1976), 42–52.

2347. Scheer, Robert. "Nelson Rockefeller Takes Care of Everybody." *Playboy,* XXII (October 1975), 76+.

2348. Schlesinger, Arthur M., Jr. "How to Control the CIA." *Current,* CLXXIV (July 1975), 12–15.

2349. _____. "What About the CIA?: Reprinted From the *Wall Street Journal,* July 2, 1975." In: Grant S. McClellan, ed. *The Right to Privacy.* Reference Shelf, v. 48, no. 1. New York: H. W. Wilson, 1976. pp. 134–139.

2350. "Secrets Congressmen Can't Get." *U.S. News and World Report,* XXXVII (July 16, 1954), 38–39.

2351. "Shaping Tomorrow's CIA: The Reorganization of the Intelligence Community." *Time,* CXI (February 6, 1978), 10–13+.

2352. Stang, Alan. "The National Security Mousetrap." *American Opinion*, XIX (November 1976), 41–45+.

2353. Szulc, Tad. "Good-bye James Bond." *New York Magazine*, XI (February 13, 1978), 13–15.

2354. _____. "Why Rockefeller Tried to Cover-up the CIA Probe." *New York Magazine*, X (September 5, 1977), 8+.

2355. Taylor, Telford. "The Crisis in Intelligence Gathering." *Columbia Journal of Law and Social Problems*, XII (Fall 1976), 451–487.

2356. Theoharis, Athan G. "Reforming the Intelligence Agencies." *U.S.A. Today*, CVII (July 1978), 6–8.

2357. "Those Charges Against the CIA: What the Record Shows." *U.S. News and World Report*, LXXIX (August 25, 1975), 38–41.

2358. Towell, Pat, jt. author. *See* Maxfield, David M. (2314).

2359. Treverton, Gregory F. "Reforming the CIA." *Millennium*, V (Winter 1976–1977), 312–317.

2360. "True-Blue Ribbon [Rockefeller Commission] Panel." *Newsweek*, LXXXV (January 20, 1975), 20+.

2361. Ungar, Sanford J. "Intelligence Tangle: The CIA and the FBI Face the Moment of Truth." *Atlantic*, CCXXXVII (April 1976), 31–42.

2362. United States. Commission on CIA Activities Within the United States [Rockefeller Commission]. *Report to the President*. Washington, D.C.: GPO, 1975. 299p.

Published commercially by the New York firm of Manor Books.

2363. _____. _____. "Rockefeller Report on the CIA [Excerpts]." In: Robert E. Cuthriell, ed. *Historic Documents of 1975*. Washington, D.C.: Congressional Quarterly, Inc., 1976. pp. 401–437.

2364. _____. Commission on the Organization of the Executive Branch of the Government. *The Hoover Commission Report on the Organization of the Executive Branch of the Government*. New York: McGraw-Hill, 1949. 524p.

Commercial publication of the government document.

2365. _____. _____. *Intelligence Activities: A Report to the Congress*. Washington, D.C.: GPO, 1955. 73p.

Part of the second Hoover Commission's findings.

2366. _____ . Commission on the Organization of the Government for the Conduct of Foreign Policy [Murphy Commission]. *Report.* Washington, D.C.: GPO, 1975. 278p.

2367. _____ . Congress. House. Committee on Armed Services. *Amending the Central Intelligence Agency Act of 1949: Report.* 89th Cong., 2nd sess. Washington, D.C.: GPO, 1966. 24p.

2368. _____ . _____ . _____ . Permanent Select Committee on Intelligence. *Annual Report.* 95th Cong., 2nd sess. Washington, D.C.: GPO, 1978. 72p.

2369. _____ . _____ . _____ . Select Committee on Intelligence. *CIA: The Pike Report.* London: Published for the Bertrand Russell Peace Foundation, by Spokesman Books, 1977. 284p.

2370. _____ . _____ . _____ . _____ . "The CIA Report the President Doesn't Want You to Read (The Pike Papers)." *The Village Voice,* (February 16, 1976), 69–92.

2371. _____ . _____ . _____ . _____ . *Committee Proceedings, September 10–November 20, 1975.* 94th Cong., 1st sess. Washington, D.C.: GPO, 1976. 344p.

2372. _____ . _____ . _____ . _____ . "House Intelligence Committee Report [Extracts]." In: Robert A. Diamond, ed. *Historic Documents of 1976.* Washington, D.C.: Congressional Quarterly, Inc., 1977. pp. 115–124.

2373. _____ . _____ . _____ . _____ . *The Pike Papers: House Select Committee on Intelligence CIA Report.* Special Supplement. New York: *The Village Voice,* 1976. 36p.

2374. _____ . _____ . _____ . _____ . *Recommendations of the Final Report.* 94th Cong., 2nd sess. Washington, D.C.: GPO, 1976. 36p.

2375. _____ . _____ . _____ . _____ . *U.S. Intelligence Agencies and Activities: The Performance of the Intelligence Community—Hearings.* 94th Cong., 1st sess. Washington, D.C.: GPO, 1976. 937p.

2376. _____ . _____ . Senate. Committee on Armed Services. *To Establish a Senate Select Committee on Intelligence: Hearings.* 94th Cong., 2nd sess. Washington, D.C.: GPO, 1976. 26p.

2377. _____ . _____ . _____ . Committee on Foreign Relations. *CIA Foreign and Domestic Activities: Hearings.* 94th Cong., 1st sess. Washington, D.C.: GPO, 1975. 39p.

2378. _____ . _____ . _____ . _____ . *National Security Act Amendment: Hearings.* 92nd Cong., 2nd sess. Washington, D.C.: GPO, 1972. 139p.

2379. _____ . _____ . _____ . Committee on Government Operations. *Oversight of U.S. Government Intelligence Functions: Hearings.* 94th Cong., 2nd sess. Washington, D.C.: GPO, 1976. 535p.

2380. _____ . _____ . _____ . _____ . Subcommittee on Intergovernmental Relations. *Legislative Proposals to Strengthen Congressional Oversight of the Nation's Intelligence Agencies: Hearings.* 93rd Cong., 2nd sess. Washington, D.C.: GPO, 1975. 205p.

2381. _____ . _____ . _____ . _____ . Subcommittee on National Policy Machinery. *Intelligence and National Security: Report.* 86th Cong., 2nd sess. Washington, D.C.: GPO, 1960.

2382. _____ . _____ . _____ . Committee on Rules and Administration. *Proposed Standing Committee on Intelligence Activities: Hearings.* 94th Cong., 2nd sess. Washington, D.C.: GPO, 1976. 228p.

2383. _____ . _____ . _____ . Joint Committee on Central Intelligence Agency. *Report.* 84th Cong., 2nd sess. Washington, D.C.: GPO, 1956.

2384. _____ . _____ . _____ . Select Committee on Intelligence. *Annual Report.* 95th Cong., 1st sess. Washington, D.C.: GPO, 1977–.

2385. _____ . _____ . _____ . _____ . *National Intelligence Reorganization and Reform Act of 1978: Hearings.* 95th Cong., 2nd sess. Washington, D.C.: GPO, 1978. 1,101p.

2386. _____ . _____ . _____ . _____ . *Rules of Procedure For the Select Committee on Intelligence, United States Senate: Adopted June 23, 1976, Amended July 20, 1977.* 95th Cong., 1st sess. Washington, D.C.: GPO, 1977. 35p.

2387. _____ . _____ . _____ . Select Committee to Study Government Operations With Respect to Intelligence Activities. "CIA Assassination Plots, NSA Cable Intercepts, FBI Abuses, and the CIA in Chile." In: Robert E. Cuthriell, ed. *Historic Documents of 1975.* Washington, D.C.: Congressional Quarterly, Inc., 1976. pp. 709–805, 873–915.

2388. _____ . _____ . _____ . _____ . *Final Report.* 94th Cong., 1st and 2nd sess. 6 pts. Washington, D.C.: GPO, 1975–1976.

2389. _____ . _____ . _____ . _____ . *Hearings.* 94th Cong., 1st and 2nd sess. 7 pts. Washington, D.C.: GPO, 1975–1976.

The testimony was mostly classified.

2390. _____ . _____ . _____ . _____ . "Senate Intelligence Committee Report." In: Robert A. Diamond, ed. *Historic Documents of 1976.* Washington, D.C.: Congressional Quarterly, Inc., 1977. pp. 235–287.

2391.   Unna, Warren. "CIA: Who Watches the Watchmen?" *Harper's*, CCXVI (April 1958), 46–53.

2392.   "Why the Spy Agencies are being Shaken-up." *U.S. News and World Report*, LXXIV (May 7, 1973), 78–80.

2393.   Wiedrich, Robert. "CIA's Entitled to a Kinder Suicide: Reprinted From the *Chicago Tribune*, October 3, 1975." *Congressional Record*, CXXI (October 3, 1975), 31751–31752.

2394.   Wolfe, Alan. "Exercise in Gentility: The Rockefeller CIA Report." *Nation*, CCXXI (August 16, 1975), 108–112.

F. *Intelligence and Covert Operations Around the World*

Introduction

The American Intelligence Community has several terms to cover the activities cited here and which were referenced in the CIA coverage in Section III.

A "clandestine operation" is an aggregate term encompassing clandestine collection and covert action and refers to "a preplanned secret intelligence information collection activity or covert political, economic, propaganda, or paramilitary action conducted so as to assure the secrecy of the operation."[1] "Clandestine collection" is "the acquisition of intelligence information in ways designed to assure the secrecy of the operation"[2] while "covert action" is "a clandestine operation designed to influence foreign governments, events, organizations, or persons. . . ."[3] The Carter reorganization plan retitled covert action "special activities," defined as activities "conducted abroad in support of national foreign policy objectives which are designed to further official United States programs and policies abroad and which are planned and executed so that the role of the United States Government is not apparent or acknowledged publicly. . . ."[4]

Despite public opinion in America, the United States has not been the only nation to engage in covert operations. Britain, France, Russia, China, Israel, the Warsaw Pact countries, West Germany, and others have engaged in intelligence operations which have also been exposed on occasion. Clandestine operations have been tricky and sensitive affairs since their expansion as part of the British Special Operations Executive and American Office of Strategic Services operations during World War II. In peacetime, they are particularly risky if they are exposed since an international crisis may result. Governments do not officially admit being involved in the internal affairs of other countries and when the facts suggest otherwise the resulting embarrassment can be acute.

On occasion, the secret services of various Western nations have become involved in illegal counterintelligence activities at home. When they are discovered as in Britain, Australia, Canada, and the U.S., domestic political upheaval, outrage, and legislative investigation almost certainly follow. In totalitarian countries like the Soviet Union and China internal surveillance is a fact of life, institutionalized as part of the secret service.

The number of clandestine operations mounted by the intelligence agencies of various countries since 1945 is uncertain. All such special activities are secret and the success of incidents "brought in from the cold," even if several years old, is usually compromised. Judging from the amount of public literature available some nations have been successful in guarding their special activities. For example, Britain employs a special form of censorship known as the "D Notice" given to journalists.

The citations in this section cover the literature on exposed special activities, espionage, clandestine collection, and some war-related military intelligence (Korea, Vietnam, Yom Kippur). These operations are referenced under six geographical regions: 1) Europe; 2) Middle East; 3) Africa; 4) Asia and the Pacific; 5) Latin America; and 6) North America. Each region begins with a general section covering operations which do not fit any given locale followed by citations to operations in various countries.

Readers seeking additional information on those activities may consult the citations in Part II, Part III, and Part IV. The chronology cites a selected list of incidents since 1945.

Notes

1. U.S. Central Intelligence Agency. "Glossary of Intelligence Terms and Definitions." In: U.S. Congress. House. Permanent Select Committee on Intelligence, *Annual Report* (95th Cong., 2nd sess. Washington, D.C.: GPO, 1978), p. 29.
2. *Ibid.*
3. *Ibid.,* p. 32.
4. *Ibid.,* p. 50.

1. Europe

a. General Works

2395.   Agee, Philip and Steve Weissman. "The CIA in Europe." *Oui,* VI (January 1977), 54+.

2396. _____ and Louis Wolf. *Dirty Work: The CIA in Western Europe.* Secaucus, NJ: Lyle Stuart, 1979. 736p.

2397. Campbell, Duncan. "Sabotage, Submarines, and the Secret Norwegian Connection." *New Statesman and Nation,* XCV (June 2, 1978), 730+.

2398. Cave-Brown, Anthony and Christopher Felix, pseud., eds. *The CIA vs. the KGB: An Encounter in History.* New York: Delta Books, 1979.

2399. Conquest, Robert. "The Secret War Between the KGB and the CIA." *Human Events,* XXXV (September 13, 1975), 5+.

2400. De Borchgrave, Arnaud. "Geneva's Soviet Agents." *Newsweek,* XCIII (May 7, 1979), 56–58.

2401. Felix, Christopher, pseud., jt. editor. *See* Cave-Brown, Anthony (2398).

2402. Hagen, Louis E. *The Secret War For Europe: A Dossier of Espionage.* New York: Stein and Day, 1969. 287p.

2403. Institute For the Study of Conflict. *New Dimensions of Security in Europe: An I.S.C. Special Report.* London: 1976. 56p.

2404. McRory, George W. *Strategic Intelligence in Modern European History.* Washington, D.C.: 1957. 74p.

2405. "Sleepers in NATO: Soviet Agents Subverting Western Europe's Armies." *Newsweek,* LXXXVII (March 8, 1976), 42–43.

2406. Steven, Stewart. *Operation Splinter Factor.* Philadelphia: Lippincott, 1974. 249p.

CIA operations in Eastern Europe.

2407. Waring, Ronald. "The Problems of Security Within NATO." *NATO's Fifteen Nations,* VIII (December 1963–January 1964), 22–25; IX (April–May 1964), 94–96.

2408. Weissman, Steve, jt. author. *See* Agee, Philip (2395).

2409. "What It Takes to Catch a Spy: Spying is Easier in Europe." *U.S. News and World Report,* XXXV (December 4, 1953), 26–30.

2410. Wolf, Louis, jt. author. *See* Agee, Philip (2396).

2411. "The World's Biggest Spy System—How It Feeds Secrets to the Reds: Soviet Espionage in Scandanavia." *U.S. News and World Report,* XXXVIII (April 1, 1955), 22–24.

b. Czechoslovakia

2412. "Limits of Intelligence: Why No One Knew—The Invasion of Czechoslovakia." *Time,* XCII (August 30, 1968), 33.

2413. Littell, Robert, ed. *The Czech Black Book: Prepared by the Institute of the History of the Czechoslovak Academy of Sciences.* New York: Praeger, 1969. 318p.

Examines the role of the KGB in the Czech invasion.

2414. "The Russian Invasion: A Failure in U.S. Intelligence?" *U.S. News and World Report,* LXV (September 2, 1968), 8.

2415. Schwartz, Harry. *Prague's 200 Days: The Struggle For Democracy in Czechoslovakia.* New York: Praeger, 1969. 274p.

c. France

2416. Boumaza, Bechir. "Torture in Paris: An Excerpt from 'La Gangrène.'" *Harper's,* CCXX (March 1960), 87+.

2417. Hess, John L. "CIA, Satice, and Scandal: Why Le Canard Endorses Domestic Intelligence." *Politicks,* I (March 14, 1978), 27+.

2418. Howe, Quincy. "At Random: The CIA in France." *Atlas,* XXIII (March 1976), 5+.

2419. Williams, Philip M. *Wars, Plots, and Scandals in Post-War France.* Cambridge and New York: Cambridge University Press, 1970. 232p.

d. Germany

2420. "Berlin, the Spy Story." *Newsweek,* LIII (June 15, 1959), 39–40.

2421. "Big Haul in Bonn: A Russian Spy Ring." *Newsweek,* LXX (October 30, 1967), 31–32.

2422. Cook, Jess, jt. author. *See* Durham, Michael (2424).

2423. Dallin, David J. "Operation Kidnap: Berlin's Soviet Underworld." *American Mercury,* LXXIV (May 1952), 55–62.

2424. Durham, Michael and Jess Cook. "A Covey of Spies is Flushed in Germany." *Life,* LXIII (November 3, 1967), 65–66+.

2425. "Espionage, Costly Baby: Spies For Russia in West Germany." *Newsweek,* LXII (July 22, 1963), 40–41.

2426. German Democratic Republic. *Espionage in West Berlin: A White Book.* East Berlin: 1959.

2427. German Federal Republic. *East Berlin: Propaganda and Subversion Center, a White Book.* Bonn: 1959.

2428. _____ . *Eastern Underground Activity Against West Berlin: A Black Book.* Bonn, 1959.

2429. Hauser, Richard F. and Frederick Sondern, Jr. "Wilhelm Zaisser, the Red Himmler." *Reader's Digest,* LXII (January 1953), 72–76.

2430. "Mischa Meets His Match: East German Spies in West Germany." *Time,* CX (July 25, 1977), 37–38.

2431. Newman, Bernard. *The Sosnowski Affair: Inquest on a Spy.* London: Laurie, 1954. 203p.

2432. Schoenbaum, David. *The Spiegel Affair.* Garden City, NY: Doubleday, 1968. 239p.

2433. Schorr, Daniel. "Five Thousand Spies a Month: Espionage in West Germany." *Reporter,* XXIII (December 8, 1960), 56–57.

2434. Singer, Kurt D. "Berlin's Spy Market." *American Mercury,* LXXVII (July 1953), 124–125.

2435. Sondern, Frederick, Jr. "Why Nerves are Raw in West Berlin." *Reader's Digest,* LXXVI (June 1960), 247–248+.

2436. _____ , jt. author. *See* Hauser, Richard F. (2429).

2437. "The Spider's Web: Spy Hunting in West Germany." *Newsweek,* LXXXVII (June 28, 1976), 44.

2438. "Spooks Galore: Spy Exposés in West Germany." *Time,* XCIII (May 16, 1969), 44+.

2439. Ungeheuer, Friedel. "Spies By the Thousand: A Report From Germany." *Harper's,* CCXLII (June 1971), 26–29.

2440. United States. Congress. Senate. Committee on the Judiciary. Subcommittee to Investigate the Administration of the Internal Security Act and Other Internal Security Laws. *Soviet Terrorism in Free Germany: Hearings and the Testimony of Theodor Hans.* 86th Cong., 2nd sess. Washington, D.C.: GPO, 1960. 39p.

e. Great Britain

2441. Alan, R. "Mrs. [Margaret] Thatcher and the CIA." *New Leader,* VI (December 4, 1978), 12–13.

2442. Bulloch, John. *Akin to Treason.* London: Barker, 1966. 188p.

2443. _____ and Henry Miller. *Spy Ring: The Full Story of the Naval Secrets Case.* London: Secker and Warburg, 1961. 224p.

2444. "The Case of the Underwater Secrets." *Newsweek,* LVII (February 20, 1961), 52–53.

2445. Charters, David A. "Intelligence and Psychological Warfare Operations in Northern Ireland." *Journal of the Royal United Service Institution for Defence Studies,* CXXII (September 1977), 22–27.

2446. Fairfield, Cecily I. *A Train of Powder.* By Rebecca West, pseud. New York: Viking Press, 1953. 310p.

2447. Great Britain. MI5. *Their Trade is Treachery.* London, 1964. 59p.

2448. Hamilton, Peter. *Espionage and Subversion in an Industrial Society.* London: Hutchinson, 1967.

2449. Hutton, Joseph B. *Danger From Moscow.* London: Burns, 1960. 261p.

2450. Kennedy, C. "High Casualty Rate Among the Exiles [in London]: Deaths of Bulgarian Defectors." *Macleans,* XCI (October 16, 1978), 32–33.

2451. Lucas, Norman. *The Great Spy Ring.* London: Barker, 1966. 284p.

2452. Miller, Henry, jt. author. *See* Bulloch, John (2443).

2453. Newman, Bernard. *Spies in Britain.* London: Hale, 1964. 190p.

2454. "Poisonous Umbrella: Deaths of Bulgarian Defectors." *Time,* CXII (October 16, 1978), 75–76.

2455. Pratt, Denis N. *Spies and Informers in the Witness Box.* London: Bernard Hanison, 1958. 96p.

2456. West, Rebecca, pseud. *See* Fairfield, Cecily I. (2446).

2457. White, John B. *Sabotage is Suspected.* London: Evans, 1957. 224p.

2458. Wynne, Barry. *The Spies Within.* London: Jenkins, 1964. 175p.

f. Greece

2459. Argyropoulos, Kaitz. *From Peace to Chaos: A Forgotten Story.* New York: Vantage Press, 1975. 195p.

2460. O'Ballance, Edgar. *The Greek Civil War: 1944–1949.* New York: Praeger, 1966. 237p.

2461. Stern, Laurence. *The Wrong Horse: The Politics of Intervention and the Failure of American Diplomacy.* New York: Times Books, 1977. 170p.

2462.   Zotos, Stephanos. *Greece: The Struggle For Freedom.* New York: Crowell, 1967. 194p.

g. Italy

2463.   Buckley, William F., Jr. "$Six Million: The Controversy Over CIA Payments to Italian Political Parties." *National Review,* XXVIII (February 6, 1976), 110–111.

2464.   Campbell, Duncan. "Friendly [U.S.] Penetration." *New Statesman and Nation,* XCVII (March 2, 1979), 280+.

h. Portugal

2465.   Hammond, John L. and Nicole Szulc. "The CIA in Portugal." In: Howard Frazier, ed. *Uncloaking the CIA.* New York: Free Press, 1978. pp. 135–147.

i. USSR

(1) GENERAL WORKS AND INTERNAL DISSENT

2466.   Agar, Augustus W. S. *Baltic Episode: A Classic of Secret Service in Russian Waters.* London: Hodder and Stoughton, 1963. 255p.

2467.   Amalrik, Andrei A. "Arrest on Suspicion of Courage: Detention By the KGB." *Harper's,* CCLIII (August 1976), 37–44+.

2468.   _____ . *Involuntary Journey to Siberia.* Translated From the Russian. New York: Harcourt, Brace, 1970. 297p.

2469.   Anderson, James K. "Unknown Soldiers of an Unknown [Ukrainian People's] Army." *Army,* XVIII (May 1968), 62–67.

2470.   Armstrong, John A. *Ukrainian Nationalism.* 2nd ed. New York: Columbia University Press, 1963. 361p.

2471.   "Aspects of Intellectual Ferment and Dissent in the Soviet Union." *Problems of Communism,* XVII (September–October 1968), 55–57.

2472.   Barron, John. "Russia's Voices of Dissent." *Reader's Digest,* CIV (May 1974), 139–143.

2473.   Block, Sidney and Peter Reddaway. *Psychiatric Terror: How Soviet Psychiatry is Used to Suppress Dissent.* New York: Basic Books, 1977.

2474.   Breslauer, George W., jt. author. *See* Dallin, Alexander (2481).

2475.   Byrnes, Robert F. "American Scholars in Russian Soon Learn About the KGB." *New York Times Magazine,* (November 16, 1969), 84–85+.

2476.   Chalidze, Valery. *To Defend These Rights: Human Rights and the Soviet Union.* Translated From the Russian. New York: Random House, 1974. 348p.

2477.   Chubatyi, Nicholas D. "The Ukrainian Underground." *Ukrainian Quarterly,* II (Winter 1946), 154–166.

2478.   Conquest, Robert. *The Human Cost of Soviet Communism.* Washington, D.C.: GPO, 1971. 33p.

2479.   _____ . *Kolynia: The Arctic Death Camps.* New York: Viking, 1978. 254p.

2480.   Copp, Dewitt S. *Incident at Boris Gleb: The Tragedy of Newcomb Mott.* Garden City, NY: Doubleday, 1968. 280p.

2481.   Dallin, Alexander and George W. Breslauer. *Political Terror in Communist Systems.* Stanford, CA: Stanford University Press, 1970. 172p.

2482.   Daumantas, Juozas. *Fighters For Freedom: Lithuanian Partisans vs. the U.S.S.R.* [1944–1947]. Translated From the Lithuanian. Woodhaven, NJ: Manylands Books, 1975. 254p.

2483.   Dolgun, Alexander. *Alexander Dolgun's Story: An American in the Gulag.* New York: Knopf, 1975. 370p.

2484.   Domberg, John. "In the Soviet Isolation Ward." *Newsweek* LXXXIV (December 28, 1970), 25–26.

2485.   Falk, John C. *Incident at Bokhara.* New York: Exposition Press, 1970. 93p.

2486.   Great Britain. *Security Advice About Visits to Communist Countries.* London: H.M Stationery Office, 1969.

2487.   Gross, Feliks. *Violence in Politics: Terror and Political Assassination in Eastern Europe and Russia.* The Hague: Mouton, 1972. 139p.

2488.   Hoover, J. Edgar. "U.S. Businessmen Face the Soviet Spy." *Harvard Business Review,* XLII (January 1964), 140–146+.

2489.   Hurst, Lynda. "The CIA Asked Me to Spy on Russia—Cyrus Eaton: Reprinted From the *Toronto Star,* June 16, 1975." *Congressional Record,* CXXI (July 14 1975) 22706–22707.

2490.   "It [Security Leaks] Could Never Happen in Russia." *U.S. News and World Report,* XXXIV (June 26, 1953), 32–35.

184 Intelligence and Covert Operations Around the World

2491. Kaplan, Howard. "Caught Trying to Smuggle a Manuscript Out of Russia [and] Arrested By the KGB: An Interview." *Publisher's Weekly,* CCXIV (September 18, 1978), 130–132.

2492. Knight, Robert. "For Agents in Moscow, Snooping is Risky Work." *U.S. News and World Report,* LXXXVI (May 7, 1979) 26–27.

2493. Reddaway, Peter. "The KGB in Georgia [U.S.S.R.]." *New York Review of Books,* XXIV (March 31, 1977), 35+.

2494. _____ . *Uncensored Russia: Protest and Dissent in the Soviet Union.* New York: American Heritage Press, 1972. 499p.

2495. _____ , jt. author. *See* Block, Sidney (2473).

2496. Rothberg, Abraham. *The Heirs of Stalin: Dissidence and the Soviet Regime, 1953–1970.* Ithaca, New York: Cornell University Press, 1972. 450p.

2497. Sadecky, Petr. "KGB." In: *Octobriana and the Russian Underground.* New York: Harper & Row, 1971. p. 7.

2498. Sayers, Michael and Aly E. Kahn. *The Great Conspiracy: The Secret War Against Soviet Russia.* Boston: Little Brown, 1946. 433p.

2499. Solzhenitsyn, Alexandr I. *The Gulag Archipelago 1918–1956: An Experiment in Literary Investigation.* Translated From the Russian. 7 pts. in 3 vols. New York: Harper & Row, 1974–1978.

2500. _____ . "Solzhenitsyn vs. the KGB." *Time,* CIII (May 27, 1974), 51.

2501. "Spies Behind the Iron Curtain." *Time,* LVIII (December 31, 1951), 20+.

2502. Union of Soviet Socialist Republics. Ministry of Information. *Caught in the Act: Facts About U.S. Espionage and Subversion Against the U.S.S.R.* Moscow: 1960. 83p.

2503. _____ . _____ . *U.S. Espionage and Subversion Against Russia.* Moscow, 1960.

2504. United States. Commission on Security and Co-Operation in Europe. *Basket III: Implementation of Helsinki Accords.* 4 vols. Washington, D.C.: GPO, 1977.

2505. _____ . _____ . *Implementation of the Final Act of the Conference on Security and Co-Operation in Europe: Findings and Recommendations Two Years After Helsinki.* 3 vols. Washington, D.C.: GPO, 1977.

2506. _____ . _____ . *Reports of Helsinki Accord Monitors in the Soviet Union: Documents of the Public Groups to Promote Observance of the Helsinki Agreements in the U.S.S.R.* 2 vols. Washington, D.C.: GPO, 1977.

2507. _____ . Congress. Senate. Committee on the Judiciary. Subcommittee to Investigate the Administration of the Internal Security Act and Other Internal Security Laws. *The Abuse of Psychiatry For Political Repression in the Soviet Union: Hearings.* 92nd Cong., 2nd sess. Washington, D.C.: GPO, 1972. 257p.

Available commercially from the New York firm of Arno Press.

2508. _____ . _____ . _____ . _____ . *U.S.S.R. Labor Camps: Hearings.* 93rd Cong., 1st sess. 2 pts. Washington, D.C.: GPO, 1973.

(2) U-2 Affair

2509. Alsop, Joseph. "The Dulles Testimony: Reprinted From the *Washington Post,* February 5, 1960." *Congressional Record,* CVI (February 9, 1960), 2297.

Further references to this incident will be found in Part IV under Francis Gary Powers.

2510. Anderson, Jack. "The United States Heard the Russians Chasing the U-2: Reprinted From the *Washington Post,* May 12, 1960." *Congressional Record,* CVI (June 23, 1960), 13937–13938.

2511. Asanov, D., *et al.,* comps. *No Return For U-2 —The Truth About the Provocative Penetration of Soviet Air Space by an American Plane: Prepared For Publication by the Union of Journalists of the U.S.S.R.* Moscow: Foreign Languages Publishing House, 1960. 174p.

2512. Blanchard, William H. "National Myth, National Character, and National Policy: A Psychological Study of the U-2 Incident." *Journal of Conflict Resolution,* VI (Spring 1962), 143–148.

2513. Cater, Douglas. "Chronicle of Confusion: U.S. Treatment of the U-2." *Reporter,* XXII (June 9, 1960), 15–17.

2514. "Chronological Account of U.S. Reports on the U-2." *Congressional Record,* CVI (May 23, 1960), 10792.

2515. "CIA's Powers." *Economist,* CCII (March 10, 1962), 906–907.

2516. "Cold War." *Newsweek,* LV (May 30, 1960), 21–28+.

2517. "Cold War Candor: The Flight to Sverdlovsk." *Time,* LXXV (May 23, 1960), 15–18.

2518. Cook, Fred J. *The U-2 Incident.* New York: Watts, 1973. 64p.

2519.   Eisenhower, Dwight D. and Christian A. Herter. *President Eisenhower's Report to the Nation May 2 5, 1 9 6 0* [and] *Secretary Herter's Report to the Senate Foreign Relations Committee.* Department of State Publication 7010, General Foreign Policy Series 151. Washington, D.C.: Department of State, 1960. 25p.

2520.   "The Flight of the U-2." *Newsweek,* LV (May 16, 1960), 27–29.

2521.   "The Flight to Sverdlovsk." *Time,* LXXV (May 16, 1960), 15–18.

2522.   Green, William. "The U-2: Facts (and Fiction)." *R.A.F. Flying Review,* XV (August 1960), 18–19, 22.

2523.   Herter, Christian A. "Official Account of the U-2 and the Summit Breakup: Testimony Before the Senate Foreign Relations Committee." *U.S. News and World Report,* XLVIII (June 6, 1960), 68–70.

2524.   _____ , jt. author. *See* Eisenhower, Dwight D. (2519).

2525.   Hotz, Robert. "Lockheed U-2 Over Sverdlovsk: A Study in Fabrication." *Aviation Week and Space Technology,* LXXII (May 16, 1960), 20–21.

2526.   Khrushchev, Nikita S. *Statement and Replies to Questions, Gorky Park, Moscow, May 1 1, 1 9 6 0: The U-2 Incident.* New York: Crosscurrents Press, 1960. 32p.

2527.   "Khrushchev's Pre-Summit Spy Cry." *Life,* XLVIII (May 16, 1960), 38–41.

2528.   Lippmann, Walter. "The Spy Business: Reprinted From the *Washington Post,* May 2, 1960." *Congressional Record,* CVI (May 23, 1960), 10786.

2529.   "'May Day! May Day!'" *Newsweek,* LV (May 16, 1960), 28–29.

2530.   Mezerik, Avraham G., ed. *U-2 and Open Skies: U.N. Action, Chronology.* New York: International Review Service, 1960. 46p.

2531.   Nathan, James A. "A Fragile Detente: The U-2 Incident Reexamined." *Military Affairs,* XXXIX (October 1975), 97–104.

2532.   Randle, Devin D. "What Really Happened to Gary Powers and His U-2." *Air Classics,* XV (April 1979), 64–67.

2533.   Ransom, Harry H. "How Intelligent is Intelligence?" *New York Times Magazine,* (May 22, 1960), 26, 80–83.

2534.   Roberts, Chalmers M. "Who Was Responsible?—Chronology of the U-2 Incident Traced in the Tangled Web of the Summit Dispute: Reprinted From the *Washington Post,* May 27, 1960." *Congressional Record,* CVI (June 23, 1960), 13951–13952.

2535. Ross, Thomas B., jt author. *See* Wise, David (2545).

2536. Shearer, Lloyd. "The U-2 Revisited." *Parade,* (October 15, 1978), 17.

2537. *Soviet Weekly,* Editors of. *American Spy Plane on Exhibition in Moscow.* A *Soviet Weekly* Booklet. London: *Soviet Weekly,* 1960. 7p.

2538. Spaatz, Carl. "Reasons the U-2 Flew." *Newsweek,* LV (May 23, 1960), 42.

2539. Taylor, Telford. "Long-Range Lessons of the U-2 Affair." *New York Times Magazine,* (July 24, 1960), 20+.

2540. "Tracked Toward Trouble." *Time,* LXXV (May 23, 1960), 12–13.

2541. "The U-2 Must Fly Again: An Interview With U.S. Officials." *U.S. News and World Report,* XLVIII (June 27, 1960), 44–49.

2542. "U.S. to Continue U-2 Flights Over the Soviet Union: Reprinted From *Aviation Week and Space Technology,* May 16, 1960." *Congressional Record,* CVI (June 7, 1960), 11976–11977.

2543. United States. Congress. Senate. Committee on Foreign Relations. *Events Incident to the Summit Conference: Hearings.* 86th Cong., 2nd sess. Washington, D.C.: GPO, 1960.

2544. Willoughby, Charles A. "Khrushchev and the Flight to Sverdlovsk." *American Mercury,* XCI (August 1960), 34–43.

2545. Wise, David and Thomas B. Ross. "The Secret History of the U-2." *Look,* XXVI (May 8 and May 22, 1962), 128+, 101–102+.

2546. _____. *The U-2 Affair.* New York: Random House, 1962. 269p.

2547. Wright, Quincy. "Legal Aspects of the U-2 Flight." *American Journal of International Law,* LIV (October 1960), 836–854.

(3) RB-47 INCIDENT

2548. "Nikita and the RB-47." *Time,* LXXVI (July 25, 1960), 21–22.

2549. Norman, L. B. "Mystery of the RB-47." *Newsweek,* LVI (July 25, 1960), 36–37.

2550. "Russians Stir Up a Phony Spy Crisis: Shooting Down an RB-47 Over the Barents Sea." *Life,* XLIX (July 25, 1960), 30–31.

2551. White, William L. *The Little Toy Dog: The Story of Two RB-47 Flyers, Captain John R. McKone and Captain Truman B. Olmstead.* New York: E. P. Dutton, 1962. 304p.

j. Yugoslavia

2552.   Dewhurst, C.H. *Close Contact.* London: Allen & Unwin, 1954. 173p.

Examines failure of the KGB during the 1948 break with Russia.

k. Cyprus

2553.   Stern, Laurence. "Bitter Lessons—How We Failed in Cyprus: Reprinted From *Foreign Policy,* Summer 1975." In: U.S. Congress. Senate. Committee on the Judiciary. Subcommittee to Investigate Problems Connected With Refugees and Escapees. *Crisis on Cyprus, 1975—One Year After the Invasion: A Staff Report.* 94th Cong., 1st sess. Washington, D.C.: GPO, 1975. pp. 125–142.

2554.   United States. Congress. House. Select Committee on Intelligence. "The 1974 Cyprus Crisis." In: *U.S. Intelligence Agencies and Activities,* Part II: *The Performance of the Intelligence Community.* 94th Cong., 1st sess. Washington, D.C.: GPO, 1975. pp. 759–766.

2555.   _____ . _____ . Senate. Committee on the Judiciary. Subcommittee to Investigate Problems Connected With Refugees and Escapees. *Crisis on Cyprus, 1975—One Year After the Invasion: A Staff Report.* 94th Cong., 1st sess. Washington, D.C.: GPO, 1975. 142p.

2. The Middle East

a. General Works

2556.   Adie, W. A. C. "China, Israel, and the Arabs." *Conflict Studies,* no. 12 (May 1971), 1–18.

2557.   Ben-Porath, Y., jt author. *See* Dan, Uri (2560).

2558.   Charteris, M. M. C. "A Year as a [British] Intelligence Officer in Palestine." *Journal of the Middle East Society,* I (October 1946), 15–23.

2559.   Copeland, Miles. *The Game of Nations: The Amorality of Power Politics.* New York: Simon and Schuster, 1970. 318p.

2560.   Dan, Uri and Y. Ben-Porath. *The Secret War: The Spy Game in the Middle East.* New York: Amis Press, 1971. 250p.

2561.   Dayan, Moshe. *Diary of the Sinai Campaign.* New York: Harper & Row, 1966. 236p.

2562.   "The Deadly Battle of the Spooks." *Time,* CI (February 12, 1973), 28+.

2563.   Dupuy, Trevor N. *Elusive Victory: The Arab-Israeli Wars, 1947–1974.* New York: Harper & Row, 1978. 672p.

2564. "Fatal Error: The Murder of Ahmed by Israeli Killers." *Time,* CII (August 6, 1973), 31–32.

2565. Heckelman, A. Joseph *American Volunteers and Israel's War of Independence.* New York: Ktav Publishing House, 1974. 304p.

2566. Hussein of Jordan, King. "Hussein on His CIA Money." *Newsweek,* LXXXIX (March 7, 1977), 16–18.

2567. Kagan, Benjamin. *The Secret Battle For Israel.* Translated From the French. Cleveland, OH: World Publishing Co., 1966. 299p.

2568. Kirkpatrick, Lyman B., Jr. "Communism and the Near East." *Naval War College Review,* XXI (October 1968), *passim.*

2569. Moore, John M., ed *The Arab-Israeli Conflict.* Princeton, NJ: Princeton University Press, 1974. 1,193p.

2570. "One Big Fishbowl." *Newsweek,* LXXVII (June 14, 1971), 44+.

2571. Osborne, John. "Carter's Oversight: The Intelligence Oversight Board's Review of CIA Payments to Hussein." *New Republic,* CLXXVI (March 19, 1977), 8–10.

2572. Rabin, Yitzhak. *Memoirs.* Boston: Little, Brown, 1979. 344p.

2573. "Sabra Spies: Israelis Spying For Syria." *Time,* C (December 25, 1972), 25–26.

2574. "Spies and Circuses: The Spy Hunt in Arab States." *Newsweek,* LXXIII (January 6, 1969), 32.

2575. United Arab Republic. Maslahat al-Istilamat. *The French Spy Ring in the U.A.R.: A Conspiracy Confirmed by Confessions.* Cairo: Information Department, 1962. 18p.

2576. Wagner, Abraham. *Crisis Decision-Making: Israel's Experience in 1967 and 1973.* New York: Praeger, 1974. 186p.

2577. "What U.S. Officials Really Knew About the Surprise Attack on Egypt." *U.S.News and World Report,* XLI (December 7, 1956), 98–100.

2578. "You Were Expecting Maybe James Bond?": Israeli-Egyptian Espionage." *Time,* LXXXIII (June 5, 1964), 33–34.

b. Yom Kippur War (1973)

2579. Brigman, James L. *Why Israel Slept: An Analysis of Israel's Unpreparedness For the Yom Kippur War.* Research Study. Maxwell AFB, AL: Air Command and Staff College, Air University, 1976. 50p.

2580. Bulloch, John. *The Making of a War.* London: Longmans, Green, 1974. 220p.

2581.   Cline, Ray S. "Policy Without Intelligence." *Foreign Policy,* XVII (Winter 1974–1975), 121–135.

2582.   Coleman, Herbert J. "Israeli Inquiry [Agranat Commission] Hits Intelligence Unit." *Aviation Week and Space Technology,* C (April 15, 1974), 26–27.

2583.   Handel, Michael I. *Perception, Deception, and Surprise: The Case of the Yom Kippur War.* Jerusalem Paper, no. 19. Jerusalem: Leonard Davis Institute of International Relations, 1976. 40p.

2584.   _____ . "Yom Kippur and the Inevitability of Surprise." *International Studies Quarterly,* XXI (September 1977), 461–502.

2585.   Heikal, Mohamed. *The Road to Ramadan.* New York: Times Books, 1975. 285p.

2586.   Herzog, Chaim. "The Middle East War, 1973." *Journal of the Royal United Service Institution for Defence Studies,* CXX (March 1975), 3–13.

2587.   _____ . *The War of Atonement, October 1973.* Boston: Little, Brown, 1975. 300p.

2588.   Israel. Agranat Commission of Inquiry. *Interim Report.* Jerusalem, 1974.

2589.   Leslie, S. C. "Crisis in the Middle East—The Israeli Dimension: Facing the Facts." *Round Table,* CCLIII (January 1974), 25–34.

2590.   *London Sunday Times,* Insight Team of. *The Yom Kippur War.* Garden City, NY: Doubleday, 1974. 514p.

2591.   "Looking Back in Anger: The Report of the Agranat Commission." *Time,* CIII (April 15, 1974), 42+.

2592.   McKenzie-Smith, Robert H. "Crisis Decisionmaking in Israel: The Case of the October 1973 Middle East War." *Naval War College Review,* XXIX (Summer 1976), 39–52.

2593.   "The Middle East War." *Armed Forces Journal International,* CXI (January 1974), 33–38.

2594.   Middleton, Drew. "Who Lost the Yom Kippur War?" *Atlantic,* CCXXXIII (March 1974), 45–47+.

2595.   "Missing the Arabs' War Signals." *Time,* CII (October 22, 1973), 48–49.

2596.   O'Ballance, Edgar. *No Victor, No Vanquished: The Yom Kippur War.* San Rafael, CA: Presidio Press, 1979. 383p.

2597. Perlmutter, Amos. "Israel's Fourth War, October 1973: Political and Military Misperceptions." *Orbis,* XIX (Summer 1975), 434–460.

2598. Ropelewski, Robert R. "Egypt Assesses Lessons of the October War." *Aviation Week and Space Technology,* XCIX (December 17, 1973), 14–17.

2599. Salmans, S. "Four Little Words: Congressional Declassification of the CIA Report Concerning the Outbreak of the 1973 Arab-Israeli War." *Newsweek,* LXXXVI (September 22, 1975), 28.

2600. Sax, Samuel W. "Arab-Israeli Conflict Four: A Preliminary Assessment." *Naval War College Review,* XXVI (January–February 1974), 7–16.

2601. Schiff, Zeev. *October Earthquake: Yom Kippur, 1973.* Tel Aviv: University Publishing Projects, 1974.

2602. Shlaim, Avi. "Failures in National Estimates: The Case of the Yom Kippur War." *World Politics,* XXVIII (April 1976), 348–380.

2603. Sobel, Lester A., ed. *Israel and the Arabs: The October 1973 War.* New York: Facts on File, Inc., 1974. 185p.

2604. Szulc, Tad. "Seeing and Not Believing: Misjudging Arab Intentions." *New Republic,* CLXIX (December 22, 1973), 13–14.

2605. United States. Congress. House. Select Committee on Intelligence. "Performance of the Intelligence Community: The 1973 Mideast War." In: Part 2 of *U.S. Intelligence Agencies and Activities—The Performance of the Intelligence Community: Hearings.* 94th Cong., 1st sess. Washington, D.C.: GPO, 1975. pp. 631–682.

2606. _____ . Defense Intelligence Agency. *A Summary of Lessons Learned in the Arab-Israeli War of 1973.* DI-646-71-74. Washington, D.C.: 1974. 47p.

2607. Viksne, J. "The Yom Kippur War in Retrospect." *Army Journal,* no. 324 (May 1976), 25–28.

2608. Whetten, Lawrence. "Military Lessons of the Yom Kippur War." *World Today,* XXX (March 1974), 101–109.

c. Iran

2609. Amnesty International. *Iran.* Briefing Paper, no. 7. London, 1976.

2610. Atyeo, Henry C. "Political Developments in Iran, 1951–1954." *Middle East Affairs,* V (August–September 1954), 249–259.

2611.   Butler, William J. and Georges Levasseur. *Human Rights and the Legal System in Iran.* 2 pts. Geneva: International Commission of Jurists, 1976.

2612.   Faroughy, Ahmad. "Repression and Iran." *Index on Censorship,* III (Winter 1974), 9–18.

2613.   Graham, Robert. *Iran: The Illusion of Power.* New York: St. Martin's Press, 1979. 224p.

2614.   Heinl, Robert D., Jr. "What the U.S. and the West May Have 'Lost' in Iran." *Sea Power,* XXII (February 1979), 15–16.

2615.   Hodgshon, Susan G. "The Tensions Between Britain and America in the Middle East, 1945–1954, With Special Reference to Iran." Unpublished PhD Dissertation, Sussex University, 1977.

2616.   "How Our Man [Kermit Roosevelt] in Tehran Brought Down a Demagogue: The CIA vs. Mohammed Mossedegh." *Esquire,* XCI (June 1975), 90+.

2617.   "Inside Ali's Suitcase: Tudeh Spies on Iran's Army." *Time,* LXIV (September 20, 1954), 42.

2618.   "Iranian Monitor Loss Minimized." *Aviation Week and Space Technology,* CX (April 30, 1979), 30.

2619.   Khalili, Parvis K. "Red Star Over Iran." *American Mercury,* LXXIX (July 1954), 77–81.

2620.   Kurzman, Dan. "Kashani of Iran: Master of Intrigue." *Nation,* CLXXVIII (April 3, 1954), 274–276.

2621.   Laqueur, Walter. "Why the Shah Fell." *Commentary,* LXVII (March 1979), 47–55.

2622.   Lenczowski, George. "United States Support For Iran's Independence and Integrity, 1945–1959." *Annals of the American Academy of Political and Social Science,* XDI (May 1972), 45–55.

2623.   Levasseur, Georges, jt. author. *See* Butler, William J. (2611).

2624.   McWilliams, Carey. "Second Thoughts: The Failure of the CIA to Interpret the Situation in Iran." *Nation,* CCXXVIII (Februry 10, 1979), 134.

2625.   Mansur, Abul K. "The Crisis in Iran: Why the U.S. Ignored a Quarter Century of Warning." *Armed Forces Journal International,* CXVI (January 1979), 26–33.

2626.   Morganthau, Tom. "[Ross] Perot's Mission Impossible." *Newsweek,* XCIII (March 5, 1979), 47–49.

2627. _____ . "Secrets of Kabkan." *Newsweek,* XCIII (March 12, 1979), 43.

    NSA/CIA listening posts.

2628. "The Royal Comeback." *Life,* XXXV (August 31, 1953), 14–17.

2629. Rudolph, James D. "Public Order and Internal Security." In: Richard F. Nyrop, ed. *Iran: A Country Profile.* DAPAM 550-68. Washington, D.C.: GPO, 1978. pp. 359–389.

2630. "Shah Returns in Triumph as the Army Kicks Out Mossadegh." *Newsweek,* XLII (August 31, 1953), 30–31.

2631. Shwadran, Benjamin. "Iran." In: *The Middle East, Oil, and the Great Powers.* New York: Council for Middle Eastern Affairs, 1955. pp. 103–152.

2632. Steele, Richard. "Fumbling the Crisis?" *Newsweek,* XCIII (January 29, 1979), 44–46.

2633. Thornburg, Max W. "The Shah Joins the Revolution." *Reader's Digest,* LXIII (December 1953), 112–117.

2634. United States. Central Intelligence Agency. *Iran After the Shah.* Washington, D.C.: 1978. 23p.

2635. _____ . _____ . *Iran in the 1980s.* Washington, D.C.: 1977. 60p.

2636. _____ . Congress. House. Committee on International Relations. Subcommittee on International Organizations. *Human Rights in Iran: Hearings.* 94th Cong., 2nd sess. Washington, D.C.: GPO, 1976.

2637. _____ . _____ . _____ . Permanent Select Committee on Intelligence. Subcommittee on Evaluation. *Iran: Evaluation of U.S. Intelligence Performance Prior to November 1978—A Staff Report.* 96th Cong., 1st sess. Washington, D.C.: GPO, 1979. 8p.

2638. "The United States and Iran's Revolution: A Symposium." *Foreign Policy,* XXXIV (Spring 1979), 3–34.

3. Africa

a. General Works

2639. Briggs, Kenneth A. "Churches, Angered By Disclosures, Seek to Bar Further CIA Use of Missionaries in Intelligence Work: Reprinted From the *New York Times,* January 29, 1976." *Congressional Record,* CXXII (February 5, 1976), 2533–2534.

2640. Greig, Ian. *The Communist Challenge to Africa.* Sandton, South Africa: Southern Africa Freedom Foundation, 1977. 384p.

2641.   Hatfield, Mark O. "Missionaries and the CIA." *Christian Herald*, XCIX (March 1976), 13+.

2642.   Hyer, Marjorie. "Clergy Wary of CIA Approaches: Reprinted From the *Washington Post*, August 5, 1975." *Congressional Record*, CXXI (December 15, 1975), 40437–40438.

2643.   Keller, Bill. "Clergy Back Hatfield—CIA Use of Missionaries Opposed: Reprinted From the Portland *Oregonian*, January 25, 1976." *Congressional Record*, CCXXII (February 5, 1976), 2534.

2644.   Kempster, Norman. "Jesuit [Rev. Roger Vekemann], 'I Got $5 Million From the CIA': Reprinted From the Washington *Evening-Star*, July 23, 1975." *Congressional Record*, CXXI (December 15, 1975), 40436–40437.

2645.   Kirkpatrick, Lyman B., Jr. "Communism in Africa." *Naval War College Review*, XXI (September 1968), *passim*.

2646.   Lemarchand, René. "The CIA in Africa: How Central? How Intelligent?" *Journal of Modern African Studies*, XIV (September 1976), 401–426.

2647.   MacEoin, Gary. "How the CIA's Dirty Tricks Threaten Mission Efforts." *Christian Century*, XCII (March 5, 1975), 217–223.

2648.   Monterio, Tony. "The CIA in Africa." In: Howard Frazier, ed. *Uncloaking the CIA*. New York: Free Press, 1978. pp. 126–134.

2649.   Rashke, Richard L. "CIA Funded, Manipulated Missionaries: Reprinted From the *National Catholic Reporter*, August 1975." *Congressional Record*, CXXI (December 15, 1975), 40434–40444.

2650.   Robison, James. "Spy Role of Missionaries Told: Reprinted From the *Chicago Tribune*, August 2, 1975." *Congressional Record*, CXXI (December 15, 1975), 40438–40439.

2651.   "U.S. Espionage." *Biblical Society*, XII (March 1975), 7–8+, 26–80.

b. Algeria

2652.   "Blame the U.S.: Another French Plot." *U.S. News and World Report*, L (May 15, 1961), 84+.

2653.   Brady, Thomas F. "Paris Rumors on CIA—Despite U.S. Denials, Speculation Persists Agency Aided Algiers Revolt: Reprinted From the *New York Times*, May 2, 1961." *Congressional Record*, CVII (May 2, 1961), 7023–7024.

2654.   Horne, Alistair. *A Savage War of Peace: Algeria, 1954–1962*. New York: Viking Press, 1978. 604p.

2655.   "Rumor or Fact: Did the CIA Interfere in Algeria?" *Newsweek*, LVII (May 15, 1961), 50–51.

2656.   Werth, Alexander. "The CIA in Algeria." *Nation*, CXCII (May 20, 1961), 433–435.

c. Angola

2657.   Bender, G. J. "Angola: A Story of Stupidity." *New York Review of Books*, XXV (December 21, 1978), 26–30.

2658.   Halperin, Morton H. and Daniel N. Hoffman. *Top Secret: National Security and the Right to Know.* New York: Simon and Schuster, 1977. 158p.

2659.   Harsch, Ernest and Tony Thomas. *Angola: The Hidden History of Washington's War.* New York: Pathfinder Press, 1976. 157p.

2660.   Hodges, Tony, jt. author. *See* Legum, Colin (2664).

2661.   Hoffman, Daniel N., jt. author. *See* Halperin, Morton H. (2658).

2662.   Ignatyev, Oleg. "Angola Retrospect." *New Times* (Moscow), no. 34 (August 1976), 27–30.

2663.   Kilpatrick, James J. "Time and Tide in Angola: Reprinted From the *Augusta Chronicle*, December 2, 1975." *Congressional Record*, CXXI (December 12, 1975), 40352.

2664.   Legum, Colin and Tony Hodges. *After Angola: The War Over Southern Africa.* New York: Africana, 1976. 85p.

2665.   Morris, Roger. "A Rare Resignation in Protest: [Assistant Secretary of State for African Affairs] Nat Davis and Angola." *Washington Monthly*, VII (February 1976), 22–30+.

2666.   Oudes, Bruce. "The CIA and Africa." *Africa Report*, XIX (July 1974), 49–52.

2667.   Scheer, Robert. "Naming Names: The CIA's Men in Charge in Angola." *New Times*, VI (February 20, 1976), 13+.

2668.   Stockwell, John. "The CIA and the Violent Option." *Africa*, (September 1978), 52–54.

2669.   _____ . *In Search of Enemies: A CIA Story.* New York: Norton, 1978. 285p.

2670.   _____ . "Our War in Angola." *Time*, CXI (May 22, 1978), 51–52.

2671.   United States. Congress. House. Committee on Foreign Relations. Special Subcommittee on Investigations. *Mercenaries in Africa: Hearings.* 94th Cong., 2nd sess. Washington, D.C.: GPO, 1976. 75p.

2672.   _____ . _____ . Senate. Committee on Foreign Relations. Subcommittee on African Affairs. *Angola: Hearings on U.S. Involvement in the Civil War in Angola.* 94th Cong., 2nd sess. Washington, D.C.: GPO, 1976. 212p.

2673.   Willey, Frederick. "Dogs of War." *Newsweek,* LXXXVI (August 25, 1975), 34–35.

d. Congo-Zaire

2674.   Abi-Saab, Georges. *United Nations Operations in the Congo, 1960–1964.* London and New York: Oxford University Press, 1978. 200p.

2675.   Adelman, Kenneth L. "Zaire's Year of Crisis." *African Affairs,* LXXVII (January 1978), 36–44.

2676.   Dayal, Rajeshwar. *Mission For Hammerskjold: The Congo Crisis.* Princeton, NJ: Princeton University Press, 1976. 335p.

2677.   Enahoro, Peter. "Did the CIA Kill Lumumba?" *Africa,* (October 1975), 11–13.

2678.   Havens, Murray C., *et al.* "The Assassination of Patrice Lumumba of the Congo." In: *Assassination and Terrorism: The Modern Dimensions.* Manchaca, TX: Sterling Swift, 1975. pp. 127–136.

2679.   House, Arthur H. *The U.N. in the Congo: The Political and Civilian Efforts.* Washington, D.C.: University Press of America, 1978. 435p.

2680.   Hovey, Graham. "CIA Denies Aiding Recruitment of Mercenaries to Fight in Zaire: Reprinted From the *New York Times,* April 18, 1977." In: U.S. Congress. House. Permanent Select Committee on Intelligence. Subcommittee on Oversight. *The CIA and the Media: Hearings.* 95th Cong., 1st and 2nd sess. Washington, D.C.: GPO, 1978. p. 358.

2681.   Joshua, Wynfred, jt. author. *See* Lefever, Ernest W. (2683).

2682.   Kanja, Thomas. *Conflict in the Congo: The Rise and Fall of Lumumba.* Baltimore, MD: Penguin Books, 1972. 160p.

2683.   Lefever, Ernest W. and Wynfred Joshua. *United Nations Peacekeeping in the Congo, 1960–1964: An Analysis of Political, Executive, and Military Control.* 4 vols. Washington, D.C.: Brookings Institution, 1966.

2684. "The Proxy War in Zaire." *Newsweek,* LXXXIX (April 25, 1977), 32–33.

2685. United States. Congress. Senate. Select Committee to Study Government Operations With Respect to Intelligence Activities. "Assassination Planning and Plots: The Congo." In: *Alleged Assassination Plots Involving Foreign Leaders: An Interim Report.* 94th Cong., 1st sess. Washington, D.C.: GPO, 1975. pp. 13–70.

2686. Volkman, Ernest. "CIA is Said to Aid Recruiting of U.S. Mercenaries For Zaire: Reprinted From the *Washington Post,* April 17, 1977." In: U.S. Congress. House. Permanent Select Committee on Intelligence. Subcommittee on Oversight. *The CIA and the Media: Hearings.* 95th Cong., 1st and 2nd sess. Washington, D.C.: GPO, 1978. p. 358.

2687. Weissman, Stephen R. *American Foreign Policy in the Congo, 1960–1964.* Ithaca, NY: Cornell University Press, 1974. 325p.

e. Somalia

2688. Crozier, Brian. "The Soviet Presence in Somalia." *Conflict Studies,* no. 54 (February 1975), 3–19.

2689. Payton, Gary D. "Soviet Military Presence Abroad: The Lessons of Somalia." *Military Review,* LIX (January 1979), 67–77.

f. South Africa

2690. "Carter's Desperate Crusade: Charges of American Spying on Nuclear Installations." *Time,* CXIII (April 23, 1979), 37.

2691. "Mystery Over a U.S. Spy Plane." *U.S. News and World Report,* LXXXVI (April 23, 1979), 16.

2692. "Nuclear Secrets in the Sand." *Maclean's,* XCII (April 23, 1979), 36–37.

4. Asia and the Pacific

a. General Works

2693. Asian Peoples' Anti-Communist League. *Let the Record Speak For Itself: Russian Spies All Over.* New Delhi, India: 1967. 137p.

2694. Cornwell, David J. M. "The KGB in Asia: Mightier Than the Sword." By John LeCarré, pseud. *Far Eastern Economic Survey,* LXXXVII (January 3, 1975), 20–27; XCIV (December 31, 1976), 20–24+.

2695. Hoffman, Steven A. "Anticipation, Disaster, and Victory: India, 1962–1971." *Asian Survey,* XII (1972), 960–979.

2696. Johnson, Russell. "U.S. Intervention in Cambodia and the Philippines." In: Howard Frazier, ed. *Uncloaking the CIA.* New York: Free Press, 1978. pp. 86–89.

2697. Kirkpatrick, Lyman B., Jr. "Communism in Asia and South Asia." *Naval War College Review,* XXI (November 1968), *passim.*

2698. LeCarré, John. *See* Cornwell, David J. M. (2694).

2699. Shaffer, Samuel. "Footlocker Preview: Red Spy Files For the Orient." *Newsweek,* XXXVII (May 28, 1951), 22–24.

2700. Short, Frisco W. *Crisis Resolution: Presidential Decision-Making in the Mayaguez and Korean Confrontations* [1975–1976]. Boulder, CO: Westview Press, 1978. 300p.

2701. "The Soviets in Bangkok: Undercover Diplomacy." *Far Eastern Economic Review,* LXXXIX (September 26, 1975), 8–9.

b. Australia

2702. Australia. Royal Commission on Espionage. *Official Transcript of Proceedings.* Sydney: A. H. Pettifer, 1955. 126p.

2703. _____. _____. *Report.* Sydney: A. H. Pettifer, 1955. 483p.

2704. Moskin, J. Robert. "World Beat: The CIA Down Under." *Atlas,* XXVII (July 1977), 4+.

2705. "Now Australia Has a Spy Ring." *U.S. News and World Report,* XXXVI (April 23, 1954), 82+.

2706. "Theresa and Miss X: Skripov and Australian Intelligence." *Time,* LXXXI (February 15, 1963), 32+.

2707. Warner, David. "Australian Lord Haw-Haw: Wilfred Burchett's Alleged Work For the Communists." *National Review,* XXVII (April 11, 1975), 395–397+.

2708. Werner, F. Andrew. "Lesson for the Free World: Australia Thwarts Communism." *American Mercury,* LXXXIV (January 1957), 128–132.

2709. Wilkie, Douglas. "The Soviet Spy Case That Shook Australia." *Reporter,* XII (March 24, 1955), 28–33.

c. China

2710. "Enemies of the People: Taiwanese Spies in the Peoples' Republic of China." *Time,* CV (January 13, 1975), 27–28.

2711. Seng-wen, Ch'en. "The Chinese Communist Investigation System." *Issues and Studies* (Taiwan), VIII (August–September 1972), 50–59, 66–70.

PRC espionage.

2712. "Spying in Peking: Chinese Accusations Against the Russians." *Time*, CIII (February 4, 1974), 49–50.

2713. "U.S. Transfers Five [CIA Officers] in Taiwan Unrest—Men Said to be Accused of Aiding Dissidents: Reprinted From the *New York Times*, June 1, 1971." *Congressional Record*, CXVII (July 15, 1971), 25532–25533.

2714. Whiting, Allen S. "New Light on Mao-Quemoy, 1958: Mao's Miscalculations." *China Quarterly*, LXII (1975), 263–270.

d. Glomar Explorer *Affair*

2715. Alpern, David M. "The CIA's Mission Impossible: 'Project Jennifer,' the Effort to Raise a Sunken Soviet Submarine." *Newsweek*, LXXXV (March 31, 1975), 24+.

2716. "Behind the Great Submarine Snatch: The *Glomar Explorer* and 'Project Jennifer.'" *Time*, CVIII (December 6, 1976), 23.

2717. Burleson, Clyde W. *The Jennifer Project.* Englewood Cliffs, NJ: Prentice-Hall, 1977. 179p.

2718. "Did Hughes Really Build a Mining Ship? *Business Week*, (April 7, 1975), 26–27.

2719. "The CIA Sub Caper: Its Effects on Research." *Science News Letter*, CVII (March 29, 1975), 204–205.

2720. "The CIA was Doing Its Job: Reprinted From the *Washington Star*, March 21, 1975." *Congressional Record*, CXXI (March 22, 1975), 8344–8345.

2721. Collier, Wayne, jt. author. *See* Varner, Roy (2743).

2722. Drosnin, Michael. "The Great Hughes Heist." *New Times*, VIII (January 21, 1977), 26+.

2723. DuBois, Larry and Lawrence Gonzales. "The Puppet—and the Puppetmasters: Uncovering the Secret World of Nixon, Hughes, and the CIA." *Playboy*, XXIII (September 1976), 74+.

2724. "The *Glomar Explorer:* Reprinted From the *Washington Post*, March 23, 1975." *Congressional Record*, CXXI (March 24, 1975), 8381.

2725. "The *Glomar* Mystery." *Time,* CVIII (December 20, 1976), 27.

2726. Gonzales, Lawrence, jt. author. *See* DuBois, Larry (2723).

2727. "The Great Submarine Snatch: 'Project Jennifer,' the Salvaging of a Russian Submarine." *Time,* CV (March 31, 1975), 20–21+.

2728. Henthoff, Nat. "The CIA's Soviet Sub Caper: Everybody Knew—Except the Public." *True Magazine,* LVII (July 1975), 76–77+.

2729. Kraft, Joseph. "Lessons From the Soviet Submarine Incident: Reprinted from the *Washington Post,* March 23, 1975." *Congressional Record,* CXXI (April 17, 1975), 10779–10780.

2730. Latham, Aaron. "How *Glomar* Really Surfaced." *New York Magazine,* VIII (April 7, 1975), 72–74.

2731. Lipsyte, Robert. "That Championship Season." *More,* V (April 1975), 27+.

2732. Miller, A. S. "Servile Press: The 'Project Jennifer' Incident." *Progressive,* XXXIX (May 1975), 6–7.

2733. Mueller, William B. "Howard Hughes, CIA, and the Incredible *Glomar Explorer.*" *Sea Classics,* XI (September 1978), 26–38.

Illustrated.

2734. "National Insecurity: 'Project Jennifer.' " *Progressive,* XXXIX (May 1975), 5–6.

2735. Newman, Barry. "Behind the *Glomar* Sub Hunt." *Nation,* CCXXI (October 11, 1975), 329–333.

2736. O'Toole, Thomas. "*Glomar* Roots Go Back to 1962 Scheme: Reprinted From the *Washington Post,* May 22, 1977." In: U.S. Congress. House. Permanent Select Committee on Intelligence. Subcommittee on Oversight. *The CIA and the Media: Hearings.* 95th Cong., 1st and 2nd sess. Washington, D.C.: GPO, 1978. pp. 363–364.

2737. Phelan, James. "How Howard Hughes Blew His CIA Cover." *True Magazine,* LVII (October 1975), 18+.

2738. " 'Project Jennifer': Reprinted from the *New York Times,* March 20, 1975." *Congressional Record,* CXXI (March 20, 1975), 7883.

2739. Rubin, A. P. "Sunken Soviet Submarines and Central Intelligence: Laws of Property and the Agency." *American Journal of International Law,* LXIX (October 1975), 855–858.

2740.   Shearer, Lloyd. "CIA Snafu." *Parade,* (March 25, 1979), 22.

Printing of classified *Glomar* remarks in the French edition of William Colby's memoirs.

2741.   "Show and Tell?: The Press Dilemma Raised by the 'Project Jennifer' Story." *Time,* CV (March 31, 1975), 60.

2742.   "Trying to Swipe a Russian Sub is Just Part of the CIA Saga." *U.S. News and World Report,* LXXVIII (March 31, 1975), 16–17.

2743.   Varner, Roy and Wayne Collier. *A Matter of Risk: The Incredible Inside Story of the CIA's Hughes Glomar Explorer Mission to Raise a Russian Submarine.* New York: Random House, 1978. 260p.

2744.   _____ . "The Secret That Nearly Sank the CIA." *Pittsburg Press Roto,* (January 7, 1979), 20–22.

2745.   Wade, Nicholas. "Deep-Sea Salvage: Did CIA Use Mohole Techniques to Raise Sub?" *Science,* CLXXXVIII (May 16, 1975), 710–713.

e. Indonesia

2746.   Karnow, Stanley. "Espionage Attempts in the 1950's Recalled—U.S. Image in Southeast Asia Suffers From Clumsy Intrigues Abroad: Reprinted from the *Washington Post,* September 7, 1965." *Congressional Record,* CXI (September 20, 1965), 24421–24423.

2747.   Stevenson, William. *Bird's Nest in Their Beard.* Boston: Houghton, Mifflin, 1964. 280p.

2748.   Sukarno. *Sukarno: An Autobiography.* Indianapolis: Bobbs-Merrill, 1965. 324p.

f. Indochina

(1) GENERAL WORKS

2749.   Blackstock, Paul W. "Covert Military Operations." In: Roger W. Little, ed. *Handbook of Military Institutions.* Beverly Hills, CA: Sage Publications, 1971. pp. 455–492.

2750.   Blaufarb, Douglas S. *The Counterinsurgency Era: U.S. Doctrine and Performance, 1950 to the Present.* New York: Free Press, 1977. 356p.

2751.   Brandon, Henry. *Anatomy of Error: The Inside Story of the Asian War on the Potomac, 1954–1969.* Boston: Gambit, 1969.

2752.   Branfman, Fred. "The Secret Wars of the CIA." In: Howard Frazier, ed. *Uncloaking the CIA.* New York: Free Press, 1978. pp. 90–100.

2753. Burchett, Wilfred G. *The Furtive War: The United States in Viet-nam and Laos.* New York: International Publishers, 1963. 224p.

2754. Committee of Concerned Asian Scholars. *The Indochina Story: A Fully Documented Account.* New York: Praeger, 1971. 347p.

2755. Duncan, Donald. *The New Legion.* New York: Random House, 1967. 275p.

2756. _____. "The Whole Thing was a Lie." *Ramparts,* IV (February 1966), 13–24.

2757. Ellsberg, Daniel. *Papers on the War.* New York: Simon and Schuster, 1972. 309p.

2758. Emerson, Gloria. *Winners and Losers: Battles, Retreats, Gains, and Losses and Ruins From a Long War.* New York: Harcourt, Brace, 1978. 448p.

2759. Fitzgerald, Frances. *Fire in the Lake.* Boston: Little, Brown, 1972. 491p.

2760. Fo, Shih. *An Exposure of Chinese Communist Drug Dealings in the "Golden Triangle."* Taipei, Formosa: Hsueh Hai Publishers, 1978. 74p.

2761. Gettleman, Marvin, *et al.,* eds. *Conflict in Indochina: A Reader on the Widening War in Laos and Cambodia.* New York: Random House, 1970. 464p.

2762. Halberstam, David. *The Best and the Brightest.* New York: Random House, 1972. 688p.

2763. _____. *The Making of a Quagmire.* New York: Random House, 1964.

2764. Hersh, Seymour. "CIA Aides Assail Asia Drug Charge of Hero-in Traffic Among Allies of the United States: Reprinted From the *New York Times,* July 22, 1972." *Congressional Record,* CXVIII (August 2, 1972), 26395–26396.

2765. Hing, Sokhom. "The CIA Against Cambodia." In: Howard Frazier, ed. *Uncloaking the CIA.* New York: Free Press, 1978. pp. 79–85.

2766. Hoopes, Townsend. *The Limits of Intervention.* Rev. ed. New York: McKay, 1973. 264p.

2767. Karnow, Stanley. "Record of CIA in Southeast Asia Places U.S. Name in Disrepute: Reprinted From the *Providence Journal,* September 7, 1965." *Congressional Record,* CXI (September 13, 1965), 23486–23487.

2768.   Kirk, Donald. *The Wider War: The Struggle For Cambodia, Thailand, and Laos.* New York: Praeger, 1971. 305p.

2769.   Laurie, James. "A Chilling Reminder From Asia." *Far Eastern Economic Review,* LXXXV (July 27, 1974), 26–27.

2770.   Lewis, Flora. "Facts Surface on the Heroin War: Reprinted From the *Washington Post,* July 14, 1971." *Congressional Record,* CXVII (July 14, 1971), 24940–24941.

2771.   _____ . "Is the CIA Mixed Up in Dope Traffic?: Reprinted From *Newsday,* May 7, 1971." *Congressional Record,* CXVII (September 23, 1971), 33213–33214.

2772.   McCoy, Alfred W. "Flowers of Evil." *Harper's,* CCXLV (July 1972), 47–53.

2773.   _____ . *The Politics of Heroin in Southeast Asia.* New York: Harper & Row, 1972. 464p.

2774.   Schurmacher, Emile C. *Our Secret War Against Red China.* New York: Paperback Library, 1962. 176p.

2775.   Scott, Peter D. *The War Conspiracy: The Secret Road to the Second Indochina War.* Indianapolis: Bobbs-Merrill, 1972. 238p.

2776.   Sihanouk, Norodom, as Related to Wilfred Burchett. *My War With the CIA.* London: Penguin Books, 1973.

2777.   Szulc, Tad. "Mums the War: Secret U.S. Operations in Southeast Asia." *New Republic,* CLXIX (August 18, 1973), 19–21.

2778.   "U.S. Infighting: Reprinted from the *Manchester Guardian,* August 14, 1971." *Congressional Record,* CXVII (October 13, 1971), 35962–35964.

2779.   United States. Congress. Committee on the Judiciary. Subcommittee to Investigate the Administration of the Internal Security Act and Other Internal Security Laws. *World Drug Traffic and Its Impact on U.S. Security: Hearings.* 92nd Cong., 2nd sess. 6 pts. Washington, D.C.: GPO, 1972–1973.

(2) LAOS

2780.   Adams, Nina and Alfred W. McCoy, eds. *Laos: War and Revolution.* New York: Published for the Committee of Concerned Asian Scholars by Harper & Row, 1970. 482p.

2781.   Allman, T. D. "U.S. Backed Lao Troops Capture Two Rebel Areas: Reprinted From the *New York Times,* September 18, 1969." In: U.S. Congress. House. Permanent Select Committee on Intelligence.

Subcommittee on Oversight. *The CIA and the Media: Hearings.* 95th Cong., 1st and 2nd sess. Washington, D.C.: GPO, 1978, p. 349.

2782.   Arbuckle, Tammy. "Hiding the U.S. Role in Laos: Reprinted From the *Washington Evening Star,* February 21, 1971." In: U.S. Congress. House. Committee on the Judiciary. Subcommittee to Investigate Problems Connected With Refugees and Escapees. *War-Related Civilian Problems in Indochina–Part II, Laos and Cambodia: Hearings.* 92nd Cong., 1st sess. Washington, D.C.: GPO, 1971. pp. 149–151.

2783.   Black, Edwin F. "Laos: A Case Study." *Military Review,* XLIV (December 1964), 49–59.

2784.   Branfman, Fred. "America's Secret War." *Progressive,* XXXVI (June 1972), 29–33.

2785.   _____ . "The CIA's Quiet Little War in Laos." *Playboy,* XXII (August 1975), 56+.

2786.   _____ . "One Man's War." *Far Eastern Economic Review,* LXVII (March 26, 1970), 24+.

2787.   _____ . "The President's Secret Army: A Case Study—The CIA in Laos, 1962–1972." In: Robert L. Borosage and John D. Marks, eds. *The CIA File.* New York: Grossman, 1976. pp. 46–78.

2788.   Chittenden, Geoffrey M. "Laos and the Powers, 1954–1962." Unpublished PhD Dissertation, University of London, 1969.

2789.   Decornoy, Jacques. "Laos: The Forgotten War." *Bulletin of the Concerned Asian Scholars,* II (April–July 1970), 21–23.

2790.   De Hoog, John. "Secret War in the Secret Country." *Orientations,* III (July 1972), 5–9.

2791.   Dengler, Dieter. *Escape From Laos.* San Rafael, CA: Presidio Press, 1979.

2792.   Dommen, Arthur J. *Conflict in Laos: The Politics of Neutralization.* New York: Praeger, 1964. 338p.

2793.   Fall, Bernard M. *Anatomy of a Crisis: The Laotian Crisis of 1960–1961.* Edited, With an Epilogue, by Roger M. Smith. Garden City, NY: Doubleday, 1969. 283p.

2794.   _____ . "Reappraisal in Laos." *Current History,* XLII (January 1962), 8–14.

2795.   Finney, John W. "United States Said to Pay Thais Aiding Laos: Reprinted From the *New York Times,* May 22, 1971." *Congressional Record,* CXVII (June 4, 1971), 18134–18135.

2796. Goldstein, Martin E. "American Foreign Policy Towards Laos, 1954–1962: A Study of Conflict, Resolution, and Intervention." Unpublished PhD Dissertation, University of Pennsylvania, 1968.

2797. Grant, Zalin. "Report From Laos: The Hidden War." *New Republic,* CLVIII (April 20, 1968), 17–19.

2798. Hill, Kenneth L. "President Kennedy and the Neutralization of Laos." *Review of Politics,* XXXI (July 1969), 353–369.

2799. Kamm, Henry. "CIA Role in Laos—Advising an Army: Reprinted From the *New York Times,* March 12, 1971." In: U.S. Congress. House. Committee on the Judiciary. Subcommittee to Investigate Problems Connected With Refugees and Escapees. *War Related Civilian Problems in Indochina–Part II, Laos and Cambodia: Hearings.* 92nd Cong., 1st sess. Washington, D.C.: GPO, 1971. pp. 151–153.

2800. McCoy, Alfred W. "Conversation With the CIA." *New York Review of Books,* XIX (September 21, 1972), 31+.

2801. ———, jt. editor. *See* Adams, Nina (2780).

2802. Paul, Roland A. "Laos: Anatomy of an American Involvement." *Foreign Affairs,* XLIX (April 1971), 533–547.

2803. Razagopal, D. R. "A Little Fox [Gen. Kong Le] in General's Tunic." *Asia Magazine,* VII (August 6, 1967), 10–11.

2804. Rich, Spencer. "Senators Told CIA Aids Laos: Reprinted From the *Washington Post,* May 22, 1971." *Congressional Record,* CXVII (June 4, 1971), 18136–18137.

2805. Scott, Peter D. "Air America: Flying the U.S. Into Laos." *Ramparts,* VIII (February 1970), 39–42+.

2806. Shaplen, Robert. "Our Involvement in Laos." *Foreign Affairs,* XLVIII (April 1970), 478–493.

2807. Starner, Frances. "Laos: Flight of the CIA." *Far Eastern Economic Review,* LXXVIII (October 7, 1972), 23–26.

2808. Stern, Lawrence. "Flights Not Flown, Troops That Don't Exist—United States Pays For Phantom War: Reprinted From the *Washington Post,* June 11, 1973." *Congressional Record,* CXIX (June 11, 1973), 18971–18972.

2809. Stevenson, Charles A. *The End of Nowhere: American Policy Towards Laos Since 1954.* Boston: Beacon Press, 1972. 367p.

2810. _____ . "The Edge of the Precipice: American Policy Towards Laos Since 1954." Unpublished PhD Dissertation, Harvard University, 1970.

2811. Treaster, Joseph B. "The CIA's Secret War." *Penthouse,* VII (September 1975), 45+.

2812. United States. Congress. Senate. Committee on Foreign Relations. Subcommittee on U.S. Security Agreements Abroad. *Aid Activities in Laos: Hearings.* 93rd Cong., 1st sess. Washington, D.C.: GPO, 1972. 26p.

2813. _____ . _____ . _____ . _____ . *Laos—April 1971: Hearings.* 92nd Cong., 1st sess. Washington, D.C.: GPO, 1971. 23p.

2814. _____ . Department of State. Bureau of Intelligence and Research. *The Situation in Laos: A Report.* Washington, D.C., 1959. 58p.

2815. Warner, Denis. "The Catastrophic Non-War in Laos." *Reporter,* XXX (June 18, 1964), 21–24.

2816. "Our Secret War in Laos." *Reporter,* XXXII (April 22, 1965), 23–26.

2817. Woodruff, John E. "The Meo of Laos—CIA Alliance Brings Ruin to Proud Race: Reprinted From the *Baltimore Sun,* February 21–22, 25, 1971." In: U.S. Congress. House. Committee on the Judiciary. Subcommittee to Investigate Problems Connected With Refugees and Escapees. *War Related Civilian Problems in Indochina—Part II, Laos and Cambodia: Hearings.* 92nd Cong., 1st sess. Washington, D.C.: GPO, 1971. pp. 131–139.

2818. Zasloff, Joseph. "Laos: The Forgotten War Widens." *Asian Survey,* (January 1970), 65–72.

(3) VIETNAM

2819. Adams, Samuel A. "Vietnam Cover-Up: Playing War With Numbers—Statistics on Viet Cong Strength Ignored by the CIA." *Harpers,* CCL (May, July 1975), 41–44+, 14+.

2820. Ball, George W. "Top Secret: The Prophecy the President Rejected [in 1964]." *Atlantic,* CCXXX (July 1972), 35–49.

2821. Bennett, Donald G. "Spot Report: Intelligence, Vietnam." *Military Review,* XLVI (August 1966), 72–77.

2822. Blackman, Morris J. "The Stupidity of Intelligence." In: Charles Peters and Timothy J. Adams, eds. *Inside the System: A Washington Monthly Reader.* New York: Praeger, 1970. pp. 271–280.

2823. Blackstock, Paul W. "The CIA Looks Good in the *Pentagon Papers.*" *Baltimore Sun Perspective,* (July 18, 1971), K1.

2824. Borin, V. L. "Who Killed Diem and Why?" *National Review,* XVI (June 2, 1964), 441–446.

2825. Branfman, Fred. "South Vietnam's Police and Prison System: The U.S. Connection." In: Howard Frazier, ed. *Uncloaking the CIA.* New York: Free Press, 1978. pp. 101–125.

2826. Brodsky, Richard. "The Saigon Connection." *Encore,* IV (August 18, 1975), 20–21.

2827. Brown, Weldon A. *The Last Chopper: The Denouement of the American Role in Vietnam, 1964–1975.* Port Washington, NY: Kennikat Press, 1976. 359p.

2828. _____. *Prelude to Disaster: The American Role in Vietnam, 1940–1963.* Port Washington, NY: Kennikat Press, 1975. 278p.

2829. Colby, William E. "The Quagmire of Vietnam." *Book Digest,* V (June 1978), 34–68.

2830. Cooper, Chester L. *The Lost Crusade: America in Vietnam.* New York: Dodd, Mead, 1970. 559p.

2831. Corson, William R. *The Betrayal.* New York: Norton, 1968. 316p.

2832. Critchfield, Richard. *The Long Charade: Political Subversion in the Vietnam War.* New York: Harcourt, Brace, 1968. 401p.

2833. Drosnin, Michael. "Phoenix: The CIA's Biggest Assassination Program." *New Times,* V (August 22, 1975), 16+.

2834. "Electronic Reconnaissance in Vietnam." *International Defense Review,* V (August 1972), 358–362.

2835. Ellsberg, Daniel. "Diemism and U.S. Arms: Impact of the Arrest, Trial, and Imprisonment of Tran Ngoc Chau." In: U.S. Congress, Senate. Committee on Foreign Relations. *Impact of the War in Southeast Asia on the U.S. Economy, Part II: Hearings.* 91st Congress, 2nd sess. Washington, D.C.: GPO, 1970. pp. 334–365.

2836. "The Enemy Within: CIA Report on Communist Spies Operating Inside the Government of South Vietnam." *Newsweek,* LXXVI (November 2, 1970), 65.

2837. "The Failure of Intelligence." *Nation,* CCVI (March 4, 1968), 292–293.

Tet offensive.

2838. Falk, Richard A. "What We Should Learn From Vietnam." In: Robert W. Gregg and Charles W. Kegley, Jr., eds. *After Vietnam: The Future of American Foreign Policy.* New York: Anchor Books, 1971. pp. 324–339.

2839. Fall, Bernard B. *Viet-Nam Witness, 1953–1956.* New York: Praeger, 1966.

2840. "Folly in Vietnam." *New Republic,* CXLIX (September 21, 1963), 6–7.

2841. Galloway, John. *The Gulf of Tonkin Resolution.* Rutherford, NJ: Fairleigh Dickinson University Press, 1970. 578p.

2842. _____ , ed. *The Kennedys and Vietnam.* New York: Facts on File, Inc., 1971. 150p.

2843. Goulden, Joseph C. *Truth is the First Casualty: The Gulf of Tonkin Affair—Illusion and Reality.* Chicago: Rand McNally, 1969, 285p.

2844. "Green Berets on Trial." *Time,* XCIV (August 22, 1968), 11–12.

For executing double-agent Thai-khac-Chuyen.

2845. Grinter, Lawrence E. "The Pacification of South Vietnam: Dilemmas of Counterinsurgency and Development." Unpublished PhD Dissertation, University of North Carolina at Chapel Hill, 1972.

2846. Gurtov, Melvin. *The First Vietnam Crisis.* New York: Columbia University Press, 1967. 228p.

2847. Halloran, Bernard F. "Soviet Armor Comes to Vietnam: A Surprise That Needn't Have Been." *Army,* XXII (August 1972), 19–23.

2848. Hammer, Richard. *One Morning in the War.* New York: Coward, McCann, 1970. 207p.

2849. Hay, John H., Jr. *Tactical and Material Innovations.* Vietnam Studies, Department of the Army. Washington, D.C.: GPO, 1974. 197p.

2850. Head, Simon. "Pacifying Vietnam." *Far Eastern Economic Review,* LVI (May 4, 1967), 259–263.

2851. _____ . "Unhappy Harbingers." *Far Eastern Economic Review,* LVI (June 1, 1967), 495–498.

2852. Heilbrunn, Otto. "Tactical Intelligence in Vietnam." *Military Review,* XLVIII (October 1968), 85–87.

2853. Hien, Anh. *The Coup d'Etat of November 1, 1963.* Saigon: U.S. Embassy, 1971. 132p.

2854.   Hinckle, Warren, *et al.* "Michigan State: University on the Make." *Ramparts,* IV (April 1966), 11–21.

2855.   Horowitz, Irving L. "Michigan State and the CIA: A Dilemma For Social Science." *Bulletin of the Atomic Scientists,* XXII (September 1966), 26–29.

2856.   Hosmer, Stephen T., *et al. The Fall of South Vietnam: Statements By Vietnamese Military and Civilian Leaders.* RAND Report R-2208-OSD. Santa Monica, CA: RAND Corporation, 1978. 131p.

2857.   Hurley, Robert M. "President John F. Kennedy and Vietnam, 1961–1963." Unpublished PhD Dissertation, University of Hawaii, 1971.

2858.   Joseph, Paul. "The Politics of Good and Bad Information: The National Security Bureaucracy and the Vietnam War." *Politics and Society,* VII (Spring 1977), 105–127.

2859.   Kelly, Francis J. *U.S. Army Special Forces, 1961–1971.* Vietnam Studies: Department of the Army. Washington, D.C.: GPO, 1973. 227p.

2860.   Kissinger, Henry, with the N.S.C. Staff. "National Security Study Memorandum-1 (N.S.S.M.-1)." *Congressional Record,* CVIII (May 10-11, 1972), 16748–16836, 17186–17189.

2861.   Knoll, Erwin. "The Mysterious Project Phoenix." *Progressive,* XXXIV (February 1970), 19–21.

2862.   Kondracke, Morton and Thomas B. Ross. "How John F. Kennedy and Aides Helped Topple Diem: Reprinted From the *Chicago Sun-Times,* June 23, 1971." *Congressional Record,* CXVII (June 29, 1971), 22785–22786.

2863.   Lansdale, Edward G. *In the Midst of Wars: An American's Mission to Southeast Asia.* New York: Harper & Row, 1972. 386p.

2864.   Lewis, Thomas J. *Year of the Hare: Bureaucratic Distortion in the U.S. Military View of the Vietnam War in 1963.* Virginia Beach, VA: 1972. 134p.

2865.   Lewy, Guenther. *America in Vietnam.* New York and London: Oxford University Press, 1979. 540p.

2866.   "Lifting the Veil: Long Tieng, Headquarters of the CIA's Secret Army." *Newsweek,* LXXIX (January 31, 1972), 33–34.

2867.   Long, Ngo-Vinh. "The CIA and the Vietnam Debacle." In: Howard Frazier, ed. *Uncloaking the CIA.* New York: Free Press, 1978. pp. 69–78.

2868.   McChristian, Joseph A. *The Role of Military Intelligence, 1965–1967*. Vietnam Studies: Department of the Army. Washington, D.C.: GPO, 1974. 182p.

2869.   "Martin File—Secret Documents in Stolen Car: Ambassador Glen A. Martin's Papers."*Newsweek,* XCII (September 25, 1978), 41–42.

2870.   Mathews, T. "Psst! Vietnam Secrets?"*Newsweek,* XC (November 28, 1977), 71.

2871.   Meany, Neville. "From the *Pentagon Papers:* Reflections on the Making of America's Vietnam Policy." *Australian Outlook,* XXVI (August 1972), 163–192.

2872.   "Misfiled Secrets: Copies of Communications Between Washington and the U.S. Embassy in Saigon in Glen A. Martin's Possession." *Time,* CXII (September 25, 1978), 26+.

2873.   Mohr, Charles. "Saigon Takes Reins of CIA's School: Reprinted From the *New York Times,* July 18, 1966."*Congressional Record,* CXII (July 18, 1966), 15998–15999.

2874.   Nighswonger, William A. *Rural Pacification in Vietnam.* New York: Praeger, 1966. 320p.

2875.   Oberdorfer, Don. *Tet!* Garden City, NY: Doubleday, 1971.

2876.   *The Pentagon Papers: The Defense Department History of United States Decision-Making on Vietnam.* The Senator [Mike] Gravel Edition. 5 vols. Boston: Beacon Press, 1971.

2877.   Prouty, L. Fletcher. "The CIA and the Green Berets: A Strange Case of Mistaken Identities?" *Armed Forces Journal,* CVII (October 4, 1969), 16–17.

2878.   _____ . "Green Berets and the CIA." *New Republic,* CLXI (August 23, 1969), 9–10.

2879.   Ross, Thomas B., jt. author. *See* Kondracke, Morton (2862).

2880.   "Saigon and the CIA."*Newsweek,* LXII (October 21, 1963), 38+

2881.   Schandler, Herbert Y. *The Unmaking of a President: Lyndon Johnson and Vietnam.* Princeton, NJ: Princeton University Press, 1977. 419p.

2882.   Scheer, Robert. "The Genesis of United States Support For Ngo Dinh Diem." In: Marvin Gettleman, ed. *Vietnam.* Rev. ed. New York: Fawcett Books, 1970. pp. 235–253.

2883. _____ . *How the United States Got Involved in Vietnam.* Santa Barbara, CA: Center for the Study of Democratic Institutions, 1965. 79p.

2884. Schemmer, Benjamin F. *The Raid* [on Son Tay]. New York: Harper & Row, 1976. 326p.

2885. Schlesinger, Arthur M., Jr. *The Bitter Heritage: Vietnam and American Democracy, 1941–1966.* Boston: Houghton, Mifflin, 1967. 126p.

2886. Sharron, Marc. "The Fall of the House of Ngo: A Case History." *Institute of Applied Psychology Review,* IV (Summer 1964), 83–92.

2887. Sheehan, Neil, *et al. The Pentagon Papers, the Secret History of the Vietnam War: The Complete and Unabridged Series as Published by the New York Times.* New York: Quadrangle Books, 1971. 677p.

2888. Sheinbaum, Sam. "University on the Make; or, How Michigan State University Helped Arm Madame Nhu." *Ramparts,* VII (January 25, 1969), 52–60.

2889. Sheriff, Ruth. "How the CIA Makes Friends and Influences Countries." *Viet-Report,* (January-February 1967), 15+.

2890. Smith, Joseph B. "The CIA in Vietnam: Nationbuilders, Old Pros, Paramilitary Boys, and Misplaced Persons." *Washington Monthly,* IX (February 1978), 22–30.

2891. Snepp, Frank W., 3rd. *Decent Interval: An Insider's Account of Saigon's Indecent End.* New York: Random House, 1977. 590p.

2892. Stein, Jeffrey. "From the Ashes, Phoenix: A CIA Operation." *Commonweal,* XCVIII (April 20, 1973), 154–160.

2893. Sutton, Horace. "Ghostly War of the Green Berets." *Saturday Review of Literature,* LII (October 18, 1969), 23–25+.

2894. Thomson, James C. "How Could Vietnam Happen?" In: Morton Halperin and Arnold Kanter, eds. *Readings in American Foreign Policy.* Boston: Little, Brown, 1971. pp. 98–110.

2895. Treaster, Joseph B. "The Phoenix Murders." *Penthouse,* VII (December 1975), 76+.

2896. Tu, Le-Anh. "Aid to Thieu." *Congressional Record,* CXVIII (October 11, 1972), 34841–34854.

2897. "Under Restraint [Thai-khac Chuyen]." *Newsweek,* LXXIV (September 1, 1969), 35–36.

2898. United States. Central Intelligence Agency. "Capabilities of the Vietnamese Communists For Fighting in South Vietnam: Excerpts From CIA Special National Intelligence Estimate No. 14.3–67, November 13, 1967." In: U.S. Congress. House. Select Committee on Intelligence. *U.S. Intelligence Agencies and Activities—Part V, Risks and Control of Foreign Intelligence: Hearings.* 94th Cong., 1st sess. Washington, D.C.: GPO, 1975. pp. 1981–1991.

2899. _____ . _____ . "Intelligence Warnings of the Tet Offensive in South Vietnam: Interim Report Declassified December 3, 1975." In: U.S. Congress. House. Select Committee on Intelligence. *U.S. Intelligence Agencies and Activities—Part V, Risks and Control of Foreign Intelligence: Hearings.* 94th Cong., 1st sess. Washington, D.C.: GPO, 1975. pp. 1993–2001.

2900. _____ . Congress. House. Select Committee on Intelligence. "The 1968 Tet Offensive in South Vietnam." In: *U.S. Intelligence Agencies and Activities—Part II, The Performance of the Intelligence Community: Hearings.* 94th Cong., 1st sess. Washington, D.C.: GPO, 1975. pp. 683–719.

2901. _____ . _____ . _____ . Committee on Foreign Relations. Subcommittee on Asian and Pacific Affairs. *The Treatment of Political Prisoners in South Vietnam by the Republic of South Vietnam: Hearings.* 93rd Cong., 1st sess. Washington, D.C.: GPO, 1973.

2902. _____ . _____ . _____ . Committee on International Relations. Special Subcommittee on Investigations. *Vietnam Evacuation: Hearings and Testimony of Ambassador Graham A. Martin.* 94th Cong., 2nd sess. Washington, D.C.: GPO, 1976. 87p.

2903. _____ . _____ . Senate. Committee on Foreign Relations. *U.S. Involvement in the Overthrow of Diem: A Staff Study Based on the Pentagon Papers.* Washington, D.C.: GPO, 1972. 73p.

2904. _____ . _____ . _____ . *Vietnam Commitments, 1961: A Staff Study Based on the Pentagon Papers.* Washington, D.C.: GPO, 1972. 38p.

2905. _____ . _____ . _____ . _____ . *Vietnam Policy and Prospects, 1970: Hearings on Civil Operations and Rural Development Support Program (CORDS).* 91st Cong., 2nd sess. Washington, D.C.: GPO, 1970.

2906. _____ . _____ . _____ . Select Committee to Investigate Government Operations With Respect to Intelligence Activities. "Assassination Planning and Plots: Diem." In: *Alleged Assassination Plots Involving Foreign Leaders: An Interim Report.* 94th Cong., 1st sess. Washington, D.C.: GPO, 1975. pp. 217–224.

2907. _____ . Department of Defense. *United States-Vietnam Relations, 1945–1967.* 12 vols. Washington, D.C.: GPO, 1971.

The Pentagon Papers

2908. _____ . Government Accounting Office. *Suggestions For Changes in U.S. Funding and Management of Pacification and Development Programs in Vietnam: A Report to Congress.* Washington, D.C.: GPO, 1972. 70p.

2909. Warner, Denis A. *Certain Victory: How Hanoi Won the War.* London: Sheed, Andrews, and McMeel, 1978. 295p.

2910. _____ . "Vietnam: The Ordeal of Pacification." *Reporter,* XXXV (December 1, 1966), 25–28.

2911. Warner, Geoffrey. "The United States and the Fall of Diem: The Coup That Never Was." *Australian Outlook,* XXVIII (December 1974), 245–258; XXIX (April 1975), 3–17.

2912. _____ . "The United States and Vietnam, 1945–1965." *International Affairs* (London), (July, October 1972), 379–395, 593–615.

2913. Welsh, David. "Pacification in Vietnam." *Ramparts,* VI (October 1967), 36–41.

2914. Westmoreland, William C. *A Soldier Reports.* Garden City, NY: Doubleday, 1976. 446p.

2915. Windchy, E. G. *Tonkin Gulf.* Garden City, NY: Doubleday, 1971. 358p.

2916. "With Cap and Cloak in Saigon: [CIA] Participation in MSU Program." *Time,* LXXXVII (April 22, 1966), 20.

g. Korea

2917. Brandt, Raymond P. "Intelligence Reports are Futile Unless They Lead to Decisions: Reprinted From the *Washington Star,* July 2, 1950." *Congressional Record,* XCVI (July 5, 1950), 9641.

2918. Cagle, Malcolm W. "Errors of the Korean War." *U.S. Naval Institute Proceedings,* LXXXIV (March 1958), 31–35.

2919. Conde, David. "The Convenient Spy Plot." *Eastern Horizon,* VII (January 1968), 49–54.

2920. DeWeerd, Harvey. "Strategic Surprise in the Korean War." *Orbis,* VI (Fall 1962), 435–452.

2921. Gardner, Lloyd C., comp. *The Korean War.* New York: Quadrangle Books, 1972. 242p.

2922.   George, Alexander L. *The Chinese Communist Army in Action: The Korean War and Its Aftermath.* New York: Columbia University Press, 1967. 255p.

2923.   Higgins, Trumbull. *Korea and the Fall of MacArthur: A Precis in Limited War.* New York and London: Oxford University Press, 1960. 229p.

2924.   Hillenhoetter, Roscoe H. "Ex-Head Asserts CIA Reports Should Have Gone to MacArthur: Reprinted From the *Washington Star,* May 10, 1951." *Congressional Record,* XCVII (1951), A2683–A2684.

2925.   "Intelligence Responsibility: Reprinted From the *Washington Star,* June 28, 1950." *Congressional Record,* XCVI (1950), A5026–A5027.

2926.   MacArthur, Douglas. *Reminiscences.* New York: McGraw-Hill, 1964. 438p.

2927.   _____ . *A Soldier Speaks: Public Papers.* New York: Praeger, 1965. 367p.

2928.   McGovern, James. *To the Yalu: From the Chinese Invasion of Korea to MacArthur's Dismissal.* New York: Morrow, 1972. 225p.

2929.   Manchester, William. "Sunset Gun, 1950–1951." In: *American Caesar: Douglas MacArthur, 1880–1964.* Boston: Little, Brown, 1978. pp. 545–629.

2930.   Marshall, Samuel L. A. "Our Mistakes in Korea." *Atlantic,* CXCII (September 1953), 46–49.

2931.   _____ . *The River and the Gauntlet: Defeat of the Eighth Army by the Chinese Communist Forces, November 1950, in the Battle of the Chongchon River, Korea.* New York: Morrow, 1953.

2932.   O'Neill, Robert. "The Chongchon River." In: Noble Frankland and Christopher Dowling, eds. *Decisive Battles of the Twentieth Century.* New York: McKay, 1976. pp. 289–304.

2933.   Paige, Glenn D. *The Korean Decision, June 24–30, 1950.* New York: Free Press, 1968. 394p.

2934.   _____ , jt. author. *See* Snyder, Richard C. (2941).

2935.   Poteat, George H. "Strategic Intelligence and National Security: A Case Study of the Korean Crisis (June 25-November 24, 1950)." Unpublished PhD Dissertation, St. Louis University, 1973.

2936.   Ransom, Harry H. *Can American Democracy Survive Cold War?* Garden City, NY: Doubleday, 1963.

2937. Rees, David. *Korea: The Limited War.* New York: St. Martin's Press, 1964. 511p.

2938. Ridgeway, Matthew B. *The Korean War.* Garden City, NY: Doubleday, 1967. 291p.

2939. Roberts, John M., Jr. "Is the United States of America Still a Babes-in-the-Woods in the Spy Business?: Reprinted from the *Ansonia* (CT) *Sentinel*, July 26, 1950." *Congressional Record*, XCVI (1950), A5431.

2940. Ruetten, R. T. "General Douglas MacArthur's 'Reconnaissance in Force': The Rationalization of a Defeat in Korea." *Pacific Historical Review*, XXXVI (1967), 79–93.

2941. Snyder, Richard C. and Glenn D. Paige. "The United States Decision to Resist Aggression in Korea." In: Richard C. Snyder, ed. *Foreign Policy Decision-Making: An Approach to the Study of International Politics.* New York: Free Press, 1962. pp. 206–248.

2942. Spanier, John W. *The Truman-MacArthur Controversy and the Korean War.* Cambridge, MA: Belknap Press, 1959. 311p.

2943. "U.S. Intelligence Blamed For Surprise in Korean Conflict." *U.S. News and World Report*, XXIX (July 21, 1950), 26–27.

2944. United States. Congress. Senate. Committee on Armed Services. *The Military Situation in the Far East: Hearings.* 82nd Cong., 1st sess. 5 vols. Washington, D.C.: GPO, 1951.

2945. _____ . _____ . _____ . _____ . _____ . 8 reels, 35mm microfilm. Washington, D.C.: University Publications of America, 1977.

Eight thousand pages of declassified transcripts.

2946. Whiting, Allen S. *China Crosses the Yalu.* Stanford, CA: Stanford University Press, 1968. 219p.

h. Singapore

2947. "Shaky Domino: CIA Agents Plotting Subversion in Singapore." *Newsweek*, LXVI (September 13, 1965), 44–45.

i. Tibet

2948. Dalai Lama of Tibet. *My Land and My People.* New York: McGraw-Hill, 1962. 271p.

2949. "A God Escapes." *Newsweek*, LIII (April 13, 1959), 46+.

2950. "God-King Finds Safety." *Life*, XLVI (May 4, 1959), 26–37.

2951. Mullin, Chris. "CIA's Tibet Campaign: Remote Underfinanced Exercise in Futility." *Atlas*, XXIII (March 1976), 15+.

1952. _____ . "The CIA Tibetan Conspiracy." *Far Eastern Economic Review,* LXXXIX (September 5, 1975), 30–34.

2953. Peissel, Michael. *The Secret War in Tibet.* Boston: Little, Brown, 1973. 258p.

2954. Thomas, Lowell, Jr. *The Silent War in Tibet.* Garden City, NY: Doubleday, 1959. 284p.

5. Latin America

a. General Works

2955. Agee, Philip. *Inside the Company: A CIA Diary.* New York: Stonehill, 1975. 640p.

Mexico, Ecuador, and Uruguay, 1960–1968.

2956. "CIA Assassination Plots in Latin America: Report." *Current History,* LXX (February 1976), 79+.

2957. Chalmers, Douglas A. "Developing on the Periphery: External Factors in Latin American Politics." In: James N. Rosenau, ed. *Linkage Politics.* New York: Free Press, 1969. p. 71+.

2958. Einaudi, L. R., jt. author. *See* Ronfeldt, D. R. (2968).

2959. Gerassi, John. *The Great Fear in Latin America.* Rev. ed. New York: Collier Books, 1965. 478p.

2960. Harding, Timothy. "The New Imperialism in Latin America: A Critique of Connor Cruise O'Brien." In: K. T. Faun and Donald C. Hodges, eds. *Readings in U.S. Imperialism.* Boston: Porter Sargent, 1971. pp. 13–23.

2961. Horowitz, David. "Malvenido Rockefeller." *Ramparts,* VIII (February 1970), 20–25.

2962. Horowitz, Irving L., ed. *The Rise and Fall of Project Camelot: Studies in the Relationship Between Social Science and Practical Politics.* Cambridge, MA: M.I.T. Press, 1967. 385p.

2963. Kirkpatrick, Lyman B., Jr. "Communism in Latin America." *Naval War College Review,* XX (June 168), *passim.*

2964. Mallin, Jay. "Phases of Subversion: The Castro Drive on Latin America." *Air University Review,* XXV (November–December 1973), 54–62.

2965. O'Brien, Connor Cruise. "Contemporary Forms of Imperialism." In: K.T. Faun and Donald C. Hodges, eds. *Readings in U.S. Imperialism.* Boston: Porter Sargent, 1971. pp. 1–13.

2966.   Ridenhour, Robert. "Yes, We Have No Maranas." *New Times*, III (July 12, 1974), 18+.

2967.   Riesel, Victor. "Defense of the CIA—Saved Latin Unions: Reprinted From the *New York World,* March 2, 1967." *Congressional Record,* CXIII (March 8, 1967), A1140–A1141.

2968.   Ronfeldt, D. R. and L. R. Einaudi. *International Security and Military Assistance to Latin America in the 1970s.* RAND Report R–924–ISA. Santa Monica, CA: RAND Corporation, 1971. 55p.

2969.   Saxe-Fernandez, John. "From Counterinsurgency to Counterintelligence." In: Julio Cotter and Richard Ragan, eds. *Latin America and the United States: The Changing Political Realities.* Stanford, CA: Stanford University Press, 1974. pp. 347–360.

2970.   "Soviet Espionage [in Latin America]." *Military Review,* XLI (June 1961), 18–19.

2971.   United States. Congress. Senate. Committee on Foreign Relations. *U.S. Relations With Latin America: Hearings.* 94th Cong., 1st sess. Washington, D.C.: GPO, 1975. 235p.

2972.   Vallance, Theodore R. "Light on the [Project Camelot] Twilight War." *Army Information Digest,* XVIII (January 1963), 36–41.

2973.   Volkman, Ernst. "Terror, Inc." *Penthouse,* X (June 1979), *passim.*

b. Bolivia and Che Guevera

2974.   Arguedas, Antonio. "With the CIA in Bolivia." *Ramparts,* VII (November 17, 1968), 47–48+.

2975.   Debray, Regis. *Che's Guerrilla War.* Translated from the French. Drayton, Middlesex, England: Penguin Books, 1975. 157p.

2976.   Gadea, Hilda. *Ernesto: A Memoir of Che Guevera.* Translated from the Spanish. Garden City, NY: Doubleday, 1972. 222p.

2977.   Gall, Norman. "The Legacy of Che Guevera." *Commentary,* (December 1967), 21–44.

2978.   Gonzalez, Luis J. and G. A. Sanchez-Salazar. *The Great Rebel: Che Guevera in Bolivia.* Translated from the Spanish. New York: Grove Press, 1969. 254p.

2979.   Harris, Richard L. *Death of a Revolutionary: Che Guevera's Last Mission.* New York: W. W. Norton, 1970. 219p.

2980.   Hodges, Donald C. *The Legacy of Che Guevera: A Documentary Study.* London: Thames and Hudson, 1977. 216p.

2981. James, Daniel. *Che Guevera: A Biography.* New York: Stein and Day, 1969. 380p.

2982. _____ , ed. *The Complete Bolivian Diaries of Che Guevera and Other Captured Documents.* New York: Stein and Day, 1968. 330p.

2983. Ray, Michele. "In Cold Blood: The Execution of Che by the CIA." *Ramparts,* VI (March 1968), 21–37.

2984. Rodriguez-Calderon, Mirta, jt. editor. *See* Rojas-Rodriguez, Marta (2985).

2985. Rojas-Rodriguez, Marta and Mirta Rodriguez-Calderon, eds. *Tania* [Tamara Bunke]: *The Unforgettable Guerrilla.* New York: Random House, 1971. 212p.

2986. Rojo, Richardo. *My Friend Che.* Translated from the Spanish. New York: Dial Press, 1968. 220p.

2987. Sanchez-Salazar, G. A., jt. author. *See* Gonzalez, Luis J. (2978).

2988. Sauvage, Leo. *Che Guevera: The Failure of a Revolutionary.* Translated from the French. Englewood Cliffs, NJ: Prentice-Hall, 1973. 282p.

2989. "Tool [Antonio Arguedas] of the Agency?" *Newsweek,* LXXII (September 2, 1968), 36.

c. Brazil

2990. Garvey, Ernest. "The CIA Bungles On: Meddling in Brazil." *Commonweal,* LXXXVII (February 9, 1964), 553–554.

2991. Quartim, Joao. *Dictatorship and Armed Struggle in Brazil.* Translated from the French. New York: Monthly Review Press, 1972. 250p.

d. British Guiana

2992. Hirsch, Fred and Richard Fletcher. *The CIA and the Labour Movement.* London: Spokesman Books, 1977. 71p.

2993. Morris, George. *CIA and American Labor: The Subversion of the AFL/CIO's Foreign Policy.* Little New World Paperbacks, LNW-12. New York: International Publishers, 1967. 159p.

2994. Reno, Philip. *The Ordeal of British Guiana.* New York: Monthly Review Press, 1964. 132p.

e. Chile

2995. Alexander, Robert J. "The Boycott, the CIA, and Other Yankee Activities." In: *The Tragedy of Chile.* Westport, CT: Greenwood Press, 1978. Chpt. XX.

2996. "Bloody End of a Marxist Dream." *Time,* CII (September 24, 1973), 35–38+.

2997. Bock, P. G. "Transnational Corporation and Private Foreign Policy: ITT in Chile." *Society,* XI (January 1974), 44–49.

2998. Borosage, Robert L. and John D. Marks. "Destablishing Chile." In: Robert L. Borosage and John D. Marks, eds. *The CIA File.* New York: Grossman, 1976. pp. 79–89.

2999. Borovskiy, V. "The Chile Operation." *New Times* (Moscow), no. 16 (April 14, 1972), 25–27.

3000. Buckley, William F., Jr. "The CIA in Chile." *National Review,* XXVI (October 11, 1974), 1188–1189.

3001. "The CIA's New Bay of Pigs." *Newsweek,* LXXXIV (September 23, 1974), 51–52.

3002. "Chile: Blood on the Peaceful Road." *Latin American Perspectives,* I (Summer 1974), 1–160.

3003. "Chile: A Case Study [of] CIA Intervention." *Time,* CIV (September 30, 1974), 21–22.

3004. "Chile—What was the U.S. Role?: A Symposium." *Foreign Policy,* XVI (Fall 1974), 126–156.

3005. "The Crisis That is Bringing Basic Changes to the CIA." *U.S. News and World Report,* LXXVII (September 16, 1974), 31–33.

3006. De Allende, Hortensia B. "The Facts About Chile." In: Howard Frazier, ed. *Uncloaking the CIA.* New York: Free Press, 1978. pp. 55–68.

3007. Fagen, Richard R. "The United States and Chile: Roots and Branches." *Foreign Affairs,* LIII (January 1975), 297–313.

3008. "Furor Over the CIA—What It is All About." *U.S. News and World Report,* LXXVII (September 30, 1974), 33–34.

3009. Garrett, Patricia, jt. author. *See* Schisch, Adam (3041).

3010. Goldberg, Peter A. "The Politics of the Allende Overthrow in Chile." *Political Science Quarterly,* XC (Spring 1975), 93–117.

3011. Goldwater, Barry. "On Covert Action in Chile, 1963–1973." *Inter-American Economic Affairs,* XXX (Summer 1976), 85–95.

3012. Greider, William, jt. author. *See* Lardner, George, Jr. (3020).

3013.   Horrock, Nicholas M. "Helms Linked to CIA Memo For Kissinger and [John] Mitchell on Plot in Chile: Reprinted From the *New York Times,* July 27, 1975." *Congressional Record,* CXXI (October 28, 1975), 33899.

3014.   ———— . "Pentagon Role Reported in '70 Plot Against Allende: Reprinted From the *New York Times,* September 3, 1975." *Congressional Record,* CXXI (October 28, 1975), 33899–33900.

3015.   ———— . "'70 Nixon Orders to CIA to Balk Allende Reported—President's Authorization Termed Cause of Agency's Role in Military Plots to Thwart Marxist's Election: Reprinted From the *New York Times,* July 23, 1975." *Congressional Record,* CXXI (October 28, 1975), 33898–33899.

3016.   "ITT: Now the Chile Papers." *Newsweek,* LXXIX (April 3, 1972), 18–20.

3017.   Kaplan, Carl and Randall Rothenberg. "The [Robert] Berrellez Case: The Black Art of Graymail—Involvement of CIA and ITT in the Chilean Coup." *Nation,* CCXXVIII (February 24, 1979), 193+.

3018.   Kay, Cristobal. "Chile: The Making of a *Coup d'Etat." Science and Society,* XXXIX (Spring 1975), 3–25.

3019.   Korry, Edward. "The Sell-Out of Chile and the American Taxpayers." *Penthouse,* IX (March 1978), 70+.

3020.   Lardner, George, Jr. and William Grieder. "CIA Link Seen in '70 Chile Plot [to Kill Gen. René Schneider]: Reprinted From the *Washington Post,* August 1, 1975." *Congressional Record,* CXXI (August 1, 1975), 27069.

3021.   Lupinovich, V. "CIA Diplomacy in Action." *International Affairs* (Moscow), no. 6 (June 1972), 994–996.

3022.   MacEoin, Gary. "The U.S. Government and Chile." *Christianity and Crisis,* XXXIV (October 14, 1974), 219–223.

3023.   Marks, John D., jt. author. *See* Borosage, Robert L. (2998).

3024.   Miller, Judith. "Criminal Negligence: Congress, Chile, and the CIA." *Progressive,* XXXVIII (November 1974), 15–19.

3025.   Morley, Morris and Steven Smith. "The 'Imperial Reach': U.S. Policy and the CIA in Chile." *Journal of Political and Military Sociology,* V (Fall 1977), 203–216.

3026.   Morris, Roger. "The Aftermath of the CIA Intervention." *Society,* XII (March 1975), 76–80.

3027.   Moss, Robert. "Cloak and Dagger Controversy." *International Review,* (Winter 1974), 19–24+.

3028.   "Non-Involvement: The CIA Role in Chile." *Commonweal,* CI (October 18, 1974), 51–52.

3029.   "Notes and Comments: The CIA Intervention in Chile." *New Yorker,* L (September 30, 1974), 27–28.

3030.   O'Leary, Jeremiah. "ITT 'Stop Allende' Role Unfolds: Reprinted From the *Washington Evening Star,* March 21, 1973." *Congressional Record,* CXIX(April 10, 1973), 11587–11588.

3031.   Petras, James F. "The CIA, [Eduardo] Frei, and the Junta." *New Politics,* XI (Fall 1976), 25–35.

3032.   _____ . "Chile: Crime, Class Consciousness, and the Bourgeoisie." *Crime and Social Justice,* VII (Spring–Summer 1977), 14–22.

3033.   _____ and Morris Morley. *The United States and Chile: Imperialism and the Overthrow of the Allende Government.* New York: Monthly Review Press, 1975. 217p.

3034.   Piedra, Alberto M. "Chile." *Strategic Review,* III (Winter 1975), 25–38.

3035.   Richards, Henry. "The Chilean Tragedy." *Center Magazine,* IX (November 1976), 9–14.

3036.   Rojas-Sandford, Robinson. *The Murder of Allende and the End of the Chilean Way to Socialism.* New York: Harper & Row, 1976. 286p.

3037.   Rothenberg, Randall, jt. author. *See* Kaplan, Carl (3017).

3038.   Roxborough, Ian. *Chile: The State and the Revolution.* New York: Holmes and Meier, 1977. 304p.

3039.   Sampson, Anthony. *The Sovereign State of ITT.* New York: Stein and Day, 1973. 323p.

3040.   Schakne, Richard. "Chile: Why We Missed the Story." *Columbia Journalism Review,* XIV (March 1976), 60–62.

3041.   Schisch, Adam and Patricia Garrett. "The Case of Chile." In: Howard Frazier, ed. *Uncloaking the CIA.* New York: Free Press, 1978. pp. 36–54.

3042.   Shanahan, Eileen. "CIA Aide [William V. Broe] Says He Gave Anti-Allende Plan to ITT: Reprinted From the *New York Times,* March 29, 1973." *Congressional Record,* CXIX (April 10, 1973), 11588–11589.

3043.   Sigmund, Paul E. "The CIA in Chile." *Worldview,* XIX (April 1976), 11–17.

3044.   _____ . *The Overthrow of Allende and the Politics of Chile, 1964– 1976.* Pittsburgh, PA: University of Pittsburgh Press, 1977. 326p.

3045.   Smith, Steven, jt. author. *See* Morley, Morris (3025).

3046.   "Somebody is Lying: ITT in Chile." *Newsweek,* LXXXI (April 9, 1973), 36+.

3047.   Stern, Laurence. "ITT and CIA on Chile—A Semblance of Influence Over Policy" Reprinted From the *Washington Post,* April 1, 1973." *Congressional Record,* CXIX (April 10, 1973), 11590–11591.

3048.   _____ . "What's Good For America." *New Statesman and Nation,* LXXXVIII (September 27, 1974), 404–405.

3049.   Stickler, Jim, ed. *Allende and the Saga of Chile.* Corpus Christie, TX: Hemisphere House, 1978. 210p.

3050.   Szulc, Tad. "Exporting Revolution: William E. Colby vs. Henry Kissinger on CIA Involvement in the 1973 Chilean Coup." *New Republic,* CLXXI (September 21, 1974), 7–9.

3051.   _____ . "ITT Under the Gun." *New Republic,* CLXXVII (August 6, 1977), 18–22.

3052.   _____ . "Project Chile." *Penthouse,* VII (October 1975), 52+.

3053.   _____ . "The US and ITT in Chile." *New Republic,* CLXVIII (June 30, 1973), 21–23.

3054.   _____ . "The View From Langley." *Washington Post Outlook,* (October 21, 1973), C1–C5.

3055.   _____ . "Where President Ford is Wrong: Candid But Mistaken About Chile." *New Republic,* CLXXI (September 28, 1974), 13–15.

3056.   United States. Congress. House. Committee on Armed Services. Special Subcommittee on Intelligence. *Inquiry Into Matters Regarding Classified Testimony Taken on April 23, 1974 Concerning the CIA and Chile: Hearings.* 93rd Cong., 2nd sess. Washington, D.C.: GPO, 1975. 38p.

3057.   _____ . _____ . _____ . Committee on Foreign Affairs. Subcommittee on Inter-American Affairs. *United States and Chile During the Allende Years, 1970–1973: Hearings.* 94th Cong., 1st sess. Washington, D.C.: GPO, 1975. 677p.

3058. _____ . _____ . Senate. Committee on Foreign Relations. Subcommittee on Multinational Corporations. *The International Telephone and Telegraph Company and Chile, 1970–1971: Hearings.* 93rd Cong., 1st sess. Washington, D.C.: GPO, 1973. 20p.

3059. _____ . _____ . _____ . Select Committee to Investigate Government Operations With Respect to Intelligence Activities. "Assassination Planning and Plots: [Gen. René] Schneider." In: *Alleged Assassination Plots Involving Foreign Leaders: An Interim Report.* 94th Cong., 1st sess. Washington, D.C.: GPO, 1975. pp. 225–254.

3060. _____ . _____ . _____ . _____ . *Covert Action: Hearings.* 94th Cong., 1st sess. Washington, D.C.: GPO, 1976. 230p.

3061. _____ . _____ . _____ . _____ . *Covert Action in Chile, 1963–1973: A Staff Report.* 94th Cong., 1st sess. Washington, D.C.: GPO, 1975. 62p.

3062. Uribe-Arce, Armando. *The Black Book of American Intervention in Chile.* Translated From the Spanish. Boston: Beacon Press, 1975. 163p.

3063. Varas, Florencia and J. M. Vergara. *Coup! Allende's Last Day.* New York: Stein and Day, 1975. 182p.

3064. "War Over Secret Warfare." *Newsweek,* LXXXIV (September 30, 1974), 37+.

3065. "Window on the CIA." *Nation,* CCXIX (September 7, 1974), 163–164.

f. Cuba

(1) GENERAL WORKS

3066. Kirkpatrick, Lyman B., Jr. "The Cuban Case History." *Naval War College Review,* XX (March 1968), *passim.*

3067. Matthews, Herbert L. *Fidel Castro.* New York: Simon and Schuster, 1969.

3068. Miller, Warren. *Ninety Miles From Home: The Face of Cuba Today.* Boston: Little, Brown, 1971. 279p.

3069. Pearson, Drew. "Kennedy, Khrushchev, and Cuba." *Saturday Review of Literature,* LII (March 29, 1969), 12–15.

3070. Rivero, Nicholas. *Castro's Cuba: An American Dilemma.* Washington, D.C.: R. B. Luce, 1962. 239p.

3071. Sobel, Lester A., ed. *Cuba, the U.S., and Russia, 1960–1963.* New York: Facts on File, Inc., 1964. 138p.

3072. Tetlow, Edwin. *Eye on Cuba.* New York: Harcourt, Brace, 1966. 291p.

3073. Thomas, Hugh. *Cuba: The Pursuit of Freedom.* New York: Harper & Row, 1971. 1,696p.

3074. _____ . "The U.S. and Castro, 1959–1962." *American Heritage,* XXIX (October 1978), 26–35.

3075. United States. Central Intelligence Agency. National Foreign Assessment Center. *Cuban Chronology.* Reference Aid. Washington, D.C., 1978. 94p.

3076. Ward, Fred. *Inside Cuba Today.* New York: Crown, 1979. 308p.

(2) BAY OF PIGS (1961)

3077. "'The Air Will Be Ours': Cuban Fighters Tell Why They Expected Air Cover." *U.S. News and World Report,* LIV (February 4, 1963), 33–36.

3078. Alsop, Stewart. "Lessons of the Cuban Disaster." *Saturday Evening Post,* CCXXXIV (June 24, 1961), 26–27+.

3079. "The Bay of Pigs Disaster." *Reporter,* XXVIII (February 14, 1963), 16+.

3080. "The Bay of Pigs Revisited—Lessons From a Failure: A *Time* Essay." *Time,* LXXXVI (July 30, 1965), 16–17.

3081. "Bitter Week: The Cuban Invasion." *Time,* LXXVII (April 28, 1961), 11–13.

3082. Cook, Fred J. "CIA: The Case Builds Up." *Nation,* XCVIII (June 22, 1964), 616–618.

3083. "Cover-Up: Deaths of Four U.S. Flyers." *Time,* LXXXI (April 9, 1963), 23–25.

3084. "Cuba: The Consequences." *Newsweek,* LVII (May 1, 1961), 23–28.

3085. De Toledano, Ralph. "The Cuba Story: Wraps Off." *National Review,* XIV (April 9, 1963), 288–289.

3086. Draper, Theodore. *Castro's Revolution: Myths and Realities.* New York: Praeger, 1962. 211p.

3087. Flaherty, Thomas. "Anatomy of a Snafu." *Life,* LIV (May 10, 1963), 80–83.

3088. _____ . "What We Learned From the Bay of Pigs." *Reader's Digest,* LXXXIII (July 1963), 92–94.

3089. Halle, Louis J. "Lessons of the Cuban Blunder." *New Republic,* CXLIV (June 5, 1961), 13–17.

3090. Handleman, H. "The Real Story of the Bay of Pigs." *U.S. News and World Report,* LIV (January 7, 1963), 38–41.

3091. Hinckle, Warren and William W. Turner. *The Cuba Project.* Boston: Houghton, Mifflin, 1979.

3092. " 'How Could I Have Been So Stupid': The Bay of Pigs Invasion." *Newsweek,* LXVI (August 2, 1965), 46–47.

3093. "How President Kennedy Upset the Cuban Invasion of April 1961." *U.S. News and World Report,* LIV (February 4, 1962), 29–30+.

3094. Hunt, E. Howard. *Give Us This Day.* New Rochelle, NY: Arlington House, 1973. 235p.

3095. "In Cuban Invasion: The Fatal Mistakes." *U.S. News and World Report,* L (May 29, 1961), 76.

3096. "Inquest: Cuban Invasion Fiasco." *Time,* LXXVII (May 9, 1961), 58–59.

3097. Johnson, Haynes B., *et al. The Bay of Pigs: The Leaders' Story of Brigade 2506.* New York: W. W. Norton, 1964. 368p.

3098. Keerdoja, Edward. "Brigade 2506: Survivors of the Bay of Pigs." *Newsweek,* XC (December 12, 1977), 20+.

3099. Kirkpatrick, Lyman B., Jr. "Paramilitary Case Study: The Bay of Pigs." *Naval War College Review,* XXV (November–December 1972), 32–42.

3100. Kurland, Gerald. *The Bay of Pigs Invasion.* Indianapolis, IN: Howard W. Sams Co., 1974. 32p.

3101. Lazo Mario. "Decision For Disaster." *Reader's Digest,* LXXXV (September 1964), 241–244+.

3102. Meyer, Karl E., jt. author. *See* Szulc, Tad (3123).

3103. Minor, Dale. *The Information War.* New York: Hawthorn Books, 1970. 212p.

3104. Miro-Cardona, José. "Refugee Leader Blames U.S. For Broken Promises: Excerpt From Statement, April 18, 1963." *U.S. News and World Report,* LIV (April 29, 1963), 65–67+.

3105. Muckerman, Joseph E. "The Bay of Pigs Revisited." *Military Review,* LI (April 1971), 77–85.

3106. Novina, Stephen. "The Invasion That Could Not Succeed." *Reporter,* XXIV (May 11, 1961), 19–23.

3107. "Operation Cuba." *Nation,* CXCII (April 29, 1961), 361–363.

3108. O'Rourke, John T. "Who Bungled the Cuban Invasion?: Another Version." *U.S. News and World Report,* LI (July 31, 1961), 56–57.

3109. Penabay, Manuel. "We Were Betrayed: The Story of One Cuban Invader." *U.S. News and World Report,* LIV (January 14, 1963), 46–49.

3110. Radosh, Ronald. "[Arthur M.] Schlesinger and Kennedy: Historian in the Service of Power, With a Reply." *Nation,* CCXXV (August 6, 20, 1977), 104–109, 147–148.

3111. Ransom, Harry H. "Secret Mission in an Open Society." *New York Times Magazine,* (May 21, 1961), 20, 77–79.

3112. Ross, Thomas B., jt. author. *See* Wise, David (3133).

3113. Rovere, Richard H. "Letter From Washington: The Attempted Invasion of Cuba." *New Yorker,* XXXVII (May 6, 1961), 139–146.

3114. Schlesinger, Arthur M., Jr. "The Bay of Pigs: A Horribly Expensive Lesson." *Life,* LIX (July 23, 1965), 62–70+.

3115. Smith, Jean E. "The Bay of Pigs: The Unanswered Questions." *Nation,* CXCVIII (April 13, 1964), 360–363.

3116. ———. "The CIA on Trial." *Reporter,* XXX (June 18, 1964), 53–56.

3117. Smith, Malcolm E., Jr. "The Bay of Pigs." In: *Kennedy's 13 Great Mistakes in the White House.* New York: The National Forum of American, Inc., 1968. pp. 46–74.

3118. Sorensen, Theodore. "Kennedy's Worst Disaster: The Bay of Pigs." *Look,* XXIX (August 10, 1965), 42–50.

3119. "Specter and Flashback: Four Who Didn't Return." *Newsweek,* LXI (March 11, 1963), 25–26.

   CIA B-26 pilots.

3120. "Spotlight on the CIA." *Senior Scholastic,* LXXIX (September 13, 1961), 18–19+.

3121. "The Story of Americans at the Bay of Pigs." *U.S. News and World Report,* LIV (March 11, 1963), 33–34.

3122. Szulc, Tad. "Cuba: Anatomy of a Failure." *Look,* XXV (July 18, 1961), 76–82.

3123. _____ and Karl E. Meyer. *The Cuban Invasion: The Chronicle of a Disaster.* New York: Praeger, 1962. 160p.

3124. "Talking to Cubans." *New Republic,* CXLIV (May 15, 1961), 3–4.

3125. Tanner, Hans. *Counter-Revolutionary Agent: Diary of the Events Which Occurred in Cuba Between January and July 1961.* New York: Universal Distributors, 1962. 161p.

3126. Turner, William, jt. author. *See* Hinckle, Warren (3091).

3127. "Up to Others: Questions About Cuba." *Time,* LXXXI (March 15, 1963), 19–20.

3128. Welzer, Michael. *Cuba: The Invasion and the Consequences.* New York: Dissent, 1961. 15p.

3129. "We Who Tried." *Life,* LIV (May 10, 1963), 20–34+.

3130. "What Went Wrong?" *New Republic,* CXLIV (May 1, 1961), 1+.

3131. Wheeler, Kenneth. "Hell of a Beating in Cuba." *Life,* L (April 28, 1961), 16–25.

3132. "Where the U.S. Went Wrong on Cuba." *U.S. News and World Report,* L (May 8, 1961), 54–56.

3133. Wise, David and Thomas B. Ross. "Strange Case of the CIA's Widows: Husbands at the Bay of Pigs." *Look,* XXVIII (June 30, 1964), 77–78+.

3134. Wyden, Peter. *Bay of Pigs: The Untold Story.* New York: Simon and Schuster, 1979. 441p.

(3) The Cuban Missile Crisis (1962)

3135. Abel, Ellie. *The Missile Crisis.* New York: McClelland, 1966. 220p.

3136. Allison, Graham T. *Essence of Decision: Explaining the Cuban Missile Crisis.* Boston: Little, Brown, 1971. 338p.

3137. Bernstein, Barton J. "The Cuban Missile Crisis." In: L. H. Miller and R. W. Pruessen, eds. *Reflections on the Cold War: A Quarter Century of American Foreign Policy.* Philadelphia: Temple University Press, 1974. pp. 130–134.

3138. _____ . "The Week We Almost Went to War." *Bulletin of the Atomic Scientists,* XXXII (February 1976), 13–21.

3139.   Christol, C. Q. and C. R. Davis. "Maritime Quarantine: The Naval Interdiction of Offensive Weapons and Associated Materials to Cuba, 1962." *American Journal of International Law,* LVII (July 1963), 525–545.

3140.   Crane, Robert D. "The Cuban Crisis: A Strategic Analysis of American and Soviet Policy." *Orbis,* VI (Winter 1963), 528–563.

3141.   Crosby, Ralph D., Jr. "The Cuban Missile Crisis: A Soviet View." *Military Review,* LVI (September 1976), 58–70.

3142.   Daniel, James and John G. Hubble. *Strike in the West: The Complete Story of the Cuban Crisis.* New York: Holt, 1963. 180p.

3143.   Davis, C. R., jt. author. *See* Christol, C. Q. (3139).

3144.   Detzer, David. *The Brink: The Cuban Missile Crisis, 1962.* New York: Crowell, 1979. 304p.

3145.   Divine, Robert A., ed. *The Cuban Missile Crisis.* New York: Quadrangle Books, 1971. 248p.

3146.   Greene, Fred. "The Intelligence Arm: The Cuban Missile Crisis." In: Roger Hilsman and Robert C. Good, eds. *Foreign Policy in the Sixties: The Issues and the Instruments.* Baltimore, MD: Johns Hopkins University Press, 1965. pp. 127–140.

3147.   Hilsman, Roger. "The Cuban Missile Crisis: The Intelligence Story." In: *To Move a Nation: The Politics of Foreign Policy in the Administration of John F. Kennedy.* Garden City, NY: Doubleday, 1967. pp. 159–183.

3148.   Horelick, Arnold L. *The Cuban Missile Crisis: An Analysis of Soviet Calculations and Behavior.* RAND Memorandum RM-3779-PR. Santa Monica, CA: RAND Corporation, 1963. 60p.

3149.   Hubble, John G., jt. author. *See* Daniel, James (3142).

3150.   Kahan, Jerome H. and Anne K. Long. "The Cuban Missile Crisis: A Study of Its Strategic Context." *Political Science Quarterly,* LXXXVII (December 1972), 564–590.

3151.   Kennedy, Robert F. *Thirteen Days: A Memoir of the Cuban Missile Crisis.* New York: W. W. Norton, 1969. 224p.

3152.   Knorr, Klaus E. "Failures in National Intelligence Estimates: The Case of the Cuban Missiles." *World Politics,* XVI (April 1964), 455–467.

3153.   Lantzer, Lawrence A. "The Cuban Missile Crisis: The Soviet View." Unpublished thesis, U.S. Naval War College, 1972.

3154. Larson, David L., ed. *The "Cuban Crisis" of 1962: Selected Documents and Chronology.* Boston: Houghton, Mifflin, 1963. 333p.

3155. Levesque, Jacques. *The U.S.S.R. and the Cuban Revolution: Soviet Ideology and Strategic Perspectives.* New York: Praeger, 1978. 220p.

3156. Long, Anne K., jt. author. *See* Kahan, Jerome H. (3150).

3157. Moeser, William. "First Person Stories by the Pilots: The Aerial Reconnaissance of Cuba." *Life,* LIII (December 7, 1962), 38–39.

3158. Moser, Don. "Time of the Angel: The U-2, Cuba, and the CIA." *American Heritage,* XXVIII (October 1977), 4–15.

3159. Nathan, H. J. "The Missile Crisis." *World Politics,* XXVII (1965), 256–281.

3160. Pachter, Henry M. *Collision Course: The Cuban Missile Crisis and Coexistence.* New York: Praeger, 1963. 261p.

3161. Trainor, James. "Cuba Missile Threat Detailed." *Missiles and Rockets,* (October 29, 1962), 12–14, 47.

3162. United States. Congress. Senate. Committee on Armed Services. Subcommittee on the Cuban Military Buildup. *Interim Report.* 88th Cong., 1st sess. Washington, D.C.: GPO, 1963. 18p.

3163. Waters, H. R. "Fact and Fancy." *Newsweek,* LXXXIV (December 23, 1974), 53–54.

3164. Wohstetter, Roberta. *Cuba and Pearl Harbor: Hindsight and Foresight,* RAND Memorandum RM-4328-ISA. Santa Monica, CA: RAND Corporation, 1965. 41p.

(4) OTHER ANTI-CUBAN OPERATIONS (1961–1969)

3165. Ayers, Bradley E. *The War That Never Was: An Insider's Account of CIA Covert Operations Against Cuba.* Indianapolis: Bobbs-Merrill, 1976. 235p.

3166. Branch, Taylor and George Crile, 3rd. "Kennedy Vendetta: How the CIA Waged a Silent War Against Cuba." *Harper's,* CCLI (August 1975), 49–63.

3167. Brown, Robert K. "The Phantom Navy of the CIA." *Sea Classics,* VIII (May 1975), 50–62.

3168. Buchanan, Patrick. "Kennedy 'Secret War' Against Castro Documented by CBS [Special 'The CIA's Secret Army']." *TV Guide,* XXV (January 25, 1977), A3+.

3169. Castro, Fidel. "Fidel Castro Denounces Aggressions Against Cuba." *Black Scholar,* VIII (December 1976), 10–17.

3170. "Castro Removal Plan—Ex-General [Edward G. Lansdale] Cites Kennedy Orders: Reprinted From the *Los Angeles Times,* May 31, 1975." *Congressional Record,* CXXI (October 28, 1975), 33897–33898.

3171. "CIA's Apprentices." *Nation,* CCXXIV (June 25, 1977), 770–772.

3172. Crile, George, 3rd, jt. author. *See* Branch, Taylor (3166).

3173. Kantor, Seth. *Who Was Jack Ruby?* New York: Everest House, 1978. 324p.

3174. "Kennedy Connection: The Question of Assassination Attempts Against Castro Authorized by the Kennedys." *Time,* CV (June 2, 1975), 10–11.

3175. Malone, William S. "The Secret Life of Jack Ruby: Involvement With the FBI, CIA, and Mafia in Plots Against Castro." *New Times,* X (January 23, 1978), 46–50+.

3176. Poyo, Gerald E. "Key West and the Cuban Ten Years War." *Florida Historical Quarterly,* LVII (January 1979), *passim.*

3177. Scheer, Robert. "Why Kill Castro?" *New Times,* V (October 31, 1975), 13.

3178. Schorr, Daniel. "The Assassins." *New York Review of Books,* XXIV (October 13, 1977), 14–22.

3179. Schulz, Donald E. "Kennedy and the Cuban Connection." *Foreign Policy,* XXVI (Spring 1977), 57–64, 121–139.

3180. Szulc, Tad. "Kennedy's Cold War." *New Republic,* CLXXVII (December 24, 1977), 19–21.

3181. "Tremendous Insanity." *Newsweek,* XCII (October 2, 1978), 62.

3182. United States. Congress. Senate. Select Committee to Investigate Government Operations With Respect to Intelligence Activities. "Assassination Planning and Plots: Cuba." In: *Alleged Assassination Plots Involving Foreign Leaders: An Interim Report.* 94th Cong., 1st sess. Washington, D.C.: GPO, 1975. pp. 71–180.

3183. Vogel, David. "The Set Up Castro." In: David Wallechinsky and Irving Wallace. *The People's Almanac 2.* New York: Morrow, 1978. pp. 714–715.

3184. Watson, Robert. "CIA: A Target Named Castro." *Newsweek,* LXXXV (June 2, 1975), 27–28.

3185. Wicker, Tom. "Murder by Any Other Name: Reprinted from the *New York Times,* June 3, 1975." *Congressional Record,* CXXI (June 4, 1975), 17125.

g. Dominican Republic

3186. Crassweller, Robert D. *Trujillo: The Life and Times of a Carribbean Dictator.* New York: Macmillan, 1966. 468p.

3187. Gall, Norman. "How Trujillo Died." *New Republic,* CXVIII (April 13, 1963), 19–20. Reprinted in the June 28, 1975 issue, pp. 12–13.

3188. Havens, Murray C., *et al.* "The Assassination of Rafael Leonidas Trujillo Molina of the Dominican Republic." In: *Assassination and Terrorism: The Modern Dimensions.* Manchaca, TX: Sterling Swift, 1975. pp. 137–147.

3189. Lardner, George, Jr. "JFK Pulled Out of U.S. Role in Trujillo Death, Aide [Richard Goodwin] Says: Reprinted From the *Boston Globe,* July 19, 1975." *Congressional Record,* CXXI (October 25, 1975), 33896–33897.

3190. Lowenthal, Abraham F. *The Dominican Intervention.* Cambridge, MA: Harvard University Press, 1972. 246p.

3191. Martin, John B. *Overtaken by Events: The Dominican Crisis From the Fall of Trujillo to Civil War.* Garden City, NY: Doubleday, 1966. 821p.

3192. Sanford, David. "The Death of Trujillo: Kennedy Complicity?" *New Republic,* CLXXII (June 28, 1975), 7–8.

3193. Slater, J. *Intervention and Negotiation: The United States and the Dominican Intervention.* New York: Harper & Row, 1970. 254p.

3194. United States. Congress. Senate. Select Committee to Investigate Government Operations With Respect to Intelligence Activities. "Assassination Planning and Plots: Trujillo." In: *Alleged Assassination Plots Involving Foreign Leaders: An Interim Report.* 94th Cong., 1st sess. Washington, D.C.: GPO, 1975. pp. 191–216.

3195. Whitney, Thomas P. "In the Wake of Trujillo." *New Republic,* CXLV (December 11, 1961), 7–8.

h. Guatemala

3196. Alexander, Robert J. "The Guatemalan Revolution and Communism." *Foreign Policy Bulletin,* XXXIII (April 1, 1954), 5–7.

3197.   Ayban de Soto, José M. *Dependency and Intervention: The Case of Guatemala in 1954.* Boulder, CO: Westview Press, 1978. 350p.

3198.   "Battle in the Backyard." *Time,* LXIII (June 28, 1954), 38–40+.

3199.   "Charges of Intervention in Guatemala Denied." *Department of State Bulletin,* XXX (February 15, 1954), 251.

3200.   De Toledano, Ralph. "Unconventional Ambassador [John E. Peurifoy]." *American Mercury,* LXXIX (October 1954), 28–32.

3201.   Dulles, John Foster. "Events in Guatemala." *Vital Speeches,* XX (July 15, 1954), 591–592.

3202.   Dwiggins, Don. "Guatemala's Secret Airstrip: The Retalhuleu Base." *Nation,* CXCII (January 7, 1961), 7–9.

3203.   Frankel, Anita. "Political Development in Guatemala, 1944–1954: The Impact of Foreign, Military, and Religious Elites." Unpublished PhD Dissertation, University of Connecticut, 1969.

3204.   Galeano, Eduardo. *Guatemala: Occupied Country.* Translated from the Spanish. New York: Monthly Review Press, 1969. 159p.

3205.   Gordon, Max. "A Case History of U.S. Subversion: Guatemala, 1954." *Science and Society,* XXXV (Summer 1971), 129–155.

3206.   "The Guatemalan Revolution That Everybody Expected." *Life,* XXXVI (June 28, 1954), 12–15.

3207.   "How Reds Use Terror Near U.S." *U.S. News and World Report,* XXXVI (May 28, 1954), 26–28+.

3208.   "Jack [John E. Peurifoy] the Nimble." *Newsweek,* XLIV (July 12, 1954), 18–20.

3209.   McDermott, Louis M. "Guatemala, 1954: Intervention or Aggression?" *Rocky Mountain Social Science Journal,* IX (January 1972), 79–88.

3210.   "Middleman in a Successful Revolution: Ambassador Peurifoy." *U.S. News and World Report,* XXXVII (July 9, 1954), 46+.

3211.   Peurifoy, John E. "The Communist Conspiracy in Guatemala." *Department of State Bulletin,* XXXI (November 8, 1954), 690–696.

3212.   _____ . "Meeting the Communist Challenge in the Western Hemisphere." *Department of State Bulletin,* XXXI (September 6, 1954), 333–336.

3213.   "Red's Priority: Pin War on the U.S." *Life,* XXXVII (July 5, 1954), 8–13.

3214. Rosen, Bernard. "The Counter-Revolution." *Nation,* CLXXIX (July 31, 1954), 87–89.

3215. Schlesinger, Stephen C. "How [Allen] Dulles Worked the *Coup d'Etat:* Guatemala." *Nation,* CCXXVII (October 28, 1972), 425–431.

3216. Schneider, Ronald M. "Guatemala: An Aborted Communist Takeover." In: Thomas T. Hammond, ed. *The Anatomy of Communist Takeovers.* New Haven, CT: Yale University Press, 1975. pp. 563–582.

3217. Scully, Michael. "The Inside Story of the Kremlin's Plot in Guatemala." *Reader's Digest,* LXVI (February 1955), 73–78.

3218. Tobis, David. "Foreign Aid: The Case of Guatemala." In: K. T. Fann and Donald C. Hodges, eds. *Readings in U.S. Imperialism.* Boston: Porter Sargent, 1971. pp. 237–249.

3219. United States. Department of State. *The Intervention of International Communism in Guatemala.* Department of State Publication 5556, Inter-American Series, 48. Washington, D.C.: GPO, 1954. 96p.

3220. Westerfield, H. Bradford. "Sublimited War to Overthrow the Government of Guatemala." In: *The Instruments of America's Foreign Policy.* New York: Crowell, 1963. pp. 422–442.

i. Jamaica

3221. Allman, T. D. "Killing Jamaica With Kindness." *Harper's,* CCLVIII (May 1979), 30–36.

Cuban intelligence.

3222. Brickhill, Joan. "Trouble in Jamaica: Is the CIA Harassing the Island's Socialist Regime?" *Atlas,* XXIV (March 1977), 44.

3223. Volkman, Ernest and John Cummings. "Murder as Usual." *Penthouse,* IX (December 1977), 112+.

j. Mexico

3224. Asinoff, Eliot, Warren Hinckle, and William Turner. *The Ten Second Jailbreak: The Helicopter Escape of Joel David Kaplan.* New York: Manor Books, 1975. 268p.

3225. Barron, John. "The Soviet Plot to Destroy Mexico." *Reader's Digest,* XCIX (November 1971), 227–232+.

k. Uruguay

3226. Langguth, A. J. *Hidden Terrors.* New York: Pantheon, 1979. 352p.

l. Venezuela

3227.   Branch, Taylor. "Incident: Investigating the Cuban Connection to the Orlando Letelier Murder in Venezuela." *Esquire,* LXXXVII (March 1977), 55–58+.

The role of Cuban intelligence agents.

6. North America

a. Canada

3228.   Alsop, Stewart. "Five Steps That Make a Spy." *Science Digest,* XIX (June 1946), 27–30.

3229.   Barros, James. "Alger Hiss and Harry Dexter White: The Canadian Connection." *Orbis,* XXI (Fall 1977), 593–605.

3230.   Brown, Sanborn and Kenneth Scott. "Count [Benjamin T.] Rumford: International Informer." *New England Quarterly,* XXI (March 1948), 34–49.

3231.   Canada. Royal Commission on Security. *Report: Abridged.* Ottawa: The Queen's Printer, 1969.

3232.   _____ . Royal Commission to Investigate Disclosures of Secret and Confidential Information to Unauthorized Persons. *Documents Relating to the Proceedings . . . Including the First and Second Interim Reports.* Ottawa: E. Cloutier, 1946. 25p.

3233.   _____ . _____ . *The Report of the Royal Commission.* Ottawa: E. Cloutier, 1946. 733p.

3234.   _____ . _____ . *Third Interim Report.* Ottawa: E. Cloutier, 1946. 10p.

3235.   _____ . Royal Commission to Investigate Matters Relating to One Gerda Munsinger. *Report.* Ottawa: The Queen's Printer, 1966.

3236.   "Canadian Exposure of Spy Ring Turns Doubting Eyes on Russia." *Newsweek,* XXVII (February 26, 1946), 38+.

3237.   "Don't Go Near the Water: Soviet Naval Lt. N. G. Redin." *Time,* XLVII (April 8, 1946), 19.

3238.   Eggleston, Wilfred. "Report of the Royal Commission on Espionage." *Queen's Quarterly,* LIII (August 1946), 369–378.

3239.   "Five Red Rings: The Canadian Spy Melodrama." *Time,* XLVII (July 29, 1946), 34.

3240. Gouzenko, Igor. "The 'Neighbors' in Canada." In: Julien Steinberg, ed. *Verdict of Three Decades.* New York: Duell, 1950. pp. 527–545.

3241. "The Growth of Soviet Espionage: The Search For Data on the Atom." *U.S. News and World Report,* XXI (August 16, 1946), 20–21.

3242. Hirsch, Richard. "Soviet Spies: The Story of Russian Espionage in North America." *Reader's Digest,* L (May 1947), 127–152.

3243. Hoover, J. Edgar. "The Trigger-Finger Clue." *Reader's Digest,* L (June 1947), 65–68.

3244. "How Canada Fights Spies." *U.S. News and World Report,* LXXIX (November 25, 1954), 70–72.

3245. "I Spy: Red Spies in Canada." *Newsweek,* XXVII (March 4, 1946), 62–63.

3246. "Instructions From Moscow." *Time,* XLVII (March 11, 1946), 36.

3247. Johnson, Thomas M. "Red Spy Net." *Reader's Digest,* LI (July 1947), 59–63.

3248. "Just Across the Border." *U.S. News and World Report,* XXI (October 11, 1946), 26–27.

3249. Labreche, Jean. "Dirty Work North: How the CIA Keeps Tabs on Canada." *Macleans,* XCI (October 9, 1978), 28+.

3250. Lee, Henry. "Smashing the Biggest Spy Ring." *Coronet,* XXXI (December 1951), 130–134.

3251. Lindley, Ernest K. "Effects of the Spy Case." *Newsweek,* XXVII (March 4, 1946), 26.

3252. Phillips, L. H. "Preventive Detention in Canada." *Canadian Forum,* XXVI (June 1946), 56–57.

3253. "Red Circles: The Canadian Spy Case." *Newsweek,* XXVIII (July 29, 1946), 42.

3254. "Red Faces: Some Canadians Supplied Atomic Bomb Secrets to Russia." *Time,* XLVII (March 4, 1946), 25.

3255. "The Red Web in Canada." *Newsweek,* XXVII (March 11, 1946), 50.

3256. "The Russian Bear Trap." *Newsweek,* XXVII (April 8, 1946), 22–23.

3257. Sandwell, B. K. "The Canadian Spy Case." *Nation*, CLXII (May 4, 1946), 536–538.

3258. Scott, Kenneth, jt. author. *See* Brown, Sanborn (3230).

3259. Shalett, Sidney M. "How the Russians Spy on Their Allies." *Saturday Evening Post*, CCXIX (January 25–February 1, 1947), 18–19+, 24+.

3260. "The Spy Business in Ottawa." *Canadian Forum*, XXVI (April 1946), 3+.

3261. Urquhart, Ian. "Mounties Still Can Get Their Man, or 13, if Need Be: Trapping KGB Agents." *Macleans*, XCI (February 20, 1978), 22–23.

3262. Viorst, Milton. "An Analysis of American Intervention in the Matter of Quebec: In the Beginning There was the CIA." *Macleans*, LXXXV (December 1972), 22–23+.

3263. Voigt, F. A. "The Royal Commission." *19th Century*, CXL (December 1946), 302–313.

3264. White, John B. *The Soviet Spy System*. London: Falcon Press, 1948. 133p.

b. United States

(1) ESPIONAGE/SUBVERSION/TREASON

3265. Alsop, Stewart. "Soviet Spymasters: The Soviet Espionage Apparatus in the United States." *Saturday Evening Post*, CCXXXVIII (May 22, 1965), 16+.

3266. Beilenson, L. W. *Power Through Subversion*. New York: Public Affairs Press, 1972. 310p.

3267. Bruslov, Y. M., *et al.* "The Practice of Recruiting Americans in the U.S.A. and Third Countries [: A KGB Training Manual]." In: John Barron. *KGB: The Secret Work of Soviet Secret Agents*. New York: Reader's Digest Press; dist. by Dutton, 1973. pp. 346–378.

3268. Burnham, James. *The Web of Subversion: Underground Networks in the U.S. Government*. New York: John Day, 1954. 248p.

3269. Buzek, Antonin. "Diplomacy and Espionage." *East Europe*, XI (August 1962), 10–11.

3270. _____ . _____ . *Military Review*, XLIII (January 1963), 85–88.

3271. Carpenter, John. *Washington Babylon.* Phoenix, AZ: Ron-San Corp., 1965. 219p.

3272. Carpozi, George. *Red Spies in the U.S.* New Rochelle, NY: Arlington House, 1973. 251p.

3273. _____ . *Red Spies in Washington.* New York: Simon and Schuster, 1968. 253p.

3274. _____ , jt. author. *See* Huss, Pierre J. (3289).

3275. "The Case of the 'Atom Spies.' " *Newsweek,* LXVI (August 23, 1965), 82.

3276. Cave Brown, Anthony and Charles B. McDonald. *The Secret History of the Atomic Bomb.* New York: Dial Press, 1977. 788p.

3277. Copeland, Miles. "CIA: The Case of Intelligence—Soviet Tactics in the United States." *National Review,* XXVII (July 4, 1975), 712–719.

3278. Crozier, Brian. "Power and National Security: [Soviet] Infiltration of the Anti-Nuclear Movement." *National Review,* XXXI (February 2, 1979), 164–167.

3279. De Toledano, Ralph. *The Greatest Plot in History.* New York: Duell, 1963. 306p.

3280. "Espionage Doesn't End With Detente." *Air Force Times,* XXXVIII (May 15, 1978), 22.

3281. "Foreign Agents in America: Shady Tactics and Worse." *U.S. News and World Report,* LXXXIII (July 4, 1977), 23–24.

3282. Green, Murray. "Intelligence For Sale at the Corner Newsstand." Air Force, XXXIX (November 1955), 82–86.

3283. Hanrahan, John D. "Foreign Agents in Our Midst." *Progressive,* XLI (November 1977), 31–35.

3284. Hirsch, Richard. *Soviet Spies: The Story of Russian Espionage in North America.* New York: Duell, 1947. 92p.

3285. Hoover, J. Edgar. "The 'Crime of the Century': The Case of the A-bomb Spies." *Reader's Digest,* LVIII (May 1951), 149–168.

3286. _____ . "How Red China Spies on the U.S." *Nation's Business,* LIV (June 1966), 84–88.

3287. _____ . "Red Spy Masters in America." *Reader's Digest,* LXI (August 1952), 83–87.

3288. "How Detente Opens Doors For Soviet Spies in the U.S." *U.S. News and World Report,* LXXX (February 23, 1976), 18–19.

3289. Huss, Pierre J. and George Carpozi. *Red Spies in the U.N.* New York: Coward-McCann, 1965. 287p.

3290. "If It's Spies That You're Wondering About: Excerpts From Report to Congress." *U.S. News and World Report,* LXVIII (June 27, 1960), 70–73.

3291. Jordan, George A. *From Major Jordan's Diaries.* New York: Harcourt, 1952. 284p.

3292. _____ . "We Gave the Reds Everything." *Reader's Digest,* LXI (December 1952), 55–61.

3293. "The KGB's United Nations Base." *Soviet Analyst,* IV (July 3, 1975), 1–3.

3294. Kirk, Donald. "Dirty Tricks Korean Style: The Involvement of the KCIA in American Affairs." *Saturday Review,* IV (January 8, 1977), 8+.

3295. Ledeen, Michael A. "Hiss, Oswald, the KGB, and Us." *Commentary,* LXV (May, August, 1978), 30–36, 8–10.

3296. Lee, Jai H. "The Activities of the Korean Central Intelligence Agency in the United States." In: Irving L. Horowitz, ed. *Science, Sin, and Scholarship: The Politics of Reverend Moon and the Unification Church.* Cambridge, MA: M.I.T. Press, 1978. pp. 120–147.

3297. Loane, Jabez W., 4th. "Treason and Aiding the Enemy." *Military Law Review,* XXX (1964), 43+.

3298. Lucas, Norman. *The Great Spy Ring.* London: Barker, 1966. 284p.

3299. McDonald, Charles B., jt. author. *See* Cave Brown, Anthony (3276).

3300. Newman, Bernard. *Soviet Atomic Spies.* London: Hale, 1952. 239p.

3301. Pilat, Oliver R. *Atom Spies.* New York: Putnam, 1952. 312p.

3302. Ranard, Donald L. "The Korean Central Intelligence Agency in the U.S.A." *Worldview,* XIX (November 1976), 19–21.

3303. "Red Terror Inside the U.S.: Secret Doings of Top Diplomats." *U.S. News and World Report,* XL (June 8, 1956), 51–52+.

3304. Reinhardt, Guenther. *Crime Without Punishment: The Secret Soviet Terror Against America.* Translated from the German. New York: Hermitage House, 1952. 322p.

3305. Reuben, William A. *The Atom Spy Hoax.* New York: Action Books, 1955. 504p.

3306. "Russian Spies Roam U.S." *U.S. News and World Report,* XXXII (February 15, 1952), 32–35.

3307. Schultz, D. O. *Subversion.* Springfield, IL: C. C. Thomas, 1973. 107p.

3308. "Soviet Spying on Capitol Hill." *Time,* CVII (March 22, 1976), 16–17.

3309. "Spying on the U.S. is Easy For Russia." *U.S. News and World Report,* XXVIII (April 21, 1950), 14–15.

3310. Stang, Alan. "Serpent in the House: The KGB." *American Opinion,* XXI (June 1978), 11–13+.

3311. Steinberg, John. "Soviet Espionage." *American Mercury,* LXXII (June 1951), 706–717.

3312. Thompson, Francis J. *Destination Washington.* London: Allen and Unwin, 1960. 222p.

3313. Tietzen, Arthur. *Soviet Spy Ring.* New York: Coward-McCann, 1961. 190p.

3314. "True Tales of the Other Side: Soviet Intelligence at Work in the U.S." *Newsweek,* LXXXVI (August 4, 1975), 28–29.

3315. Tully, Andrew M. *The FBI's Most Famous Cases.* New York: Morrow, 1965. 242p.

3316. _____ . *White Tie and Dagger.* New York: Morrow, 1967. 257p.

3317. Udell, Gilman G., comp. *Laws Relating to Espionage, Sabotage, Etc.*[1917–1976]. U.S. House of Representatives Special Publication, no. 7. Rev. ed. Washington, D.C.: GPO, 1976. 171p.

3318. United States. Congress. House. Committee on International Relations. Subcommittee on International Organizations. *Activities of the Korean Central Intelligence Agency in the United States: Hearings.* 94th Cong., 2nd sess. 2 pts. Washington, D.C.: GPO, 1976.

3319. _____ . _____ . _____ . _____ . _____ . *Korean-American Relations.* 95th Cong., 1st sess. 7 pts. Washington, D.C.: GPO, 1977–1978.

3320. _____ . _____ . _____ . _____ . _____ . _____ : *Appendices.* 95th Cong., 2nd sess. 2 pts. Washington, D.C.: GPO, 1978.

3321. _____ . _____ . _____ . Committee on Standards of Official Conduct. "Korean Influence Investigation: Report." In: Patricia A. O'Connor, ed. *Historic Documents of 1978.* Washington, D.C.: Congressional Quarterly, Inc., 1979. pp. 845–908.

3322. _____ . _____ . _____ . Committee on Un-American Activities. *Communist Espionage: Hearings.* 81st Cong., 1st and 2nd sess. Washington, D.C.: GPO, 1951. 70p.

3323. _____ . _____ . _____ . _____ . *Communist Espionage in the United States Government: Hearings.* 80th Cong., 2nd sess. 2 pts. Washington, D.C.: GPO, 1948.

3324. _____ . _____ . _____ . _____ . *Communist Espionage in the United States: Hearings and Testimony of Frantisek Tisler, Former Military and Air Attaché, Czechoslovak Embassy in Washington, D.C.* 86th Cong., 2nd sess. Washington, D.C.: GPO, 1960. 9p.

3325. _____ . _____ . _____ . _____ . *The Conduct of Espionage Within the United States by Agents of Foreign Communist Governments: Hearings.* 90th Cong., 1st sess. Washington, D.C.: GPO, 1967. 160p.

3326. _____ . _____ . _____ . _____ . *The Investigation of Soviet Espionage: Hearings.* 85th Cong., 1st and 2nd sess. 2pts. Washington, D.C.: GPO, 1958.

3327. _____ . _____ . _____ . _____ . *The Shameful Years: Thirty Years of Soviet Espionage in the United States.* 81st Cong., 2nd sess. Washington, D.C.: GPO, 1951.

3328. _____ . _____ . _____ . _____ . *Soviet Espionage Activities in Connection With Jet Propulsion and Aircraft: Hearings.* 81st Cong., 1st sess. Washington, D.C.: GPO, 1949. 27p.

3329. _____ . _____ . _____ . _____ . *Soviet Espionage Activities in Connection With the Atomic Bomb: Report.* 80th Cong., 2nd sess. Washington, D.C.: GPO, 1948. 23p.

3330. _____ . _____ . _____ . _____ . *Spotlight on Spies.* 81st Cong., 1st sess. Washington, D.C.: GPO, 1949. 17p.

3331. _____ . _____ . Senate. Committee on the Judiciary. Subcommittee to Investigate the Administration of the Internal Security Act and Other Internal Security Laws. *Communist Bloc Intelligence Activities in the United States: Hearings.* 94th Cong., 1st sess. Washington, D.C.: GPO, 1975. 64p.

3332. _____ . _____ . _____ . _____ . *Communist Infiltration in the Nuclear Test Ban Movement: Hearings.* 86th Cong., 2nd sess. 2 pts. Washington, D.C.: GPO, 1960–1961.

3333. _____ . _____ . _____ . _____ . *Espionage Activities of Personnel Attached to Embassies and Consulates Under Soviet Domination in the United States: Hearings.* 82nd Cong., 1st and 2nd sess. Washington, D.C.: GPO, 1952. 52p.

3334. _____ . _____ . _____ . _____ . *The Scope of Soviet* [Espionage] *Activity in the United States: Hearings.* 84th Cong., 2nd sess. to 85th Cong., 1st sess. 95 pts. Washington, D.C.: GPO, 1956–1959.

3335. _____ . _____ . _____ . Select Committee on Ethics. *Korean Influence Inquiry.* 95th Cong., 2nd sess. Washington, D.C.: GPO, 1978. 180p.

3336. _____ . _____ . _____ . Select Committee on Intelligence. *Activities of "Friendly"* [KCIA] *Foreign Intelligence Services in the United States: A Case Study.* 95th Cong., 2nd sess. Washington, D.C.: GPO, 1978. 24p.

3337. _____ . _____ . _____ . _____ . "Prosecutions For Violations of the Espionage Statutes [1951–1963 and] Provisions of the Atomic Energy Act [1962–1977]." In: *The Use of Classified Information in Litigation: Hearings.* 95th Cong., 2nd sess. Washington, D.C.: GPO, 1978. pp. 227–235.

3338. _____ . Department of Justice. *Report of the Attorney General to the Congress of the United States on the Administration of the Foreign Agents Registration Act of 1938, as Amended, For the Calendar Year 1972.* Washington, D.C.: GPO, 1973. 208p.

3339. _____ . Federal Bureau of Investigation. *Expose of Soviet Espionage, May 1960.* Washington, D.C.: GPO, 1960. 63p.

3340. Weyl, Nathaniel. "Pro-Soviet Espionage." In: *Treason: The Story of Disloyalty and Betrayal in American History.* New York: Public Affairs Press, 1950. pp. 412–423.

3341. Willoughby, Charles A. "Espionage and the American Communist Party." *American Mercury,* LXXXVIII (January 1959), 117–123.

3342. _____ . "Soviet Espionage." *Vital Speeches,* XXIII (March 15, 1957), 344–347.

(2) INTERNAL SECURITY AND INDIVIDUAL RIGHTS

3343. Agee, Philip. "CIA vs. U.S.A." *Oui,* IV (September 1975), 72+.

3344. "Ahead, New Drive on Spies: [William E.] Jenner Carrying the Ball." *U.S. News and World Report,* XXXV (December 4, 1953), 49–51.

3345. Albergotti, Robert D. "Search and Seizure: Warrantless Foreign National Security Wiretaps." *Tulane Law Review,* XLIX (May 1975), 1153–1160.

3346. Alpern, David M. "Bella's File: The CIA File on Bella Abzug." *Newsweek,* LXXXV (March 17, 1975), 22–23.

3347. Archer, Jules. *Superspys: The Secret Side of Government.* New York: Delacorte Press, 1977. 252p.

3348. Armer, Paul. "Computer Technology and Surveillance.' *Computers and People,* XXIV (September 1975), 8–11.

3349. Ashmore, Harry S., ed. *The William O. Douglas Inquiry Into the State of Individual Freedom.* Boulder, CO: Westview Press, 1979. 250p.

3350. Association of the Bar of the City of New York. Committee on Civil Rights. "Military Surveillance of Civilian Political Activities: Report and Recommendations for Congressional Action." *Record of the Association of the Bar of the City of New York,* XXVIII (October 1973), 651–676.

3351. ———. Committee on Federal Legislation. "Judicial Procedures For National Security Electronic Surveillance." *Record of the Association of the Bar of the City of New York,* XXIX (December 1974), 751–774.

3352. Bain, Donald. *The Control of Candy Jones.* Chicago: Playboy Press, 1976. 267p.

3353. Baskir, Lawrence M. "Reflections on the Senate Investigation of Army Surveillance." *Indiana Law Journal,* XLIX (Summer 1974), 618–653.

3354. Becker, Louis G., jt. author. *See* Kaiser, Frederick M. (3427).

3355. Bernstein, Barton J. "The Road to Watergate and Beyond: The Growth and Abuse of Executive Authority Since 1940." *Law and Contemporary Problems,* XL (Spring 1976), 58–86.

3356. Blackstock, Paul W. "Political Surveillance and the Constitutional Order." *Worldview,* XIV (May 1971), 11–14.

3357. Blum, Richard H. *Deceivers and Deceived.* Stanford University Institute of Public Policy Analysis Publications. Springfield, IL: C. C. Thomas, 1971. 328p.

3358. ——— , ed. *Surveillance and Espionage in a Free Society: A Report by the Planning Group to the Policy Council of the Democratic National Committee.* New York: Praeger, 1972. 319p.

3359. Blumenthal, Fred. "How We Outsmart Red Spies." *Parade,* (February 11, 1962), 6+.

3360. Boeth, Richard. "The Assault on Privacy: Snoops, Bugs, Wiretaps, Dossiers, Data Banks—and Specters of 1984." *Newsweek,* LXXVI (July 27, 1970), 15–20.

3361. Boggs, Timothy A., jt. author. *See* Lehman, Bruce A. (3438).

3362. Bontecou, Eleanor. *The Federal Loyalty-Security Program.* Ithaca, NY: Cornell University Press, 1953. 377p.

3363. Borosage, Robert L. "Secrecy vs. the Constitution." *Society,* XII (March–April 1975), 71–75.

3364. _____ , jt. author. *See* Raskin, Marcus G. (3474).

3365. Bottom, N. R. "Security Intelligence." *Security Management,* XX (July 1976), 36–39.

3366. Brown, Ralph S. *Loyalty and Security.* New Haven, CT: Yale University Press, 1958. 524p.

3367. Brown, Robert M. *The Electronic Invasion.* New York: John F. Rider, 1967. 184p.

3368. Burlingham, Bo. "Paranoia in Power: [Tom C.] Huston's Domestic Spy Plan." *Harper's,* CCXLIX (October 1974), 26+.

3369. Burnham, David. "Fourteen City Policemen Got CIA Training: Reprinted From the *New York Times,* December 17, 1972." *Congressional Record,* CXIX (February 6, 1973), 3558–3559.

3370. Carroll, John M. *The Third Listener: Personal Electronic Espionage.* New York: E. P. Dutton, 1969. 179p.

3371. Caute, David. *The Great Fear: The Anti-Communist Purge Under Truman and Eisenhower.* New York: Simon and Schuster, 1978. 697p.

3372. Cherry, William A. "The Military: A Source of Equipment and Training." *Police Chief,* XLII (April 1975), 53–55.

3373. Christie, George C. "Government Surveillance and Individual Freedom." *New York University Law Review,* XLVII (November 1972), 871–902.

3374. *Civil Liberties Review,* Editors of. "Rx for Surveillance: A *Civil Liberties Review* Feature." *Civil Liberties Review,* I (Summer 1974), 7–78.

3375. Colby, Jonathan E. "The Developing International Law on Gathering and Sharing Security Intelligence." *Yale Studies in World Public Order,* I (1974), 49–92.

3376.   Colby, William E. "Intelligence Secrecy and Security in a Free Society." *International Security,* I (Fall 1976), 3–14.

3377.   *Columbia Human Rights Law Review* Staff, eds. *Surveillance, Data-veillance, and Personal Freedoms: The Use and Abuse of Information Technology—A Symposium.* Fair Lawn, NJ: R. E. Burdick, 1973. 247p.

3378.   Cook, Blanche W. "Surveillance and Mind Control." In: Howard Frazier, ed. *Uncloaking the CIA.* New York: Free Press, 1978. pp. 174–189.

3379.   Cott, Lawrence V. "Espionage—An Old Problem Still With Us." In: Richard O. Wright, ed. *Whose FBI?* La Salle, IL: Open Court Publications, 1974. pp. 96–138.

3380.   Cotter, Richard D. "Notes Toward a Definition of National Security." *Washington Monthly,* VII (December 1975), 4–16.

3381.   Cowan, Paul. *State Secrets: Police Surveillance in America.* New York: Holt, Rinehart, and Winston, 1974. 333p.

3382.   Cox, Arthur M. *The Myths of National Security: The Peril of Secret Government.* Boston: Beacon Press, 1975. 231p.

3383.   Cragan, John F. and Donald C. Shields. *Government Surveillance of U.S. Citizens: Issues and Answers.* Minneapolis: Campus Press, 1971. 111p.

3384.   Crewdson, John M. "FBI Checking of Radicals [COINTEL-PRO] Went on Beyond Deadline: Reprinted From the *New York Times,* October 6, 1975." In: Frank S. McClellan, ed. *The Right to Privacy.* Reference Shelf, v. 48, no. 1. New York: H. W. Wilson, 1976. pp. 106–109.

3385.   _____ . "Opening of Mail is Traced to FBI—Agency Concedes Operation—Declares Purpose was to Thwart Espionage: Reprinted From the *New York Times,* August 6, 1975." *Congressional Record,* CXXI (October 28, 1975), 33901–33902.

3386.   Cunningham, John E. *Security Electronics.* Indianapolis, IN: H. W. Sams, 1970. 159p.

3387.   Dash, Samuel, *et al. The Eavesdroppers.* New York: DeCapo Press, 1974. 484p.

3388.   Davidson, Bill. "The Real Story of How the U.S. Catches Spies." *Look,* XXI (September 17, 1957), 23–27.

3389.   Dershowitz, A. M. "Unchecked Wiretapping: Before Watergate and After." *New Republic,* CLXXII (May 31, 1975), 13–17.

3390.   Donner, Frank. "Domestic Political Intelligence." In: Howard Frazier, ed. *Uncloaking the CIA.* New York: Free Press, 1978. pp. 165–173.

3391.   _____ . "Electronic Surveillance: The National Security Game." *Civil Liberties Review,* II (Summer 1975), 15–47.

3392.   _____ . "Memos to the Chairman: The Issue, of Course, is Power." *Nation,* CC (February 22, 1975), 200–204.

3393.   _____ . "Political Intelligence: Cameras, Informers, and Files." *Civil Liberties Review,* I (Summer 1974), 8–25.

3394.   Dorman, Michael. *Dirty Politics: From 1776 to Watergate.* New York: Delacorte, 1979. 301p.

3395.   Dorsen, Norman and Stephen Gillers, ed. *None of Your Business: Government Secrecy in America.* New York: Viking Press, 1974. 362p.

3396.   "Electronic Eavesdropping: Watergate Comes Full Circle." *Congressional Quarterly Weekly Report,* XXXI (August 25, 1973), 2321–2324.

3397.   Ellison, James M. "A Report From the Wiretap Subculture." *Washington Monthly,* VII (December 1975), 27–33.

3398.   Emerson, Thomas I. "Controlling the Spies." *Center Magazine,* XII (January 1979), 60–74.

3399.   "The FBI's Political Abuses: Full Text of Official Report." *U.S. News and World Report,* LXXIX (December 15, 1975), 61–64.

3400.   Fink, Robert. "The Unsolved Breakins, 1970–1974." *Rolling Stone,* (October 10, 1974), *passim.*

3401.   Footlick, J. K. "Counterspy's Dilemma: Investigating Foreign Agents in the U.S." *Newsweek,* LXXXVIII (November 22, 1976), 43+.

3402.   "Foreign Security Surveillance and the Fourth Amendment." *Harvard Law Review,* LXXXVII (March 1974), 976–1000.

3403.   "Foreign Security Surveillance—Balancing Executive Power and the Fourth Amendment." *Fordham Law Review,* XLV (1977), 1179–1201.

3404.   Freeland, R. M. *The Truman Doctrine and the Origins of McCarthyism: Foreign Policy, Domestic Politics, and Internal Security, 1946–48.* New York: Knopf, 1972. 419p.

3405.   French, Scott R. *The Big Brother Game.* San Francisco, CA: Gnu Publishers, 1975. 237p.

3406. Fry, Ron, jt. author. *See* LeMond, Alan (3439).

3407. Gaines, J. R. "The CIA's Letter Bombs: The Mail-Opening Program." *Newsweek,* LXXXVI (October 6, 1975), 40 .

3408. George, Willis D. *Surreptitious Entry.* New York: Appleton-Century, 1946. 214p.

3409. Gillers, Stephen, jt. author. *See* Dorsen, Norman (3395).

3410. "The Growing Alarm Over Official 'Snooping.' " *U.S. News and World Report,* LXX (February 22, 1971), 38–41.

3411. Haltom, John F. "National Security and Civil Liberty: Government Techniques Employed to Combat Subversive Activities, 1938–1953." Unpublished PhD Dissertation, University of Texas, 1954.

3412. Harper, Alan D. *The Politics of Loyalty: The White House and the Communist Issue, 1946–1952.* Westport, CT: Greenwood Press, 1969. 318p.

3413. Hodges, David P. "Electronic Visual Surveillance and the Fourth Amendment: The Arrival of Big Brother?" *Hastings Constitutional Law Quarterly,* III (Winter 1976), 261–299.

3414. Hoover, J. Edgar. *Masters of Deceit.* New York: Holt, 1958. 374p.

3415. Horrock, Nicholas M. "Electronic Surveillance—Scope of Wiretapping and Bugging an Issue of Rising Concern: Reprinted From the *New York Times,* February 20, 1975." In: Grant S. McClellan, ed. *The Right to Privacy.* Reference Shelf, v. 48, no. 1. New York: H. W. Wilson, 1976. pp. 81–86.

3416. _____ . "National Security Agency Reported Eavesdropping on Most Private Cables: Reprinted From the *New York Times,* August 30, 1975." In: U.S. Congress. Senate. Committee on the Judiciary. Subcommittee on Constitutional Rights. *Surveillance Technology, 1976.* 94th Cong., 2nd sess. Washington, D.C.: GPO, 1976. pp. 1108–1111.

3417. Hougan, James. *Spooks: The Haunting of America—The Private Use of Secret Agents.* New York: Morrow, 1978. 478p.

3418. _____ . "A Surfeit of Spies." *Harper's,* CCXLIX (November 1974), 51–67.

3419. "How the U.S. Army Spies on Citizens." *Life,* LXX (May 26, 1971), 20–27.

3420. Huck, S. L. M. "Gambling With Subversion." *American Opinion,* XX (May 1977), 9–14+.

3421. "Incursions on Privacy: Computers, Army, Wiretaps." *Congressional Quarterly Weekly Report,* XXIX (February 19, 1971), 425–430.

3422. Janov, Gwenellen P. "Electronic Surveillance." *George Washington Law Review,* XLI (October 1972), 119–134.

3423. Jenner, William E. "Rat Hunt, Not Witch Hunt: An Address." *Vital Speeches,* XXXVI (January 1, 1954), 48–50.

3424. Jordan, Don. "Looking In on Us: Surveillance, Surveillance—All is Surveillance." *Environment,* XIX (August 1977), 6–11.

3425. "Judicial Review of Military Surveillance of Civilians: Big Brother Wears Modern Army Green." *Columbia Law Review,* LXXII (October 1972), 1009–1047.

3426. Jung, John. "Snoopology." *Human Behavior,* IV (October 1975), 56–59.

3427. Kaiser, Frederick M. and Louis G. Becker. "Surveillance Technology, 1976: An Overview." In: U.S. Congress. Senate. Committee on the Judiciary. Subcommittee on Constitutional Rights. *Surveillance Technology, 1976.* 94th Cong., 2nd sess. Washington, D.C.: GPO, 1976. pp. 13–94.

3428. Katz, Harvey. "Big Brother is Listening: The Wiretappers are Loose in the Land and 1984 May Be Closer Than You Think." *Washingtonian,* V (June 1970), 44–45, 73–78.

3429. Kelly, Clarence M. "FBI's Illegal Activities." In: Robert A. Diamond, ed. *Historic Documents of 1976.* Washington, D.C.: Congressional Quarterly, Inc., 1977. pp. 321–331.

3430. Kelly, John. *The CIA in America.* Westport, CT: Laurence Hill, 1979.

3431. Kenny, Gerald J. "The 'National Security Wiretap': Presidential Prerogative or Judicial Responsibility?" *Southern California Law Review,* XLV (Summer 1972), 888–913.

3432. Lacovara, Philip A. "Presidential Power to Gather Intelligence: The Tension Between Article II and Amendment IV." *Law and Contemporary Problems,* XL (Summer 1976), 106–131.

3433. Lambie, William K., Jr. "Electronic Surveillance for National Security." *Journal of Police Science Administration,* III (September 1975), 346–350.

3434. Lapidus, Edith J. *Eavesdropping on Trial.* Rochelle Park, NJ: Hayden Book Co., 1974. 287p.

3435. Lasky, Victor. *It Didn't Start With Watergate.* New York: Dell, 1977. 478p.

3436. Latham, Earl. *The Communist Controversy in Washington: From the New Deal to McCarthy.* Cambridge, MA: Harvard University Press, 1966. 446p.

3437. Laturno, Gary M. "Presidential Authority to Authorize Investigative Techniques in Foreign Intelligence Investigations." *FBI Law Enforcement Bulletin,* XLV (June 1976), 27–31.

3438. Lehman, Bruce A. and Timothy A. Boggs. "How Uncle Sam Covers the Mails." *Civil Liberties Review,* IV (May–June 1977), 20–28.

3439. LeMond, Alan and Ron Fry. *No Place to Hide.* New York: St. Martin's Press, 1975. 278p.

3440. Levine, Jack. "[J. Edgar] Hoover and the Red Scare." *Nation,* CXCV (October 20, 1962), 232–235.

3441. Lewin, Nathan. "Pulling the Plug on the FBI's Bug." *New Republic,* CLXVII (July 15, 1972), 12–15.

3442. Long, Edward V. *The Intruders.* New York: Praeger, 1967. 230p.

3443. Marks, John D. "The CIA at Home." In: Howard Frazier, ed. *Uncloaking the CIA.* New York: Free Press, 1978. pp. 159–164.

3444. Mathews, David J. "Civilians' Claims That Army's Data Gathering System Works a Chilling Effect on Their First Amendment Rights Held Not to be a Justifiable Controversy. Absent Showing of Objective Present Harm or Threat of Future Harm." *Villanova Law Review,* XVIII (February 1973), 479–491.

3445. Meisel, Alan. "Political Surveillance and the Fourth Amendment." *University of Pittsburgh Law Review,* XXXV (Fall 1973), 53–71.

3446. Merced, Florencio. "The CIA in Puerto Rico." In: Howard Frazier, ed. *Uncloaking the CIA.* New York: Free Press, 1978. pp. 26–32.

3447. Mikva, Abner J. "A Nation in Fear: An Interview on Military Spying." *Progressive,* XXXV (February 1971), 18–20.

3448. Miller, Arthur R. *The Assault on Privacy: Computers, Data Banks, and Dossiers.* Ann Arbor: University of Michigan Press, 1971. 333p.

3449. Mollenhoff, Clark. "Counterintelligence: The Key to National Security." *Human Events,* XXXV (July 12, 1975), 8+.

3450. Munves, James. *The FBI and the CIA: Secret Agents and American Democracy.* New York: Harcourt, 1975. 185p.

3451. Nathanson, Nathaniel L. "Freedom of Association and the Quest for Internal Security: Conspiracy From Dennis to Dr. Spock." *Northwestern University Law Review*, LXV (May–June 1970), 153–192.

3452. "The National Security Interest and Civil Liberties." *Harvard Law Review*, LXXXV (April 1972), 1130–1284.

3453. Neler, Aryeh. *Dossier: The Secret Files They Keep on You.* New York: Stein and Day, 1975. 216p.

3454. Nelson, Gaylord. " 'National Security' and Electronic Surveillance: The Need For Corrective Legislation." *Intellect*, CIII (January 1975), 230–233.

3455. _____ . "Warrantless Bugs: The Invisible Pests." *Trial*, XI (March–April 1975), 64–65+.

3456. Nesson, Charles R. "Aspects of the Executive's Power Over National Security Matters: Secrecy Classification and Foreign Intelligence Wiretaps." *Indiana Law Journal*, XLIX (Spring 1974), 399–421.

3457. "New CIA Furor." *Newsweek*, LXXXV (January 6, 1975), 10+.

3458. " 'Operation Chaos': Reprinted From the *New York Times*, June 11, 1975." *Congressional Record*, CXXI (June 11, 1975), 18284–18285.

3459. Osolin, Charles. "Military Snooping—Pentagon Listening in on America's Calls: Reprinted From the *Atlanta Constitution*, September 14, 1975." In: U.S. Congress. Senate. Committee on the Judiciary. Subcommittee on Constitutional Rights. *Surveillance Technology: 1976*. 94th Cong., 2nd sess. Washington, D.C.: GPO, 1976. pp. 1056–1059.

3460. O'Toole, George. "Harmonica Bugs, Cloaks, and Silver Boxes: Eavesdropping in Post-Watergate America." *Harper's*, CCL (June 1975), 36–39.

3461. Ottenberg, Miriam. *The Federal Investigators.* Englewood Cliffs, NJ: Prentice-Hall, 1962. 348p.

3462. Owen, Stephen T. "Eavesdropping at the Government's Discretion: First Amendment Implications of the National Security Eavesdropping Power." *Cornell Law Review*, LVI (November 1970), 161–170.

3463. Perkus, Cathy, ed. *Cointelpro: The FBI's Secret War on Political Freedom.* New York: Monad Press, 1976. 190p.

3464. Pincus, Walter. "Spies and Presidents: Reprinted From the *Washington Post*, January 26, 1975." *Congressional Record*, CXXI (January 27, 1975), 1430–1431.

3465. Plate, Thomas. "Wired [New York] City: The Invasion of the Privacy Snatchers." *New York Magazine*, VI (July 9, 1973), 28–33.

3466. Pollock, David A. *Methods of Electronic Audio Surveillance.* Springfield, IL: C. C. Thomas, 1975. 385p.

3467. Powers, Thomas. "The Government is Watching: Is There Anything the Police [FBI and CIA] Don't Want to Know?" *Atlantic,* CCXXX (October 1972), 51–63.

3468. "Present and Proposed Standards for Foreign Intelligence Electronic Surveillance." *Northwestern University Law Review,* LXXI (March–April 1974), 109–133.

3469. Pyle, Christopher H. "CONUS Intelligence: The Army Watches Civilian Politics." *Washington Monthly,* II (January 1970), 5+.

3470. _____ . "CONUS Revisited: The Army Covers Up." *Washington Monthly,* II (July 1970), 49–58.

3471. _____ . "Military Surveillance of Civilian Politics, 1967–1970." Unpublished PhD Dissertation, Columbia University, 1974.

3472. _____ . "Spies Without Masters: The Army Still Watches Civilian Politics." *Civil Liberties Review,* I (Summer 1974), 38–49.

3473. Raskin, Marcus G. *National Security Emergence as an Instrument of State Power.* Edison, NJ: Transaction Books, 1979.

3474. _____ and Robert L. Borosage. "National Security and Official Accountability: Can We Return to Government Ruled By Law?" *Vital Issues,* XXIII (September 1973), 1–4.

3475. "Rattling Skeletons in the CIA Closet: Charges of Illegal Spying on American Citizens Within the U.S." *Time,* CV (January 6, 1975), 44–46.

3476. Redlick, Norman. "Spies in Government." *Nation,* CLXXVIII (February 6, 1954), 109–111.

3477. Roebuck, Julian B. *Political Crime in the United States: Analyzing Crimes By and Against the Government.* New York: Praeger, 1978. 224p.

3478. Rorvik, David. "Bringing the War Home: Reprinted From *Playboy,* September 1974." In: U.S. Congress. Senate. Committee on the Judiciary. Subcommittee on Constitutional Rights. *Surveillance Technology: 1976.* 94th Cong., 2nd sess. Washington, D.C.: GPO, 1976. pp. 957–966.

3479. Ross, Thomas B. "Spying in the United States." *Society,* XII (March–April 1975), 64–70.

3480. _____ . "Surreptitious Entry: The CIA's Operations in the United States." In: Robert L. Borosage and John D. Marks, eds. *The CIA File.* New York: Grossman, 1976. pp. 93–108.

3481.   Rule, James B. *Private Lives and Public Surveillance.* New York: Schocken Books, 1974. 382p.

3482.   St. George, Andrew. "How Does It Feel to be Bugged, Watched, Followed, Hounded and Pestered by the CIA?" *Esquire*, LXXXIII (June 1975), 118–122+.

3483.   Sale, Kirkpatrick. "Spies With and Without Daggers." In: Howard Frazier, ed. *Uncloaking the CIA.* New York: Free Press, 1978. pp. 148–158.

3484.   Schwarz, Frederick A. O., Jr. "Intelligence Activities and the Rights of Americans." *Christianity and Crisis*, XXXVII (February 7, 1977), 8–13.

3485.   Schwartz, Herman. "Six Years of Tapping and Bugging." *Civil Liberties Review*, I (Summer 1974), 26–37.

3486.   Scott, Peter D. "From Dallas to Watergate: The Longest Cover-Up." *Ramparts*, XII (November 1973), 12–17+.

3487.   Scoville, Herbert, Jr. "The Technology of Surveillance." *Society*, XII (March–April 1975), 58–63.

3488.   Seamans, Andrew. "Developing the Internal Security Mission." In: Richard O. Wright, ed. *Whose FBI?* La Salle, IL: Open Court Publishers, 1974. pp. 139–172.

3489.   "A Secret Dossier on Every American?" *U.S. News and World Report*, LXXV (August 27, 1973), 54–55.

3490.   Shapiro, Ira. "Civil Liberties and National Security: The Outlook in Congress." *Intellect*, CV (February 1977), 230–233.

3491.   Shattuck, John H. F. "Tilting at the Surveillance Apparatus." *Civil Liberties Review*, I (Summer 1974), 59–73.

3492.   _____. "Uncovering Surveillance." *Trial*, XI (January 1975), 40–41+.

3493.   Sheridan, Thomas I., 3rd. "Electronic Intelligence Gathering and the Omnibus Crime Control and Safe Streets Act of 1968." *Fordham Law Review*, XLIX (1976), 331–354.

3494.   Shields, Donald C., jt. author. *See* Cragan, John F. (3383).

3495.   Shils, Edward A. *The Torment of Secrecy: The Background and Consequences of American Security Policies.* Carbondale, IL: University of Southern Illinois Press, 1974. 238p.

3496.   Shloss, Leon. "DOD Security: The New Look." *Government Executive*, I (October 1969), 44–46.

3497. "Sloppy Spies: The FBI Arrest of Three Soviet Agents." *Time*, CXI (June 5, 1978), 19–20.

3498. Smith, R. C. "The Wired Nation: Wiretaps." *Privacy Journal*, no. 9 (July 1975), 1+.

3499. Spindel, Bernard B. *The Ominous Ear.* New York: Award House, 1968. 268p.

3500. "Spying at White House Orders: When It Started and Why." *U.S. News and World Report*, LXXIV (June 11, 1973), 19–21.

3501. Sterling, James W., *et al. Protecting Dissent–Policing Disorder.* Gaithersburg, MD: Professional Standards Division, International Association of Chiefs of Police, 1974. 485p.

3502. Stern, Laurence. "A Sense of Deja Vu at CIA—Watergate Disclosures Raise Questions [About the Huston Plan]: Reprinted From the *Washington Post*, July 10, 1973." *Congressional Record*, CXIX (July 11, 1973), 23412–23413.

3503. Stokes, Dillard. "How to Insure Security in Government Service: Past Failures and Present Remedies." *Commentary*, XVII (January 1954), 25–36.

3504. Stout, Jared. "Keeping Tabs on Civilians: The Army Security Agency." *Nation*, CCXI (December 28, 1970), 681–683.

3505. Stout, Richard L. "Extracts From the Rockefeller CIA Report: Reprinted From the *Christian Science Monitor*, June 11, 1975." In: Grant S. McClellan, ed. *The Right to Privacy.* Reference Shelf, v. 48, no. 1. New York: H. W. Wilson, 1976. pp. 110–117.

3506. Szulc, Tad. "The Spy Among Us." *Penthouse*, VI (July 1975), 44+.

3507. Theoharis, Athan G. "Bureaucrats Above the Law: Double-Entry Intelligence Files." *Nation*, CCXXV (October 22, 1977), 393–397.

3508. _____ . "The Essentials of the Loyalty Program." In: Barton J. Bernstein, ed. *Politics and Policies of the Truman Administration.* Rev. ed. Chicago: Quadrangle Books, 1978. pp. 242–268.

3509. _____ . "The FBI's Stretching of Presidential Directives, 1936–1953." *Political Science Quarterly*, XCI (Winter 1977), 649–673.

3510. _____ . "From the Cold War to Watergate: National Security and Civil Liberties." *Intellect*, CIII (October 1974), 20–26.

3511. _____ . "The Quest For Absolute Security." In: *Seeds of Repression: Harry S. Truman and the Origins of McCarthyism.* Chicago: Quadrangle Books, 1974. pp. 98–123.

3512. _____ . "The Rhetoric of Politics: Foreign Policy, Internal Security, and Domestic Politics in the Truman Era, 1945–1950." In: Barton J. Bernstein, ed. *Politics and Policies of the Truman Administration.* Chicago: Quadrangle Books, 1970. pp. 196–241.

3513. _____ . *Spying on Americans: Political Surveillance From Hoover to the Huston Plan.* Philadelphia, PA: Temple University Press, 1978. 360p.

3514. Ungar, Sanford J. "Counterintelligence and Internal Security." In: *FBI: An Uncensored Look Behind the Walls.* Boston: Little, Brown, 1976. pp. 111–146.

3515. United States. Comptroller General. *FBI Domestic Intelligence Operations, Their Purpose and Scope: Issues That Need to Be Resolved.* Washington, D.C.: GPO, 1976. 48p.

3516. _____ . Congress. House. Committee on Government Operations. Subcommittee on Foreign Operations and Government Information. *Telephone Monitoring Practices by Federal Agencies: Hearings.* 93rd Cong., 2nd sess. Washington, D.C.: GPO, 1974. 293p.

3517. _____ . _____ . _____ . _____ . _____ . *The Use of Polygraphs and Similar Devices by Federal Agencies: Hearings.* 93rd Cong., 2nd sess. Washington, D.C.: GPO, 1974. 790p.

3518. _____ . _____ . _____ . _____ . _____ . *The Use of Polygraphs and Similar Devices by Federal Agencies: Report.* 94th Cong., 2nd sess. Washington, D.C.: GPO, 1976. 61p.

3519. _____ . _____ . _____ . _____ . Subcommittee on Government Information and Individual Rights. *The Interception of Nonverbal Communications by Federal Intelligence Agencies: Hearings.* 94th Cong., 1st and 2nd sess. Washington, D.C.: GPO, 1976. 344p.

3520. _____ . _____ . _____ . _____ . _____ . *Justice Department Treatment of Criminal Cases Involving CIA Personnel and Claims of National Security: Hearings.* 94th Cong., 1st sess. Washington, D.C.: GPO, 1975. 431p.

3521. _____ . _____ . _____ . _____ . _____ . *Notification to Victims of Improper Intelligence Agency Activities: Hearings.* 94th Cong., 2nd sess. Washington, D.C.: GPO, 1976. 506p.

3522. _____ . _____ . _____ . Committee on Internal Security. *Domestic Intelligence Operations For Internal Security Purposes: Hearings.* 93rd Cong., 2nd sess. Washington, D.C.: GPO, 1974. 590p.

3523. _____ . _____ . _____ . Committee on the Judiciary. Subcommittee on Courts, Civil Liberties, and the Administration of Justice. *Foreign Intelligence Surveillance Act: Hearings.* 95th Cong., 2nd sess. Washington, D.C.: GPO, 1978. 183p.

3524. _____ . _____ . _____ . _____ . Subcommittee on Civil and Constitutional Rights. *FBI Counterintelligence Programs: Hearings.* 93rd Cong., 2nd sess. Washington, D.C.: GPO, 1974. 47p.

3525. _____ . _____ . _____ . _____ . _____ . *Military Surveillance: Hearings.* 93rd Cong., 2nd sess. Washington, D.C.: GPO, 1974. 397p.

3526. _____ . _____ . _____ . _____ . _____ . *Military Surveillance of Civilian Politics: Report.* 93rd Cong., 1st sess. Washington, D.C.: GPO, 1973. 150p.

3527. _____ . _____ . _____ . _____ . _____ . *Political Intelligence in the Internal Revenue Service—The Special Service Staff: A Documentary Analysis.* 93rd Cong., 2nd sess. Washington, D.C.: GPO, 1974. 344p.

3528. _____ . _____ . _____ . _____ . _____ . *Surveillance Technology, 1976: Policy and Implications—An Analysis and Compendium of Materials—A Staff Report.* 94th Cong., 2nd sess. Washington, D.C.: GPO, 1976. 1,280p.

3529. _____ . _____ . _____ . _____ . _____ . *Wiretapping, Eavesdropping, and the Bill of Rights: Hearings.* 86th Cong., 1st sess. Washington, D.C.: GPO, 1959. 2,008p.

3530. _____ . _____ . _____ . _____ . _____ . *Wiretapping For National Security: Hearings.* 83rd Cong., 2nd sess. Washington, D.C.: GPO, 1954. 91p.

3531. _____ . _____ . _____ . _____ . Subcommittee on Criminal Laws and Procedures and on Constitutional Rights. *Electronic Surveillance For National Security Purposes: Joint Hearings.* 93rd Cong., 2nd sess. Washington, D.C.: GPO, 1974. 577p.

3532. _____ . _____ . _____ . _____ . _____ . *Foreign Intelligence Surveillance Act of 1976: Hearings.* 94th Cong., 2nd sess. Washington, D.C.: GPO, 1976. 144p.

3533. _____ . _____ . _____ . Select Committee on Intelligence. Subcommittee on Intelligence and the Rights of Americans. *Electronic Surveillance Within the United States For Foreign Intelligence Purposes: Hearings.* 94th Cong., 2nd sess. Washington, D.C.: GPO, 1976. 301p.

3534. _____ . _____ . Joint Committee on Internal Revenue Taxation. *Investigation of the Special Service Staff [1969–1973] of the Internal Revenue Service: Hearings.* 94th Cong., 1st sess. Washington, D.C.: GPO, 1975.

3535. _____ . _____ . Senate. Committee on Foreign Relations. *Dr. Kissinger's Role in Wiretapping: Hearings.* 93rd Cong., 2nd sess. Washington, D.C.: GPO, 1974. 409p.

3536. _____ . _____ . _____ . _____ . *Report on the Inquiry Concerning Dr. Kissinger's Role in Wiretapping, 1969–1971: Review and Findings.* 93rd Cong., 2nd sess. Washington, D.C.: GPO, 1974. 6p.

3537. _____ . _____ . _____ . _____ . *CIA Foreign and Domestic Activities: Hearings.* 94th Cong., 1st sess. Washington, D.C.: GPO, 1975. 39p.

3538. _____ . _____ . _____ . _____ . Subcommittee on Surveillance. *Warrantless Wiretapping and Electronic Surveillance: Report.* 94th Cong., 1st sess. Washington, D.C.: GPO, 1975. 11p.

3539. _____ . _____ . _____ . Committee on the District of Columbia. *Wiretapping in the District of Columbia: Report.* 81st Cong., 2nd sess. Washington, D.C.: GPO, 1951. 7p.

3540. _____ . _____ . _____ . Committee on the Judiciary. Subcommittee on Administrative Practices and Procedures. *Warrantless Wiretapping: Hearings.* 92nd Cong., 2nd sess. Washington, D.C.: GPO, 1973. 221p.

3541. _____ . _____ . _____ . _____ . _____ . _____ . 93rd Cong., 2nd sess. Washington, D.C.: GPO, 1974. 519p.

3542. _____ . _____ . _____ . _____ . Subcommittee on Constitutional Rights. *Army Surveillance of Civilians: A Documentary Analysis.* 92nd Cong., 2nd sess. Washington, D.C.: GPO, 1972. 97p.

3543. _____ . _____ . _____ . _____ . _____ . *Federal Data Banks, Computers, and the Bill of Rights: Hearings.* 92nd Cong., 1st sess. 2 pts. Washington, D.C.: GPO, 1972.

3544. _____ . _____ . _____ . _____ . _____ . *Surveillance: Hearings on the Matter of Wiretapping, Electronic Eavesdropping, and Other Surveillance.* 94th Cong., 1st sess. 2 pts. Washington, D.C.: GPO, 1975.

3545. _____ . _____ . _____ . _____ . _____ . *Wiretapping and Electronic Surveillance: Hearings.* 93rd Cong., 2nd sess. Washington, D.C.: GPO, 1974. 275p.

3546. _____ . _____ . _____ . _____ . Subcommittee to Investigate the Administration of the Internal Security Act and Other Internal Security Laws. *Interlocking Subversion in Government Departments: Hearings.* 83rd Cong., 1st sess. 30 pts. Washington, D.C.: GPO, 1953.

3547. _____ . _____ . _____ . _____ . Subcommittee to Investigate the Circumstances With Respect to the Disposition of the Charges of Espionage and the Possession of Documents Stolen From Secret Government Files. *Report.* 79th Cong., 2nd sess. Washington, D.C.: GPO, 1946. 16p.

3548. _____ . _____ . _____ . Committee on Post Office and Civil Service. Subcommittee on Postal Facilities, Mail, and Labor Management. *Postal Inspection Service's Monitoring and Control of Mail Surveillance and Mail Cover Programs: Hearings.* 94th Cong., 1st sess. Washington, D.C.: GPO, 1975. 238p.

3549. _____ . _____ . _____ . _____ . Subcommittee on Postal Operations. *Privacy in the Mail: Hearings.* 90th Cong., 2nd sess. Washington, D.C.: GPO, 1968. 33p.

3550. _____ . _____ . _____ . Committee on Ways and Means. Subcommittee on Oversight. *Internal Revenue Service Intelligence Operations: Hearings.* 94th Cong., 1st sess. Washington, D.C.: GPO, 1975. 100p.

3551. _____ . _____ . _____ . Select Committee on Intelligence. *U.S. Intelligence Agencies and Activities, Part V—Risks and Control of Foreign Intelligence: Hearings.* 94th Cong., 1st sess. Washington, D.C.: GPO, 1975. 468p.

3552. _____ . _____ . _____ . _____ . *U.S. Intelligence Agencies and Activities, Part III—Domestic Intelligence Programs: Hearings.* 94th Cong., 1st sess. Washington, D.C.: GPO, 1975. 175p.

3553. _____ . _____ . _____ . _____ . Subcommittee on Security and Disclosure. *National Security Secrets and the Administration of Justice: Report.* 95th Cong., 2nd sess. Washington, D.C.: GPO, 1978. 51p.

3554. _____ . _____ . _____ . Select Committee to Study Government Operations With Respect to Intelligence Activities. *Domestic Intelligence Programs.* 94th Cong., 1st sess. Washington, D.C.: GPO, 1976. 285p.

3555. _____ . _____ . _____ . _____ . *The Huston Plan.* 94th Cong., 1st sess. Washington, D.C.: GPO, 1976. 403p.

3556. _____ . _____ . _____ . _____ . *Intelligence Activities and the Rights of Americans.* 94th Cong., 2nd sess. Washington, D.C.: GPO, 1976. 396p.

3557. _____ . _____ . _____ . _____ . *Mail Opening.* 94th Cong., 1st sess. Washington, D.C.: GPO, 1976. 260p.

3558. _____ . Department of the Army. "Department of the Army Civil Disturbance Information Collection Plan." *Congressional Record,* CXVIII (March 3, 1971), E1401–E1411.

3559. _____ . Government Accounting Office. *FBI Domestic Intelligence Operations: An Uncertain Future.* Washington, D.C.: GPO, 1977. 95p.

3560. _____ . _____ . *Personal Security Investigations: Inconsistent Standards and Procedures.* Washington, D.C.: GPO, 1974. 18p.

3561. Watters, David L. "Microwave Eavesdropping." In: U.S. Congress. Senate. Select Committee on Intelligence. Subcommittee on Intelligence and the Rights of Americans. *Foreign Intelligence Surveillance Act of 1978: Hearings.* 95th Cong., 2nd sess. Washington, D.C.: GPO, 1978. pp. 148–178.

3562. Westin, Alan F. *Privacy and Freedom.* New York: Atheneum, 1967.

3563. Weyl, Nathaniel. *The Battle Against Disloyalty.* New York: Crowell, 1951. 378p.

3564. Wicker, Tom. "The Undeclared Witch-Hunt." *Harper's,* CCXXXIX (November 1969), 108–110.

3565. Wills, Gary. "Someone to Watch Over You." *New York Review of Books,* XXII (November 13, 1975), 20–22.

3566. Wise, David. *The American Police State: The Government Against the People.* New York: Random House, 1976. 437p.

3567. _____ . "The Kissinger Wiretaps." *New Times,* VII (October 29, 1976), 24+.

3568. _____ . *The Politics of Lying: Government Deception, Secrecy, and Power.* New York: Random House, 1973. 440p.

3569. Woodward, Bob. "Messages of Activists [Jane Fonda, Benjamin Spock] Intercepted [by NSA]: Reprinted from the *Washington Post,* October 13, 1975." *Congressional Record,* CXXI (October 28, 1975), 33900.

3570. Woolf, Leonard S. "Espionage, Security, and Liberty." *Political Quarterly,* XXVII (April 1956), 152–162.

3571. Wright, Richard O. "The Domestic Intelligence Mission." In: Richard O. Wright, ed. *Whose FBI?* LaSalle, IL: Open Court Publishers, 1974. pp. 92–96.

3572. _____ . "Internal Security Today." In: Richard O. Wright, ed. *Whose FBI?* LaSalle, IL: Open Court Publishers, 1974. pp. 173–219.

(3) THE ASSASSINATION OF PRESIDENT KENNEDY

3573. Bugge, Brian K. *The Mystique of Conspiracy: Oswald, Castro, and the CIA.* Staten Island, NY: 1978. 135p.

3574. Duncan, Susanna. "Oswald the Secret Agent." *New York Magazine,* XI (March 6, 1978), *passim.*

3575.   Eddowes, Michael. *The Oswald File.* New York: Clarkson N. Potter, 1977. 240p.

3576.   Epstein, Edward J. *Inquest: The Warren Commission and the Establishment of Truth.* New York: Viking Press, 1966. 224p.

3577.   _____ . *Legend: The Secret World of Lee Harvey Oswald.* New York: Reader's Digest Press; dist. by McGraw-Hill, 1978. 382p.

3578.   _____ . _____ . *Reader's Digest,* XII (March–April 1978), 82–92+, 153–164+.

3579.   Fensterwald, Bernard. *Coincidence or Conspiracy.* New York: Zebra Books, 1977. 210p.

3580.   Lane, Mark. "Was the CIA Involved in Dallas?" In: Howard Frazier, ed. *Uncloaking the CIA.* New York: Free Press, 1978. pp. 210–222.

3581.   Manchester, William R. *The Death of a President: November 20–25, 1963.* New York: Harper & Row, 1967. 710p.

3582.   O'Toole, George. *The Assassination Tapes.* New York: Penthouse Press, 1975. 265p.

3583.   Scott, Peter D., *et al. The Assassinations: Dallas and Beyond.* New York: Random House, 1976. 732p.

3584.   Snyder, Richard E. "The Soviet Sojourn of Citizen Oswald." *Washington Post Magazine,* (April 1, 1979), 28–35.

3585.   Szulc, Tad. "Death of JFK: CIA and FBI Failure to Report Anti-Castro Conspiracies to the Warren Commission." *New Republic,* CLXXIV (June 5, 1976), 6–8.

3586.   United States. Congress. House. Select Committee on Assassinations. *Investigations of the Assassination of President John F. Kennedy, Part IV: Hearings.* 95th Cong., 2nd sess. Washington, D.C.: GPO, 1978. 608p.

3587.   _____ . _____ . _____ . _____ . "Summary of Findings and Recommendations." In: Patricia A. O'Connor, ed. *Historic Documents of 1978.* Washington, D.C.: Congressional Quarterly, Inc., 1979. pp. 909–922.

3588.   _____ . Presidential Commission on the Assassination of President Kennedy. *Hearings and Report.* 26 vols. Washington, D.C.: GPO, 1964.

3589.   _____ . _____ . *Report of the Warren Commission.* New York: McGraw-Hill, 1964. 726p.

3590.   Vanbemmelen, J. M. "Did Lee Harvey Oswald Act Without Help?" *New York University Law Review,* XL (May 1965), 466–476.

(4) WATERGATE

3591.   "Animals in the Forest: The CIA's Watergate Tapes." *Time,* CIII (February 11, 1974), 26.

3592.   Baker, Howard H., Jr. "Some Foolish Mistakes: Report on the Relationship Between the CIA and the Watergate Break In." *Time,* CIV (July 15, 1974), 19.

3593.   Barker, Bernard and Eugenio R. Martinez. "Mission Impossible: The Watergate Burglers—Excerpts From Interviews." *Harpers,* CCXLIX (October 1974), 50–58.

3594.   Bernstein, Carl and Bob Woodward. *All the President's Men.* New York: Simon and Schuster, 1975. 382p.

3595.   _____ . *The Final Days.* New York: Simon and Schuster, 1976. 476p.

3596.   Buckley, William F., Jr. "Colson, Nixon, and the CIA." *National Review,* XXVII (August 2, 1974), 884–885.

3597.   "The Colson Saga: CIA." *National Review,* XXVI (July 19, 1974), 794+.

3598.   "Colson's Weird Scenario: Blaming the Watergate Break In on the CIA." *Time,* CIV (July 8, 1974), 16.

3599.   Congressional Quarterly, Inc. *Watergate: Chronology of a Crisis.* Washington, D.C.: 1975. 1,039p.

3600.   Copeland, Miles. "Unmentionable Uses of the CIA." *National Review,* XXV (September 14, 1973), 990–997.

3601.   Dean, John, III. *Blind Ambition: The White House Years.* New York: Simon and Schuster, 1976. 415p.

3602.   _____ . "Interview." *Playboy,* XXII (January 1975), 65+.

3603.   Ehrlichman, John. "Erlichman on the CIA." *Congressional Quarterly Weekly Report,* XXXI (June 2, 1973), 1351–1357.

3604.   Haldeman, H. R. *The Ends of Power.* New York: Times Books, 1977. 326p.

3605.   Hempstead, Smith. "New Bay of Pigs For CIA?" *Congressional Record,* CXIX (May 9, 1973), 15085.

3606.   Hersh, Seymour M. "[Gen. Robert E.] Cushman Okayed CIA Aid to Hunt: Reprinted From the *New York Times,* May 9, 1973." *Congressional Record,* CXIX (May 9, 1973), 15084–15085.

3607.   Jaworski, Leon. *The Right and the Power: The Prosecution of Watergate.* New York: Reader's Digest Press; dist. by McGraw-Hill, 1976. 305p.

3608.   "Kid Gloves: The Watergate Testimony of William E. Colby." *New Republic,* CLXIX (July 21, 1973), 9–10.

3609.   Knappman, Edward, *et al.,* eds. *Watergate and the White House.* 3 vols. New York: Facts on File, Inc., 1973–1974.

3610.   Loory, Stuart H. "CIA's Man [Alexander Butterfield] in the White House." *Columbia Journalism Review,* XIV (September 1975), 11–14.

3611.   Lukas, John A. *Nightmare: The Underside of the Nixon Years.* New York: Viking Press, 1976. 626p.

3612.   McCord, James W., Jr. "Watergate and the Intelligence Community." *Armed Forces Journal International,* CX (August 1973), 57–58.

3613.   Magruder, Jebb S. *An American Life: One Man's Road to Watergate.* New York: Atheneum, 1974. 338p.

3614.   _____ . *From Power to Peace.* Waco, TX: World Books, 1978. 224p.

3615.   _____ . "Means: Watergate Reflections." *New York Times Magazine,* (May 20, 1974), 103–104+.

3616.   Mankiewicz, Frank. *U.S. vs. Richard M. Nixon: The Final Crisis.* New York: Quadrangle Books, 1975. 276p.

3617.   Martinez, Eugenio R., jt. author. *See* Barker, Bernard (3593).

3618.   *New York Times* Staff. *The Watergate Hearings.* New York: Bantam Books, 1973. 886p.

3619.   _____ . *The White House Transcripts.* New York: Bantam Books, 1973. 877p.

3620.   Osborne, John. "Nixon's Devils." *New Republic,* CLXXV (August 7, 1976), 11–12.

3621.   Pincus, William. "The Cold War Brought Home." *New Republic,* CLXVIII (June 23, 1973), 12–15.

3622. _____ . "Getting to the Bottom of the CIA Coverup: The Break In at the Office of Daniel Ellsberg's Psychiatrist." *New Republic,* CLXXI (September 28, 1974), 11–13.

3623. _____ . "How the FBI and CIA Played the Game." *New Republic,* CLXVIII (June 16, 1973), 19–23.

3624. Prouty, L. Fletcher. "An Inside Look: Watergate and the World of the CIA." *Ramparts,* XII (October 1973), 21–23.

3625. Safire, William. *Before the Fall: An Inside View of the Pre-Watergate White House.* Garden City, NY: Doubleday, 1975. 704p.

3626. _____ . "Exposing FBI Surveillance." *Current,* CXXXV (October 1973), 33–36.

3627. Sherrill, Robert. "Zealots For Nixon: Gaudy Night at the Watergate." *Nation,* CCXV (September 25, 1972), 230–234.

3628. Sirica, John J. *To Set the Record Straight.* New York: W. W. Norton, 1979. 394p.

3629. "Spy in the White House?: The Question of Alexander Butterfield's Contact With the CIA." *Time,* CVI (July 21, 1975), 14.

3630. Szulc, Tad. "CIA and the Plumbers." *New Republic,* CLXIX (December 29, 1973), 19–21.

3631. _____ . "How Nixon Used the CIA." *New York Magazine,* VIII (January 20, 1975), 28+.

3632. Thompson, Fred D. *At That Point in Time: The Inside Story of the Senate Watergate Committee.* New York: Quadrangle Books, 1975. 275p.

3633. United States. Congress. House. Committee on Armed Services. Special Subcommittee on Intelligence. *Inquiry Into the Alleged Involvement of the Central Intelligence Agency in the Watergate and Ellsberg Matters: Hearings.* 94th Cong., 1st sess. Washington, D.C.: GPO, 1975. 1,131p.

3634. _____ . _____ . _____ . _____ . _____ . _____ :   *Report.* 94th Cong., 1st sess. Washington, D.C.: GPO, 1975. 23p.

3635. _____ . _____ . _____ . Committee on the Judiciary. *Impeachment of Richard M. Nixon, President of the United States* [Article I]. 93rd Cong., 2nd sess. Washington, D.C.: GPO, 1974. 528p.

3636. _____ . _____ . Senate. Select Committee on Presidential Campaign Activities. *Presidential Campaign Activities of 1972: Hearings.* 93rd Cong., 1st sess. 26 pts. Washington, D.C.: GPO, 1973.

3637. _____ . _____ . _____ . *Draft of Final Report.* 93rd Cong., 2nd sess. 3 pts. Washington, D.C.: GPO, 1974.

3638. _____ . _____ . _____ . *The Senate Watergate Report: The Final Report of the Ervin Committee.* 2 vols. New York: Dell, 1976.

3639. "What the CIA Knew." *Newsweek,* LXXXIV (July 15, 1974), 29.

3640. White, Theodore H. *Breach of Faith: The Fall of Richard Nixon.* New York: Atheneum, 1975. 373p.

3641. Winter, Robert K., Jr. *Watergate and the Law.* Washington, D.C.: American Enterprise Institute for Public Policy Research, 1974. 85p.

3642. Woodward, Bob, jt. author. *See* Bernstein, Carl (3594).

IV/Some Personalities of the Secret Wars

Introduction

This section brings together in a single unit many useful and interesting biographies and autobiographies published since 1945. Section A is devoted to collective biography and Section B is an alphabetically-arranged guide to specific personalities.

A word of caution. Many biographies, especially those of defectors or agents who were exposed, were penned with specific national disinformation or propaganda goals in mind. The same caution applies to autobiographies with even more emphasis. For example, see the autobiographies of Harold "Kim" Philby and Oleg Penkovskiy, and the published testimony of foreign agents interviewed by the Senate Internal Security Subcommittee.

A. General Biographies

Introduction

This subsection cites collected biographies devoted to personnel involved in intelligence and covert operations since the end of World War II. A few of the titles cited here are further analyzed in Subsection B, Specific Personalities.

3643. *Army Times,* Editors of. *Modern American Secret Agents.* New York: Dodd, Mead, 1966. 143p.

3644. Bakeless, John. *Turncoats, Traitors, and Heroes.* Philadelphia: Lippincott, 1959. 406p.

3645. Barron, John. "Soviet Citizens Engaged in Clandestine Operations Abroad." In: *KGB: The Secret Work of Soviet Secret Agents.* New York: Reader's Digest Press; dist. by E. P. Dutton, 1973. pp. 379–415.

3646. Coffin, Tristram. "America Has Ace Spies, Too." *Coronet,* XXX (August 1951), 37–41.

3647. Cookridge, E. H. pseud. *See* Spiro, Edward (3676).

3648. Denniston, Elinor. *Famous American Spies.* By Rae Foley, pseud. New York: Dodd, Mead, 1962. 158p.

3649. De Toledano, Ralph. *Spies, Dupes, and Diplomats.* Rev. ed. New Rochelle, NY: Arlington House, 1967. 258p.

3650. Fairfield, Cecily I. *The New Meaning of Treason.* By Rebecca West, pseud. New York: Viking Press, 1964. 374p.

3651. Foley, Rae, pseud. *See* Denniston, Elinor (3648).

3652. Franklin, Charles. *The Great Spies.* New York: Hart, 1967. 272p.

3653. Gribble, Leonard R. *Stories of Famous Spies.* London: Barker, 1964. 208p.

3654. Hinchley, Vernon. *Spies Who Never Were.* New York: Dodd, Mead, 1965. 211p.

3655. Hoehling, Adolph A. *Women Who Spied.* New York: Dodd, Mead, 1967. 204p.

3656. Hutton, Joseph B. *Women in Espionage.* New York: Macmillan, 1972. 192p.

3657.   Institut zur Erforschung der U.S.S.R., Munich. *Party and Government Officials of the Soviet Union, 1917–1967.* Metuchen, NJ: The Scarecrow Press, 1969. 214p.

3658.   _____. *The Soviet Diplomatic Corps, 1917–1967.* Metuchen, NJ: The Scarecrow Press, 1970. 240p.

3659.   _____. *Who Was Who in the U.S.S.R.* Metuchen, NJ: The Scarecrow Press, 1972. 687p.

3660.   *The International Who's Who.* London: Europa Publications, 1945–. v. 10–.

3661.   Lewytzkyj, Borys and Juliusz Stroynowski, eds. *Who's Who in the Socialist Countries.* New York: K. G. Sauer, 1978. 1,200p.

3662.   Maclean, Fitzroy. *Take Nine Spies.* New York: Atheneum, 1978. 341p.

3663.   Mauerstr, Julius M. *Who's Who in CIA: A Biographical Reference Work on 3,000 Officers of the Civil and Military Branches of the Secret Service of the U.S.A. in 120 Countries.* Translated From the German. East Berlin: German Democratic Republic, 1968. 605p.

3664.   Moorehead, Alan. *The Traitors.* Rev. ed. New York: Harper's, 1963. 236p.

3665.   *New York Times,* Editors of. *Obituary Index, 1858–1968.* New York: New York Times, Inc., 1970. 1,136p.

3666.   Newman, Joseph. *Famous Soviet Spies: The Kremlin's Secret Weapon.* Washington, D.C.: Books by *U.S. News and World Report,* 1976. 223p.

3667.   Nolen, Barbara, ed. *Spies, Spies, Spies.* New York: Watts, 1965. 250p.

3668.   Orsag, Carol. "An International Array of Spies." In: David Wallechinsky and Irving Wallace. *The Peoples' Almanac.* Garden City, NY: Doubleday, 1975. pp. 646–650.

3669.   Packer, Herbert. *Ex-Communist Witness.* Stanford, CA: Stanford University Press, 1962. 279p.

3670.   Pinto, Oreste. "The Secrets of Super Spies." *Science Digest,* XXXV (May 1954), 57–62.

3671.   Singer, Kurt D. *Communist Agents in America, 1947: A Who's Who of American Communists.* New York: News Background, 1947. 20p.

3672.   _____. *The Men in the Trojan Horse.* Boston: Beacon Press, 1953. 258p.

3673. _____. *Spies For Democracy.* Minneapolis: Denison, 1960. 272p.

3674. _____. *The World's 30 Greatest Women Spies.* New York: Holt, 1951. 318p.

3675. Sparrow, Gerald. *The Great Spies.* London: Long, 1969. 183p.

3676. Spiro, Edward. *Sisters of Delilah.* By E. H. Cookridge, pseud. London: Oldbourne Press, 1959. 224p.

3677. Steele, Richard. "Swapping Spies For Dissidents." *Newsweek,* XCIII (May 7, 1979), 49.

3678. Strong, Kenneth W. D. *Men of Intelligence: A Study of the Roles and Decisions of Chiefs of Intelligence From World War I to the Present Day.* London: Cassell, 1970. 183p.

3679. Stroynowski, Juliusz, jt. editor. *See* Lewytzkyj, Borys (3661).

3680. "These Men Run the CIA." *Esquire,* LXV (May 1966), 84–85+.

3681. *The Times,* Editors of. *Obituaries From the Times, 1961–1970.* Reading, Berkshire, England: Newspaper Archive Developments, 1976. 952p.

3682. United States. Department of State. *Biographic Register.* Washington, D.C.: GPO, 1945–.

3683. West, Rebecca, pseud. *See* Fairfield, Cecily I. (3650).

3684. Weyl, Nathaniel. *Treason: The Story of Disloyalty and Betrayal in American History.* Washington, D.C.: Public Affairs Press, 1950. 491p.

3685. "Who Spies and Why." *Senior Scholastic,* XCVI (February 9, 1970), 4–9.

3686. Wighton, Charles. *The World's Greatest Spies: True-Life Dramas of Outstanding Secret Agents.* New York: Taplinger, 1966. 319p.

3687. Wilkinson, Burke, comp. *Cry Sabotage!* Scarsdale, NY: Bradbury Press, 1972. 265p.

3688. _____. *Cry Spy!* Scarsdale, NY: Bradbury Press, 1969. 271p.

3689. Zahn, Gordon C. "007's of Real Life: The Non-Fiction List." *Commonweal,* (December 8, 1972), 229–232.

B. Specific Personalities

Introduction

This sub-section cites some interesting individuals who have participated in espionage, treason, disinformation, covert operations, and other aspects of the secret war since 1945. Most of these people were agents (caught or defected), some were traitors or fools, several were military personnel or diplomats involved in intelligence operations, and a number were (are) directors of national intelligence organizations. The list of references is arranged alphabetically by surname with cross references between some aliases.

To facilitate the use of this part, the following national breakdown is provided.

U.S.

Andrew Adams
Philip Agee
Donald A. Allen
Ulius L.'Amoss
James J. Angleton
Walter Bedell-Smith
Elizabeth Bentley
Robert R. Bowie
Christopher J. Boyce
V. L. Bullough
George Bush
John W. Butenko
Whittaker Chambers
Ray Cline
William E. Colby
Peer De Silva
Martha E. Dodd
William J. Donovan
John Downey
Allen Dulles
Jack Dunlap
Noel Field
Harry Gold
Sidney Gottlieb
John F. Hasey
Richard Helms
Frank Hirt
Alger Hiss
J. Edgar Hoover
John Humnik
Ronald Humphrey
E. Howard Hunt
Sam Jaffe

Robert L. Johnson
William P. Kampiles
Joseph D. Kauffman
E. Henry Knocke
Irving Kristol
William L. Langer
Andrew D. Lee
Flora Lewis
Joseph A. McChristian
John McCone
Marion Miller
James Mintkenbaugh
Bernon Mitchell/William Martin
Boris Morros
Frank J. Mrvka
Bruce T. Odell
Frank R. Olson
Robert Oppenheimer
Otto F. Otepka
Saul K. Padover
John A. Paisley
Joseph S. Peterson, Jr.
Martha Peterson
Herbert A. Philbrick
David A. Phillips
Francis Gary Powers
William F. Rayburn
Kermit Roosevelt
Julius and Ethel Rosenberg
Michael Selzer
Joseph B. Smith
Morton Sobell
Robert Soblen
Frank Snepp
Theodore Sorensen

Robert G. Thompson
Stansfield Turner
Vernon K. Walters
Richard S. Welch
Harry D. White

Britain

David J. Bingham
George Blake
Elizabeth P. Brousse
Guy Burgess/Donald Maclean
Lionel K. Crabbe
Kenneth J. Lennon
Keith and Kenneth Littlejohn
Banda Macleod
Maurice Oldfield
Harold "Kim" Philby
John D. Profumo
Reginald C. Thomas
William Vassall
Stephen Ward
George Watt
Grenville Wynne

Bulgaria

Ivan A. H. Georgiev

Canada

Sam Carr
John K. Starnes
Emma Woikin

China

China Pi-hwei
Kim Suim
Li Tsung-jen
Hung Wang
Eva Wu

Cuba

Mirtha A. Borras y Almanza
Orlando Castro-Hidalgo

Czechoslovakia

Lawrence Britt
Alfred Frenzel
Josep Frolik
Lazlo Szabo
Frantisek Tisler

France

Ben Barka
Phillippe T. De Vosjoli
Jean Dides
René Duchez
Magda Fontanges
Georges Pacques

Germany

Herbert Boeckenhaupt
Reinhard Gehlen
Guenther Guillaume
Erich Helbig
Uwe Holst
Otto John
Ursel Lorenzen
Lothar and Renate Lutze
Hermann Luedke
Richard Meier
Günther Nollau
Helga Pohl-Wennenmacher
Hannsheinz Porst
Hans K. Ronblom
Irmgard M. Schmidt
Martha Schneider
Horst Schwirkman
Rupert Sigl
Werner Stillers
Jurgen Wiegel

Israel

Eli Cohen
Avri El-Ad
Alfred Frauenknecht
Iser Harel
Wolfgang Lotz
Aharon Yariv

Italy

Francisco Constamtini
Georgio Rinaldi

Korea

Sang K. Kim
Kim H. Wook

Norway

Gunvor G. Haavik

Poland

Michael Golemewski
Izyador Modelski
Pawel Monat
Jerzy Sosnowski
Alexander Steele

Rhodesia

John H. P. Brumer

USSR

Rodolf Abel
K. M. Alexeev
Nikolai Artamonov (N. Shadrin)
Lavrenty P. Beria
Dmitri Buligin
Petr S. Deriabin
Anatoli Dolnytsin
Anatoly Filatov
Klaus Fuchs
Igor Gouzenko
Anatoli Granovsky

Petr G. Gugorenko
George Karlin
Alexsandr Kasnakheyev
Nikolai E. Khokhlov
Urii Krotkov
Mikhail M. Lebedev
Yuri Loginov
Konon T. Molody (G. Lonsdale)
Alexei Myagkov
Yuri I. Nosenko
Alexander Orlov
Oleg Penkovskiy
Vladimir M. Petrov
Yuri A. Rastvorov
A. I. Romanov
Yevgeny Y. Runge
Vladimir N. Sarkharov
Ivan A. Serov
Arhady Shevchenko
Bogdan N. Stasinskii
Vasilii V. Tarasov

Sweden

Ernest H. Andersson
Stig Wennerstrom

Switzerland

Jean L. Jeanmarie

Syria

Farhan Attassi

Turkey

Nahit Imre

Rudolf Abel

3690. "Abel For Powers." *Time,* LXXIX (February 16, 1962), 15–16.

3691. "American Example." *Newsweek,* LXIII (March 30, 1964), 75–76.

3692. "Artist in Brooklyn." *Time,* LXX (August 19, 1957), 13–14.

3693.   Bernikow, Louise. *Abel.* New York: Trident Press, 1970. 347p.

3694.   "Big Spy, A Bigger Game." *Newsweek,* L (August 19, 1957), 21–23.

3695.   Donovan, James B. *Strangers on a Bridge: The Case of Col. Abel.* New York: Atheneum, 1964. 432p.

3696.   Franklin, Charles. "Rudolf Abel." In: *Great Spies.* London: Hart, 1967. pp. 207–210.

3697.   "Freedom Bridge." *Newsweek,* LIX (February 19, 1962), 19–21.

3698.   Gibney, Frank. "Intimate Portrait of a Russian Spymaster." *Life,* XLIII (November 17, 1957), 122–130.

3699.   "The Great Spy Swap: An Album of Intrigue." *Life,* LII (February 16, 1962), 30–36.

3700.   "Guilty as Charged." *Newsweek,* L (November 4, 1957), 32+.

3701.   Hoover, J. Edgar. "The Case of the Faceless Spy." *Reader's Digest,* LXXVIII (January 1961), 61–64.

3702.   Hutton, J. Bernard. *The Traitor Trade.* New York: J. Obolensky, 1963. 223p.

3703.   Lindeman, Bard. "He [James B. Donovan] Defended a Soviet Spy." *Coronet,* XLVIII (October 1960), 46–51.

3704.   Morgan, Ted. "Rudolf Abel." By Sanche de Gramont, pseud. In: Burke Wilkinson, ed. *Cry Spy.* Scarsdale, NY: Bradbury Press, 1969. pp. 205–224.

3705.   "The Rise and Ruin of a Successful Spy." *Life,* XLIII (August 19, 1957), 18–23.

3706.   Wighton, Charles. "Rudolf Abel." In: *World's Greatest Spies.* New York: Taplinger, 1965. pp. 299–313.

3707.   Wittenberg, Ernest. "The Thrifty Spy on the Sixth Avenue El." *American Heritage,* XVII (January 1965), 60–64, 100–101.

Andrew Adams

3708.   "Haiti and the CIA: The Case of Andrew Adams." *Nation,* CC (January 11, 1965), 22–23.

Philip Agee

3709.   Agee, Philip. "Interview." *Playboy,* XXII (August 1975), 49+.

3710. _____ . "Why I Split the CIA and Spilled the Beans." *Esquire,* LXXXIII (June 1975), 128–130.

3711. "Dirty Work." *Time,* CXII (October 2, 1978), 32+.

3712. Evans, Rowland and Robert Novak. "Philip Agee—CIA's First Defector: Reprinted From the *Boston Globe,* March 19, 1977." In: U.S. Congress. House. Permanent Select Committee on Intelligence. Subcommittee on Oversight. *The CIA and the Media: Hearings.* 95th Cong., 1st and 2nd sess. Washington, D.C.: GPO, 1978. p. 360.

3713. Halperin, Morton H. "Led Astray by the CIA." *New Republic,* CLXXII (June 28, 1975), 8–11.

3714. Jones, Jereme. "Philip Agee: A Spy Who Quit Unmasks the CIA He Served." *People,* III (February 3, 1975), 23–25.

3715. Latham, Aaron. "A Defection in the Family." *New York Magazine,* VIII (August 11, 1975), 8–10.

3716. Nossiter, Bernard. "Outcasts of the Island." *New York Review of Books,* XXIV (April 14, 1977), 31+.

3716a. "Philip Agee." *People,* VII (February 7, 1977), 26–31.

K. M. Alexeev

3717. Alexeev, K. M. "How We Duped Our American Friends." *Saturday Evening Post,* CCXXI (July 10, 1948), 30+.

3718. _____ . "Why I Deserted the Soviet." *Saturday Evening Post,* CCXX (June 26, 1948), 18–19+.

Donald A. Allen

3719. "A Young Reporter's Decision to Join CIA Led to Strain, Anger, and Regret." *New York Times Biographical Service,* VIII (December 1977), 1583.

Ulius L. Amoss

3720. "Cloak, Dagger, and $5,000." *Newsweek,* XLII (October 5, 1953), 21–23.

3721. Klaw, S. "International Private Eye: The Adventures of Colonel Amoss." *Reporter,* X (February 2, 1954), 27–31.

3722. Kobler, J. "He Runs a Private OSS." *Saturday Evening Post,* CCXXVII (May 21, 1955), 31+.

Ernest H. Andersson

3723. "Judas, j.g." *Time,* LVIII (November 12, 1951), 31–32.

3724. "Red Traitor." *Newsweek*, XXXVIII (November 12, 1951), 50–51.

James J. Angleton

3725. "Angleton: The Quiet American." *Newsweek*, LXXXV (January 6, 1975), 11.

3726. Hersh, Seymour M. "The Angleton Story." *New York Times Biographical Service*, IX (June 1978), 688–694.

3727. Latham, Aaron. "Politics and the CIA: Was Angleton Spooked by State?" *New York Magazine*, VIII (March 10, 1975), 32+.

3728. Murphy, Charles J. V. "The Making of a Master Spy: James J. Angleton, Chief of Counterintelligence." *Time*, CV (February 24, 1975), 18–19.

3729. "New CIA Furor." *Newsweek*, LXXXV (January 6, 1975), 10+.

3730. "The Spy Whom Came Into the Heat." *Time*, CV (January 6, 1975), 45.

Nikolai Artamonov

3731. "Double Trouble." *Time*, CXI (May 22, 1978), 29.

3732. "Espionage." *Time*, CX (July 25, 1977), 38.

3733. Szulc, Tad. "The [Nicholas] Shadrin Affair: A Double Agent Double-Crossed." *New York Magazine*, XI (May 8, 1978), 42–48.

Farhan Attassi

3734. "The Man From SKUNK: The Case of Syrian-Born Farhan Attassi." *Time*, LXXXV (February 26, 1965), 35.

Povi Bang-Jensen

3735. United States. Congress. Senate. Committee on the Judiciary. Subcommittee to Investigate the Administration of the Internal Security Act and Other Internal Security Laws. *The Bang-Jensen Case: Report.* 87th Cong., 1st sess. Washington, D.C.: GPO, 1961. 120p.

Ben Barka

3736. "The Ben Barka Scandal and Other Cloak-and-Dagger Affairs." *Atlantic*, CCXVII (April 1966), 30+.

3737. "Diminished Fifth: L'Affaire Ben Barka Erupts Into Scandal." *Newsweek*, LXVII (January 31, 1966), 44+.

3738. "Enter the CIA: The Ben Barka Affair." *Newsweek,* LXVII (February 7, 1966), 32+.

3739. "L'Affaire Ben Barka." *Time,* LXXXVII (January 28, 1966), 33.

3740. Sterling, Claire. "The Ben Barka Affair." *Reporter,* XXXIV (March 10, 1966), 22–28.

3741. Werth, Alexander. "Ben Barka is Dead: Charges Against the CIA." *Nation,* CCII (March 28, 1966), 350–352.

3742. _____ . "DeGaulle and L'Affaire: The Ben Barka Scandal." *Nation,* CCII (February 21, 1966), 200–204.

Walter Bedell-Smith

3743. Laurence, William H. "Bedell is Back on the Eisenhower Team." *New York Times Magazine,* (March 1, 1953), 11+.

Elizabeth Bentley

3744. Alsop, Joseph. "Miss Bentley's Bondage." *Commonweal,* LV (November 9, 1951), 120–122.

3745. Bentley, Elizabeth. *"Out of Bondage: The Story of Elizabeth Bentley.* New York: Devin-Adair, 1951. 311p.

3746. "The Case of Mary and the Spy Ring Shrinks to the Case Against the Reds." *Newsweek,* XXXII (August 2, 1948), 20+.

3747. "Spy Story (Unproven)." *Newsweek,* XXXII (August 9, 1948), 19–20.

3748. Stripling, Robert E. "Elizabeth Bentley." In: *Red Plot Against America.* New York: Bell Publishing Co., 1949. pp. 89–94.

Lavrenty P. Beria

3749. "Behind the Beria Affair." *U.N.World,* VII (August 1953), 4–5.

3750. "The Fight Inside Russia." *U.S. News and World Report,* XXXV (July 17, 1953), 15–18.

3751. Khokhlov, Nikolai E. "Executioners' Shots Reveal New Struggle Inside the Kremlin: An Interview." *U.S. News and World Report,* XXXVIII (January 21, 1955), 42–47.

3752. Liebling, A. J. "Wayward Press: The Arrest of Beria." *New Yorker,* XXIX (August 1, 1953), 46–53.

3753. "Mr. Dulles Thinks Twice About the Meaning of Beria's Downfall." *Nation,* CLXXVII (July 25, 1953), 62–64.

3754. Orlov, Alexander. "The Beria I Knew." *Life*, XXXV (July 20, 1953), 33+.

3755. "The Ouster of Lavrenty P. Beria: The Committee's Communique, the Presidium's Communique, and Part of the *Pravda* Editorial of July 10." *Current History*, XXV (August 1953), 122–124.

3756. "The Purge of the Purger." *Time*, LXII (July 20, 1953), 21–24.

3757. Salisbury, Harrison E. "Russia Re-Viewed." *Reader's Digest*, LXV (December 1954), 146–149.

3758. Wittlin, Thaddeus. *Commissar: The Life and Death of Lavrenty Pavlovich Beria*. New York: Macmillan, 1972. 566p.

David J. Bingham

3759. "Henpecked Spy: The Case of David J. Bingham in England." *Time*, XCIX (March 27, 1972), 52+.

George Blake

3760. "The Blake Case: Spying in Great Britain." *America*, CV (May 27, 1961), 359–360.

3761. Bourke, Sean. *The Springing of George Blake*. New York: Viking Press, 1970. 379p.

3762. "End of a Spy." *Newsweek*, LVII (May 15, 1961), 52–53.

3763. "Escape Into the Cold." *Newsweek*, LXVIII (November 7, 1966), 52–54.

3764. Franklin, Charles. "George Blake." In: *Great Spies*. London: Hart, 1967. pp. 222–227.

3765. Mok, Michael. "The Irish 'Who' in a British Whodunit." *Life*, LXVI (January 24, 1969), 59–63.

3766. "A Question of Identity." *Time*, LXXXVIII (November 4, 1966), 38+.

3767. Spiro, Edward. *The Many Sides of George Blake, Esq.* By E. H. Cookridge, pseud. New York: Vortex Press, 1970. 250p.

3768. _____. *Shadow of a Spy: The Complete Dossier on George Blake*. By E. H. Cookridge, pseud. London: Frewin, 1967. 254p.

3769. "Spy Escapes From Wormwood Scrubs." *Illustrated London News*, CCXLIX (October 29, 1966), 10.

Herbert Boeckenhaupt

3770. "Sergeant's Revenge: The Arrest of Herbert Boeckenhaupt." *Newsweek,* LXVIII (November 14, 1966), 37–38.

Mirtha M. Borras Y Almanza

3771. St. George, Andrew. "Girl Spy Against Castro." *Look,* XXVIII (December 29, 1964), 60–65.

Robert R. Bowie

3772. *Facts on File,* Editors of. "Robert Richardson Bowie." In: their *Political Profiles: The Eisenhower Years.* New York, 1977. pp. 56–57.

3773. Morris, Roger. "Deputies are Forever." *New Republic,* CLXXVI (April 23, 1977), 15–17.

Christopher Boyce

3774. Lindsey, Robert. "To Be Young, Rich—and a Spy." *New York Times Magazine,* (May 22, 1977), 18+.

3775. Randall, Kenneth. "The Hush-Hush Controversy." *Far Eastern Economic Review,* XCVI (May 20, 1977), 30+.

3776. "Stealing the Company Store." *Time,* CIX (May 9, 1977), 19.

3777. Steele, Richard. "The Pyramider Spy Case." *Newsweek,* LXXXIX (April 18, 1977), 29.

Lawrence Britt

3778. United States. Congress. Senate. Committee on the Judiciary. Subcommittee to Investigate the Administration of the Internal Security Act and Other Internal Security Laws. *Testimony of* [Czech Agent] *Lawrence Britt: Hearings.* 92nd Cong., 1st sess. Washington, D.C.: GPO, 1971. 19p.

Elizabeth P. Brousse

3779. "The Blond Bond." *Time,* LXXXII (December 20, 1963), 17–18.

John H. P. Brumer

3780. Christie, Roy. *For the President's Eyes Only: The Story of* [Rhodesian] *John Brumer, Agent Extraordinary.* London: Hugh Keartland Publications, 1971. 183p.

Dmitri Buligin

3781. Buligin, Dmitri. "I Was a Free Russian." *American Mercury,* LXV (August 1947), 163–171.

3782. _____ . "Life of a Soviet Professor." *American Mercury,* LXVI (March 1948), 328–336.

V. L. Bullough

3783. Bullough, V. L. "How I Became a Security Risk." *Nation,* CCXXII (February 7, 1976), 140–142.

Guy Burgess and Donald Maclean

3784. "Britain Explains Burgess-Maclean Flight: Text of White Paper." *U.S. News and World Report,* XXXIX (September 30, 1955), 76–79.

3785. "British Officials Criticized in Burgess-Maclean Case: Editorial From *The Times* of London." *U.S. News and World Report,* XXXIX (October 7, 1955), 130–131.

3786. Connolly, Cyril. *The Missing Diplomats.* London: Queen Anne Press, 1952. 49p.

3787. Driberg, Tom. *Guy Burgess: A Portrait With Background.* London: Weidenfeld and Nicolson, 1956. 123p.

3788. "Five Minute Press Conference Ends a Five Year Mystery: Text of Discussion in Parliament and Summary of Editorial Comment in Britain." *U.S. News and World Report,* XL (February 24, 1956), 32–36+.

3789. Flugel, Edna R. "The Burgess-Maclean Case." *American Mercury,* LXXXIV (February-April 1957), 7–13, 127–134, 69–77.

3790. "The Great Spy Scandal." *U.S. News and World Report,* XL (February 17, 1956), 120–167.

3791. Hamilton, Gerald. "Guy Burgess as I Knew Him." *Spectator,* XCV (November 4, 1955), 578+.

3792. Hoare, Geoffrey. *The Missing Macleans.* New York: Viking Press, 1955. 247p.

3793. "How Two Spies Cost the U.S. a [Korean] War." *U.S. News and World Report,* XXXIX (September 30, 1955), 21–24.

3794. Hughes, Richard. "How I Broke the Burgess-Maclean Case: Excerpts From the *Sunday Times,* London." *U.S. News and World Report,* XL (March 2, 1956), 28–29.

3795. Maclean, Fitzroy. "Guy Burgess and Donald Maclean." In: *Take Nine Spies.* New York: Atheneum, 1978. pp. 222–277.

3796. "The Missing Spies." *Time,* LXVI (October 3, 1955), 23–24.

3797. "More Light on the Missing Diplomats: Excerpts From the Debate in the House of Commons, November 7, 1955." *U.S. News and World Report,* XXXIX (November 18, 1955), 158–167.

3798. Petrov, Vladimir M. "Mystery of the Missing Diplomats Solved." *U.S. News and World Report,* XXXIX (September 23, 1955), 21–27.

3799. Purdy, Anthony and Douglas Sutherland. *Burgess and Maclean.* Garden City, NY: Doubleday, 1963. 182p.

3800. Roth, Andrew G. "The Burgess-Maclean Case." *Nation,* CLXXXI (October 15, 1955), 318–320.

3801. "Traitors on Display." *Newsweek,* XLVII (February 20, 1956), 43–44.

George Bush

3802. Evans, Rowland and Robert Novak. "Overlooked Political Realities: Reprinted From the *Washington Post,* November 12, 1975." *Congressional Record,* CXXI (November 13, 1975), 36439.

3803. United States. Congress. Senate. Committee on Armed Services. *Nomination of George Bush to be Director of Central Intelligence: Hearings.* 94th Cong., 1st sess. Washington, D.C.: GPO, 1975. 94p.

3804. Will, George F. "George Bush, Political Ambitions: Reprinted From the *Washington Post,* November 12, 1975." *Congressional Record,* CXXI (November 13, 1975), 36438–36439.

John W. Butenko

3805. "The Quiet Man." *Newsweek,* LXII (November 11, 1963), 44+.

Sam Carr

3806. "What Made [Canadian Spy] Sam Run?" *Time,* LIII (February 7, 1949), 30–31.

Orlando Castro-Hidalgo

3807. Castro-Hidalgo, Orlando. *Spy For Fidel.* Translated From the Spanish. Miami, FL: E. A. Seemann, 1971. 110p.

3808. United States. Congress. Senate. Committee on the Judiciary. Subcommittee to Investigate the Administration of the Internal Security Act and Other Internal Security Laws. *Communist Threat to the United States Through the Caribbean: Hearings and Testimony of Orlando Castro-Hidalgo.* 91st Cong., 1st sess. Washington, D.C.: GPO, 1969. 34p.

Whittaker Chambers *See* Alger Hiss

Ray Cline

3809. Cline, Ray. *Secrets, Spies, and Scholars: Blueprint of the Essential CIA.* Washington, D.C.: Acropolis Books, 1976. 294p.

Eli Cohen

3810. Aldouby, Zwy and Jerrold Ballinger. *The Shattered Silence: The Eli Cohen Affair.* New York: Coward-McCann, 1971. 453p.

3811. Ben-Hanan, Eli. *Our Man in Damascus.* Tel Aviv: A.D.M. Publishing House, 1968. 191p.

3812. Dan, Ben. *Spy From Israel.* London: Vallentine, Mitchell, 1969. 212p.

3813. "Of Hate and Espionage." *Time,* LXXXV (March 5, 1965), 31–32.

3814. Rouleau, Eric. "The Double Life of Eli Cohen." *Atlas,* X (July 1965), 10–12.

3815. Salpeter, E. "The Kibbutz Boy Who Became a Spy." *New Leader,* LVI (January 8, 1973), 4–6.

3816. "Spy Season." *Newsweek,* LXV (March 8, 1965), 44–45.

William E. Colby

3817. Alpern, David M. "Light of Day." *Newsweek,* LXXXVI (July 7, 1975), 14–15.

3818. Colby, William E. "America's Top Intelligence Chief Sizes Up the World's Trouble Spots." *U.S. News and World Report,* LXXVII (December 2, 1974), 30–31.

3819. _____ . "The CIA's Mr. Colby: An Interview." *New Republic,* CLXXIV (March 13, 1976), 12–21.

3820. _____ . "Director Colby on the Record: Excerpts From an Interview." *Time,* CIV (September 30, 1974), 18–19.

3821. _____ . "Good and Bad Secrets: An Interview." *Newsweek,* LXXXV (January 20, 1975), 21.

3822. _____ . "In His Own Words: An Interview." *People,* IX (May 29, 1978), 47–48+.

3823. _____ . "Why I was Fired From the CIA." *Esquire,* LXXXIX (May 9, 1978), 59–62+.

3824. _____ . "Spotlight on CIA: An Interview." *U.S. News and World Report*, LXXVII (December 2, 1974), 29–32+.

3825. _____ and Peter Forbath. *Honorable Men: My Life in the CIA.* New York: Simon and Schuster, 1978. 493p.

3826. _____ . _____ . London: Hutchinson, 1978. 493p.

Contains additional material unpublished in the U.S.

3827. "Directors Defend Themselves: William E. Colby's Report." *Time*, CV (January 27, 1975), 29+.

3828. *Facts on File*, Editors of. "William E. Colby." In: *Political Profiles: The Johnson Years.* New York, 1976. pp. 120–121.

3829. "Ford's Costly Purge." *Time*, CVI (November 15, 1975), 8–12+.

3830. Osborne, John. "Backing and Filling." *New Republic*, CLXXIII (November 22, 1975), 12–13.

3831. _____ . "Jerry's Guys." *New Republic*, CLXXIII (November 15, 1975), 9–12.

3832. "Scenario of the Shake-Up." *Time*, CVI (November 17, 1975), 12+.

3833. Sherrill, Robert. "With All Due Respect—Stonewall Colby of the CIA." *Nation*, CCXIX (October 5, 1974), 300–303.

3834. "Shivering From Overexposure." *Time*, CV (March 31, 1975), 27.

3835. "Supersleuth Takes Over at CIA." *U.S. News and World Report*, LXXV (August 13, 1975), 29.

3836. "Tales of an Old Soldier." *Time*, CVI (July 7, 1975), 8.

3837. "Trying to Govern as the Fires Grow Hotter." *Time*, CI (May 21, 1973), 13–14.

3838. Szulc, Tad. "Firings and Foreign Policy." *New Republic*, CLXXIII (November 15, 1975), 7–9.

3839. United States. Congress. Senate. Committee on Armed Services. *Nomination of William E. Colby to be Director of Central Inelligence: Hearings.* 93rd Cong., 1st sess. Washington, D.C.: GPO, 1973. 186p.

3840. "William Colby." *Current Biography*, XXXVI (January 1975), 12–15.

3841. Wise, David. "Colby of CIA, CIA of Colby." *New York Times Magazine*, (July 1, 1973), 8–9+.

Francisco Constantini

3842. "The Tactful [Italian] Servant." *Time,* LXX (December 9, 1957), 31–32.

Lionel K. Crabbe

3843. Hutton, Bernard J. *Frogman Spy: The Incredible Case of Commander Crabbe.* New York: McDowell, Obolensky, 1960. 180p.

3844. "Mystery of the Frogman's Dive For Red Secrets." *Life,* XL (May 28, 1956), 38–42.

3845. Singer, Kurt D. "The Frogman." In: *Spies For Democracy.* Minneapolis: Dennison, 1960. pp. 217–238.

Sahag Dedeyan

3846. Salmans, S. "The Armenian Connection." *Newsweek,* LXXXVI (July 7, 1975), 19–20.

Petr S. Deriabin

3847. Deriabin, Petr S., with Frank Gibney. "Red Agent's Vivid Tale of Terror." *Life,* XLVI (March 23, 1959), 110–112+.

3848. _____. *The Secret World.* Garden City, NY: Doubleday, 1959. 334p.

Peer De Silva

3849. De Silva, Peer. *Sub Rosa: The Uses of Intelligence.* New York: Times Books, 1978. 288p.

Phillippe T. De Vosjoli

3850. Barry, John. "The Broad Impact of 'Martel': Everywhere But France." *Life,* LXIV (April 26, 1968), 38–39.

3851. De Vosjoli, Phillippe T. "The Head That Holds Some Sinister Secrets: The 'Martel' Affair." *Life,* LXIV (April 26, 1968), 30–39.

3852. _____. *Lamia.* Boston: Little, Brown, 1970. 344p.

3853. _____. "NATO Scenario of Spies and Suicide." *Life,* LXV (December 13, 1968), 26–29.

3854. _____. "The Strange Case of De Gaulle and the Soviet Spies." *Reader's Digest,* XCIII (July 1968), 95–100.

3855. "The Fourth Man?" *National Review,* XX (May 7, 1968), 434–435.

3856. "The Sapphire Affair: Report of Soviet Spies in the Highest Echelons of the French Government." *Time*, XCI (August 26, 1968), 30+.

3857. Scali, John. "Spies Around DeGaulle." *Look*, XXXII (May 14, 1968), 44–45+.

3858. "Stranger Than Fiction: Alleged Soviet Spy in the French Government." *Newsweek*, LXXI (April 29, 1968), 40+.

Jean Dides

3859. "Dark Trial of Treason in France." *Newsweek*, XLIV (October 11, 1954), 40–42.

3860. "Letter From Paris: *L'Affaire de la Trahison Genet.*" *New Yorker*, XXX (October 9, 1954), 158+.

3861. "Rot at the Heart: The Dides Case." *Time*, LXIV (October 18, 1954), 30+.

3862. Taylor, Edmond. "L'Affaire Dides." *Reporter*, XI (November 4, 1954), 27–32.

3863. "Why Red Spies Found Easy Pickings in France." *U.S. News and World Report*, XXXVII (October 22, 1954), 53+.

Martha E. Dodd

3864. "Ex-Ambassador's Daughter—a Red Spy." *Newsweek*, L (August 26, 1957), 28–30.

3865. "Travellers." *Time*, LXX (September 2, 1957), 17–18.

Anatoli Dolnytsin

3866. " 'D' For Dolnytsin: Spies For Britain and Russia." *Newsweek*, LXII (July 22, 1963), 40.

William J. Donovan

3867. Dulles, Allen W. "William J. Donovan and National Security: Speech to the Erie County Bar Association, Buffalo, New York, May 4, 1959." *Congressional Record*, CV (May 14, 1959), 8103–8105.

3868. Ford, Corey. *Donovan of OSS*. Boston: Little, Brown, 1970. 366p.

John Downey

3869. Baranski, Larry. "In His Own Words: An Interview." *People*, X (December 18, 1978), 45–46+.

René Duchéz

3870.   Perrault, Geoffrey. "The Housepainter of Caen." In: Burke Wilkinson, ed. *Cry Spy!* Scarsdale, NY: Bradbury Press, 1969. pp. 140–147.

Allen W. Dulles

3871.   "Allen W. Dulles." *Current Biography,* X (March 1949), 13–15.

3872.   Baker, Russell. "The Other Mr. Dulles—of CIA." *New York Times Magazine,* (March 16, 1958), 17+.

3873.   Dulles, Allen W. "We Tell Russia Too Much." *U.S. News and World Report,* XXXVI (May 19, 1954), 62–68.

3874.   Edwards, Robert and Kenneth Dunne. *A Study of a Master Spy: Allen Dulles.* London: Housmans, 1961. 79p.

3875.   *Facts on File,* Editors of. "Allen W. Dulles." In: *Political Profiles: The Eisenhower Years.* New York, 1977. pp. 161–163.

3876.   Franklin, Charles. "Allen Dulles." In: *Great Spies.* London: Hart, 1967. pp. 252–255.

3877.   "The Hearty Professional." *Time,* XCIII (February 7, 1969), 18–19.

3878.   "The Man With the Innocent Air." *Time,* LXII (August 3, 1953), 12–15.

3879.   Mosley, Leonard. *Dulles: A Biography of Eleanor, Allen, and John Foster Dulles and Their Family Network.* New York: Dial Press, 1978. 530p.

3880.   Phillips, Cabell. "Mr. Dulles of the Silent Service." *New York Times Magazine,* (March 29, 1953), 12+.

3881.   Singer, Kurt D. "Allen W. Dulles." In: *Men in the Trojan Horse.* Boston: Beacon Press, 1953. pp. 74–77.

3882.   "A Spy Goes to Heaven." *Newsweek,* LXXIII (February 10, 1969), 26+.

3883.   "The Story of Allen Dulles and the CIA." *U.S. News and World Report,* XLVIII (May 23, 1960), 25–26.

3884.   United States. Central Intelligence Agency. Library. *Allen Welsh Dulles, Director of Central Intelligence.* Washington, D.C., 1962. 84p.

Jack Dunlap

3885.   "The Invisible Man." *Newsweek,* LXII (October 21, 1963), 43–44.

3886.   Oberdorfer, Delbert. "The Playboy Sergeant Who Spied For Russia: Jack Dunlap." *Saturday Evening Post,* CCXXXVII (March 1964), 40+.

Avri El-Ad

3887.   El-Ad, Avri, with James Creech. *Decline of Honor: Autobiography.* Chicago: Contemporary Books, 1976. 364p.

Noel Field

3888.   De Toledano, Ralph. "The Noel Field Story." *American Mercury,* LXXX (April 1955), 5–8.

3889.   Field, Noel. "I Was Condemned to Death by a Soviet Court: An Interview." *U.S. News and World Report,* XXXIX (December 9, 1955), 68–70+.

3890.   Lewis, Flora. *Red Pawn: The Story of Noel Field.* Garden City, NY: Doubleday, 1965. 283p.

Anatoly Filatov

3891.   Martin, D. C. "The Filatov File." *Newsweek,* XCII (July 31, 1978), 31.

Magda Fontanges

3892.   "Agent F8006." *Newsweek,* XXIX (February 10, 1947), 38.

3893.   "Duce's Old Flame Convicted as a [French] Spy." *Life,* XXII (February 17, 1947), 34–35.

Alfred Frauenknecht

3894.   Erdman, Paul. "The True Story of a Spy Coup: How Israel Got the Blueprints For France's Hottest Fighter Plane." *New York Magazine,* IX (August 30, 1976), 35–45.

Alfred Frenzel

3895.   "The Diligent [Czech] Deputy." *Time,* LXXVI (November 14, 1960), 27–28.

Josep Frolik

3896.   Frolik, Josep. *The Frolik Defection: The Memoirs of an* [Czech] *Agent.* London: Leo Cooper, 1975. 184p.

Klaus Fuchs

3897. Bohn, William E. "Why Stalin was not Surprised." *Reader's Digest,* LIX (July 1951), 25–26+.

3898. "The Case of the World's Greatest Secret." *Life,* XXX (April 16, 1951), 53–56.

3899. Curran, Charles G. "Stalin Merely Smiled: Fuchs at Los Alamos." *Spectator,* CCIII (September 18, 1959), 363–366.

3900. Fairfield, Cecily I. "The Terrifying Import of the Fuchs Case." By Rebecca West, pseud. *New York Times Magazine,* (March 4, 1951), 10+.

3901. "Fourteen Years For Fuchs." *Newsweek,* LXIV (March 13, 1950), 34.

3902. "Fourteen Years For 'Grossest Treachery.'" *Life,* XXIX (March 13, 1950), 42–43.

3903. Freed, Louis I. "Russia's Spy Master." *Coronet,* XXXI (February 1952), 98–102.

3904. "How Russia Got U.S. Secrets." *U.S. News and World Report,* XXVIII (February 17, 1950), 11–13.

3905. Huie, William B. "Who Gave Russia the A-bomb?" *American Mercury,* LXXII (April–May 1951), 413–421, 593–602.

3906. Moorehead, Alan. "Traitor Klaus Fuchs: He Gave Stalin the A-bomb." *Saturday Evening Post,* CCXXIV (May 24–June 14, 1952), 22–23+, 32–33+, 36–37+, 34+.

3907. "Red Shadows on a Worried World." *Newsweek,* XXXV (February 20, 1950), 17–19.

Reinhard Gehlen

3908. "Der Doktor." *Time,* LXXVI (July 11, 1960), 36+.

3909. "Failure of Intelligence: The Gehlen Organization." *Newsweek,* LXII (August 5, 1963), 34.

3910. Gehlen, Reinhard. *The Service: Memoirs.* Translated From the German. Cleveland, OH: World Publishing Co., 1972. 386p.

3911. Harrison, George. "Our Man Beelzebub." *New Republic,* CLXVI (April 22, 1972), 25–27.

3912. Hohne, Heinz and Herman Zolling. *The General was a Spy: The Truth About General Gehlen and His Spy Ring.* Translated from the German. New York: Coward-McCann, 1972. 347p.

3913.   "In From the Cold: The Chief of West German Intelligence Retires." *Time,* XCI (January 26, 1968), 30.

3914.   "The Invisible Man." *Newsweek,* LXXI (May 6, 1968), 56+.

3915.   Joesten, Joachim. "The Mysterious Herr Gehlen." *New Republic,* XIII (October 4, 1954), 11–14.

3916.   Johnson, Thomas M. "Our Silent Partner in the Secret War Against Communism." *American Mercury,* XCI (September 1960), 3–10.

3917.   Spiro, Edward. *Gehlen, Spy of the Century.* By E. H. Cookridge, pseud. New York: Random House, 1972. 402p.

Ivan A. H. Georgiev

3918.   "Name That Tune." *Time,* LXXXIII (January 3, 1969), 37–38.

3919.   "Price to Pay." *Newsweek,* LXIII (January 6, 1964), 32.

3920.   "Tomorrow is Forever." *Newsweek,* LXIII (January 13, 1964), 31–32.

Harry Gold

3921.   Brelis, Dean. "The Making of a Spy: Communists Befriended Harry Gold." *Life,* XXVIII (June 12, 1950), 7–8+.

3922.   Slack, A. D. "Inside Story of a Native American Who Turned Spy." *U.S. News and World Report,* XXIX (November 24, 1950), 15–17.

Michael Golemewski

3923.   Richards, Guy. *Imperial Agent: The Golemewski-Romanov Case.* New York: Devin-Adair, 1966. 284p.

Sidney Gottlieb

3924.   "Key Witness in CIA Inquiry." *New York Times Biographical Service,* VIII (September 1977), 1237.

Igor Gouzenko

3925.   Gouzenko, Igor. *The Iron Curtain.* New York: E. P. Dutton, 1948. 279p.

3926.   _____ . "Stalin Sent Me to Spy School." *Coronet,* XXXIII (March 1953), 85–92.

3927.   _____ . *This Was My Choice.* 2nd ed. Montreal: Palm Publishers Press Service, 1968. 238p.

Anatoli Granovsky

3928. Granovsky, Anatoli. *All Pity Choked: The Memoirs of a Soviet Secret Agent.* London: Kimber, 1955. 248p.

3929. _____. *I was an NKVD Agent: A Top Soviet Spy Tells His Story.* New York: Devin-Adair, 1962. 343p.

Petr G. Grigorenko

3930. Grigorenko, Petr G. *The Grigorenko Papers.* Boulder, CO: Westview Press, 1976. 194p.

Günter Guillaume

3931. Brandt, Willy. *People and Politics:The Years 1960–1975.* Translated From the German. Boston: Little, Brown, 1978. 524p.

3932. "Brandt Comes In From the Cold." *Newsweek,* LXXXIII (May 20, 1974), 51–52+.

3933. Drath, Viola H. *Willy Brandt: Prisoner of His Past.* Philadelphia: Chilton, 1975. 364p.

3934. "My Friend the Spy." *Newsweek,* LXXXIII (May 6, 1974), 43.

3935. "Spy in the Closet: Günter Guillaume, East German Spy on Willy Brandt's Staff." *Time,* CIII (May 6, 1974), 34+.

Gunvor G. Haavik

3936. "From Russia With Lovers: The Arrest of Gunvor G. Haavik, Soviet Spy [in Norway]." *Time,* CIX (February 28, 1977), 32–33.

Iser Harel

3937. Bar-Zohar, Michael. *Spies in the Promised Land: Iser Harel and the Israeli Secret Service* [1948–1963]. Translated From the French. Boston: Houghton, Mifflin, 1972. 292p.

3938. Harel, Iser. *The House on Garibaldi Street: The First Full Account of the Capture of Adolf Eichmann, Told by the Former Head of Israel's Secret Service.* New York: Viking Press, 1975. 265p.

John F. Hasey

3939. Karnow, Stanley. "An Odd Bit of Hidden History—DeGaulle's CIA Aide: The Views of John F. Hasey." *New Republic,* CLXX (June 29, 1974), 17–18.

Abu Hassan

3940.   Carroll, Raymond. "Death of a Terrorist: The Murder of Abu Hassan is Charged to the Mossad." *Newsweek,* XCIII (February 5, 1979), 61.

3941.   "Death of a Terrorist: The Murder of Abu Hassan in Beirut." *Time,* CXIII (February 5, 1979), 111–112.

Erich Helbig

3942.   "Domestic Scandal: Erich Helbig on Trial in West Germany." *Newsweek,* LXV (April 12, 1965), 56+.

Richard Helms

3943.   Alpern, David M. "Constant Witness: Richard M. Helms." *Newsweek,* LXXXV (February 24, 1975), 21.

3944.   Birns, Laurence. "How to Lie in Washington and Get Away With It." *New York Review of Books,* XXII (July 17, 1975), 39+.

3945.   Boeth, Robert and V. E. Smith. "The Helms File." *Newsweek,* XC (October 10, 1977), 31–32.

3946.   "The Brotherhood of Liars." *Nation,* CCXXIV (February 26, 1977), 226–227.

3947.   "CIA's New Super Spook." *Newsweek,* LXXXI (January 1, 1973), 17.

3948.   "The Cool Pro Who Runs the CIA." *Newsweek,* LXXVIII (November 22, 1971), 30–31.

3949.   "Counterattack and Counterpoint." *Time,* CII (August 13, 1973), 15–17.

3950.   *Facts on File,* Editors of. "Richard Helms." In: *Political Profiles: The Johnson Years.* New York, 1976. pp. 266–268.

3951.   _____ . _____ . In: *Political Profiles: The Kennedy Years.* New York, 1976. pp. 219–220.

3952.   Getlein, Frank. "Helmsmen, What Quarry?" *Commonweal,* CIV (November 25, 1971), 740–741.

3953.   "Guarding the Secrets: The Testimony of Richard Helms." *Nation,* CCXXV (November 12, 1977), 482–484.

3954.   Halperin, Morton H. "Did Helms Commit Perjury?" *New Republic,* CLXXIV (March 6, 1976), 14–17.

3955. Helms, Richard M. "Global Intelligence: The Democratic Society, an Address, April 14, 1971." *Vital Speeches,* XXXVII (May 15, 1971), 450–454.

3956. _____ . "Spying and a Free Society: The CIA Chief Speaks Out." *U.S. News and World Report,* LXX (April 26, 1971), 84–86.

3957. "Helms Makes a Deal." *Time,* CX (November 14, 1977), 18+.

3958. "The High Price of Security." *Newsweek,* LXXXI (May 28, 1973), 33+.

3959. "The Importance of Richard Helms." *National Review,* XXIX (November 25, 1977), 1348–1349.

3960. Larson, Janet K. "Up Against Citizen Helms." *Christian Century,* XCIV (November 30, 1977), 1108–1110.

3961. Lewis, Anthony. "Lying in State: Reprinted From the *New York Times,* July 14, 1975." *Congressional Record,* CXXI (July 21, 1975), 22917–22918.

3962. Madden, Robert. "A Man Known For Reliability." *New York Times Biographical Service,* VIII (November 1977), 1512–1513.

3963. Osborne, John. "Carter and Helms." *New Republic,* CLXXVII (November 19, 1977), 10–13.

3964. Pincus, William. "Dealing With Liars." *New Republic,* CLXXII (March 1, 1975), 14–16.

3965. _____ . "The Duping of Richard Helms." *New Republic,* CLXXII (February 15, 1975), 12–14.

3966. Powers, Thomas. *The Man Who Kept the Secrets: Richard Helms and the CIA.* New York: Knopf, 1979. 416p.

3967. _____ . "The Rise and Fall of Richard Helms: Survival and Sudden Death in the CIA." *Rolling Stone,* (December 16, 1976), 46+.

3968. "Richard M. Helms." *People,* VIII (November 21, 1977), 40–41.

3969. "Spare That Spook: The Case of Richard M. Helms." *New Republic,* CLXXVII (November 19, 1977), 5+.

3970. Steel, Ronald. "Public Interest Perjury: Scarlet Letter Brings Honor to Helms." *Politicks,* I (January 17, 1978), 8–9.

3971. "They Never Laid a Hand on Him: Richard Helms." *Nation,* CCXXV (November 19, 1975), 514–515.

3972. United States. Congress. Senate. Committee on Foreign Relations. *Nomination of Richard Helms to Be Ambassador to Iran and CIA International and Domestic Activities: Hearings.* 93rd Cong., 2nd sess. Washington, D.C.: GPO, 1974. 109p.

3973. Wells, Benjamin. "H-L-S of the CIA." *New York Times Magazine,* (April 18, 1971), 34–54.

3974. "Written in Blood: The Testimony of Richard Helms." *Nation,* CCXXI (October 4, 1975), 292–293.

Frank Hirt

3975. Asbury, Herbert and Willis D. George. "Doodles That Caught a Spy." *Collier's,* CXVII (January 5, 1946), 16+.

3976. "G.I. Spy: Frank Hirt." *Newsweek,* XXVII (January 7, 1946), 24–25.

Alger Hiss

3977. "Alger Hiss." *Current Biography,* VIII (February 1947), 28–30.

3978. Altman, G. T. "Added Witness." *Nation,* CXCI (October 1, 1960), 201–209.

3979. "And Now For Hiss' Side." *Newsweek,* XXXIII (June 27, 1949), 23–24.

3980. Andrews, Bert and Peter. *A Tragedy of History: A Journalist's Confidential Role in the Hiss-Chambers Case.* New York: David McKay, 1962. 235p.

3981. Arthur, Robert A. "Hanging Out." *Esquire,* LXXVIII (July 1972), 26+.

3982. Atkins, Ollie. "The Pumpkin Papers and a Generation on Trial." *Saturday Evening Post,* CCXLVIII (January 1976), 40–41+.

3983. Bendiner, Robert. "The Ordeal of Alger Hiss." *Nation,* CLXX (February 4–11, 1950), 100–103, 123–125.

3984. _____. "The Trial of Alger Hiss." *Nation,* CLXVIII (June 11–25, July 15, 1949), 650–651, 699–700, 52–55.

3985. Boulton, W. K. and C. D. Williams. "Two Experts Examine the Alger Hiss Story." *Saturday Review of Literature,* XL (May 18, 1957), 25+.

3986. Buckley, William F., Jr. "Assault on Whittaker Chambers." *National Review,* XVI (December 15, 1964), 1098–2000.

3987. _____ . "The End of Whittaker Chambers." *Esquire,* LVIII (September 1962), 77–80+.

3988. Busch, Francis X. "Alger Hiss." In: *Guilty or Not Guilty?* Indianapolis: Bobbs-Merrill, 1952. pp. 197–287.

3989. Bychowski, Gustav. "The Potential of Psychoanalytic Biography: [Dorothy F.] Zeligs on Chambers-Hiss." *American Image,* XXVI (Fall 1969), 233–241.

3990. "The Case of Alger Hiss." *Time,* LV (February 13, 1950), 22–23.

3991. Chambers, Whittaker. *Cold Friday.* New York: McGraw-Hill, 1964. 327p.

3992. _____ . "Herring and the Thing." *Look,* XVII (December 29, 1953), 14–18.

3993. _____ . "I Was the Witness." *Saturday Evening Post,* CCXXIV (February 9–April 12, 1952), 17–19+, 22–23+, 22–23+, 20–21+, 24–25+, 36–37+, 36–37+, 32–33+, 40–41+.

3994. _____ . "Odyssey of a Friend: Letters to William F. Buckley, Jr., 1954–1955." *National Review,* XXII (January 13, 1970), 22–32.

3995. _____ . "Whittaker Chambers Meets the Press." *American Mercury,* LXVIII (February 1949), 153–160.

3996. _____ . *Witness.* Chicago: Regnery, 1968. 808p.

3997. Cook, Fred J. "Haunting the Hiss Case: The Ghost of a Typewriter." *Nation,* CXCIV (May 12, 1962), 416–421.

3998. _____ . "Hiss: New Perspectives on the Strangest Case of Our Times." *Nation,* CLXXXV (September 21, 1957), 142–180.

3999. _____ . "Nixon Kicks a Hole in the Hiss Case." *Nation,* CXCIV (April 7, 1962), 296+.

4000. _____ . *The Unfinished Story of Alger Hiss.* New York: Morrow, 1958. 184p.

4001. Cooke, Alastair. *A Generation on Trial: The U.S.A. vs. Alger Hiss.* 2nd ed. New York: Knopf, 1952. 356p.

4002. Cooney, T. E. "Alger Hiss' Story." *Saturday Review of Literature,* XL (May 11, 1957), 16+.

4003. Costello, William A. "The Hiss Case: Climax of Nixon's Career in the House." *New Republic,* CXLI (December 7, 1959), 12–16.

4004. Countryman, Vern. "One Small Step For Alger Hiss." *New Republic,* CLXXIII (August 30, 1975), 14–17.

4005. De Toledano, Ralph. "The Alger Hiss Story." *American Mercury,* LXXVI (June 1953), 13–20.

4006. _____ , and Victor Lasky. *Seeds of Treason: The True Story of the Hiss-Chambers Tragedy.* A Newsweek Book. New York: Funk and Wagnalls, 1950. 270p.

4007. _____ . _____ . Rev. ed. Chicago: Regnery, 1962. 314p.

4008. _____ . _____ . *Reader's Digest,* LVI (May 1950), 148–180.

4009. "Face to Face Test." *Newsweek,* XXXII (August 30, 1948), 15–16.

4010. Fielder, L. A. "Hiss, Chambers, and the Age of Innocence: Who was Guilty—and of What?" *Commentary,* XII (August, December 1951), 109–119, 597–598.

4011. Footlick, J. K. "The Pumpkin Papers." *Newsweek,* LXXXVI (August 11, 1975), 57.

4012. Hiss, Alger. *In the Court of Public Opinion.* New York: Harper & Row, 1970. 424p.

4013. Hiss, Anthony. *Laughing Last: Alger Hiss.* Boston: Houghton, Mifflin, 1977. 194p.

4014. "The Hiss File." *Nation,* CCXV (December 18, 1972), 613–614.

4015. Hook, Sidney. "The Case of Alger Hiss." *Encounter,* LI (August 1978), 48–55.

4016. Jewitt, William A. J. *The Strange Case of Alger Hiss.* Garden City, NY: Doubleday, 1953. 380p.

4017. Kinsley, M. "Alger Hiss and the Smoking Gun Fallacy." *Washington Monthly,* VII (October 1975), 52–60.

4018. Lansner, Kenneth. "Alger Hiss Argues His Innocence." *Newsweek,* XLIX (May 13, 1957), 40+.

4019. Lowenthal, J. "What the FBI Knew and Had." *Nation,* CCXXII (June 26, 1976), 776–782.

4020. McColloch, C. "The Strange Case of Alger Hiss: A Reply to Lord Jewitt." *American Bar Association Journal,* XL (March 1954), 199–202+.

4021. McHughes, Lee M. "The Hiss Act and Its Application to the Military." *Military Law Review,* XIV (1962), 67+.

4022.   McWilliams, Carey. "Post-Mortem on the Hiss Case." *Nation,* CCXXII (April 3, 1976), 389–390.

4023.   _____. "Will Nixon Exonerate Hiss?" *Nation,* CCXXI (September 20, 1975), 229–231.

4024.   Millis, Walter, Fred Rodell, and Victor Lasky. "Was Hiss Framed?: A Debate." *Saturday Review of Literature,* XLI (May 31, June 21, July 12, and October 18, 1958), 14–17+, 27–28, 21+, 21–22.

4025.   Nixon, Richard M. "The Hiss Case." In: *Six Crises.* Garden City, NY: Doubleday, 1962. pp. 1–72.

4026.   _____. "Quizzing Nixon: An Interview." *U.S. News and World Report,* XXXIII (August 29, 1952), 34–37+.

4027.   _____. "The Strange Case of Alger Hiss." *Reader's Digest,* LXXXI (November 1962), 88–93+.

4028.   Nobile, Philip. "The State of the Art of Alger Hiss." *Harper's,* CCLII (April, June 1976), 67–68+, 4+.

4029.   "One Spy of Many: The Chambers Report." *Newsweek,* XXXIII (January 10, 1949), 18–19.

4030.   Phillips, William. "In and Out of the Underground: The Confessions of Whittaker Chambers." *American Mercury,* LXXIV (June 1952), 92–99.

4031.   Ratcliffe, S. K. "The Tragedy of Alger Hiss." *Fortnightly,* CLXXIII (March 1950), 168–173.

4032.   Reuben, William A. *Honorable Mr. Nixon and the Alger Hiss Case.* New York: Action Books, 1956. 72p.

4033.   Schlesinger, Arthur M., Jr. "Espionage or Frame-up?: The Case of Alger Hiss and Whittaker Chambers." *Saturday Review of Literature,* XXXIII (April 15, 1950), 21–24.

4034.   Seth, Ronald. *The Sleeping Truth: The Hiss-Chambers Affair.* New York: Hart Publishing Co., 1968. 292p.

4035.   Sherrill, Robert. "Alger Hiss." *New York Times Book Review,* (April 25, 1976), 31–32+.

4036.   "The Slander of a Dead Man." *Time,* LXXXIX (February 10, 1967), 102+.

4037.   Smith, John C. *Alger Hiss: The True Story.* New York: Holt, 1976. 485p.

4038. "Stolen Secrets of the U.S." *U.S. News and World Report,* XXV (December 17, 1948), 19–21.

4039. "Story Against Story." *Newsweek,* XXXII (August 16, 1948), 17–18.

4040. Theoharis, Athan G. "Abuse of Power: What the New Hiss Suit Uncovers." *Nation,* CCXXVII (October 7, 1978), 336–340.

4041. _____ . "Classification Restrictions and the Public's Right to Know: A New Look at the Alger Hiss Case." *Intellect,* CIV (September 1975), 86–89.

4042. Trilling, David. "Memorandum on the Hiss Case." *Partisan Review,* XVII (May 1950), 484–500.

4043. "Two Men." *Time,* LII (December 20, 1948), 17–21.

4044. "Verdict: Hiss Has Been Lying." *Time,* CVII (March 29, 1976), 30–31.

4045. Weinstein, Allen. "The Alger Hiss Case Revisited." *American Scholar,* XLI (Winter 1971), 121–132.

4046. _____ . "Hiss and the Rosenberg Files: On the Search For Smoking Guns." *New Republic,* CLXXIV (February 14, May 15–22, 1976), 16–17+, 30–32, 31–32.

4047. _____ . "Nixon vs. Hiss." *Esquire,* LXXXIV (November 1975), 73–80+.

4048. _____ . *Perjury: The Hiss-Chambers Case.* New York: Knopf, 1978. 674p.

4049. Werchen, Raymond A. and Fred J. Cook. "New Light on the Hiss Case." *Nation,* CCXVI (May 28, 1973), 678–684.

4050. Weyl, Nathaniel. "The Case of Alger Hiss." In: *Treason: The Story of Disloyalty and Betrayal in American History.* New York: Public Affairs Press, 1950. pp. 424–441.

4051. _____ . "I Was in a Communist Unit With Hiss: An Interview." *U.S. News and World Report,* XXXIV (January 9, 1953), 22–40.

4052. Wills, G. "The Hiss Connection Through Nixon's Life." *New York Times Magazine,* (August 25, 1974), 8–9+.

4053. "Woodstock Mystery: How the FBI Broke the Hiss Case." *Newsweek,* XXXII (December 27, 1948), 19–20.

4054. Younger, Irving. "Was Alger Hiss Guilty?, with Discussion." *Commentary,* LX (August, December 1975), 23–37, 4+.

4055. Zeligs, Meyer A. *Friendship and Fratricide: An Analysis of Whittaker Chambers and Alger Hiss.* New York: Viking Press, 1967. 476p.

Uwe Holstz

4056. Birnbaum, Norman. "The Case of the Media's Agents: [West German] Espionage Scandal Involving Uwe Holstz." *Nation,* CCXXVII (November 4, 1978), 457+.

4057. Grenard, Peter. "Spies in the Ointment." *Macleans,* XCI (September 18, 1978), 36+.

J. Edgar Hoover

4058. Demaris, Ovid. *The Director: An Oral Biography of J. Edgar Hoover.* New York: Harper & Row, 1975. 405p.

4059. De Toledano, Ralph. *J. Edgar Hoover: The Man and His Times.* New Rochelle, NY: Arlington House, 1973. 384p.

4060. Donner, Frank. "How J. Edgar Hoover Created His Intelligence Powers." *Civil Liberties Review,* III (February–March 1977), 34–51.

4061. "Hoover and His FBI: An Era Ends." *Newsweek,* LXXIX (May 15, 1972), 26–28+.

4063. "The Long Reign of J. Edgar Hoover." *Time,* XCIX (May 15, 1972), 18–19.

4064. Nash, Jay Robert. *Citizen Hoover: A Critical Study of the Life and Times of J. Edgar Hoover and His FBI.* Chicago: Nelson-Hall, 1972. 298p.

John Huminik

4065. Huminik, John. *Double Agent.* New York: New American Library, 1967. 181p.

4066. _____ . _____ ; [Excerpt]. In: Burke Wilkinson, ed. *Cry Spy!* Scarsdale, NY: Bradbury Press, 1969. pp. 254–260.

Ronald Humphrey

4067. "Affair of the Heart: The Case of Ronald Humphrey." *Newsweek,* XCI (February 13, 1978), 25–26.

4068. Coburn, Judith. "Jimmy Carter's Tet Offensive: The Case of Ronald Humphrey and David Troung." *New Times,* X (April 17, 1978), 27–36.

4069. Stein, Jeffrey. "The Espionage Circus." *Inquiry,* I (April 2, 1978), 6–7.

E. Howard Hunt

4070. Hunt, E. Howard. *Undercover: The Memoirs of an American Secret Agent.* New York: Berkeley Publishing Co.; dist. by Putnam, 1974. 338p.

4071. Szulc, Tad. *Compulsive Spy: The Strange Career of E. Howard Hunt.* New York: Viking Press, 1974. 180p.

Nahit Imre

4072. Acoca, M. "The Turk With a Taste For Scotch and Secrets." *Life,* LXV (December 13, 1968), 30–31.

Sam Jaffe

4073. Branch, Taylor. "The Man Who Called Walter Cronkite a Spy: Sam Jaffe." *Esquire,* LXXXVII (April 1977), 34–36+.

4074. _____ . "Sam Jaffe and the New Blacklist." *Esquire,* LXXXVII (March 1977), 36+.

4075. Friedman, Robert. "The Reporter Who Came in From the Cold." *More,* VII (March 1977), 46–48.

Jean Louis Jeanmarie

4076. Barron, John. "Portrait of a [Swiss] Traitor." *Reader's Digest,* CXIII (August 1978), 111–115.

Otto John

4077. John, Otto. *Twice Through the Lines.* New York: Harper & Row, 1972. 340p.

James F. Johnson

4078. Johnson, James F. *The Man Who Sold the Eiffel Tower.* Garden City, NY: Doubleday, 1961. 216p.

Robert L. Johnson

4079. Barron, John. "The Sergeant Who Opened the Door." *Reader's Digest,* CIV (January 1974), 187–194+.

William P. Kampiles

4080. Buckley, William F., Jr. "Skullduggery: The Sale of a Spy Satellite Manual to the Russians—Case of William P. Kampiles." *National Review,* XXXI (January 5, 1979), 48.

4081. "Former CIA Officer Arrested in Secret Satellite Manual Sale: The Case of William P. Kampiles." *Aviation Week and Space Technology,* CIX (August 28, 1978), 22–23.

4082. Hurt, Henry. "CIA in Crisis: The Kampiles Case." *Reader's Digest,* CXIV (June 1979), 65–72.

4083. Ledeen, Michael A. "Mole in Our Midst?" *New York Magazine,* XI (October 2, 1978), 55–57.

4084. Ott, John. "Espionage Trial Highlights CIA Problems: The Case of William P. Kampiles." *Aviation Week and Space Technology,* CIX (November 27, 1978), 21–23.

George Karlin

4085. United States. Congress. Senate. Committee on the Judiciary. Subcommittee to Investigate the Administration of the Internal Security Act and Other Internal Security Laws. *Hearings and Testimony of George Karlin.* 91st Cong., 1st and 2nd sess. Washington, D.C.: GPO, 1970. 258p.

Alexsandr Y. Kasnakheyev

4086. Kaznakheyev, Alexsandr Y. *Inside a Soviet Embassy: Experiences of a Russian Diplomat in Burma.* Philadelphia: Lippincott, 1962. 250p.

4087. United States. Congress. Senate. Committee on the Judiciary. Subcommittee to Investigate the Administration of the Internal Security Act and Other Internal Security Laws. *Soviet Intelligence in Asia: Hearings and Testimony of Alexsandr Yurievich Kasnakheyev.* 86th Cong., 1st sess. Washington, D.C.: GPO, 1959. 25p.

4088. _____ . _____ . _____ . _____ . _____ . *Conditions in the Soviet Union, the New Class: Hearings and Further Testimony of Alexsandr Y. Kasnakheyev.* 86th Cong., 2nd sess. Washington, D.C.: GPO, 1960. 42p.

Joseph P. Kauffman

4089. Cook, Fred J. "The Ordeal of Captain Kauffman." *Nation,* CXCVII (September 14, 1963), 123–138.

Christine Keeler *See* John Profumo

Nikolai E. Khokhlov

4090. "Case History of a Red Assassin." *U.S. News and World Report,* XXXVI (May 7, 1954), 71–74.

4091. "How Russia Uses Assassins." *U.S. News and World Report,* XXXVI (May 7, 1954), 27–29.

4092. "I Have Come to Kill." *Newsweek,* XLIII (May 3, 1954), 46–48.

4093. Kathov, George. *The Khokhlov Case.* St. Anthony's Papers on Soviet Affairs. London: St. Anthony's College, 1954. 42p.

4094. Khokhlov, Nikolai E. "Cold-Blooded Murder is Part of Russia's Cold War in the West." *American Mercury,* LXXIX (September 1954), 144–157.

4095. _____ . "I Would Not Murder For the Soviets." *Saturday Evening Post,* CCXXVII (November 20–December 11, 1954), 27–29+, 34–35+, 30+, 30+.

4096. _____ . *In the Name of Conscience: The Testament of a Soviet Secret Agent.* New York: David McKay, 1959. 365p.

4097. "Rebellious Assassin." *Newsweek,* XLIII (May 31, 1954), 24.

4098. United States. Congress. House. Committee on Un-American Activities. *Investigation of Communist Activities in the Los Angeles, Calif., Area, Part VIII—Thought Control in Soviet Art and the Liberation of Russia: Hearings and the Testimony of Nikolai Khokhlov.* 84th Cong., 2nd sess. Washington, D.C.: GPO, 1956. 49p.

4099. _____ . _____ . Senate. Committee on the Judiciary. Subcommittee to Investigate the Administration of the Internal Security Act and Other Internal Security Laws. *Activities of the Soviet Secret Service: Hearings and Testimony of Nikolai Eugeniyevich Khokhlov, Former MGB Agent.* 83rd Cong., 2nd sess. Washington, D.C.: GPO, 1954. 48p.

4100. _____ . _____ . _____ . _____ . _____ . *Scope of Soviet Activities in the United States: Hearings and Testimony of Nikolai Khokhlov.* 85th Cong., 1st sess. Washington, D.C.: GPO, 1957. 24p.

4101. "Whistler." *Time,* LXIII (May 3, 1954), 27–29.

Sang K. Kim

4102. "Seoul's School For Scandal." *Time,* CVIII (December 13, 1976), 16+.

4103. Szulc, Tad. "Inside South Korea's CIA." *New York Times Magazine,* (March 6, 1977), 41–42+.

Lyman B. Kirkpatrick, Jr.

4104. Kirkpatrick, Lyman B., Jr. *The Real CIA.* New York: Macmillan, 1968. 312p.

E. Henry Knocke

4105. United States. Congress. Senate. Select Committee on Intelligence. *Nomination of E. Henry Knocke to be Deputy Director of Central Intelligence: Hearings.* 94th Cong., 2nd sess. Washington, D.C.: GPO, 1976. 33p.

Irving Kristol

4106. Kristol, Irving. "Memoirs of a Cold Warrior." *New York Times Magazine,* (February 11–25, 1968), 25+, 22+.

Urii Krotkov

4107. United States. Congress. Senate. Committee on the Judiciary. Subcommittee to Investigate the Administration of the Internal Security Act and Other Internal Security Laws. *Hearings and Testimony of George Karlin.* 91st Cong., 1st and 2nd sess. Washington, D.C.: GPO, 1970. 258p.

William L. Langer

4108. Langer, William L. *In and Out of the Ivory Tower: The Autobiography of William L. Langer.* New York: Neale Watson Academic Publications, 1977. 268p.

Mikhail M. Lebedev

4109. Lebedev, Mikhail M. *Treason—For My Daily Bread.* Translated From the Russian. Guernsey, British Isles: Vallancez Press, 1977. 407p.

Andrew D. Lee *See* Christopher J. Boyce

Kenneth J. Lennon

4110. "Informer: Kenneth Lennon." *Time,* CIII (April 29, 1974), 35–36.

4111. Robertson, Geoffrey. "Lennon, a Case to Answer." *New Statesman and Nation,* LXXXVIII (November 15, 1974), 690+.

4112. _____ . *Reluctant Judas: The Life and Death of Special Branch Informer Kenneth Lennon.* London: Temple Smith, 1976. 228p.

Flora Lewis

4113. Lewis, Flora. *Red Pawn.* Garden City, NY: Doubleday, 1965.

Keith and Kenneth Littlejohn

4114. "Dial-a-[British] Spy." *Newsweek,* LXXXII (August 13, 1973), 38+.

Yuri Loginov

4115. "Man of the World." *Newsweek,* LXX (September 25, 1967), 56.

Gordon Lonsdale, pseud. *See* Konon T. Molody

Ursel Lorenzen

4116. Bruning, Fred. "A Model [East German] Spy." *Newsweek,* XCIII (March 19, 1979), 50–51.

Wolfgang Lotz

4117. "The Champagne Spy." *Time,* XCVI (November 23, 1970), 27–28.

4118. Lotz, Wolfgang. *The Champagne Spy: Israel's Master Spy Tells His Story.* New York: St. Martin's Press, 1972. 240p.

Lothar and Renate Lutze

4119. "Spies With Many Secrets." *Time,* CX (December 26, 1977), 25.

Hermann Lüdke

4120. All Honorable Men." *Newsweek,* LXXII (November 4, 1968), 50.

4121. Kolcum, Edward H. "NATO Plans Shaken by Espionage." *Aviation Week and Space Techology,* LXXXIX (November 11, 1968), 26–28.

4122. "Of Suicide and Espionage." *Time,* XCII (November 1, 1968), 38.

Joseph A. McChristian

4123. Norman, Lloyd H. "Westmoreland's J-2." *Army,* XVII (May 1967), 21–25.

Donald Maclean *See* Guy Burgess

Banda Macleod

4124. Singer, Kurt D. "The Daughter of Mata Hari." In: *Spies For Democracy.* Minneapolis: Dennison, 1960. pp. 93–104.

4125. _____ . "Mata Hari's Daughter, Too, Died at Dawn." In: *Spies Over Asia.* London: W. H. Allen, 1956. pp. 88–124.

John A. McCone

4126. "CIA's New Boss." *Time,* LXXVIII (October 6, 1961), 22–23.

4127. McCone, John A. "We Must Know Everything: An Interview." *Progressive,* XL (March 1976), 5–6.

4128. "Why John McCone?" *New Republic,* CXLV (October 23, 1961), 7–8.

William H. Martin *See* Bernon Mitchell

Richard Meier

4129. " 'Mischa' [Markus Wolf] Meets His Match." *Time,* CX (August 8, 1977), 37–38.

Marion Miller

4130. Miller, Marion. *I Was a Spy.* Indianapolis: Bobbs-Merrill, 1960. 224p.

James Mintkenbaugh

4131. "The Spy Who Broke and Told." *Time,* LXXXV (April 16, 1965), 25.

Bernon F. Mitchell

4132. United States. Congress. House. Committee on Un-American Activities. *Security Practices in the National Security Agency: Report.* 87th Cong., 1st sess. Washington, D.C.: GPO, 1962. 23p.

Izyador Modelski

4133. United States. Congress. House. Committee on Un-American Activities. *Hearings and Documentary Testimony of Izyador Modelski, Former Military Attaché of the Polish Embassy, Washington, D.C.* 81st Cong., 1st sess. Washington, D.C.: GPO, 1949. 100p.

Konon T. Molody

4134. Franklin, Charles. "Gordon Lonsdale." In: *Great Spies.* London: Hart, 1967. pp. 211–222.

4135. "Honest-to-Badness." *Time,* LXXXVI (November 12, 1965), 44–45.

4136. Maclean, Fitzroy. "Gordon Lonsdale." In: *Take Nine Spies.* New York: Atheneum, 1978. pp. 278–303.

4137. Molody, Konon T. *Spy: Twenty Years in the Soviet Secret Service.* By Gordon Lonsdale, pseud. New York: Hawthorn Books, 1965. 220p.

Like the memoirs of Kim Philby these were written with KGB assistance—some say they were edited by Philby himself!

Pawel Monat

4138. Monat, Pawel, with John Dille. "Americans Talk Too Much." *Life,* LI (August 18, 1961), 7–8+.

4139. _____ . *Spy in the U.S.* New York: Harper & Row, 1962. 208p.

4140. United States. Congress. Senate. Committee on the Judiciary. Subcommittee to Investigate the Administration of the Internal Security Act and Other Internal Security Laws. *Soviet Espionage Though Poland: Hearings and the Testimony of Pawel Monat.* 86th Cong., 1st sess. Washington, D.C.: GPO, 1960. 41p.

Boris Morros

4141. Cook, Fred J. "Boris Morros: Hero or Myth?" *Nation,* CLXXXVI (January 25, 1958), 70–74.

4142. Morros, Boris. *My Ten Years as a Counterspy, as Told to Charles Samuels.* New York: Viking Press, 1959. 248p.

Frank J. Mrkva

4143. "Czechs Bamboozled by a Man Named Mrkva." *Life,* LXI (July 22, 1966), 22–23.

Aleksei Myagkov

4144. Myagkov, Aleksei. *Inside the KGB: An Exposé by an Officer of the Third Directorate.* New Rochelle, NY: Arlington House, 1977. 131p.

Günther Nollau

4145. Nollau, Günther. *International Communism and World Revolution.* Translated from the German. New York: Praeger, 1961. 357p.

By a West German intelligence official.

Yuri I. Nosenko

4146. "The De-Briefing Process for the U.S.S.R.'s Defectors." *Newsweek,* LXIII (February 24, 1964), 40–41.

4147. "Defector: Yuri Ivanovich Nosenko." *Time,* LXXXIII (February 21, 1964), 34+.

4148. Epstein, Edward J. "Nosenko: The Red Herring." *New York Magazine,* XI (February 27, 1978), 34–35.

Bruce T. Odell

4149. Beecher, William. "Former Spy Tells of Being Left in the Cold: Reprinted From the *Washington Evening Star,* October 25, 1976." In: U.S. Congress. Senate. Committee on the Judiciary. Subcommittee on Constitutional Rights. *Surveillance Technology: 1976.* 94th Cong., 2nd sess. Washington, D.C.: GPO, 1976. pp. 1098–1104.

Maurice Oldfield

4150. "The Honourable Grammar Schoolboy." *New Statesman and Nation,* XCVI (July 7, 1978), 12–13.

Frank R. Olson

4151. Gaines, J. R. "Casualty: Frank R. Olson." *Newsweek,* LXXXVI (July 21, 1975), 17+.

4152. "No One Told Them: Death of Frank R. Olson Linked to CIA Drug Experiment." *Time,* CVI (July 21, 1975), 15+.

Robert Oppenheimer

4153. Alsop, Joseph and Stewart. "We Accuse." *Harper's,* CCIX (October 1954), 25–45.

4154. _____ . _____ . *U.S. News and World Report,* XXXVII (December 24, 1954), 86–103.

4155. Ascoli, Max. "The Jurisprudence of Security, With Excerpts From the AEC Board's Findings in the Oppenheimer Case." *Reporter,* XI (July 6, 1954), 7–9.

4156. "Atlantic Report on Washington: The Oppenheimer Case." *Atlantic,* CXCIV (August 1954), 6+.

4157. Boskin, Joseph. *The Oppenheimer Affair: A Political Play in Three Acts.* Beverly Hills, CA: Glencoe Press, 1968. 145p.

4158. "The Case of Robert Oppenheimer." *New Republic,* CXXX (April 26, 1954), 8–15.

4159. "Findings in the Case of Dr. Oppenheimer: Full Text of Findings of the Personnel Security Board, Dissent, and Appeal." *U.S. News and World Report,* XXXVI (June 11, 1954), 82–101.

4160.   Groves, Leonard R. "General Groves Sizes Up Scientists: From the Oppenheimer Hearings." *U.S. News and World Report*, XXXVII (July 2, 1954), 79–84.

4161.   Hewlett, Richard G. and Francis Duncan. *A History of the United States Atomic Energy Commission, 1939–1952*. 2 vols. State College, PA: Pennsylvania State University Press, 1962–1969.

4162.   Kalven, Harry, Jr. "The Case of J. Robert Oppenheimer Before the Atomic Energy Commission." *Bulletin of the Atomic Scientists*, X (September 1954), 259–269.

4163.   Lilienthal, David E. *The Atomic Energy Years*. Vol. II of the *Journals of David E. Lilienthal*. New York: Harper & Row, 1964. 678p.

4164.   _____ . "Mystery in the Oppenheimer Case." *U.S. News and World Report*, XXXVII (July 9, 1954), 89–95.

4165.   McWilliams, Carey. "The Oppenheimer Case." *Nation*, CLXXVIII (May 1, 1954), 373–379.

4166.   Major, John. *The Oppenheimer Hearing*. New York: Stein and Day, 1971. 336p.

4167.   Matthews, Joseph B. "The Oppenheimer Story." *American Mercury*, LXXIX (October 1954), 136–143.

4168.   Michelmore, Peter. *The Swift Years: The Robert Oppenheimer Story*. New York: Dodd, Mead, 1969. 273p.

4169.   Nichols, Kenneth D. "In the Matter of J. Robert Oppenheimer: Findings and Recommendations." *Bulletin of the Atomic Scientists*, X (September 1954), 271–274.

4170.   _____ . "This is What the Government Says: Text of Letter to Dr. Oppenheimer." *U.S. News and World Report*, XXXVI (April 23, 1954), 55–59.

4171.   Oppenheimer, J. Robert. "This is What Dr. Oppenheimer Says: Full Text of Dr. Oppenheimer's Letter to General [Kenneth D.] Nichols." *U.S. News and World Report*, XXXVI (April 23, 1954), 59–68.

4172.   "The Oppenheimer Case." *Bulletin of the Atomic Scientists*, X (May 1954), 173–187+.

4173.   "The Oppenheimer Paradox: Sense and Senselessness." *Newsweek*, XLIII (April 26, 1954), 28–29.

4174.   "Oppenheimer's Security." *Science News Letter*, LXV (April 24, June 12–26, 1954), 259–261, 371–374, 403.

4175. Robb, Roger. "Former AEC Counsel Explains Why Oppenheimer was Ousted." *U.S. News and World Report*, XXXVIII (April 1, 1955), 92–95.

4176. Schlesinger, Arthur M., Jr. "The Oppenheimer Case." *Atlantic*, CXCIV (October 1954), 29–36.

4177. Shepley, James R. and Clay Blair, 3rd. *Hydrogen Bomb: The Men, the Menace, the Mechanism.* New York: David McKay, 1954. 244p.

4178. Stern, Philip M. *The Oppenheimer Case: Security on Trial.* New York: Harper & Row, 1969. 591p.

4179. "The Strange Case of Dr. Oppenheimer." *U.S. News and World Report*, XXXVI (April 23, 1954), 20–22+.

4180. "Testimony That Decided the Oppenheimer Case: Answers by the Scientist and His Critics in Cross-Examination Before the [AEC] Personnel Security Board." *U.S. News and World Report*, XXXVI (June 25, 1954), 79–106.

4181. United States. Atomic Energy Commission. *In the Matter of J. Robert Oppenheimer: Transcript of Hearings Before the Personnel Security Board and Texts of Principal Documents and Letters.* Cambridge, MA: M.I.T. Press, 1971. 1,084p.

4182. White, Theodore H. "U.S. Science: The Troubled Quest." *Reporter*, XI (September 23, 1954), 26–27+.

4183. "Why Dr. Oppenheimer is Called a Security Risk: Text of the Atomic Energy Commission's Decision." *U.S. News and World Report*, XXXVII (July 9, 1954), 71–81.

4184. Wilson, Thomas W. *The Great Weapons Heresy.* Boston: Houghton, Mifflin, 1970. 275p.

Alexander Orlov

4185. Orlov, Alexander. *Handbook of Intelligence and Guerrilla Warfare.* Ann Arbor: University of Michigan Press, 1963. 187p.

4186. _____ . *The Secret History of Stalin's Crimes.* New York: Random House, 1953. 366p.

4187. United States. Congress. Senate. Committee on the Judiciary. Subcommittee to Investigate the Administration of the Internal Security Act and of Alexander Orlov. 83rd Cong., 2nd sess. Washington, D.C.: GPO, 1955. 20p.

Released to the public in 1962.

4188. _____ . _____ . _____ . _____ . _____ . *The Scope of Soviet Activity in the United States—Part LI: Hearings and Testimony of Alexander Orlov.* 84th Cong., 2nd sess. Washington, D.C.: GPO, 1957. 48p.

4189. _____ . _____ . _____ . _____ . _____ . *The Legacy of Alexander Orlov.* 93rd Cong., 1st sess. Washington, D.C.: GPO, 1973. 150p.

Otto F. Otepka

4190. "CIA's Vietnam Hit LBJ, Otepka: Reprinted From the *Government Employee's Exchange,* April 30, 1969." *Congressional Record,* CXV (April 30, 1969), 10918.

4191. Gill, William J. *The Ordeal of Otto Otepka.* New Rochelle, NY: Arlington House, 1969. 505p.

4192. "Mrs. Otepka Recalls Ordeal: Reprinted From the *Washington Evening Star,* April 27, 1969." *Congressional Record,* CXV (April 28, 1969), 10529–10530.

4193. "Otepka was Major Roadblock in Takeover by a 'New Team'— *New York Times* Linked to CIA Plot on OFFL: Reprinted from the *Government Employee's Exchange,* April 16, 1969." *Congressional Record,* CXV (April 30, 1969), 10918–10919.

Georges Pacques

4194. "The Man With the Cosmic View: Georges Pacques." *Time,* LXXXII (October 4, 1963), 42+.

4195. "The Undercover Talleyrand: French Spy Georges Pacques." *Time,* LXXXIV (July 17, 1974), 31–32.

4196. "With All Due Modesty . . .: Georges Pacques." *Newsweek,* LXII (October 7, 1963), 58+.

Saul K. Padover

4197. Padover, Saul K. *Experiment in Germany: The Story of an American Intelligence Officer.* New York: Duell, Sloan, and Pearce, 1946. 408p.

John A. Paisley

4198. "The Puzzling Paisley Case." *Time,* CXIII (January 22, 1979), 30–31.

4199. "Suicide or Murder?: The Death of Consultant John A. Paisley." *Newsweek,* XCII (October 16, 1978), 45+.

4200. Szulc, Tad. "The Missing CIA Man." *New York Times Magazine,* (January 7, 1979), 13+.

Oleg V. Penkovskiy

4201. Blackstock, Paul W. "The CIA and the Penkovskiy Affair." *Worldview*, IX (February 1966), 11–15.

4202. "Fear at the Top: The Execution of Oleg Penkovskiy." *Newsweek*, LXI (June 10, 1963), 60–61.

4203. Franklin, Charles. "Oleg Penkovskiy." In: *Great Spies*. London: Hart, 1967. pp. 231–245.

4204. "The Great Western Spy Net." *Time*, LXXXI (May 15, 1963), 35–36.

4205. "Leaks at the Top?" *Newsweek*, LXI (May 13, 1963), 44.

4206. Maclean, Fitzroy. "Oleg Penkovskiy." In: *Take Nine Spies*. New York: Atheneum, 1978. pp. 304–332.

4207. "The Moscow Spy Trial." *Illustrated London News*, CCXLII (May 18, 1963), 756–757.

4208. Penkovskiy, Oleg V. *The Penkovskiy Papers*. Translated from the Russian. Garden City, NY: Doubleday, 1965. 411p.

Ghostwritten.

4209. Schwartz, Harry. "The Spy Who Came in From the Cold War." *Saturday Review of Literature*, XLIX (January 29, 1966), 36–38.

4210. "Spies in Moscow: More Than Meets the Eye." *Newsweek*, LXI (May 20, 1963), 41–42.

4211. "Spy in the Kremlin: Oleg V. Penkovskiy." *Newsweek*, LXV (November 8, 1965), 48–49.

4212. "Spy Thriller From a Moscow Courtroom: The Penkovskiy Trial." *U.S. News and World Report*, LIV (May 20, 1963), 8–9.

4213. Wynne, Grenville M. "British Agent Supports [the Authenticity of the] Penkovskiy Papers." *Publisher's Weekly*, CLXXXVIII (November 22, 1965), 39–40.

4214. _____ . *Contact on Gorky Street*. New York: Atheneum, 1967. 222p.

4215. _____ . _____ . *Reader's Digest*, XCI (August 1967), 185–190+.

4216. _____ . _____ [: Extract]. In: Burke Wilkinson, ed. *Cry Spy!* Scarsdale, NY: Bradbury Press, 1969. pp. 242–253.

4217. _____ . *The Man From Moscow: The Story of Wynne and Penkovskiy*. London: Hutchinson, 1967. 222p.

Joseph S. Peterson, Jr.

4218. "The Hush-Hush Suspect." *Newsweek,* XLIV (October 18, 1954), 32+.

4219. "Sometimes It's Easy to Get U.S. Secrets." *U.S. News and World Report,* XXXVII (October 29, 1954), 38+.

Martha Peterson

4220. Deming, Angus. "We Still Need Spies: The Arrest of Martha Peterson in Moscow." *Newsweek,* XCI (June 26, 1978), 38+.

4221. "Episodes in a Looking-Glass War." *Time,* CXI (June 26, 1978), 29–31.

Vladimir M. Petrov

4222. Bialoguski, Michael. *The Case of Colonel Petrov: How I Weaned a High MVD Official From Communism.* New York: McGraw-Hill, 1955. 238p.

4223. _____ . "How I Weaned Petrov From Communism." *Saturday Evening Post,* CCXXVIII (August 6–September 10, 1955), 17–19+, 34–35+, 30+, 30+, 30+, 36+.

4224. Brown, Wilton J., ed. *The Petrov Conspiracy Unmasked.* Sydney, Australia: Current Book Distributors, 1957. 360p.

4225. "Notes From the Downunderground." *Time,* LXIX (February 11, 1957), 100+.

4226. Petrov, Vladimir M. "Russian Spy Tells His Own Story." *U.S. News and World Report,* XXXIX (September 30, 1955), 114–130.

4227. _____ and Evdokia Petrova. *Empire of Fear.* New York: Praeger, 1957. 351p.

Herbert A. Philbrick

4228. Philbrick, Herbert A. *I Led 3 Lives: Citizen, Communist, Counter-Spy.* New York: McGraw-Hill, 1952. 323p.

Harold A. R. "Kim" Philby

4229. "Britain's Spy Scandals [Profumo and Philby]: How They Grew." *U.S. News and World Report,* LIV (June 24, 1963), 46–48.

4230. "British Spies [Philby, Burgess and Maclean] For the Soviet Union: Reprinted From the *Washington Post,* October 8, 1967." *Congressional Record,* CXIII (October 9, 1967), 28231–28233.

4231. Burn, Michael. "Philby—Why a Spy?" In: *The Debatable Land.* London: Hamilton, 1970. pp. 221–274.

4232. "Communist in MI6." *Time,* XC (October 13, 1967), 37–38.

4233. "The Establishment Man." *Newsweek,* LXX (October 16, 1967), 45–46.

4234. Giniger, K. S. "A Real-Life James Bond." *Saturday Review of Literature,* LI (August 3, 1968), 29–30.

4235. Greene, Graham and Malcolm Muggeridge. "Reflections on the Character of Kim Philby." *Esquire,* LXX (September 1968), 110–113+.

4236. "Hello, Comrade Philby: With Excerpts From an Interview." *Newsweek,* LXXI (January 1, 1968), 32–33.

4237. "The Kindly Superspy." *Time,* XCI (June 7, 1968), 108+.

4238. Kirkpatrick, Lyman B., Jr. "The Spy With the Old School Tie." *Transaction,* VI (January 1969), 57–58.

4239. Lejeune, Anthony. "Britain's Master Spy." *National Review,* XX (May 21, 1968), 505–506.

4240. "Love, Kim." *Newsweek,* LXI (March 18, 1963), 40+.

4241. McDermott, Geoffrey. "James Bond Could Have Learned From Philby." *New York Times Magazine,* (November 12, 1967), 36–37+.

4242. Maclean, Fitzroy. "Harold 'Kim' Philby." In: *Take Nine Spies.* New York: Atheneum, 1978. pp. 222–271.

4243. Maule, Henry. "Philby Admits Spying for the Reds: Reprinted From the *New York Daily News,* October 2, 1967." *Congressional Record,* CXIII (October 12, 1967), 28841–28842.

4244. Mosley, Leonard. "Letters From a Spy: The Philby Case." *Esquire,* LXXXIX (March 28, 1978), 48–49+.

4245. "The Old School Spy." *Time,* XCI (March 1, 1978), 26.

4246. Page, Bruce, with David Leitch and Phillip Knightley. *The Philby Conspiracy.* Garden City, NY: Doubleday, 1968. 300p.

4247. Philby, Eleanor. *Kim Philby, The Spy I Married.* New York: Ballantine Books, 1968. 173p.

4248. Philby, Harold A. R. "Kim." *My Silent World.* New York: Grove Press, 1968. 262p.

Written after his defection to Russia.

4249. _____ . "Whiff of the Firing Squad." In: Burke Wilkinson, ed. *Cry Spy!* Scarsdale, NY: Bradbury Press, 1969. pp. 261–268.

4250. Seale, Patrick and Maureen McConville. *Philby: The Long Road to Moscow.* New York: Simon and Schuster, 1973. 282p.

4251. Sheehan, E. R. F. "The Rise and Fall of a Soviet Agent." *Saturday Evening Post,* CCXXXVII (February 15, 1964), 30–32+.

4252. Spiro, Edward. *The Third Man.* By E. H. Cookridge, pseud. New York: Putnam, 1968. 281p.

4253. "Stranger Than Spy Fiction: The Story of Double-Agent Philby." *U.S. News and World Report,* LXIII (October 10, 1967), 19–20.

4254. Trevor-Roper, Hugh R. "The Philby Affair: Espionage, Treason, and Secret Services." *Encounter,* XXX (April 1968), 3–26.

4255. _____ . _____ . London: Kimber, 1968. 126p.

4256. Weeks, Edward A. "The Peripatetic Reviewer." *Atlantic,* CCXXI (June 1968), 116–119.

4257. Werth, Alexander. "Philby: Virtuoso of Lying and Spying." *Nation,* CCVI (May 20, 1968), 669–670.

4258. Wise, David. "The Spy Who Flew His Cage." *New Republic,* CLVIII (May 25, 1968), 36–38.

David A. Phillips

4259. Phillips, David A. "Final Act in the Theater of the Absurd." *Retired Officer,* (April 1976), 26–29.

4260. _____ . *The Night Watch: 25 Years of Peculiar Service.* New York: Atheneum, 1977. 309p.

Chin Pi-hwei

4261. "Broken Jade." *Newsweek,* XXXI (April 5, 1948), 38–39.

4262. Burke, J. "Japan's Mata Hari." *Life,* XXIII (July 28, 1947), 19–20.

4263. "Death of a Spy." *Life,* XXIV (April 26, 1948), 39–40.

4264. "The Foolish Elder Brother." *Time,* LI (April 5, 1948), 34+.

Helga Pohl-Wennenmacher

4265. Pohl-Wennenmacher, Helga. *Red Spy at Night: A True Story of Espionage and Seduction Behind the Iron Curtain.* Translated from the German. London: New English Library, 1977. 176p.

Hannsheine Porst

4266. Stolley, R. B. "The Two Faces of Hannsheine Porst." *Life*, LXV (November 22, 1968), 79–80+.

Francis Gary Powers

4267. Berman, Harold J. *Trial of the U-2: Exclusive Authentic Account of the Court Proceedings of the Case of Francis Gary Powers Heard Before the Military Division of the Supreme Court of the U.S.S.R., Moscow, August 17–19, 1960.* Chicago: Trans-World Publications, 1960. 158p.

4268. "The Boy From Virginia." *Time*, LXXVI (August 29, 1960), 18–20.

4269. Demaris, Ovid. "Going to See Gary." *Esquire*, LXV (May 1966), 88–91+.

4270. Donovan, James B. "The Powers Espionage Trial." *America*, CIV (October 29, 1960), 142–144.

4271. *Facts on File*, Editors of. "Francis Gary Powers." In: *Political Profiles: The Eisenhower Years.* New York, 1977. pp. 486–487.

4272. ———. ———. In: *Political Profiles: The Kennedy Years.* New York, 1976. pp. 414–415.

4273. "Five Lessons For America [in] the Powers Trial and Its Aftermath." *Air Force*, XLIII (October 1960), 37–41.

4274. Franklin, Charles. "Francis Gary Powers." In: *Great Spies.* London: Hart, 1967. pp. 255–258.

4275. Gillingham, Peter N. "Russia Stages a New Show Trial." *New York Times Magazine*, (August 14, 1960), 13+.

4276. "He Flew the U-2." *Newsweek*, LXXI (February 12, 1968), 12.

4277. Oldfield, Barney. "Powers: From Probe to Plowshare—an Interview." *NATO's Fifteen Nations*, XX (April–May 1975), 60–64+.

4278. "The Pilot and the Prosecuter." *Newsweek*, LXV (August 22, 1960), 27–29+.

4279. Powers, Barbara. *Spy Wife.* New York: Pyramid Books, 1965. 188p.

4280. Powers, Francis Gary. "Flight and Capture of the U-2: Testimony Before a Senate Committee." *U.S. News and World Report*, LII (March 19, 1962), 48–51.

4281. _____ . "Francis Gary Powers Tells His Story." *New York Times Magazine*, (April 19, 1970), 36–37+.

4282. _____ . "Here is Powers' Own Story—as Told by the Russians." *U.S. News and World Report*, XLIX (August 22, 1960), 53–55+.

4283. _____ . *Operation Overflight: The U-2 Pilot Tells His Story For the First Time.* New York; Holt, 1970. 375p.

4284. _____ . "The Poison Pin Decision." *Rolling Stone*, XXV (December 1, 1977), 52–53.

4285. "Powers on Trial." *Illustrated London News*, CCXXXVII (August 27, 1960), 327–329.

4286. Riesman, David. "The U-2 Affair: Aftermath and Afterthoughts." *Commonweal*, LXXVI (June 8, 1962), 273–276.

4287. *Soviet Booklets*, Editors of. *The Powers Case: Material of the Court Hearings in the Criminal Case of the American Spy-Pilot, Francis Gary Powers.* Soviet Booklet, no. 79. London, 1960. 92p.

4288. "U-2 Spy: Questions Without Answers." *Newsweek*, LIX (February 26, 1962), 19–20.

4289. United States. Congress. Senate. Committee on Armed Services. *Francis Gary Powers: Hearings.* 87th Cong., 2nd sess. Washington, D.C.: GPO, 1962. 25p.

4290. "United States Seeks Access to Francis Powers: Text of Notes Exchanged." *Department of State Bulletin*, XLIII (August 22, 1960), 276–277.

4291. "Was Powers Shot Down?" *Time*, LXXVI (October 3, 1960), 28.

4292. White, William S. "In the Dock." *Time*, LXXVI (September 5, 1960), 50–51.

John D. Profumo

4293. "Anticlimax: The [Alfred T. D.] Denning Report." *Newsweek*, LXII (October 7, 1963), 51.

4294. Behr, Edward. "Crisis Over Christine." *Saturday Evening Post*, CCXXXVI (July 13, 1963), 77–85.

4295. Bergquist, Lawrence. "Personal Report on Britain's Biggest Scandal." *Look*, XXVII (July 30, 1963), 81–86.

4296. Brogan, Colm. "The Profumo Affair." *National Review*, XIV (July 2, 1963), 528–529+.

4297. Burnet, Alastair. "The Blushing James Bond." *New Republic,* CXLIX (August 17, 1963), 9–10.

4298. Denning, Alfred T. D. *Lord Denning's Report.* London: H. M. Stationery Office, 1963. 113p.

4299. _____ . *The Profumo-Christine Keeler Affair: Lord Denning's Report, Presented to Parliament by the Prime Minister.* New York: Popular Library, 1963. 174p.

4300. "Dial 'S' For Squalor: Regina vs. Stephen Thomas Ward." *Time,* LXXXII (August 2, 1963), 22+.

4301. Fairfield, Cecily I. "Doctor Stephen Ward Returns." By Rebecca West, pseud. *Esquire,* LXII (September 1964), 138+.

4302. "Ineffectual, but Innocent: Lord Denning's Report." *Time,* LXXXII (October 4, 1963), 40–41.

4303. "Moral Post-Mortem." *Time,* LXXXII (August 16, 1963), 20–21.

4304. "The New Pornocracy." *Newsweek,* LXII (July 8, 1963), 35–36.

4305. "New Uproar in Britain Over Security: Summary of the Denning Report." *U.S. News and World Report,* LV (October 7, 1963), 8–9.

4306. "One Crowded Hour." *Time,* LXXXII (August 9, 1963), 26+.

4307. "The Price of Christine." *Time,* LXXXI (June 14, 1963), 32–33.

4308. "Theydunit." *Newsweek,* LXII (July 15, 1963), 22+.

4309. " 'What the Hell. . . .' " *Newsweek,* LXXXI (June 17, 1963), 38+.

Yuri A. Rastvorov

4310. "The Case of Russia's Missing Diplomat." *U.S. News and World Report,* XXXVI (February 12, 1954), 28–30.

4311. Eunson, Robert. "How We Nabbed Russia's Number One Spy." *Saturday Evening Post,* CCXXVII (September 25, 1954), 27+.

4312. Rastvorov, Yuri A. "Good-bye to Red Terror." *Life,* XXXVII (December 13, 1954), 49–50+.

4313. _____ . "Red Fraud and Intrigue in the Far East." *Life,* XXXVII (December 6, 1954), 174–176.

4314. "Yuri A. Rastvorov Granted Asylum: With Statement by Mr. Rastvorov." *Department of State Bulletin,* XXXI (August 23, 1954), 271–273.

William F. Rayburn

4315.   *Facts on File,* Editors of. "William Francis Rayburn." In:*Political Profiles: The Johnson Years.* New York, 1976. p. 487.

Georgio Rinaldi

4316.   "From Scandinavia to Somalia: A Soviet Spy Network Crumbles." *U.S. News and World Report,* LXII (April 24, 1967), 44–46.

A. I. Romanov

4317.   Romanov, A. I. *Nights are Longest There: A Memoir of the Soviet Security Service.* Translated From the Russian. Boston: Little, Brown, 1972. 256p.

Hans K. Ronblom

4318.   Ronblom, Hans K. *The Spy Without a Country.* Translated From the *Swedish.* New York: Coward, McCann, 1965. 222p.

Kermit Roosevelt

4319.   *Facts on File,* Editors of. "Kermit Roosevelt." In:*Political Profiles: The Eisenhower Years.* New York, 1977. pp. 525–526.

Julius and Ethel Rosenberg

4320.   "After Seventeen Years." *Nation,* CCIII (September 12, 1966), 203–204.

4321.   Anders, Roger M. "The Rosenberg Case Revisited: The Greenglass Testimony and the Protection of Atomic Secrets." *American Historical Review,* LXXXIII (April 1978), 388–400.

4322.   Busch, Francis X. "The Trial of Julius and Ethel Rosenberg and Morton Sobell For Conspiracy to Transmit Information Relative to the National Defense to Soviet Russia." In: *Enemies of the State.* Indianapolis: Bobbs-Merrill, 1954. pp. 235–299.

4323.   Countryman, Vernon. "Out Damned Spot: Judge [Irving R.] Kaufman and the Rosenberg Case." *New Republic,* CLXXVII (October 8, 1977), 15–17.

4324.   Davidson, Bill. "The First Real Story of the Big Atomic Bomb Plot: The People Who Stole It From Us."*Look,* XXI (October 29, 1957), 87–88+.

4325.   De Toledano, Ralph. *The Greatest Plot in History.* New York: Duell, Sloan, and Pearce, 1963. 306p.

4326.   *Facts on File,* Editors of. "Julius and Ethel Rosenberg." In: *Political Profiles: The Eisenhower Years.* New York, 1977. pp. 526–528.

4327.   Fairfield, Cecily I. "Annals of Treason." By Rebecca West, pseud. *New Yorker,* XXVIII (February 14, 1953), 37–40+; XXIX (February 21–28, 1953), 37–40+, 33–34+.

4328.   Fineberg, Solomon A. "Behind the Rosenberg Case." In: Victor Lasky, ed. *American Legion Reader.* New York: Hawthorn Books, 1953. pp. 418–430.

4329.   _____ . "Plain Facts About the Rosenberg Case." *Reader's Digest,* LXIII (September 1953), 9–14.

4330.   _____ . *The Rosenberg Case: Fact and Fiction.* New York: Oceana Publications, 1953. 159p.

The A.C.L.U. statement of December 7, 1952.

4331.   Footlick, J. K., *et al.* "The Rosenbergs Retried." *Newsweek,* LXXXV (May 19, 1975), 54–55.

4332.   Franklin, Charles. "Julius and Ethel Rosenberg." In: *Great Spies.* London: Hart, 1967. pp. 204–207.

4333.   _____ . _____ . In: his *World-Famous Trials.* New York: Taplinger, 1966. pp. 259–283.

4334.   "Generation on Trial." *Time,* CV (May 7, 1975), 77+.

4335.   Glackin, J. J. "How Secrecy Played Executioner." *Bulletin of the Atomic Scientists,* XXXI (June 1975), 14–16.

4336.   Goldstein, Alvin H. *The Unquiet Death of Julius and Ethel Rosenberg.* New York: Laurence Hill, 1975.

4337.   Goodman, Walter. "The Rosenberg Case: An Inquest on an Inquest." *New York Times Magazine,* (May 24–June 7, 1970), 28–29+, 7+.

4338.   Gottlieb, Jeff. "Frame-ups." *Politics Today,* V (May 1978), 12+.

4339.   Lehmann, Paul. "History's New Light: The Rosenbergs, Then and Now." *Christianity and Crisis,* XXXVIII (July 17, 1978), 185–187.

4340.   Meerpol, Robert and Michael. *We Were Your Sons: The Legacy of Julius and Ethel Rosenberg.* Boston: Houghton, Mifflin, 1975. 419p.

4341.   Morgan, Ted. "The Rosenberg Jury." *Esquire,* LXXXIII (May 1975), 105–109+.

4342.   Nizer, Louis. *Implosion Conspiracy.* Garden City, NY: Doubleday, 1973. 495p.

4343.   "No. 4." *Time,* LVI (July 31, 1950), 12–13.

4344.   Parrish, Michael E. "Cold War Justice: The Supreme Court and the Rosenbergs." *American Historical Review,* LXXXII (October 1977), 805–842.

4345.   Rabinowitz, Victor. "The Rosenberg Case and United States Policy." *Science and Society,* XXXI (Winter 1967), 67–73.

4346.   Root, Jonathan. *Betrayers: The Rosenberg Case – a Reappraisal of an American Crisis.* New York: Coward-McCann, 1963. 305p.

4347.   *The Rosenberg Atomic Spy Case.* Mount Dora, FL: Documentary Photo Cards, 1978. Sixteen 11" x 14" photographs.

4348.   "The Rosenberg Myth." *Time,* LXXXIX (February 24, 1967), 51–52.

4349.   Schardt, Arlie. "Julius Guilty, Ethel Framed?" *Newsweek,* XCIII (July 2, 1979), 64.

4350.   Schneir, Walter. "The Second Frame-Up of Julius and Ethel Rosenberg." *Ramparts,* XII (August 1973), 41–44+.

4351.   _____ and Miriam. *Invitation to an Inquest.* Garden City, NY: Doubleday, 1965. 467p.

4352.   "Spies in the U.S. Told Russia All." *U.S. News and World Report,* XXX (April 6, 1951), 13–15.

4353.   Stern, Sol and Ronald Radosh. "The Hidden Rosenberg Case: How the FBI Framed Ethel to Break Julius." *New Republic,* CLXXX (June 23, 1979), 13–26.

4354.   "The Story of Two Spies." *U.S. News and World Report,* XXXIV (January 9, 1953), 42–43.

4355.   Theoharis, Athan G. "A Break in the Rosenberg Case." *Nation,* CCXXVII (July 1, 1978), 5–6.

4356.   "The Truth, After 26 Years." *New Republic,* CLXXX (June 23, 1979), 5–8.

4357.   Wexley, John. *The Judgment of Julius and Ethel Rosenberg.* New York: Cameron and Kahn, 1955. 672p.

4358.   "Worse Than Murder." *Time,* LVII (April 16, 1951), 22–23.

Yevgeny Y. Runge

4359. United States. Congress. Senate. Committee on the Judiciary. Subcommittee to Investigate the Administration of the Internal Security Act and Other Internal Security Laws. *Testimony of Colonel Yevgeny Y. Runge: Hearings.* 91st Cong., 2nd sess. Washington, D.C.: GPO, 1970. 67p.

Vladimir N. Sakharov

4360. Barron, John. "The Spy Who Vanished." *Reader's Digest,* CVII (November 1975), 223–227+.

Irmgard M. Schmidt

4361. "Secrets For Sale in Berlin." *U.S. News and World Report,* XXXVIII (January 7, 1955), 35–36.

Martha Schneider

4362. Whitney, C. R. "Working for the CIA Ruined Her Life." *New York Times Biographical Service,* VII (December 1976), 1789–1790.

Horst Schwirkman

4363. "'Joker': The Schwirkman Incident." *Newsweek,* LXIV (September 28, 1964), 48+.

Michael Selzer

4364. Ravitch, David. "Brouhaha in Brooklyn." *New Republic,* CLXXVI (March 12, 1977), 18–21.

Ivan A. Serov

4365. "Dropping the Cop." *Time,* LXXII (December 22, 1958), 20–21.

4366. Jordan, Henry. "Ivan Serov: Hatchet Man For the Kremlin." *Reader's Digest,* LXXII (February 1958), 121–122+.

Nicholas Shadrin, pseud. *See* Nikolai Artamonov

Arhady Shevchenko

4367. Chavez, Judy. *Defector's Mistress: The Judy Chavez Story.* New York: Dell, 1979. 267p.

4368. "Defector's Lady: [CIA] Payments to Arhady Shevchenko's Female Companion." *Newsweek,* XCII (October 23, 1978), 53.

Rupert Sigl

4369. "Agent of Doom." *Newsweek,* LXXIII (May 19, 1969), 48.

4370. Sigl, Rupert. *In the Claws of the KGB: Memoirs of a* [Austrian] *Double-Agent.* Philadelphia: Dorrance, 1978. 247p.

Joseph B. Smith

4371. Smith, Joseph B. *Portrait of a Cold Warrior.* New York: Putnam, 1976. 448p.

Morton Sobell

4372. Langer, Edward. "The Case of Morton Sobell: New Queries From the Defense." *Science,* CLIII (September 23, 1966), 1501–1505.

4373. Love, Stephen. "The Sobell Case." *Nation,* CLXXXII (June 23, 1956), 526–528.

4374. Sobell, Morton. *On Doing Time.* New York: Scribner's, 1974. 525p.

Robert Soblen

4375. "Approaching the End." *Newsweek,* LX (July 30, 1962), 35–36.

4376. Higgings, Robert. "The Soblen Case." *World Today,* XVIII (October 1962), 415–427.

4377. Schneir, Walter. "The Soblen Trial." *Nation,* CXCIII (August 26, 1961), 91–94.

4378. "The Soblen Case." *New Republic,* CXLVII (September 17, 1962), 6–7.

4379. "Soblen vs. the State." *Newsweek,* LX (September 17, 1962), 47–48.

4380. Thornberry, Charles. "The Soblen Case." *Political Quarterly,* XXXIV (April 1963), 162–173.

Jerzy Sosnowski

4381. Newman, Bernard. *The Sosnowski Affair: Inquest on a* [Polish] *Spy.* London: Laurie, 1954. 203p.

Frank Snepp

4382. Emerson, Gloria. "The Spy Who Rang My Doorbell: Frank Snepp." *New York Magazine,* XI (January 23, 1978), 50–53.

4383. Snepp, Frank. "The CIA vs. Me." *Newsweek,* XCII (July 31, 1978), 13.

Theodore Sorensen

4384. Towell, Pat. "Sorensen Withdraws Nomination to Head CIA." *Congressional Quarterly Weekly Report,* XXXV (January 22, 1977), 154–155.

4385. United States. Congress. Senate. Select Committee on Intelligence. *Nomination of Theodore C. Sorensen to be Director of Central Intelligence: Hearings.* 95th Cong., 1st sess. Washington, D.C.: GPO, 1977. 43p.

John K. Starnes

4386. Lewis, Robert. "See No Evil, Hear No Evil, Speak No Evil." *Macleans,* XCI (November 20, 1978), 24–25.

Bogdan N. Stasinskii

4387. Steele, J. L. "Assassin." In: Barbara Nolen, ed. *Spies, Spies, Spies.* New York: Watts, 1965. pp. 233–250.

4388. Van Bergh, Hendrik. *Murder to Order.* Translated From the Dutch. London: Ampersand, 1965. 110p.

Alexander Steele

4389. Steele, Alexander. *How to Spy on the U.S.* New Rochelle, NY: Arlington House, 1974. 185p.

Werner Stillers

4390. "The S-Bahn Spy: Werner Stiller's Defection From East Germany to West Germany." *Time,* CXIII (February 5, 1979), 115.

Kim Suim

4391. Singer, Kurt D. "Charm School at King Jade Street." In: *Spies Over Asia.* London: W. H. Allen, 1956. pp. 161–169.

4392. Thayer, M. V. "The Korean Seductress Who Betrayed America." *Coronet,* XXVIII (October 1950), 55–58.

Vasilii V. Tarasov

4393. "Double Duty in Canada." *Time,* LXXXIII (May 8, 1964), 49–50.

Laszlo Szabo

4394. United States. Congress. House. Committee on Armed Services. Special Subcommittee on the Central Intelligence Agency. *Statement of Laszlo Szabo in Hearings Before the CIA Subcommittee.* 89th Cong., 2nd sess. Washington, D.C.: GPO, 1966. 46p.

Frantisek Tisler

4395. United States. Congress. House. Committee on Un-American Activities. *Communist Espionage in the United States: Hearings and Testimony of Frantisek Tisler, Former Military and Air Attache, Czechoslovak Embassy, in Washington, D.C.* 86th Cong., 2nd sess. Washington, D.C.: GPO, 1960. 9p.

Reginald C. Thomas

4396. Thomas, Reginald C. "I Spied on the Red Chinese." *Saturday Evening Post,* CCXXV (June 20, 1953), 27+.

Robert G. Thompson

4397. "Lenin, Mon Amour."*Newsweek,* LXV (March 22, 1965), 23–24.

4398. "The Stupid Spy." *Time,* LXXXV (March 19, 1965), 31–32.

4399. Thompson, Robert G. "I Spied For the Russians." *Saturday Evening Post,* CCXXXVIII (May 22–June 5, 1965), 23–29, 38–40+.

David Truong *See* Ronald Humphrey

Li Tsung-jen

4400. "The Chinese Lawyer." *Time,* LXXXVI (August 27, 1965), 14–15.

4401. "Propaganda Coup." *Newsweek,* LXVI (August 2, 1965), 36+.

4402. Seagrave, Sterling and R. A. Jones. "From China With Love." *Esquire,* LXV (January 1966), 42–47+.

Stansfield Turner

4403. "An Admiral For Superspook?" *Time,* CIX (February 14, 1977), 24.

4404. Alpern, David M. "Admiral For the CIA: The Stansfield Turner Nomination." *Newsweek,* LXXXIX (February 21, 1977), 17–18.

4405. Binder, David. "Carter's Choice to Head the CIA." *New York Times Biographical Service,* VIII (February 1977), 301–302.

4406.   Boeth, Robert. "Backstage at the CIA." *Newsweek,* XC (September 12, 1977), 27–28.

4407.   _____ . "How Turner Runs His Ships." *Newsweek,* XCI (February 6, 1978), 22–23.

4408.   *Congressional Quarterly Weekly Report,* Editors of. "Stansfield Turner." In: *President Carter.* Washington, D.C., 1977. pp. 39–40.

4409.   "Controversy Over Czar For Intelligence." *U.S. News and World Report,* LXXXIV (February 6, 1978), 50–52.

4410.   Getlein, Frank. "Appointment Calendar: The Nomination of Stansfield Turner." *Commonweal,* CIV (March 4, 1977), 133–134.

4411.   "Has the Admiral Gone Adrift?: Director Stansfield Turner." *Time,* CXIII (January 29, 1979), 18.

4412.   Lowther, William. "The S.O.B. of the CIA." *Macleans,* XCI (March 6, 1978), 46–48+.

4413.   "Old Salt Opens Up the Pickle Factory." *Time,* CIX (June 20, 1977), 22–25.

4414.   "Stansfield Turner." *Current Biography,* XXXIX (May 1978), 40–43.

4415.   _____ . In: Charles Moritz, ed. *Current Biography Yearbook, 1978.* New York: H. W. Wilson, 1979. pp. 431–434.

4416.   "Suetonius," pseud. "Admirable Stansfield Turner." *New Republic,* CLXXVI (March 12, 1977), 10–12.

4417.   Towell, Pat. "Carter Picks NATO Commander to Head CIA." *Congressional Quarterly Weekly Report,* XXXV (February 12, 1977), 259–260.

4418.   Turner, Stansfield. "Carter's Intelligence Chief Sizes-Up World Trouble Spots: An Interview." *U.S. News and World Report,* LXXXII (May 16, 1977), 24–26.

4419.   _____ . "A Constructive Approach to Intelligence Activities." *U.S.A. Today,* CVII (August 1978), 2–3.

4420.   _____ . "'I Will Be Criticized': An Interview." *Time,* CXI (February 6, 1978), 18.

4421.   United States. Central Intelligence Agency. Office of Public Affairs. *Biography of Admiral Stansfield Turner.* Washington, D.C., 1979. 2p.

4422. _____ . Congress. Senate. Select Committee on Intelligence. *Nomination of Admiral Stansfield Turner to be Director of Central Intelligence: Hearings.* 95th Cong., 1st sess. Washington, D.C.: GPO, 1977. 98p.

William Vassall

4423. Brogan, Colm. "Britain's Scandalous Spy Case." *National Review,* XIV (March 12, 1963) 195–196+.

4424. Fairfield, Cecily I. *The Vassall Affair.* By Rebecca West, pseud. London: Sunday Telegraph, 1963. 99p.

4425. Franklin, Charles. "William Vassall." In: *Great Spies.* London: Hart, 1967. pp. 227–231.

4426. Great Britain. Tribunal to Inquire Into the Vassall Case and Related Matters. *Minutes of Evidence Taken at Public Hearings.* Parliamentary Papers, no. 2037. London: H. M. Stationery Office, 1963. 552p.

4427. _____ . _____ . *Report.* Parliamentary Papers, no. 2009. London: H. M. Stationery Office, 1963. 87p.

4428. Hyde, H. Montgomery. "Composite Portrait of the Soviet Spy." *New York Times Magazine,* (February 16, 1964), 14+.

4429. Panter-Downes, Mollie. "Letter From London: The Vassall Case." *New Yorker,* XXXIX (May 25, 1963), 146–148.

4430. "Trial of Truth: The Vassall Case, England." *Newsweek,* LX (November 26, 1962), 34+.

4431. Vassall, William J.C. *Vassall: The Autobiography of a Spy.* London: Sidgwick and Jackson, 1975. 200p.

Vernon K. Walters

4432. Latham, Aaron. "Soldier, Spy—Tinkered Out!" *Esquire,* LXXXIX (April 25, 1978), 18+.

4433. Walters, Vernon K. *Silent Missions.* Garden City, NY: Doubleday, 1978. 654p.

Hung Wang

4434. "Enemies of the People." *Time,* CV (January 13, 1975), 27.

George Watt

4435. Watt, George. *China Spy.* London: Johnson, 1972. 208p.

Richard S. Welch

4436. Deming, Angus. "Scholar, Wit, Athlete, Spy." *Newsweek,* LXXXVII (January 5, 1976), 26.

Stig Wennerstrom

4437. Altavilla, Enrico. "The Career of a Spy." In: *The Art of Spying.* Translated From the Italian. Englewood Cliffs, NJ: Prentice-Hall, 1965. pp. 63–71, 81–91.

4438. "The Case of the Red Eagle." *Time,* LXXXIII (May 8, 1964), 30.

4439. Cort, David. "The Well-Informed Spy." *Nation,* CC (February 8, 1965), 136–138.

4440. Halacy, Daniel S. "Stig Wennerstrom." In: *Master Spy.* New York: McGraw-Hill, 1968. pp. 141–155.

4441. "A Hell of a Nice Guy." *Newsweek,* LXII (July 8, 1963), 36–37.

4442. "Include the Women." *Time,* LXXXIV (December 11, 1964), 34.

4443. "One Solitary Flaw." *Newsweek,* LXIII (May 11, 1964), 38.

4444. "Red Spy's Secret: First Win the Wives." *U.S. News and World Report,* LVII (December 7, 1964), 12.

4445. Ronblom, Hans K. *The Spy Without a Country.* Translated From the Swedish. New York: Coward-McCann, 1965. 222p.

4446. Ross, Irwin. "The Case of the Swedish Spy." *Reader's Digest,* LXXXVI (April 1965), 117–125.

4447. _____ . "The Master Spy Who Almost Got Away." *Harper's,* CCXXIX (December 1964), 47–54.

4448. "The Spy Scandal That Concerns the U.S." *U.S. News and World Report,* LX (July 8, 1963), 8.

4449. United States. Congress. Senate. Committee on the Judiciary. Subcommittee to Investigate the Administration of the Internal Security Act and Other Internal Security Laws. *The Wennerstroem Spy Case—How It Touched the United States and NATO: Excerpts From the Testimony of Stig Eric Constan Wennerstroem, a Noted Soviet Agent.* 88th Cong., 2nd sess. Washington, D.C.: GPO, 1964. 168p.

4450. Whiteside, Thomas. *An Agent in Place: The Wennerstrom Affair.* New York: Viking Press, 1966. 150p.

4451. _____ . "Annals of Espionage: The Wennerstrom Case." *New Yorker,* XLII (March 26–April 9, 1966), 58–60+, 51–52+, 92+.

4452.   Wilson, George C. "Swedish Spy Details Soviet ICBM Gamble." *Aviation Week and Space Technology,* LXXXI (December 14, 1966), 22–23.

Harry D. White

4453.   "All About the White Case: Official Statements, Testimony, and Correspondence." *U.S. News and World Report,* XXXV (November 20, 1953), 110–118+.

4454.   Bouscaren, Anthony T. "Why Did Truman Disregard Spy Warnings?" *U.S. News and World Report,* XLI (September 14, 1956), 122–123.

4455.   Brownell, Herbert and J. Edgar Hoover. "The White Case." *Time,* LXII (November 30, 1953), 19–23.

4456.   "Close-Up of a Ghost." *Life,* XXXV (November 23, 1953), 29–35.

4457.   "Did Communist Ring Circle the White House?" *U.S. News and World Report,* XXXV (November 20, 1953), 17–20.

4458.   Mundt, Karl E. "How Harry Dexter White Pulled Strings For Russia." *U.S. News and World Report,* XXXV (December 25, 1953), 82–86.

4459.   "One Man's Greed." *Time,* LXII (November 23, December 14, 1953), 21–24+, 11–12+.

4460.   "Spy Story as Told by Truman, Brownell, and FBI's Hoover: The Latest Statements by High Officials on the White Case." *U.S. News and World Report,* XXXV (November 27, 1953), 104–123.

4461.   "Truman on Trial." *New Republic,* CXXIX (November 30, 1953), 6–15.

4462.   "Who's Right in the White Case?" *U.S. News and World Report,* XXXV (November 27, 1953), 26+.

Emma Woikin

4463.   "A Scent For Secrets." *Time,* XLVII (April 22, 1946), 42.

Kim H. Wook

4464.   "Kim Hyung Wook: Former Chief of Korea's CIA." *New York Times Biographical Service,* VIII (June 1977), 838.

Eva Wu

4465. Singer, Kurt D. "The Red Chrysanthemum." In: Barbara Nolen, ed. *Spies, Spies, Spies.* New York: Watts, 1965. pp. 208–216.

4466. _____ . _____ . In: *Spies Over Asia.* London: W. H. Allen, 1956. pp. 153–160.

Grenville Wynne *See* Oleg Penkovskiy

Aharon Yariv

4467. "Master Spy." *Newsweek,* LXXX (October 16, 1972), 44+.

Appendix I:
Late Entries to February 1980

Introduction

The following citations were uncovered too late for inclusion in the main body of the bibliography. All entries are, however, keyed into the author index.

A. Books

4468. Atholl, Justin. *How Stalin Knows: The Story of the Great Atomic Spy Conspiracy.* Norwich, England: Jarrold, 1951. 181p.

4469. Barron, John. *MIG Pilot: The Final Escape of Lt.* [Viktor] *Belenko.* New York: Reader's Digest Press; dist. by McGraw-Hill, 1980. 217p.

4470. Boyle, Andrew. *The Fourth Man* [Anthony Blunt]: *The Definitive Account of Kim Philby, Guy Burgess, and Donald Maclean and Who Recruited Them to Spy for Russia.* New York: Dial Press, 1980. 504p.

4471. Brandt, Edward. *The Last Voyage of U.S.S. Pueblo.* New York: W. W. Norton, 1969. 248p.

4472. Brecker, Michael, with Benjamin Geist. *Decisions in Crisis: Israel, 1967 and 1973.* Berkeley: University of California Press, 1980. 451p.

4473. Canfield, Michael and Allan Weberman. *Coup d'Etat in America: The CIA and the Assassination of John F. Kennedy.* New York: The Third Press, Joseph Okpaky Publishing Co., 1975. 314p.

4474. Caroz, Yaakov. *The Arab Secret Services.* London: Transworld, 1978. 440p.

4475. Chomsky, N. A. and E. S. Herman. *The Political Economy of Human Rights.* 2 vols. Boston: South End Press, 1979.

4476. Cohen, Helen D. *Soviet Policy Toward Black Africa: The Focus on National Integration.* New York: Praeger, 1972. 316p.

4477. Deacon, Richard, pseud. *See* McCormick, Donald (4507).

4478. Derogy, Jacques and Hesi Carmel. *The Untold History of Israel.* Translated from the French. New York: Grove Press, 1979. 346p.

4479. Diederich, Bernard. *Trujillo: The Death of the Goat.* Boston: Little, Brown, 1978. 264p.

4480. Donner, Frank J. *The Age of Surveillance: The Aims and Methods of America's Political Intelligence System.* New York: Alfred A. Knopf, 1980. 576p.

4481. Dorey, M. A. *World Police Systems: A Factual Text.* Boston: Northeastern University, 1975. 376p.

4482. *Facts on File,* Editors of. *Day-by-Day: The Fifties.* New York, 1979. 1,000p.

4483. _____ . *Indonesia: The Sukarno Years.* New York, 1979. 140p.

4484. ———. *Political Prisoners: A World Report.* New York, 1979. 285p.

4485. ———. *Portuguese Revolution, 1974–1976.* New York, 1978. 151p.

4486. ———. *Revolt in the Congo.* New York, 1977. 187p.

4487. ———. *South Vietnam—U.S.-Communist Confrontation in Southeast Asia, 1961–1973.* 7 vols. New York, 1977.

4488. Fidler, Richard. *R.C.M.P.: The Real Subversives.* New York: Pathfinder Press, 1978. 95p.

4489. George, Alexander L. *Presidential Decisionmaking in Foreign Policy: The Effective Use of Information and Advice.* Boulder, CO: Westview Press, 1980. 268p.

4490. Golan, Aviezer and Danny Pinkas. *Shula: Code-Name "The Pearl."* New York: Delacorte Press, 1980. 352p.

4491. Gouré, Leon and Morris Rothenberg. *Soviet Penetration of Latin America.* Coral Gables, FL: Center for Advanced International Studies, University of Miami, 1975. 204p.

4492. Granger, John V. N. *Technology and International Relations.* New York: W. H. Freeman, 1979. 202p.

4493. Halliday, Fred. *Iran: Dictatorship and Development.* Harmondsworth, England: Penguin Books, 1979. 348p.

4494. Hanrieder, Wolfram F. and Larry V. Buel, eds. *Words and Arms: A Dictionary of Security and Defense Terms, With Supplemental Data.* Boulder, CO: Westview Press, 1979. 250p.

4495. Herman, E. S., jt. author. *See* Chomsky, N. A. (4475).

4496. Hoveyda, Fereydoun. *The Fall of the Shah.* New York: Wyndham Books, 1980.

4497. Kalvoda, Josef. *Czechoslovakia's Role in Soviet Strategy.* Washington, D.C.: University Press of America, 1978. 396p.

4498. Kaplan, Susan, jt. editor. *See* Macy, Christy (4508).

4494. Kelly, W. N. *Policing* [and Counterespionage] *in Canada.* Toronto: Macmillan, 1976. 712p.

4500. Kerkvliet, B. J. *The Huk Rebellion: A Study of Peasant Revolt in the Philippines.* Berkeley: University of California Press, 1977. 305p.

4501.   Kosut, Hal. *Cambodia and the Vietnam War.* New York: Facts on File, 1971. 222p.

4502.   Kraslow, David, jt. Author. *See* Loory, Stuart H. (4505).

4503.   Levitt, Morton and Michael. *A Tissue of Lies: Nixon vs. Hiss.* New York: McGraw-Hill, 1979. 344p.

4504.   Lindsey, Robert. *The Falcon and the Snowman: A True Story of Friendship and Espionage.* New York: Simon and Schuster, 1980. 340p.

Andrew Lee and Christopher Boyce.

4505.   Loory, Stuart H. and David Kraslow. *The Secret Search for Peace in Vietnam.* New York: Random House, 1968. 2,477p.

4506.   Lotz, Wolfgang. *A Handbook for Spies.* New York: Harper & Row, 1980. 160p.

4507.   McCormick, Donald. *The British Connection: Russia's Manipulation of British Individuals and Institutions.* By Richard Deacon, pseud. London: Hamilton, 1979. 291p.

4508.   Macy, Christy and Susan Kaplan, eds. *Documents* [on CIA]. Harmondsworth, England: Penguin Books, 1979.

4509.   Martin, David C. *Wilderness of Mirrors.* New York: Harper & Row, 1980. 256p.

James J. Angleton and William Harvey.

4510.   Morris, Robert. *Self Destruct: Dismantling America's Internal Security.* New Rochelle, NY: Arlington House, 1979. 348p.

4511.   Morrow, Robert. *Betrayal: A Reconstruction of Certain Clandestine Events From the Bay of Pigs to the Assassination of John F. Kennedy.* Chicago: Regnery, 1976. 229p.

4512.   Moyer, Frank A. *Foreign Weapons Handbook.* Boulder, CO: Panther Publications, 1970. 326p.

4513.   _____ and Robert J. Scroggie. *Combat Firing Techniques.* Boulder, CO: Paladin Press, 1971. 116p.

4514.   Murray, John. *Spy Called Swallow: The True Story of Norma* [Korzhenko-Murray]. London: W. H. Allen, 1978. 175p.

4515.   O'Ballance, Edgar. *The Kurdish Revolt, 1961–1970.* London: Faber and Faber, 1973. 196p.

4516.   Pinkas, Danny, jt. author. *See* Golan, Aviezer (4490).

4517.   Pirogov, Petr. *Why I Escaped.* New York: Duell, 1950. 336p.

4518.   Potter, William C., ed. *Verification and SALT.* Boulder, CO: Westview Press, 1980. 200p.

4519.   Ray, Ellen, ed. *Dirty Work 2: The CIA in Africa.* Secaucus, NJ: Lyle Stuart, 1979.

4520.   Roosevelt, Kermit. *Countercoup: The Struggle for the Control of Iran.* New York: McGraw-Hill, 1979. 217p.

4521.   Rothenberg, Morris, jt. author. *See* Gouré, Leon (4491).

4522.   *Selected Examples of Possible Approaches to Electronic Communications Interception Operations.* Boulder, CO: Paladin Press, 1980. 40p.

4523.   Smirnov, Gabriel. *The Revolution Disarmed: Chile, 1970–1973.* New York: Monthly Review Press, 1979. 256p.

4524.   Sobel, Lester A., ed. *Russia's Rulers: The Khrushchev Period.* New York: Facts on File, 1971. 394p.

4525.   Stieber, Wilhelm J. *The Chancellor's Spy.* Translated from the German. New York: Grove Press, 1980.

4526.   Taborsky, Edward. *Communist Penetration of the Third World.* New York: Robert Speller and Sons, 1973. 500p.

4527.   Theberge, James. *Soviet Penetration of Latin America.* New York: Crane, Russak, 1974. 107p.

4528.   Tiger, Edith, ed. *In Re Alger Hiss: Petition for a Writ of Error "Coram Nobis."* New York: Hill and Wang, 1979. 438p.

4529.   Valenta, Jiri. *Soviet Intervention in Czechoslovakia, 1968: Anatomy of a Decision.* Baltimore, MD: Johns Hopkins University Press, 1979. 192p.

B. Articles

4530.   Adler, Emanuel. "Executive Command and Control in Foreign Policy: The CIA's Covert Activities." *Orbis,* XXIII (Fall 1979), 671–696.

4531.   "Analysis of the Support Provided to the Warren Commission by the Central Intelligence Agency." In: U.S. Congress. House. Select Committee on Assassinations. Vol. XI of the *Investigation of the Assassination of President John F. Kennedy: Appendix to Hearings.* 95th Cong., 2nd sess. Washington, D.C.: GPO, 1979. pp. 471–504.

4532. "Anti-Castro Activists and Organizations." In: U.S. Congress. House. Select Committee on Assassinations. Vol. X of the *Investigation of the Assassination of President John F. Kennedy: Appendix to Hearings.* 95th Cong., 2nd sess. Washington, D.C.: GPO, 1979. pp. 1–146.

4533. Band, R. E. "Havana Knows: Castro's Assassins Strike Again." *American Opinion,* XVII (June 1974), 23–25.

4534. Barron, John. "MIG Pilot." *Reader's Digest,* CXVI (January 1980), 187–226.

4535. _____ . "A Tale of Two [American and Soviet] Embassies." *Reader's Digest,* CXV (December 1979), 116–120.

4536. Becker, Abraham. "The Meaning and Measure of Soviet Military Expenditures." In: U.S. Congress. Joint Economic Committee. *Soviet Economy in a Time of Change: A Compendium of Papers.* 96th Cong., 1st sess. Washington, D.C.: GPO, 1979. pp. 356–368.

4537. "Blackbirds Over Cuba: SR-71 Spy Plane." *Time,* CXIV (October 22, 1979), 46.

4538. Blakeley, Bob and G. R. "Security of Number Theoretic Public Key Cryptosystems Against Random Attack." *Cryptologia,* III (1979), 29+, 105+.

4539. Bobb, Merrick J. "Preventive Intelligence Systems and the Courts." *California Law Review,* LVIII (June 1970), 914–940.

4540. "Bonn—Spy Target No. 1." *German International,* XXIII, no. 4 (1979), 12–17.

4541. Booth, Walter B. "Allies [in Laos] or Hirelings?" *Army,* XXII (May 1972), 43–47.

4542. Branch, Tom. "The Letelier Investigation." *New York Times Magazine,* (July 16, 1978), 26–30+.

4543. Brown, F. C. "The Phoenix Program." *Military Journal,* II (Spring 1979), 19–21, 49.

4544. Bruning, Fred. "The Fourth Man [Anthony Blunt]." *Newsweek,* XCIV (November 26, 1979), 69–70.

4545. _____ . "A Spy of a Better Sort." *Newsweek,* XCIV (December 3, 1979), 78.

4546. Buchanan, Patrick. "Miserable Failures of Spymasters: Reprinted from the *Chicago Tribune,* October 16, 1979." *Congressional Record,* CXXV (October 17, 1979), E5091–E5092.

4547.   Calvert, Michael. "Some Aspects of Guerrilla Warfare: Socio-Economic Poliwar and Psywar." *Journal of the Royal United Service Institution for Defence Studies,* CXVII (September 1972), 20–24.

4548.   Campbell, Duncan. "BP Sets Up Saudi Secret Police." *New Statesman and Nation,* XCVII (March 23, 1979), 384–386.

4549.   "Canada to the Rescue." *Time,* CXV (February 11, 1980), 20–22.

Canadian agents spirit Americans out of Iran.

4550.   Carroll, Raymond. "Russian Mole in the FBI?: The Views of William C. Sullivan." *Newsweek,* XCIV (July 9, 1979), 35–36.

4551.   "CIA Eyes Growing Soviet Trade in Chemicals." *Chemical and Engineering News,* LVII (January 15, 1979), 20+.

4552.   "Change of Shift for the KGB." *Far Eastern Economic Review,* CIV (June 15, 1979), 31–32.

4553.   Clymer, Ada. "The Bombing of Joe Bananas." *Progressive,* XXXVI (August 1972), 20–25.

4554.   Colby, William E. "Verifying SALT." *Worldview,* XXII (April 1979), 4–7.

4555.   Cook, Fred J. "J. Edgar Hoover and the FBI." *Lithopinion,* VI (February 1971), 8–15, 58–63.

4556.   Corddry, Charles W. "CIA Heads Faults Plans for MX: Reprinted from the *Baltimore Sun,* August 10, 1979." *Congressional Record,* CXXV (September 14, 1979), H7932–H7933.

4557.   "The Creation of the KGB." *Institute for the Study of the U.S.S.R. Bulletin,* I (July 1954), 13–15.

4558.   Crozier, Brian. "Moscow's Aim in Greece." *Soviet Analyst,* IV (June 5, 1975), 1–2.

4559.   "Daring Escape from Iran." *Newsweek,* XCV (February 11, 1980), 26–29.

4560.   "Did Anyone Tell the Queen?: Art Historian Anthony Blunt was a Spy for the Soviets." *Life,* III (January 1980), 31–37.

4561.   Diffie, Whitfield and Martin E. Hellman. "Privacy and Authentication: An Introduction to Cryptography." *Proceedings of the Institute of Electrical and Electronics Engineers,* (March 1979), 397–427.

4562.   Evron, Yair. "Israel and the Atom: The Uses and Misuses of Ambiguity, 1957–1967." *Orbis,* XVII (Winter 1974), 1326–1334.

4563. "The Evolution and Implications of the CIA-Sponsored Assassination Conspiracies Against Fidel Castro." In: U.S. Congress. House. Select Committee on Assassinations. Vol. X of the *Investigation of the Assassination of President John F. Kennedy: Appendix to Hearings.* 95th Cong., 2nd sess. Washington, D.C.: GPO, 1979. pp. 147–196.

4564. "Fact Sheet on Disclosure of the National Foreign Intelligence Program (NFIP) Appropriation." *Congressional Record,* CXXV (June 8, 1979), E2821–E2822.

4565. *Facts on File,* Editors of. "Allen Welsh Dulles." In: *Political Profiles: The Truman Years.* New York, 1978. pp. 143–147.

4566. _____ . "Elizabeth Bentley." In: *Political Profiles: The Truman Years.* New York, 1978. p. 30.

4567. _____ . "Ethel and Julius Rosenberg." In: *Political Profiles: The Truman Years.* New York, 1978. pp. 477–480.

4568. Fialka, John J. "CIA Believed in 1974 That Israel Had Bomb: Reprinted from the *Washington Star,* January 27, 1978." *Congressional Record,* CXXV (May 14, 1979), S5744.

4569. _____ . "CIA's Top Secret 'Mistake' on Israel and the Bomb: Reprinted from the *Washington Star,* January 28, 1978." *Congressional Record,* CXXV (May 14, 1979), S5744–S5745.

4570. _____ . "Israel and the Bomb—Secret File Provoked a Storm: Reprinted from the *Washington Star,* March 2, 1978." *Congressional Record,* CXXV (May 14, 1979), S5742–S5743.

4571. _____ . "Report CIA Had Proof in '68 Israel Had A-bomb Material: Reprinted from the *Chicago Tribune,* December 9, 1977." *Congressional Record,* CXXV (May 14, 1979), S5742.

4572. Fischer, Elliot. "Language Redundancy and Cryptanalysis." *Cryptologia,* III (1979), 233+.

4573. Fritchey, Clayton. "The CIA's Way With Presidents: Reprinted from the *Washington Post,* April 14, 1979." *Congressional Record,* CXXV (April 23, 1979), E1731–E1732.

4574. "From the KGB to the FBI." *Newsweek,* XCV (March 17, 1980), 40.

4575. Garn, E. Jake. "Mr. Carter's Information Gap." *National Review,* XXXI (December 21, 1979), 1614–1615+.

4576. _____ . "The SALT Verification Myth." *Strategic Review,* VII (Summer 1979), 16–24.

4577.   Gonzales, Lawrence. "The Unappreciated Art of CIA." *Qui,* VIII (January 1979), 50–52, 108–116.

4578.   Goodman, Richard C. "Privacy and Political Freedom: Applications of the Fourth Amendment to 'National Security Investigations.'" *UCLA Law Review,* XVII (June 1970), 1205–1251.

4579.   Greider, William. "Government Claims Power to Snoop: Reprinted from the *Washington Post,* May 6, 1979." *Congressional Record,* CXXV (May 16, 1979), E2338.

4580.   Halperin, Morton H. "The CIA's Distemper." *New Republic,* CLXXXII (February 9, 1980), 21–23.

4581.   Hammond, James D. "The Human Factor in Intelligence." *Marine Corps Gazette,* LXIII (April 1979), 19–20.

4582.   Handleman, Howard. "The Soviet KGB in America." *Air Force Magazine,* LXII (June 1979), 57–60.

4583.   Hanke, Robert F. "National Technical Means of Verification." *Military Engineer,* LXXII (September–October 1979), 308+.

4584.   Hellman, Martin E., jt. author. *See* Diffie, Whitfield (4561).

4585.   "Help Wanted at the CIA." *Newsweek,* XCIV (August 20, 1979), 26.

4586.   Hitchens, Christopher. "Keeping It in the Royal Family: The Blunt Case." *Nation,* CCXXIX (December 22, 1979), 651–654.

4587.   Hoge, William. "A Soldier's About-Face." *New York Times Biographical Service,* X (March 1979), 313–314.

        Brazilian intelligence chief Oliveira-Figueiredo.

4588.   Holley, Charles. "Israel After Agranat." *The Middle East,* no. 35 (September 1977), 25–33.

4589.   "How Satellites May Help to Sell SALT." *U.S. News and World Report,* LXXXVI (May 21, 1979), 25–26.

4590.   Huddleston, Walter D. and Ted Weiss. "Pro and Con Debate: Take the Wraps off CIA?" *U.S. News and World Report,* LXXXVIII (February 25, 1980), 45–46.

4591.   Huibregtse, P. K. "Psychological Warfare in North Mozambique." *NATO's Fifteen Nations,* XVII (April–May 1972), 28–30.

4592.   Inman, Bobby R. "The NSA Perspective on Telecommunications Protection in the Nongovernment Sector." *Cryptologia,* III (1979), 129 ⌊.

4593. Kahn, David. "Cryptologia Goes Public." *Foreign Affairs,* LVIII (Fall 1979), 141–160.

4594. Kaiser, Frederick M. "The U.S. Intelligence Community." *Society,* XVI (May 1979), 31–39.

4595. Kelly, Clarence M. "Domestic Industrial Espionage." *Security Management,* XIX (November 1975), 1–3.

4596. Kelly, Orr. "The 'New' FBI Swings Into Action." *U.S. News and World Report,* LXXXVIII (February 18, 1980), 23–26.

4597. Kruh, Louis. "Cipher Devices." *Cryptologia,* III (1979), 206+.

4598. Lardner, George, Jr. "CIA Probe Into Rifled Files Called Superficial, Self-Serving: Reprinted from the *Washington Post,* June 19, 1979." *Congressional Record,* CXXV (June 28, 1979), H5401–H5402.

4599. _____ . "House Probing CIA 'Babysitter' [Regis T. Blahut]' Who Rifled Files on JFK: Reprinted from the *Washington Post,* June 28, 1979." *Congressional Record,* CXXV (June 28, 1979), H5402.

4600. Latimer, Thomas K. "U.S. Intelligence and the Congress." *Strategic Review,* VII (Summer 1979), 47–56.

4601. Lee, William T. "Intelligence: Some Issues of Performance." In: William Schneider, Jr., and Francis P. Hoeber, eds. *Arms, Men, and Military Budgets: Issues for Fiscal Year 1977.* New York: Crane, Russak, 1976. Chpt. 3.

4602. Levere, J. "Begin Uses Admen to Wage Israel's Propaganda War." *Advertising Age,* XLIX (September 11, 1978), 109+.

4603. Levin, Bob. "Israel's Spies in the U.S." *Newsweek,* XCIV (September 3, 1979), 23.

4604. "Longer Leash for the CIA." *Macleans,* XCII (May 14, 1979), 32–33.

4605. Lowenthal, Mark M. "Foreign Intelligence: Management and Organizational Issues." In: U.S. Congress. Joint Economic Committee. *The U.S. Role in a Changing World Political Economy—Major Issues for the 96th Congress.* 96th Cong., 1st sess. Washington, D.C.: GPO, 1979. pp. 635–647.

4606. McQueen, A. D. "Useful Intelligence Can Be Collected from Many Sources." *Security Management,* XXIII (September 1979), 12–14+.

4607. Mayer, Allan J. "The U.S.'s Blind Eye." *Newsweek,* XCIV (September 17, 1979), 30.

4608. Methvin, Eugene H. "'Domestic Spying': The Constitutional Imperative—the Proposed FBI Charter Would Give Every Terrorist One Free Blast." *American Spectator,* XIII (January 1980), 21–23.

4609. Mills, Bart. "Slipping Into Bulgaria, Filming on the Sly. . . ." *TV Guide,* XXVII (October 6, 1979), 11–14.

4610. Moore, John E. "The U.S. Intelligence Community: Its Problems—and Achievements." *Navy International,* LXXIX (August 1974), 11–12.

4611. Morganthau, Tom. "[KGB] Spying on U.S. Business." *Newsweek,* XCIV (November 12, 1979), 43.

4612. Nickel, H. "The U.S. Failure in Iran." *Fortune,* XCIX (March 12, 1979), 94–98+.

4613. Nossiter, Bernard D. "ABC Caper: A Secrecy Trial Leaves MI-5 with Soot on Its Face." *Progressive,* XLIII (May 1979), 41–42.

4614. O'Dell, G. W. T. "We Now Have a New Breed of O-2." *Marine Corps Gazette,* LXIII (April 1979), 15–16.

4615. Ognev, Grigori. "[American] Propaganda and Men's Good Will." *Soviet Literature,* no. 12 (December 1978), 157–161.

4616. "Oswald in the Soviet Union: An Investigation of Yuri Nosenko." In: U.S. Congress. House. Select Committee on Assassinations. Vol. XII of *Investigation of the Assassination of President John F. Kennedy: Appendix to Hearings.* 95th Cong., 2nd sess. Washington, D.C.: GPO, 1979. pp. 475–644.

4617. Porter, D. G. "Saigon's Secret Police." *Nation,* CCX (April 27, 1970), 498–500.

4618. Possony, Stefan T. "HVA (Haupt Verwaltung Aufklaerung): A Revolutionary Intelligence Service [East Germany]." *Defense and Foreign Affairs Digest,* VII (April 1979), 42–43.

4619. Powell, Bill C. "Did Israeli Intelligence Fail?: The October 1973 War." *M. I. Magazine,* IV (Summer 1976), 22–28.

4620. Powers, Thomas. "Inside the Department of Dirty Tricks: The CIA at Work." *Atlantic,* CCXLIV (August 1979), 33–64.

4621. Rees, John. "Web is Being Spun Around Washington: [Soviet] Espionage." *American Opinion,* XXII (September 1979), 1–4+.

4622. Relyea, Harold C. "The Evolution and Organization of the Federal Intelligence Function: A Brief Overview (1776–1975)." In: U.S. Congress. Senate. Select Committee to Investigate Government Operations With Respect to Intelligence Operations. *Supplemental Reports on Intelligence Activities: Report.* 94th Cong., 2nd sess. Washington, D.C.: GPO, 1976. pp. 1–292.

4623. Rey, Lucien. "The Revolution in Zanzibar." *New Left Review,* XXV (May–June 1964), 29–32.

4624. Robinson, D. F. "The Threat to Liberty and the Role of Intelligence-Gathering in Its Defence." *Army Quarterly,* CVIII (October 1978), 409–416.

4625. "Rudolph P. Chernyazev." *New York Times Biographical Service,* X (April 1979), 431.

4626. Russell, Richard. "Interview with Gerry Hemming: An Ex-CIA Man's Stunning Revelations on 'the Company,' JFK's Murder, and the Plot to Kill Richard Nixon." *Argosy,* CCLXXXIII (April 1976), 25–28, 52–54.

4627. Sanders, S. W. "CIA: Trying to Put Humpty-Dumpty Together." *Business Week,* (December 31, 1979), 52+.

4628. Schemmer, Benjamin F. "The Intelligence Community's Case Against Turner: Reprinted from the *Washington Post,* April 8, 1979." *Congressional Record,* CXXV (April 10, 1979), H2194–H2196.

4629. Schmidt, Dana A. "The Kurdish Insurgency." *Strategic Review,* II (Summer 1974), 51–58.

4631. Scott, Stephen. "Howard Marks [British Agent] Disappears." *New Statesman and Nation,* XCVIII (July 13, 1979), 40–41.

4632. _____ . "The Secret War for Ireland." *New Statesman and Nation,* XCVIII (July 13, 1979), 40–41.

4633. "Set of Rules for the FBI: Charter Proposal." *Newsweek,* XCIV (August 13, 1979), 79–80.

4634. Shearer, Lloyd. "Real-Life [Mossad] Spies Outdo James Bond." *Parade,* (July 1, 1979), 20.

4635. _____ . "Sex, Studs, and Spies [in West Germany]." *Parade,* (September 9, 1979), 16–17.

4636. Sherman, Lawrence W. "Chartering the FBI." *Criminal Law Bulletin,* XVI (January–February 1980), 53–58.

4637. Shlaim, Avi. "The Lavon Affair." *Middle East International,* no. 76 (October 1977), 12–14.

4638. Smith, Richard K. "The Violation of the *Liberty.*" *U.S. Naval Institute Proceedings,* CIV (June 1978), 62–79.

4639. "Solo Flight: A Spy [Christopher Boyce] Goes Back Into the Cold." *Time,* CXV (February 4, 1980), 32.

4640. "Soviet Propaganda and Psychological Warfare." *Air Intelligence Training Bulletin,* VI (June 1954), 34–42.

4641. Szulc, Tad. "CIA Blunders in Saudi Arabia." *New York Magazine,* XII (June 4, 1979), 69+.

4642. _____ . "The Great American Foreign Policy Machine." *Washingtonian,* VII (June 1973), 70–74, 104–118.

4643. _____ . "Guess Who's Trying to be Henry Superspy?" *Washingtonian,* IX (March 1974), 54–57, 99–106.

4644. _____ . "How Kissinger Runs Our 'Other Government.'" *New York Magazine,* VII (September 30, 1974), 59–66.

4645. _____ . "The KGB in Washington." *Washington Post Magazine,* (March 2, 1980), 12–22.

4646. _____ . "Shaking Up the CIA." *New York Times Magazine,* (July 29, 1979), 13–21, 33–35, 45–56.

4647. Tepfers, V. "The Soviet Political Police Today." *East and West,* no. 1 (1954), 42–49.

4648. Ulman, William A. "Russian Planes are Raiding Canadian Skies." *Collier's,* CXXXIII (October 16, 1953), 34–35+.

4649. "Unlocking CIA Files: How to Win (?) a FOI Case—The W. H. Ferry Case." *Nation,* CCXXIX (July 7, 1979), 11–14.

4650. Viorst, Milton. "The Mafia, the CIA, and the Kennedy Assassination." *Washingtonian,* XI (November 1975), 113–118.

4651. Waghelstein, John D. "Che's Bolivian Adventure." *Military Review,* LIX (August 1979), 39–48.

4652. Webster, William. "America's Top Cop Takes Aim at a Tough Target—Modernizing and De-Hooverizing the FBI: An Interview." *People,* XII (December 24, 1979), 94–95.

4653. Weiss, Ted, jt. author. *See* Huddleston, Walter D. (4590).

4654. Weissman, Stephen R. "CIA Covert Action in Zaire and Angola." *Political Science Quarterly,* XCV (Summer 1979), 263–286.

4655. _____ . "CIA Operations." In: René Lemarchand, ed. *American Foreign Policy in South Africa: The Stakes and the Stance.* Washington, D.C.: University Press of America, 1978. pp. 383–432.

4656. Wiegley, Richard D. "The Recovered Sunken Warship [*Glomar Explorer*]: A Legal Question." *U.S. Naval Institute Proceedings,* CV (January 1979), 26–32.

4657. Williams, George. "Intelligence and Book Learning: A Comprehensive Survey of Public Sources on Secret Activities." *Choice,* XVI (November 1979), 1125–1138.

4658. Wise, David. "Is Anybody Watching the CIA?" *Inquiry,* I (November 27, 1978), 17–21.

C. Documents, Papers, and Reports

4659. *Agent's Handbook of Black Bag Operations.* Boulder, CO: Paladin Press, 1979. 64p.

4660. *Annual Collections of Declassified Documents.* Washington, D.C.: Carrollton Press, 1975–. v. 1–.

4661. Aspin, Les. *SALT Verification: Prudence or Paranoia?* Washington, D.C., 1978. 21p.

4662. *The Declassified Documents Retrospective Collection.* 3 vols. and 1,000 microfiche. Washington, D.C.: Carrollton Press, 1976.

4663. Gambolati, Roland L. *Propaganda and Agitation in the Soviet Military.* Research Report. New York: Army Institute for Advanced Russian and East European Studies, 1975. 35p.

4664. Hart, Rosemary. "J. Robert Oppenheimer: A Case Study in the Strategies of Self-Defense in a Government Security Hearing." Unpublished PhD Dissertation, University of Minnesota, 1977.

4665. Immerman, Richard H. "From Guatemala to the Bay of Pigs: The CIA and the Cold War Ethos." Unpublished paper, 73rd Annual Meeting of the Organization of American Historians, 1980.

4666. _____ . "The United States and Guatemala, 1954: A Cold War Strategy for the Americas." Unpublished PhD Dissertation, Boston College, 1978.

4667.   Katz, Amrom H. *Verification and SALT: The State of the Art and the Art of the State.* Washington, D.C.: Heritage Foundation, 1979. 45p.

4668.   Keeshemeti, Paul. *The Soviet Approach to International Political Communication.* RAND Paper P-788. Santa Monica, CA: RAND Corporation, 1956. 25p.

4669.   Kelly, Clarence M. *Intelligence Investigations.* Washington, D.C.: Federal Bureau of Investigation, 1976. 10p.

4670.   King, Jerry K., ed. *International Political Effects of the Spread of Nuclear Weapons.* Washington, DC.: GPO for the National Foreign Assessment Center, CIA, 1979. 234p.

4671.   Kramer, Donna S., comp. *Is Israel a Nuclear Power?: Selected Bibliography, 1961 to the Present.* Washington, D.C.: Congressional Research Service, Library of Congress, 1979. 3p.

4672.   Kramer, Howard D. and John L. Houk. *Psychological Operations—Burma: Project "Prosyms."* Washington, D.C.: American University, 1959. 448p.

4673.   _____ . *Psychological Operations—Cambodia: Project "Prosyms."* Washington, D.C.: American University, 1959. 471p.

4674.   _____ . *Psychological Operations—China: Project "Prosyms."* Washington, D.C.: American University, 1959. 476p.

4675.   _____ . *Psychological Operations—South Vietnam: Project "Prosyms."* Washington, D.C.: American University, 1959. 440p.

4676.   _____ . *Psychological Operations—Thailand: Project "Prosyms."* Washington, D.C.: American University, 1960. 332p.

4677.   Lowenthal, Mark M. *The Central Intelligence Agency: Organizational History.* CRS–78–168F. Washington, D.C.: Congressional Research Service, Library of Congress, 1978. 62p.

4678.   _____ . *Intelligence Community: Congressional Oversight.* Issue Brief 77079. Washington, D.C.: Congressional Research Service, Library of Congress, 1977. 28p.

4679.   _____ . *Intelligence Community: Reform and Reorganization.* Issue Brief 76039. Washington, D.C.: Congressional Research Service, Library of Congress, 1976. 33p.

4680.   _____ . *SALT Verification.* CRS–78–142F. Washington, D.C.: Congressional Research Service, Library of Congress, 1978. 84p.

4681.   Nawful al-Sayyid, Muhammad A. *Israel's Crime Record.* Cairo: Information Department, Government of Egypt, 1965.

4682. Newman, Steven L. "The Oppenheimer Case: A Reconsideration of the Role of the Defense Department and National Security." Unpublished PhD Dissertation, New York University, 1977.

4683. Strauch, Ralph. *Strategic Warning and General War: A Look at the Conceptual Issues.* RAND Note N–1180AF. Santa Monica, CA: RAND Corporation, 1979. 51p.

4684. Todd, James C. "Soviet Propaganda Against the North Atlantic Treaty Organization: A Problem in Psychological Warfare." Unpublished MA Thesis, Tulane University, 1952.

4685. *Unconventional Warfare Devices and Techniques.* Boulder, CO: Paladin Press, 1979. 234p.

4686. United States. Army. Institute for Military Assistance. *Psychological Operations.* FM 33–1. 2 pts. Ft. Bragg, NC, 1979.

4687. _____ . _____ . Special Forces. *Special Forces Demolition Techniques.* FM 31–20. Boulder, CO: Paladin Press, 1979. 67p.

4688. _____ . Central Intelligence Agency. *CIA Ammunition and Explosive Supply Catalog.* Boulder, CO: Paladin Press, 1979. 88p.

4689. _____ . _____ . *CIA Explosives for Sabotage.* Boulder, CO: Paladin Press, 1979. 70p.

4690. _____ . _____ . *CIA Special Weapons Supply Catalog.* Boulder, CO: Paladin Press, 1979. 77p.

4691. _____ . _____ . National Foreign Assessment Center. *China: International Trade, 1977–1978.* Research Paper. Washington, D.C.: Document Expediting Project, Exchange and Gift Division, Library of Congress, 1978. 23p.

4692. _____ . _____ . _____ . *Least-Developed Countries: Economic Characteristics and Stake in North-South Issues.* Research Paper. Washington, D.C.: Document Expediting Project, Exchange and Gift Division, Library of Congress, 1978. 48p.

4693. _____ . _____ . _____ . *The Role of the LDC's in the U.S. Balance of Payments.* Research Aid. Washington, D.C.: Document Expediting Project, Exchange and Gift Division, Library of Congress, 1978. 149p.

4694. _____ . _____ . _____ . *The Scope of Poland's Economic Dilemma.* Research Paper. Washington, D.C.: Document Expediting Project, Exchange and Gift Division, Library of Congress, 1978. 14p.

4695. _____ . _____ . _____ . *Soviet Agricultural Commodity Trade, 1960–1976: A Statistical Survey.* Reference Aid. Washington, D.C.: Document Expediting Project, Exchange and Gift Division, Library of Congress, 1978. 235p.

4696. _____ . _____ . _____ . *Soviet Civil Defense.* Research Paper. Washington, D.C.: Document Expediting Project, Exchange and Gift Division, Library of Congress, 1978. 16p.

4697. _____ . Congress. House. Committee on Armed Services. Subcommittee on Intelligence and Military Application of Nuclear Energy. Panel on the Strategic Arms Limitations Talks and the Comprehensive Test Ban Treaty. *SALT II, an Interim Assessment: Report.* 95th Cong., 2nd sess. Washington, D.C.: GPO, 1978. 65p.

4698. _____ . _____ . _____ . Committee on Foreign Affairs. Subcommittee on Europe and the Middle East. *U.S. Policy Toward Iran, January 1979: Hearings.* 9th Cong., 1st sess. Washington, D.C.: GPO, 1979. 69p.

4699. _____ . _____ . _____ . Committee on Government Operations. Subcommittee on Government Information and Individual Rights. *Justice Department Treatment of Criminal Cases Involving CIA Personnel and Claims of National Security: Hearings.* 94th Cong., 1st sess. Washington, D.C.: GPO, 1975. 431p.

4700. _____ . _____ . _____ . Committee on Internal Security. *Statutory Authority for the FBI's Domestic Intelligence Activities: An Analysis.* 93rd Cong., 1st sess. Washington, D.C.: GPO, 1973. 59p.

4701. _____ . _____ . _____ . Select Committee on Intelligence. *Security Clearance Procedures in the Intelligence Agencies: Staff Report.* 96th Cong., 1st sess. Washington, D.C.: GPO, 1979. 34p.

4702. _____ . _____ . _____ . _____ . Subcommittee on Legislation. *Espionage Laws and Leaks: Hearings.* 95th Cong., 1st sess. Washington, D.C.: GPO, 1979. 280p.

4703. _____ . _____ . _____ . _____ . _____ . *Graymail Legislation: Hearings.* 96th Cong., 1st sess. Washington, D.C.: GPO, 1979. 219p.

4704. _____ . _____ . _____ . _____ . _____ . *Impact of the Freedom of Information Act and the Privacy Act on Intelligence Activities: Hearings.* 96th Cong., 1st sess. Washington, D.C.: GPO, 1979. 182p.

4705. _____ . _____ . _____ . _____ . Subcommittee on Oversight. *Intelligence on the World Energy Future: Staff Report.* 96th Cong., 1st sess. Washington, D.C.: GPO, 1979. 13p.

4706. _____ . _____ . Senate. Committee on Foreign Relations. *Diplomatic Immunity Legislation: Hearings.* 95th Cong., 2nd sess. Washington, D.C.: GPO, 1978. 111p.

4707. _____ . _____ . _____ . Select Committee on Intelligence. *Principal Findings on the Capabilities of the United States to Monitor the SALT II Treaty: Report.* 96th Cong., 1st sess. Washington, D.C.: GPO, 1979. 5p.

4708. _____ . Department of Defense. Defense Intelligence Agency. "Militarized Security Forces." In: *Handbook on the Soviet Armed Forces.* DDB–2680–40–78. Washington, D.C.: GPO, 1979. pp. 13/1–13/6.

4709. _____ . Department of State. Bureau of Public Affairs. Office of Public Communication. *SALT II Senate Testimony, July 9–11, 1979.* Current Policy, no. 72A. Rev. ed. Washington, D.C., 1979. 36p.

4710. _____ . _____ . _____ . _____ . "Verification Measures." In: *SALT II Basic Guide: A Special Report.* Rev. ed. Washington, D.C., 1979. pp. 8–9.

4711. _____ . Office of Telecommunications Policy. *Study of the Vulnerability of Electronic Communication Systems to Electronic Interception.* 2 vols. McLean, VA: Mitre Corporation, 1977.

4712. Waghelstein, John D. "A Theory of Revolutionary Warfare and Its Application to the Bolivian Adventure of Che Guevara." Unpublished Thesis, Army Command and Genral Staff College, 1973.

4713. Zickel, Raymond E. *Soviet Combat Intelligence and Reconnaissance.* New York: Army Institute for Advanced Russian and East European Studies, 1973. 41p.

Appendix II:
Magazines and Journals Containing at Least One Article Relative to This Guide

Aerospace Engineering
Africa
Africa Report
Africa Today
African Affairs
Air Classics
Air Force
Air Force and Space Digest
Air Force Magazine
Air Power Historian
Air University Quarterly Review
Air University Review
Airman
All Hands
America
American Bar Association Journal
American Education
American Heritage
American Image
American Journal of International
  Law
American Legion Magazine
American Mercury
American Opinion
American Philosophical Society
  Proceedings
American Political Science Review
American Scholar
American-Slavic Review
American Sociological Review
American Spectator
Annals of the American Academy of
  Political and Social Science
Antioch Review
Argosy
Armed Forces and Society
Armed Forces Journal International
Armor
Army
Army Information Digest
Army Quarterly
Asia Magazine
Asian Forum
Asian Survey

Astronautics
Atlantic
Atlas
Australian Outlook
Aviation Week and Space Technology

Baltimore Sun Perspective
Bell System Technical Journal
Biblical Society
Black Scholar
Book Digest
Broadcasting
Bulletin of the Atomic Scientists
Bulletin of the Concerned Asian
  Scholars
Bulletin of the Institute for the Study
  of the U.S.S.R.
Bulletin of the New York Public
  Library
Business Week

Canadian Army Journal
Canadian Forum
Catholic World
Center Magazine
Change
Chemical and Engineering News
Chicago
China Quarterly
Christian Century
Christian Herald
Christianity and Crisis
Civil Liberties Review
Collier's
Columbia Journal of Law and Social
  Issues
Columbia Journalism Review
Combat Forces
Commander's Digest
Commentary
Commonweal
Communication Quarterly
Communist Affairs
Computers and Automation

Conflict Studies
Congressional Quarterly Weekly
  Report
Congressional Record
Contact
Cornell Law Review
Coronet
Cosmopolitan
Crawdaddy
Crime and Social Justice
Criminal Law Bulletin
Cryptologia
Current
Current Biography
Current History

Data
Defense and Foreign Affairs Digest
Department of State Bulletin
Disarmament and Arms Control
Dissent

East Asian Review
East Europe
Eastern European Quarterly
Eastern Horizon
Eastern World
Ebony
Electronic Design
Electronic Warfare
Encore
Encounter
Enquirer Magazine
Environment
Esquire

FBI Law Enforcement Bulletin
Far Eastern Economic Review
Far Eastern Survey
Federal Register
Film Library Quarterly
Flight International
Florida Historical Quarterly
Fordham Law Review
Foreign Affairs

Foreign Policy
Foreign Policy Bulletin
Foreign Service Journal
Fortnightly
Fortune
Free China Review
Freedom at Issue
Freedom Front (Hong Kong)

Gazette
George Washington Law Review
German International
Government Executive

Harper's
Harper's Weekly
Harvard Law Review
Hastings Constitutional Law
  Quarterly
Hawk
History, Numbers and War
History Today
Horizon
Human Behavior
Human Events
Human Relations

Illustrated London News
Index on Censorship
Indiana Law Journal
Infantry
Infantry Journal
Inquiry
Instant Research on Peace and War
Institute of World Affairs
  Proceedings
Intellect
Inter-American Economic Affairs
Interavia
International Affairs (London)
International Affairs (Moscow)
International Conciliation
International Defense Review
International Organization
International Science and Technology

International Security
International Studies Notes
International Studies Quarterly
Israel Horizons
Israel Magazine
Issues and Studies (Taiwan)

Jerusalem Quarterly
Journal of American History
Journal of Arms Control
Journal of Broadcasting
Journal of Conflict Resolution
Journal of Contemporary Asia
Journal of Higher Education
Journal of Inter-American Studies
Journal of Modern African Studies
Journal of Police Science
    Administration
Journal of Political and Military
    Sociology
Journal of Politics
Journal of Public Law
Journal of Social Issues
Journal of Social Psychology
Journal of the Middle East Society
Journal of the Royal United Service
    Institute for Defence Studies
Journal of the United Service
    Institution
Journal of the U.S. Army Intelli-
    gence and Security Command
Journal of the United States Artillery
Journalism Quarterly

Kenyon Review

Latin American Perspectives
Law and Contemporary Problems
Library Journal
Life
Lithopinion
Look
Los Angeles Magazine

McGill Law Journal

Macleans
Mademoiselle
Mankind
Marine Corps Gazette
Mid-America
Middle East Affairs
Middle East Journal
Middle Eastern Affairs
Midway
Military Affairs
Military Law Review
Military Review
Millennium
Missiles and Rockets
Mississippi Quarterly
More

N.A.E.B. Journal
NATO's Fifteen Nations
Nation
National Review
National Security Affairs Forum
Nation's Business
Naval War College Review
Navigator
N.E.A. Journal
New England Quarterly
New Leader
New Politics
New Republic
New Statesman and Nation
New Times
New Times (Moscow)
New West
New York Magazine
New York Review of Books
New York Times Biographical
    Service
New York Times Magazine
New York University Journal of
    International Law and Politics
New York University Law Review
New Yorker
Newsweek

*Northwestern University Law
   Review*

Officer
Oklahoma Observer
Orbis
Orientations
Oui

Pacific Historical Review
Parade
Partisan Review
Penthouse
People
Pittsburgh Press Roto
Playboy
Police Chief
Policy Sciences
Political Quarterly
Political Science Quarterly
Political Studies
Politics and Society
Politics Today
Politicks
Popular Electronics
Popular Mechanics
Popular Photography
Popular Science
Present Tense
Presidential Studies Quarterly
Printers' Ink
Privacy Journal
Problems of Communism
*Proceedings of the Institute of Elec-
   trical and Electronics Engineers*
Profile
Progressive
Psychic World
Psychological Bulletin
Psychology Today
Public Opinion Quarterly
Public Relations Journal
Publishers Weekly

Quarterly Journal of Speech

Queen's Quarterly
Quest

RAF Flying Review
Ramparts
Reader's Digest
*Record of the Association of the Bar
   of the City of New York*
Redbook
Reporter
Retired Officer
Review of Politics
Ripon Forum
*Rocky Mountain Social Science
   Journal*
Rolling Stone
Round Table
Roundel
Royal Air Forces Quarterly
Russian Review

S.A.S. Review
Saturday Evening Post
Saturday Review
Saturday Review of Literature
Science
Science and Society
Science Digest
Science Newsletter
Scientific American
Sea Classics
Sea Power
Security Management
Senior Scholastic
Signal
Skeptic
Slavic Review
Social Forces
Society
Sociological Quarterly
South Atlantic Quarterly
Southern California Law Review
*Southern Speech-Communication
   Journal*
Southern Quarterly

Soviet Analyst
Soviet Literature
Soviet Military Review
Soviet Review
Soviet Studies
Space/Aeronautics
Space World
Spaceflight
Spectator
Strategic Review
Studies in International Relations
   (Warsaw)
Studies on the Soviet Union

T.V. Guide
Tactical Air Reconnaissance Digest
Temple Law Quarterly
Time
Transaction
Translations on U.S.S.R. Military
   Affairs (JPRS)
Trial
True
Tulane Law Review
Twentieth Century

UCLA Law Review
Ukrainian Review
U.N. World
United Service Institute of India
   Journal

U.S.A. Today
U.S. Army Aviation Digest
U.S. Naval Institute Proceedings
U.S. News and World Report
University of Pittsburgh Law
   Review

Vanderbilt Journal of Transnational
   Law
Viet-Report
Villanova Law Review
Virginia Law Review
Virginia Quarterly Review
Vital Issues
Vital Speeches
Washington Post Outlook
Washington Monthly
Washingtonian
Weekly Compilation of Presidential
   Documents
Western Humanities Review
Western Political Quarterly
World Marxist Review
World Politics
World Today
Worldview

Yale Law Review
Yale Review
Yale Studies in World Public Order

Appendix III:
Charts

Chart I

The Intelligence Cycle

is the process by which information is acquired, converted into intelligence, and made available to policymakers. There are usually five steps which constitute *The Intelligence Cycle*.

1. Planning and Direction

This involves the management of the entire intelligence effort, from the identification of the need for data to the final delivery of an intelligence product to a customer.

The whole process is initiated by requests or requirements for intelligence on certain subjects. These are based on the ultimate needs of the policymakers—the President, the National Security Council, and other major departments and agencies of government.

2. Collection

This involves the gathering of the raw data from which finished intelligence will be produced. There are many sources for the collection of information, including foreign radio broadcasts, newspapers, periodicals, and official government personnel stationed in American embassies abroad.

There are also secret sources, such as agents and defectors who provide information obtainable in no other way.

Finally, technical collection—photography and electronics—has come to play an indispensable part in modern intelligence by extending the Nation's sensory system—its eyes and ears.

3. Processing

This step is concerned with the conversion of the vast amount of information coming into the system to a form more suitable for the production of finished intelligence, such as in language translations, decryption, and sorting by subject matter. The information that does not go directly to analysts is sorted and made available for rapid computer retrieval.

Processing also refers to data reduction—interpretation of the information stored on film and tape through the use of highly refined photographic and electronic processes.

4. Production and Analysis

This refers to the conversion of basic information into finished intelligence. It includes the integration, evaluation, and analysis of all available data and the preparation of a variety of intelligence products. Such products or estimates may be presented as briefings, brief reports or lengthy studies.

The "raw intelligence" collected is frequently fragmentary and at times contradictory. Analysts, who are subject-matter specialists for a particular country, produce finished intelligence by evaluating and integrating the various pieces of data and interpreting their meaning and significance.

The subjects involved may concern different regions, problems, or personalities in various contexts—political, geographic, economic, military, scientific, or biographic. Current events, capabilities, or probable developments in the future may also be examined.

5. Dissemination

The last step is the distribution and handling of the finished intelligence by the consumers of intelligence, the same policymakers whose needs triggered the Intelligence Cycle. Sound policy decisions must be based on sound knowledge. Intelligence aims to provide that knowledge.

Chart II

Command Responsibilities of the Chairman of Soviet State Security (KGB)

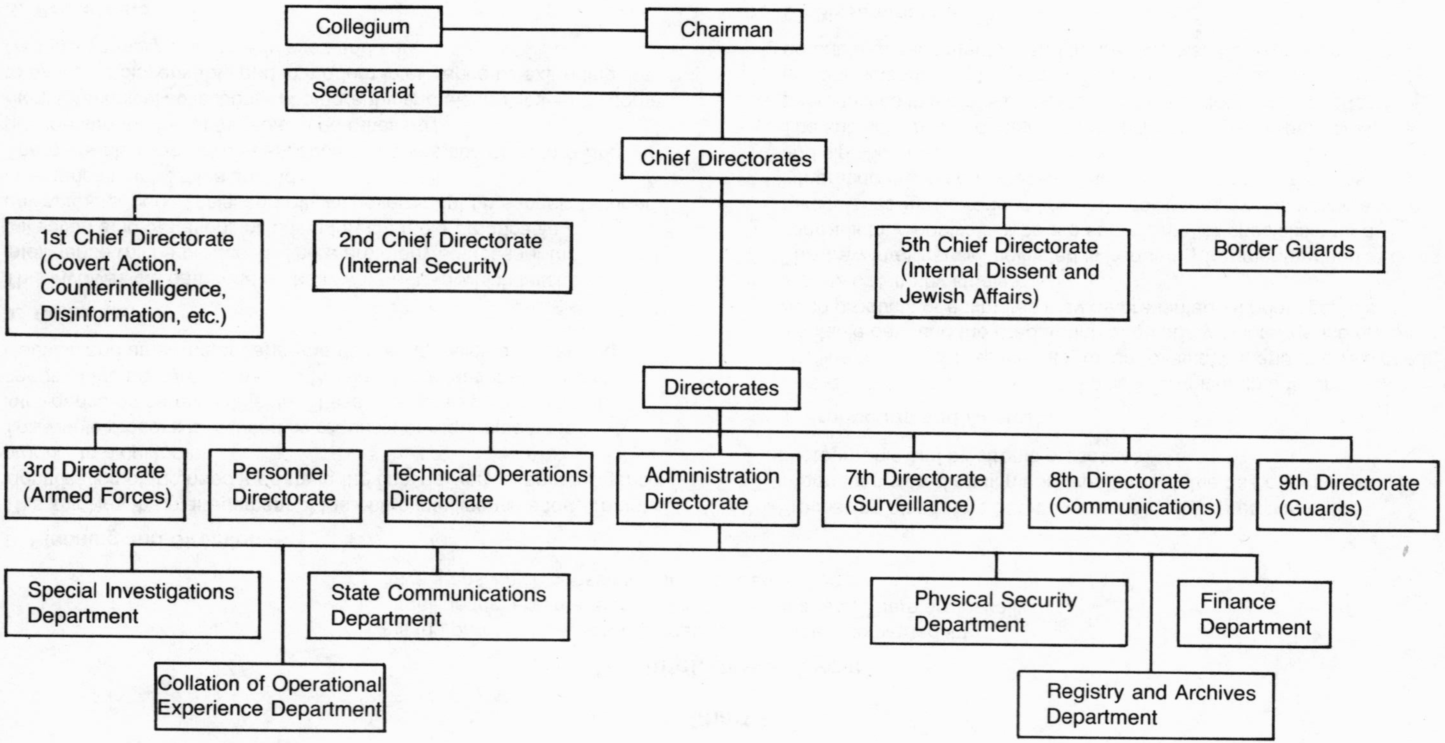

Chairman

- Collegium
- Secretariat

Chief Directorates

- 1st Chief Directorate (Covert Action, Counterintelligence, Disinformation, etc.)
- 2nd Chief Directorate (Internal Security)
- 5th Chief Directorate (Internal Dissent and Jewish Affairs)
- Border Guards

Directorates

- 3rd Directorate (Armed Forces)
- Personnel Directorate
- Technical Operations Directorate
- Administration Directorate
- 7th Directorate (Surveillance)
- 8th Directorate (Communications)
- 9th Directorate (Guards)

Departments:
- Special Investigations Department
- State Communications Department
- Collation of Operational Experience Department
- Physical Security Department
- Finance Department
- Registry and Archives Department

Chart III

Chairman and Deputies,
Soviet State Security (KGB), 1945–1980

CHAIRMEN, SOVIET STATE SECURITY
(NKVD, NKGB, MVD, MGB, KGB)

Sergei N. Kruglov
July 1945–March 1953

Vsevolod N. Merkulov
April 1943–? 1950

Viktor S. Abakumov
? 1950–? 1951

Seman D. Ignatyev
? 1951–March 1953

Lavrenti P. Beria
March 1953–June 1953

Sergei N. Kruglov
March 1953–April 1954

Ivan A. Serov
March 1954–December 1958

Aleksandr N. Shelepin
December 1958–November 1961

Vladimir Y. Semichastnyy
November 1961–April 1967

Yuri V. Andropov
April 1967–

DEPUTY CHAIRMEN

Ivan A. Serov
1941–1954

Aleksey A. Yepishev
1951–1953

Mikhail D. Ryumin
1952–1953

Konstantin F. Lunev
1953–1959

Vadim S. Tikunov
1958–1961

Sergey S. Belchenko
1958–1965

Petr I. Ivashutin
1962–1963

Nikolay S. Zakharov
1962–

Mikhail S. Rogov
1966–

Lev I. Pankratov
1967–

Aleksandr I. Perepelitsyn
1959–1967

Semen K. Tsvigun
1967–

Ardalion N. Malygin
1968–

Viktor M. Chebrikov
1969–

Vladimir P. Pirozhkov
1971–

Georgiy K. Tsinev
1971–

N. P. Yemokhonov
1974–

Chart IV

U.S. Senate and House Intelligence Committees

SENATE SELECT COMMITTEE ON INTELLIGENCE

(Formed 19 May 1976)

Birch Bayh (D., Indiana), Chairman
Barry Goldwater (R., Arizona), Vice Chairman

Daniel K. Inouye (D., Hawaii)
Adlai E. Stevenson (D., Illinois)
Walter D. Huddleston
   (D., Kentucky)
Joseph R. Biden (D., Delaware)
Daniel Patrick Moynihan
   (D., New York)
Henry M. Jackson
   (D., Washington)

Jake Garn (R., Utah)
John H. Chafee
   (R., Rhode Island)
Richard G. Lugar (R., Indiana)
Malcolm Wallop (R., Wyoming)
David F. Durenberger
   (R., Minnesota)

Robert C. Byrd (D., West Virginia), Ex Officio Member
Howard H. Baker, Jr. (R., Tennessee), Ex Officio Member

HOUSE PERMANENT SELECT COMMITTEE ON INTELLIGENCE

(Formed 14 July 1977)

Edward P. Boland (D., Massachusetts), Chairman

Clement J. Zablocki
   (D., Wisconsin)
Bill D. Burlison (D., Missouri)
Morgan F. Murphy (D., Illinois)
Les Aspin (D., Wisconsin)
Charles Rose (D., North Carolina)
Romano L. Mazzoli
   (D., Kentucky)
Norman Y. Mineta (D., California)
W. Wyche Fowler (D., Georgia)

J. Kenneth Robinson
   (R., Virginia)
John M. Ashbrook (R., Ohio)
Robert McClory (R., Illinois)
G. William Whitehurst
   (R., Virginia)
C. W. Bill Young (R., Florida)

Chart V

The American Intelligence Community

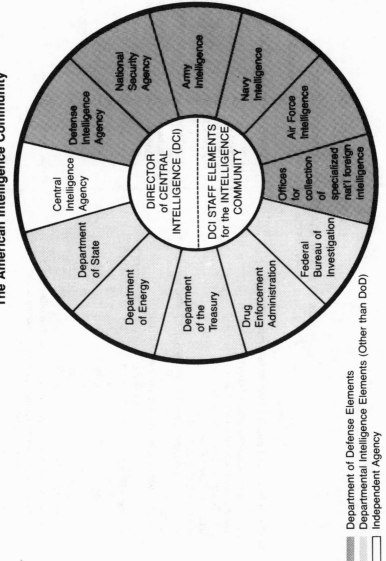

 Department of Defense Elements

 Departmental Intelligence Elements (Other than DoD)

☐ Independent Agency

Director of Central Intelligence (DCI)

DCI STAFF ELEMENTS for the INTELLIGENCE COMMUNITY

Central Intelligence Agency

Defense Intelligence Agency

National Security Agency

Army Intelligence

Navy Intelligence

Air Force Intelligence

Offices for collection of specialized nat'l foreign intelligence

Federal Bureau of Investigation

Drug Enforcement Administration

Department of the Treasury

Department of Energy

Department of State

Chart VI

How to Obtain CIA Publications and Maps
Available to the Public

To obtain individual publications or tailored services:

(for documents published after 1 February 1979)
National Technical Information Service
U.S. Department of Commerce
5285 Port Royal Road
Springfield, Virginia 22161
Telephone: NTIS Order Desk 703-557-4650; 557-4780 to obtain order number

- Cost varies with size and number of pages

Page Range	Ad Hoc or Demand	Standing Order Category
1-25	$ 4.75	$ 3.80
26-75	6.25	5.00
76-125	9.00	7.20
126-175	12.50	10.00
All Microfiche	3.00	

- Subscription and Deposit Account service offered
- May use American Express, check or money order
- Rush handling available

To obtain earlier publications:

(published before February 1979)
Hard copy and microfilm service may also be purchased from the Library of Congress Photoduplication Service, Washington, D.C. 20540; telephone: 202-426-5650. Maps and atlases may be ordered from the Superintendent of Documents, Government Printing Office, Washington, D.C. 20402; telephone 202-783-3238.

To subscribe to all CIA publications:

Document Expediting Project (DOCEX)
Exchange and Gifts Division
Library of Congress
Washington, D.C. 20540
Telephone: 202-426-5253

- Annual fee is $225 for subscription service

Chart VII

Director of Central Intelligence Command Responsibilities

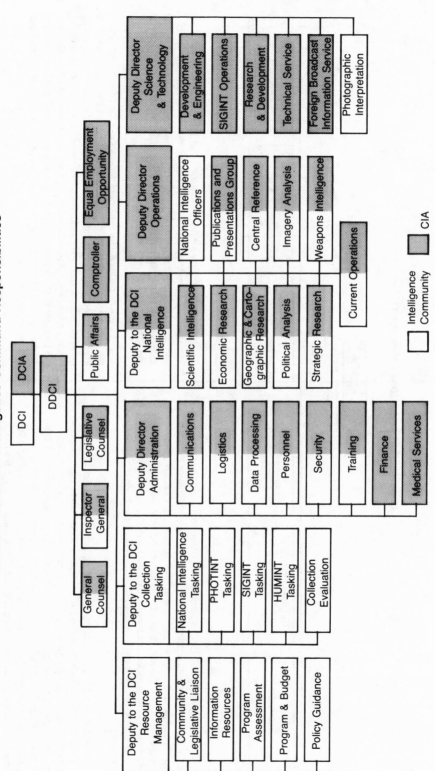

Chart VIII

Organization under New Executive Order

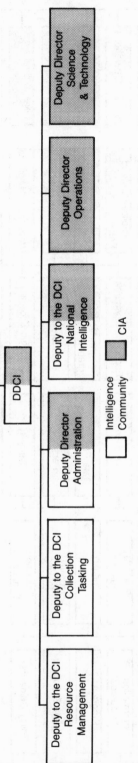

1. *The Deputy to the DCI for Resource Management* is the principal adviser to the DCI on all matters relating to the National Foreign Intelligence Program (NFIP) budget prior to its presentation to the President and Congress. He will ensure the DCI has full access to relevant information and will conduct audits and evaluations as necessary. He will also assist the DCI in arriving at budget recommendations and will oversee the execution of the budget once it is approved.

2. *The Deputy to the DCI for Collection Tasking* is the principal adviser to the DCI on all collection efforts within the Intelligence Community. He is responsible for assigning intelligence collection objectives and tasks to all intelligence elements of the Intelligence Community through the National Intelligence Tasking Center (NITC) which he heads. He establishes priorities 'for tasking national intelligence collection systems in response to the production priorities set by the National Foreign Assessment Center. Through the NITC, he ensures dissemination of the information collected.

3. *The Deputy Director for Administration* is responsible for supporting administratively those Intelligence Community components under the jurisdiction of the DCI as well as performing other tasks as assigned. He will continue to serve all his assigned functions as the Deputy Director for Administration of the CIA.

4. *The Deputy to the DCI for National Intelligence* is the principal adviser to the DCI on the production of national intelligence, both as to how it is accomplished and what it contains. He is responsible for organizing national efforts to assess and evaluate foreign intelligence data in support of national intelligence objectives as established by the National Security Council. He is the Director of the National Foreign Assessment Center and oversees the production of that Center. He also monitors product quality and evaluates product responsiveness.

5. *The Deputy Director for Operations* and the *Deputy Director for Science and Technology* will continue to serve all their presently assigned functions for the Central Intelligence Agency.

Chart IX

Directors and Deputies of
Central Intelligence, 1946–1980

DIRECTORS OF CENTRAL INTELLIGENCE

RADM Sidney W. Souers, USNR
23 January 1946–10 June 1946

LTGEN Hoyt S. Vandenburg, USA
10 June 1946–1 May 1947

RADM Roscoe H. Hillenkoetter, USN
1 May 1947–7 October 1950

GEN Walter Bedell Smith, USA
7 October 1950–9 February 1953

The Honorable Allen W. Dulles*
26 February 1953–29 November 1961

The Honorable John A. McCone
29 November 1961–28 April 1965

VADM William F. Raborn, Jr.,
(USN, Ret.)
28 April 1965–30 June 1966

The Honorable Richard Helms
30 June 1966–2 February 1973

The Honorable James R. Schlesinger
2 February 1973–2 July 1973

The Honorable William E. Colby
4 September 1973–30 January 1976

The Honorable George Bush
30 January 1976–20 January 1977

ADM Stansfield Turner,
(USN, Ret.)**
9 March 1977–

*Mr. Dulles served as Acting DCI from 9-26
February 1953

**Admiral Turner retired on 31 December
1978 while serving as DCI

DEPUTY DIRECTORS

Kingman Douglass*
2 March 1946–11 July 1946

BGEN Edwin K. Wright, USA
20 January 1947–9 March 1949

The Honorable William H. Jackson
7 October 1950–3 August 1951

The Honorable Allen W. Dulles
23 August 1951–26 February 1953

GEN Charles P. Cabell, USAF
23 April 1953–31 January 1962

LTGEN Marshall S. Carter, USA
3 April 1962–28 April 1965

The Honorable Richard Helms
28 April 1965–30 June 1966

VADM Rufus L. Taylor, USN
13 October 1966–31 January 1969

LTGEN Robert E. Cushman, Jr.,
USMC
7 May 1969–31 December 1971

LTGEN Vernon A. Walters, USA**
2 May 1972–7 July 1976

The Honorable E. Henry Knoche***
7 July 1976–31 July 1977

John F. Blake****
31 July 1977–10 February 1978

The Honorable Frank C. Carlucci
10 February 1978–

*Mr. Douglass served as Acting DDCI from 2 March–11 July 1946

**GEN Walters served as Acting DCI from 3 July 1973–3 September 1973

***Mr. Knoche served as Acting DCI from 20 January 1977–9 March 1977

****Mr. Blake served as Acting DDCI from 31 July 1977–10 February 1978

Author Index

ABC News, 2078
Abel, Ellie, 3135
Abi-Saab, Georges, 2674
Ablett, Charles B., 903
Abshire, David M., 415
Achard, James, 416
Acheson, Dean, 159–160
Acoca, M., 4072
Adam, Corinna, 2212
Adams, Nina, 2780
Adams, Samuel A., 2819
Adams, Sherman, 161
Adelman, Kenneth L., 2675
Adie, W. A. C., 2556
Adler, Emanuel, 4530
Adler, Renata, 2213
Agar, Augustus W. S., 2466
Agee, Philip, 1423, 1822, 2214, 2395–2396, 2955, 3343, 3709–3710
Aitken, Jonathan, 507
Akers, Robert W., 787
Alan, R., 2441
Albergotti, Robert D., 3345
Aldouby, Zwy, 3810
Alexander, Robert J., 363, 2995, 3195
Alexander, Yonah, 437
Alexeev, K. M., 3717–3718
Alexinsky, Gregoire, 1324
Alisky, Marvin, 306
Allen, George V., 205, 417, 647–648
Allison, Graham T., 1463, 3136
Allman, T. D., 2781
Allport, F. H., 418
Almaney, Adnan, 438
Alpern, David M., 2002, 2114–2118, 2215–2220, 2715, 3346, 3817, 3943, 4404
Alsop, Joseph, 3744, 4153–4154
Alsop, Stewart, 162, 1823–1824, 2509, 3078, 3228, 3265, 4153–4154
Altavilla, Enrico, 1127, 4437
Altman, G. T., 3978

Amalrik, Andrei A., 2467–2468
Ambrose, Stephen E., 1473
American Cryptogram Association, 904
Amnesty International, 873, 2609
Anders, Roger M., 4321
Anderson, Jack, 2120, 2510
Anderson, James K., 2469
Andregg, Charles H., 1672
Andrew, Christopher, 1243
Andrews, Bert, 3980
Andrews, Peter, 3980
Andrews, Robert H., 1798
Andrusiak, Nicholas, 558
Anisimov, Oleg, 649
Anson, Robert S., 2121
Araldsen, O. P., 559
Arbuckle, Tammy, 2782
Archer, Jules, 3347
Ardoin, Birthney, 364
Arguedas, Antonio, 2974
Argyropoulos, Kaitz, 2459
Armbrister, Trevor, 1102–1103
Armer, Paul, 3348
Armstrong, John A., 2470
Arsenian, Seth, 439
Artemiev, Vyacheslav, 1325
Arthur, Robert A., 3981
Asanov, D., 2511
Asbury, Herbert, 3975
Ascoli, Max, 4155
Ashman, Charles, 2122
Ashman, Harold L., 1474
Ashmore, Harry S., 3349
Asian Peoples' Anti-Communist League, 2693
Asinoff, Eliot, 3224
Aspin, Les, 945, 4661
Association of the Bar of the City of New York, 2222
_____ , Committee on Civil Rights, 3350
_____ , Committee on Federal Legislation, 3351

367

WITHDRAWAL